OUR MAN IN TEHRAN

ROBERT WRIGHT

OUR MAN IN
TEHRAN

KEN TAYLOR, THE CIA
AND THE IRAN HOSTAGE CRISIS

HARPER
PERENNIAL

HARPER PERENNIAL

Published by Harper Perennial, an imprint of HarperCollins Publishers Ltd.

First published in Canada in a hardcover edition by HarperCollins Publishers Ltd: 2010
This Harper Perennial trade paperback edition: 2011

Grateful acknowledgment is given to the following for permission to reproduce photographs:
Ken Taylor, pp. 17 (*Ken Taylor and the Shah of Iran*), 186 (*Ken and Pat Taylor*), 291 (*Ken and Pat Taylor*);
Canadian Press (CP), jacket (*Ayatollah Khomeini*), pp. 58 (*Shah and Empress of Iran*), 107 (*Iranians and hostage*), 209 (*helicopters*); CP/Peter Bregg, jacket (*Taylor*), pp. 3 (*Taylor*), 39 (*Iranians protesting*), 71 (*Khomeini*),
90 (*students protesting*), 125 (*Iranian women*), 153 (*women in front of Tehran University*), 173 (*Iranian students*),
273 (*Canadian embassy in Iran*), 310 (*Sadegh Ghotbzadeh*); CP/Chuck Mitchell, p. 140 (*Joe Clark*); CP/Barry
Thumma, p. 325 (*Taylor, at podium, with Ronald Reagan*); Babak, www.babak.ca, p. 341 (*Taylor*);
iStockphoto, pp. 222 (*censored document*), 243 (*handshake*), 258 (*passport*).

HarperCollins books may be purchased for educational, business,
or sales promotional use through our Special Markets Department.

HarperCollins Publishers Ltd
2 Bloor Street East, 20th Floor
Toronto, Ontario, Canada
M4W 1A8

www.harpercollins.ca

Library and Archives Canada Cataloguing in Publication
information is available upon request

ISBN 978-1-55468-300-0

Printed in the United States
RRD 9 8 7 6 5 4 3 2

For Laura, Helena, Anna and Michael

CONTENTS

PREFACE

Our *Man in Tehran* recounts the exploits of Canada's fifth ambassador to Iran, Kenneth D. Taylor, the man who, in January 1980, became the world's most celebrated diplomat for his role in rescuing six Americans during the Iran hostage crisis.

I first met Ken Taylor in March 2008, in the restaurant of Toronto's Park Hyatt hotel. We had agreed to conduct our first interview for this book over breakfast and, in typical fashion, Taylor was punctual, impeccably dressed and full of energy despite having underslept. While we were getting acquainted, sipping coffee and chatting casually about current affairs, a man in his mid-forties approached our table and asked politely if he could interrupt our conversation. He identified himself as an American businessman. He was dining with an older Canadian colleague, he said, who had pointed Taylor out to him and reminded him of the role he had played in rescuing the American diplomats from Tehran. "I am no groupie," the man told

Taylor, "but I just wanted to say thanks." Taylor shook the man's hand warmly, without so much as a hint that this scene had played out hundreds of times over the last three decades.

There is a mystique about Ken Taylor even now. Yet, like the so-called Canadian caper itself, our sense of the man remains one-dimensional, almost a caricature. When the Central Intelligence Agency (CIA) allowed some of its covert operatives to step out of the shadows in 1997 and take credit for rescuing the six Americans from Tehran, it was easy to believe that the affable ambassador had exaggerated his, and by extension Canada's, contribution. Some Canadians, in the press and even in government, turned on him, branding him an imposter. Others were quietly disillusioned. In spite of Taylor's once-ubiquitous presence in North American popular culture, we suddenly realized that he had told us almost nothing about what had actually happened in Tehran. As it turns out, Ambassador Taylor was a master of the black art magicians call *legerdemain,* or misdirection. For the whole time he was cultivating his public persona as the unassuming hero of Tehran, he was concealing more about what he had actually done there than most of us could have imagined. In piecing together this story for the first time, *Our Man in Tehran* shines a light on the real Ken Taylor, a man we never really knew.

I first met former secretary of state for external affairs Flora MacDonald several weeks after my introduction to Ken Taylor. She graciously agreed to an interview at her home, a cozy Ottawa apartment that overlooks the Rideau Canal where she still ice-skates regularly. Her place is filled with the trophies of a life spent in Canadian and international politics—gifts from former heads of state, honorary degrees, various paintings, sculptures and tapestries from around the world. Among Ms. MacDonald's many mementoes is a small, framed watercolour. It shows two Muslim women in full chador (veil and gown) walking down a city sidewalk, small trees in the foreground and mountains rising in the background. The painting is obviously the work of an amateur, out of place among MacDonald's museum-quality treasures. I asked her about it. She told me that the watercolour was painted by American chargé d'affaires Bruce Laingen during his 444 days of captivity in Iran. This streetscape, she explained, had been his only window on the world for the 15 months he was imprisoned at the Iranian foreign ministry. Laingen had given MacDonald the painting as a token of his gratitude for her decisive role in rescuing his six American colleagues.

This vignette speaks to the broader pattern I encountered at every stage of my research, of enduring personal attachments forged in cruel circumstances. Ken Taylor and Bruce Laingen have remained good friends since their time in Tehran together, as have retired Canadian diplomat Roger Lucy and two of the Americans he helped to rescue, Mark and Cora Lijek. Flora MacDonald's collaboration with U.S. secretary of state Cyrus Vance cemented a close personal bond that lasted until his death in 2002. Many of the politicians, bureaucrats, diplomats and intelligence officers connected with the hostage crisis express identical sentiments—a profound sense of camaraderie coupled with a deep reservoir of pride in what they accomplished together.

A word on sources. Like many Canadian historians, I have benefited greatly from federal access-to-information and privacy (ATIP) provisions that allow for the opening (declassifying) of archival documents upon request. *Our Man in Tehran* is largely based on hundreds of newly opened External Affairs cables that moved between Ottawa, Washington, Tehran and other world capitals in the period before, during and after the hostage crisis. Because these cables were written in diplomatic language—terse, declarative sentences, all in capital letters and without articles (*the, an*)—I have reformed them slightly for ease of reading. Articles have been inserted into cable excerpts without the use of square brackets. Thus, "MUCH OF PUBLIC REACTION

HAS FOCUSED ON SPONSOR OF RESOLUTION" becomes "Much of the public reaction has focused on the sponsor of the resolution." I have also ignored the diplomatic convention of repeating the word *not*. Thus, "EMBASSY HAS NOT/NOT BEEN AFFECTED" becomes "The embassy has not been affected." In every other respect, the sources cited in the endnotes conform to established scholarly standards. There is no invented dialogue in this book.

Our Man in Tehran could not have been written without the help of others. It gives me great pleasure to acknowledge them here.

Research funding was provided by the Ontario Arts Council, for which I am indebted. For putting themselves at my disposal early on in my research, I am grateful to Rodney Moore, Mark Entwistle and James Hyndman of Foreign Affairs and International Trade Canada (formerly the Department of External Affairs). My thanks go out as well to Paulette Dozois at Library and Archives Canada (LAC), Lisa Perry and Diane Simard of the Access to Information division of LAC, Patrick Bélanger and Jo-Anne Valentine at the Foreign Affairs Library in Ottawa, Trish Johns-Wilson and Jacquie Slater of the Bata Library at Trent University, and Karen Benacquista, Heather Gildner and Denise Drabkin of the Toronto Public Library. I am also grateful to James Carrick, Thomas Fischer, Les Harris, Deborah Hulley, Jean-Pierre Juneau, Ramanand Kamineni, Arthur Milnes, Dennis Molinaro, Dan Wright, R. K. Wright, James Yancy and Shirley Young.

Ken Taylor, Mark Lijek, Roger Lucy and William Daugherty took a keen interest in this project at every stage, sitting for long interviews, agreeing to an extensive correspondence and reading early drafts of the book in their entirety. For their unstinting generosity, I am deeply indebted.

For their willingness to be interviewed for this book, I am grateful to Kenneth Curtis, Louis Delvoie, Laverna Dollimore, Claude Gauthier, Allan Gotlieb, Erik Lang, Flora MacDonald, John

Sheardown, Zena Sheardown, Michael Shenstone, Peter Tarnoff, Douglas Taylor and Pat Taylor. My thanks go out as well to those persons who kindly agreed to be interviewed on condition of anonymity. Special thanks to my research assistants, Helena Wright, Alex Barlow and especially Rachel Horner, and to my editor at HarperCollins Canada, Jim Gifford.

My greatest debt, as ever, is to my wife, Laura, and our children, Helena, Anna and Michael. *Our Man in Tehran* will be the first of my books in which Michael will be able to read his own name in the dedication. He will be disappointed to see that it is not about dinosaurs.

All writers know that words cannot express our debt to those we love. Yet we hope that our work will be read by them above all, for they are present on every page and in every line.

This book is for you, guys.

"An ambassador is a man of virtue sent abroad to lie for his country."
—Henry Wotton, Sr. (1568–1639)

PROLOGUE

On September 11, 2001, at 10:28 a.m., the north tower of the World Trade Center crashed to the ground, its iconic 360-foot communications antenna disappearing in an almost perfect vertical drop into a monstrous column of dust and debris. The tower had been spewing black smoke into the blue Manhattan skyline since the first of al Qaeda's hijacked planes, American Airlines Flight 11, had struck it two hours earlier. The south tower, torn asunder at 9:03 a.m. by the spectacular impact of the second hijacked plane, United Airlines Flight 175, had already been reduced to rubble.

Watching the cataclysm from New Jersey's Communipaw ferry terminal, due east across the Hudson River from Ground Zero, were Ken Taylor and his wife of over forty years, Pat. The two were on their way back to their Manhattan home after a short visit to Goose Bay, Labrador. They had actually intended to return on September 10, but a fire at Newark International Airport had forced their mid-afternoon flight to return to Halifax. The morning of September 11, the Taylors again flew from Halifax to Newark, this time landing without incident at 9 a.m.—just moments before the second plane hit the World Trade Center. They later learned that theirs had been one of the last flights permitted to land in the New York City area before the Federal Aviation Administration closed the airports. Had their flight entered U.S. airspace just ten minutes later, it, too, would have been forced back to Halifax; twenty minutes later and the Taylors might well have ended up back at Goose Bay along with the thirteen thousand other bewildered travellers whose diverted flights had delivered them into the homespun hospitality of the local Newfoundlanders.

No sooner had the Taylors landed in Newark than they were swept up in the unfolding drama of the day. "When I went to get my baggage," Ken Taylor later recalled, "I overheard one of the baggage handlers saying, 'Apparently a plane flew into the World Trade towers.' His partner said, 'Don't kid me.' So we picked up our bags, we got into a cab and the driver told us what he had been hearing on the radio. We turned around the corner of the terminal, and we could see the smoke coming up from Manhattan. The driver took us to a ferry stop on the Newark side, halfway between New Jersey and New York, and he said, 'This is as far as I can go.' People were coming off the ferries. We couldn't cross. Then at 10:30 we saw the second tower crumble."[1]

Like all inbound NYC commuters that day, the Taylors found themselves stranded after the Port Authority of New York and New Jersey closed all bridges, tunnels and ferries in the area. They spent the day in the bar of the Sheraton Hotel in Jersey City, glued, like most North Americans, to CNN. At eight in the evening, a friend picked them up and welcomed them into his New Jersey home for the night. The Taylors took the train back to New York the next day, making their way through the eerily quiet city, past the smouldering ruins of Lower Manhattan, and finally back to their Park Avenue apartment. They had been absent for only three days, but the city they had called home for twenty years had been transformed. "It certainly was a profound moment for us," Ken later reflected."[2]

~ ~ ~

Like most career diplomats, Ken Taylor remains an inveterate wanderer. Since retiring from the foreign service in the mid-1980s, he has spent two decades in the boardrooms of some of North America's leading corporations. This has meant international travel on an almost full-time basis—Calgary this week, Mexico City the next. He jokingly calls the eighteenth-floor lounge of Toronto's Park Hyatt hotel "the office," a picturesque space in the heart of the city where he regularly meets new acquaintances and old friends. Taylor personified the idea of globalization long before it became *au courant*. He has friends all over the world, and from all walks of life. He is casually multilingual, multicultural and cosmopolitan, and so are those closest to him. His wife, Pat, for example, is an Australian of Chinese descent whom he met while at graduate school in California. Their son, Douglas, bears a strong resemblance to them both. Ken Taylor has never renounced his Canadian citizenship, and he feels no less Canadian for having chosen New York as his permanent home. "Why would you want to live anywhere else?" he remarks with the sort of casual candour that makes nationalists in Canada bristle. His world is borderless.

The Taylors had gone to Goose Bay on September 9, 2001, to commemorate the death of RCAF airman Newton Van Allen exactly sixty years earlier. Accompanying them from New York was Elliott Roosevelt III, great-grandson of U.S. president Franklin Delano Roosevelt. The memorial service was organized by the Taylors' friend Dr. Traer Van Allen, who had been a child of ten when his brother "Newty" was killed in action. In words that resonated personally for

Ken Taylor, Van Allen eulogized his late brother's heroism during a sombre ceremony at the 5 Wing military cemetery. "He was so dedicated to Canada, democracy and the war effort. He wanted to do something important."[3] Taylor's presence at this modest memorial service amounts to little more than a tiny vignette in a lifetime of adventurous globe-trotting. Yet it somehow encapsulates the man's entire world view. He could have been anywhere on that magnificent autumn day, but he went to Goose Bay with Pat and some expatriate Canadian friends to honour a fallen soldier he had never known. It was a quiet display of personal loyalty from a man rightly famous for his civic generosity.

~ ~ ~

Standing with Pat amid the crowd of stranded commuters two days later, watching Lower Manhattan burn, Ken Taylor was sickened by what he saw but he was not surprised. As Canada's ambassador to Iran in the late 1970s, he had borne witness to the first incarnation of modern Islamic politics,[*] and he knew its power. He had watched as Iranian zealots—elderly holy men and their devoted young acolytes—fought to establish Islam's first theocratic state, destroying their enemies and later vanquishing even some of their most prominent loyalists. He saw the innocent perish along with the guilty, and he lost many friends. Long before 9/11, Taylor understood that the lifeblood of this potent new force in the Muslim world was not merely religious fervour but an incendiary, all-consuming anti-Americanism that had

---

[*] Following the American historian Michael H. Hunt, I prefer the phrase *Islamic politics* to either *Islamic fundamentalism* or *militant Islam*, which after 9/11 evoked President George W. Bush's own militant Manicheanism. See Michael H. Hunt, "In the Wake of September 11: The Clash of What?" *Journal of American History* 89:2 (September 2002), 422–3.

cast a long shadow over the Middle East and northern Africa. It was only a matter of time before it crossed the oceans.

As he watched the World Trade Center collapse in a heap of ash and twisted steel, so obviously the handiwork of the terrorist known to American intelligence authorities as UBL (Osama bin Laden), Taylor recalled with visceral intensity how two decades earlier a band of nameless students had become national heroes in Iran for taking one hundred American diplomats hostage. September 11 would usher in a brave new world of stateless, lawless terrorism, but for Taylor, the true catalyst had come on November 5, 1979, the day Ayatollah Ruhollah Khomeini gave his blessing to the students' occupation of the U.S. embassy compound in Tehran, transforming a short-term "set-in" into an interminable international crisis. "March forward bravely and deal with devilish American power!" the ayatollah told his young followers.[4] With this pronouncement, Taylor knew that Khomeini had set in motion "a war with no holds barred."[5] It would be a war with many enemies—liberals, secularists, Marxists, ethnic minorities—but none greater than the "Great Satan," the United States.

Many members of the diplomatic corps in Tehran waffled on the 1979 hostage-taking, but there was never any doubt about where the Canadian ambassador stood. He took the view that the armed occupation of a foreign embassy marked "the death knell of diplomacy," and this he took personally.[6] From the outset of the crisis, Taylor and his colleagues at the Canadian embassy would do everything in their power to help their beleaguered American counterparts. For their role in spiriting six U.S. diplomats out of Iran in January 1980, the Canadians would be celebrated as heroes on both sides of the forty-ninth parallel. Taylor's face, framed by a mop of greying hair and sporting Coke-bottle glasses, became one of the most recognizable in North America at the time. He was christened the Canadian "Scarlet Pimpernel" for his heroics. Countless photographs were taken, movies were made, honours bestowed. Yet while he and his colleagues enjoyed the accolades, never did they forget that among the fifty-three American hostages left behind in Tehran, and, indeed, among the millions of Iranians swept up in Khomeini's grand design, were some of their closest friends.

The hostages remained front-page news for 444 days, an intensely personal drama that engrossed millions of North Americans. Yet practically from the moment the Iranians finally freed them, in January 1981, the crisis faded from public view. "Somehow, the country did not want to ask many questions," a *New York Times* report later observed. "The homecoming seemed enough."[7] Ken Taylor's moment in the spotlight came and went, as he knew it would. Life went on. Yet even today, thirty years later, he can recall his experience of the hostage crisis with a clarity and an intensity undiminished by the passage of time. Never has he second-guessed his decision to take a tough stand during the crisis, and never has he softened in his conviction that he and his Canadian colleagues were on the right side of history.

These recollections and a hundred others flooded into Ken Taylor's consciousness as he stood with Pat on that New Jersey wharf and watched the north tower of the World Trade Center vanish into dust. It was already obvious that for most North Americans the attack on America on September 11 was a watershed event. But not for Taylor and the handful of Canadians posted to Tehran all those years ago.

~ ~ ~

Our Man in Tehran tells the story of the two and a half years that Ken Taylor served as Canada's top diplomat in Iran. When he first arrived, in September 1977, the country was firmly in the grip of Shah Mohammad Reza Pahlavi, an authoritarian monarch whom everyone expected to rule into the 1980s and beyond. "Unless the Shah becomes clearly incapable either physically or mentally of making decisions," the CIA had concluded just a month before Taylor's arrival, "no one is likely to be challenging him overtly for any portion of his power."[8] Nobody—not U.S. intelligence or the KGB or even Ayatollah Khomeini—anticipated how quickly the shah's regime would collapse. By the time Ambassador Taylor left Tehran, in January 1980, the shah was in exile, Khomeini was approaching the first anniversary of his triumphant homecoming, his Islamic revolution was an accomplished fact, and fifty-three American diplomats were entering their fourth month of captivity as prisoners of Iranian militants.

Like virtually all other foreigners in Tehran after the fall of the shah, Ken Taylor and his Canadian colleagues found themselves reacting to events that they could neither anticipate nor fully comprehend. "Who is in charge in Tehran?" was the refrain from the world's capitals as they tried to make sense of Iran's secretive, Byzantine new power structure. Posted initially to Iran to promote Canadian trade, Taylor might easily have imagined spending his ambassadorial tenure on Tehran's well-established diplomatic cocktail circuit. Instead he was drawn inexorably into the paroxysms of the revolution, becoming Canada's principal crisis manager there. When Ottawa directed Taylor to organize the evacuation of Canadian nationals from Iran, in January 1979, he and his embassy colleagues exceeded their superiors' expectations by a long measure. The ambassador was, all agreed, a man who could lead under pressure. When asked in February 1979 to quietly coordinate Canada's assumption of Israel's diplomatic interests in Iran, Taylor demonstrated his penchant for efficiency and discretion.

With each new challenge, the Canadian ambassador worked closely with others in the diplomatic corps, but particularly with the Americans, Ambassador William Sullivan and, later, Chargé d'Affaires Bruce Laingen. By the time the U.S. embassy compound was seized, in November 1979, demolishing the Americans' diplomatic and intelligence capability, Ken Taylor was one of the only Westerners in Iran trusted by Washington. Within weeks, he became the Americans' most valuable asset there.

Ken Taylor did not set out to be the hero of Tehran. As he lamented repeatedly over the course of his ambassadorial tenure, Iran's tragedy was that so many talented and dedicated individuals turned out to be "the wrong person at the wrong time."[9] Taylor himself was not one of them. As his American friends attest even now, it was their good fortune that a man of Taylor's élan was posted to the Iranian capital just as the storm was breaking.

OUR MAN IN TEHRAN

PART ONE
TEHRAN

Chapter 1
THE UNLIKELY AMBASSADOR

On Thursday, November 10, 1977, Kenneth Douglas Taylor awakened early, alone in his North Tehran villa save for one or two of the eight household staff he had inherited along with the house. He groomed himself, perused the English-language Tehran newspapers and put on his finest Francesco Smalto suit. After six weeks of serving unofficially as the head of the Canadian government mission in Iran, the day had finally arrived when he would officially be accredited as ambassador.

The forty-three-year-old Taylor had spent almost twenty years—his entire working life—climbing the ranks of the Trade Commissioner Service, the rough-and-tumble branch of the diplomatic corps responsible for cutting Canada's foreign-trade deals and managing its international commerce. Taylor had worked alongside many a Canadian ambassador and high commissioner, but never before had he been appointed head of mission (HOM) himself. This morning Taylor would present his credentials as Canada's fifth ambassador to the Imperial State of Iran. And he would do so before the country's reigning sovereign, Mohammad Reza Pahlavi, the Shahanshah Aryamehr (King of Kings), Light of the Aryans.

Coiffed and confident, Taylor left his house and climbed into the back seat of a waiting limousine. Flanked by two rows of police cars, his was one of six cars dispatched by the shah to carry a group of newly appointed ambassadors to the morning ceremony. Taylor was accompanied by three colleagues from the Canadian embassy, all of them, like him, decked out in white tie. Their driver had been instructed to take them to "the palace," an address that required no elaboration. The Niavaran Palace complex in the Shemiranat district of North Tehran was the permanent home of the shah and his entourage, the seat of Western power in the Middle East and the nerve centre of one of the most security-obsessed regimes in the world. As the regal cortège passed through the massive wrought-iron gates and onto the palace grounds, past the heavily armed sentries, the imperial troops at the honour guard and the impeccably manicured gardens, Taylor mused to himself that this was not an occasion he had ever envisaged as a young boy growing up in Calgary.

His instincts were more prescient than he could ever have imagined. Nothing in his foreign-service training could have prepared him, in fact, for the thirty extraordinary months he would serve as Canada's ambassador to Iran. It would be an exciting ride, and it would start the first day he was on the job.

~ ~ ~

Richard Taylor was a first-generation Welsh immigrant who ran a commercial printing shop in Calgary, initially with his father and later with his three brothers. His wife, Nancy Taylor, was born in Ontario and trained as a nurse. An only child, Ken, born in Calgary in 1934, excelled in virtually all areas of life: academic, athletic, social.

He developed an abiding attachment to his hometown, yet he knew well before leaving high school that there was a world beyond Calgary that he had to see. "There was no better place to be brought up," he later remarked, "but I knew that if I could get in elsewhere, I was not going to go to university in Alberta."[1] Taylor got his wish, completing a BA at the University of Toronto and a master's degree in administration at Berkeley. He went straight from grad school into the Canadian foreign service in 1959, serving as a trade counsellor in Guatemala, Pakistan and the UK. In 1971 he returned to Ottawa, rising quickly through the ranks of the civil service. By 1974 he was general director of the Canadian Trade Commissioner Service, the top job in the foreign-service section of the Department of Industry, Trade and Commerce.

After seven years, it was again time for Taylor to go abroad. He put the word out early in 1977 that he would like an ambassadorial posting. He could have had his pick of any number of embassies, but he asked for Iran because he had an instinct that it was on the verge of becoming one of the world's most exciting hot spots. "He was a very skilled and well-regarded diplomat," Prime Minister Joe Clark would later say of Taylor. "No one without those qualities would have gone to a situation like Tehran. That was a wild time, and one couldn't be sure that normal diplomatic niceties—protocols—would be followed."[2] Michael Shenstone, the Ottawa mandarin who would become Taylor's closest comrade at the Department of External Affairs during the hostage crisis, agreed. "I wasn't involved in the decision to send Ken to Tehran, but it was an excellent one," Shenstone later recalled. "He was the top trade person. It was apparent that he was right on top of things."[3]

External Affairs approved Taylor's appointment; putting some teeth in Canada's trade relationship with Iran, an OPEC country, had assumed a new urgency after the oil shock of 1973–4. Prior to that, Tehran was a rather undistinguished outpost for a Canadian diplomat. Canada had not bothered sending an ambassador to Iran before 1958, and after that the bilateral relationship seldom rose above "cordial if limited," as one Canadian HOM put it.[4] Although Iran was routinely heralded as Canada's second-largest export market in the Middle East, behind Israel, the value of those exports was a paltry $4 million* annually. Fewer than one hundred Iranians emigrated to Canada each year, and only a slightly larger number studied at Canadian universities. "Tehran was even considered a possible candidate for closure under austerity pressures," an External Affairs memo later noted flatly.[5]

The one bright spot in Iranian–Canadian relations prior to the energy crisis had come in the form of high-level visits. Shah Pahlavi and his wife, Empress Farah Diba, visited Canada together in 1965, touring Ottawa, Quebec, Montreal and Toronto. Two years later, the shah returned to Montreal to attend Expo 67. In 1971 the empress also visited Montreal to inaugurate the Iranian pavilion at Terre des Hommes. Farah's visit was reciprocated later the same year when Governor General Roland Michener and his wife attended the shah's celebration at Persepolis of the 2,500th anniversary of the Persian Empire, a $200 million affair described by the shah's critics as "a meaningless extravaganza staged by an ostentatious monarch."[6] In January 1971, Prime Minister Pierre Elliott Trudeau made a one-day stop in Tehran. Three years later Iranian prime minister Amir Abbas Hoveyda reciprocated with a state visit to Ottawa, where he cemented an enduring personal friendship with Trudeau.

One person who understood that the political was personal in imperial Iran was Taylor's predecessor as Canadian ambassador, the former Rhodes Scholar and career diplomat James (Jim) George. By his own admission, George had fawned breathlessly over the shah and his retinue when he arrived in Tehran in 1972. "My first impressions

---

* Unless otherwise indicated, all figures are U.S. dollars.

of Iran and of the Shah were highly favourable," he later recalled. "An Iranian renaissance was underway thanks to rapidly increasing oil revenues but also thanks to the vision and efforts of a remarkable man, the Shahanshah Aryamehr."[7]

Ambassador George was not the only Western observer to be seduced by the shah's imperial mystique in those days. Before the mid-1970s, when the very phrase "shah of Iran" became synonymous worldwide with repressive dictatorship and human-rights atrocities on a monstrous scale, Shah Mohammad Reza Pahlavi had cultivated an aura of divine untouchability, part sun king and part tabloid jet-setter. Film footage of the shah in mid-life reveals a confident, regal face and a taut, athletic physique. His bodily movements and speech were well rehearsed—subtle, understated, calibrated to impart an impression of serene self-importance. In addition to his native Persian (Iranians prefer the term *Persian* to *Farsi*), the shah spoke English and French fluently, always with a European rather than a Persian lilt. Strangely for a man who would come to personify iron-fisted authoritarianism, there was warmth and kindness in his eyes. His face and voice bore almost nothing of the angry intensity of some of the twentieth century's better-known tyrants. "The Shah's father was a dictator pretending to be a nice man," Jim George liked to say. "The Shah himself is a nice man pretending to be a dictator."[8]

Ambassador George discovered early on that the palace was the seat of Iranian power, prestige and glamour. Everyone from movie stars to business tycoons revelled in their proximity to the shah. "My predecessor was a learned and respected man, a scholar in his own right," Ken Taylor would later say of George, noting that he had brought to the post a solid grasp of Iranian culture and politics.[9] But George was not above punctuating his official dispatches from Tehran with gossip about the shah's inner circle. In January 1973, for example, he cabled Ottawa with a report that the shah was rumoured to have fallen in love with an "18 year old beauty," whom he had installed in one of his palaces.[10] Empress Farah, the shah's third wife and official *shahbanou* (empress) because she had borne him an heir, was said to be so upset by the affair that she had flown off to Switzerland. (Both of the shah's earlier marriages had ended in divorce.) Ambassador George speculated that the shah would not likely take the teenager, if only because King Hussein of Jordan had set the respectable limit on the number of marriages for Muslim heads of state at three. Six months later, however, George conceded to his superiors at External that he had misjudged the situation. The shah had indeed married the girl, Gilda Soufi. She was not eighteen but twenty-five years old, and their marriage remained a state secret. George cautioned his colleagues against leaking the story. "The political consequences for the shah at home and abroad are likely to be rather negative," the ambassador cabled Ottawa. "Please protect this info carefully."[11] Ottawa obliged.

Though Ambassador George was not considered aggressive in his pursuit of Canadian trade with Iran, the bilateral relationship took flight during his tenure; the oil boom had made Iran fabulously rich, inflating the country's per capita GNP from $200 to $1000 in one fell swoop.[13] All of a sudden, Tehran was the place to be. Trade ministers exchanged visits, and the value of Iranian–Canadian trade vaulted. By 1975 Canadian imports from Iran— almost entirely oil—were valued at $758 million, and exports at $145 million.[14] The largest Canadian enterprise in Iran was a forest-industries program developed as a joint venture between Stadler Herter of Montreal and an Iranian Crown corporation. Situated on the Caspian Sea, less than one hundred miles from the Soviet border, this $500 million venture included a sawmill, a plywood plant and the massive Gilan pulp and paper mill, with 103 Canadian employees. Other firms doing business in Iran included Massey Ferguson, Canada Wire and Cable, Canadian General Electric, Acres International and Ircan Corporation, virtually all of them involved in large resource-management projects. Iran expressed interest in CANDU reactor technology. There was even talk of Iran buying the Come By Chance oil refinery in Newfoundland.

Despite these prospects, snags persisted in Canada's trade with Iran. In February 1977, Ambassador George appealed to the shah to invite Canadian firms into offshore oil exploration in the Caspian Sea but was rebuffed because Iran's commercial agreements with the Soviet Union precluded either country from striking outside deals unilaterally. George also pitched Canadian firms involved in petro-chemical refining but was told by the shah that Iran already had excess refinery capacity from its European and Japanese partners. On the crucial matter of oil pricing, the shah said only that he would extend to Canada the same deal he had given the Europeans, namely, that it could pay for a certain portion of its petroleum purchases in goods and services. The shah invited George to consider Canadian participation in Iranian railway development, but the idea went nowhere after it became clear that Canada had little expertise in railway electrification, the only form of rail development in which the shah had any interest.[15]

On September 10, 1977, the shah received Ambassador George for a farewell call. His Imperial Majesty seldom said goodbye in person to exiting ambassadors, but he had made an exception in George's case, as "a gesture to Canada."[16] Summarizing the current state of Iranian politics for the benefit of his successor, George speculated that the new prime minister, Dr. Jamshid Amuzegar, would "wait for orders from the shah" rather than taking his own initiative. "It is now too complex a country for one man to take all the decisions, but psychologically [the shah] has conditioned his people to believe that it can be dangerous to take initiative from below." George concluded his tenure as ambassador with a prognostication typical of almost all Western observers in those years. "The difficulties inherent in the system cannot be gainsaid," he wrote, "but I feel that the basic strength of the Iran economy will pull them through and that they will be on another euphoric upswing in about two years."[17]

~ ~ ~

By the time he was called to present his credentials in November 1977, Ken Taylor had been in Iran six weeks, long enough to imbibe his predecessors' cardinal rule of political success there. "If you really wanted something done," he would say, "you had to have connections with the palace." Iranian government ministers were highly regarded among Western diplomats in Tehran: well educated, competent and dedicated. But alongside the official Majlis (parliament) ran a parallel system. "You had the classic public service and, on the other hand, you had the palace and the minister of court," Taylor later recalled. "You really had to, one way or the other, have a sensitivity to both of their functions but also have some degree of access." Canada's new ambassador began charting his own course as soon as he arrived in Tehran. "I got to know some people, some friends of the palace," said Taylor. "I had my own relationship with the shah. It was quite different from George's, but I was on equally good terms. I was also active in the community, active socially."[18]

When Taylor took over, the Canadian diplomatic mission was composed of nine foreign-service officers—the ambassador, three External Affairs officers, three Trade and Commerce officers, an immigration officer, and an attaché from the Canadian Forces. (The attaché would be recalled in May 1978 as a cost-saving measure.) The mission also employed twenty-five Iranian staff. The chancery building, at 57 Darya-e-Noor Street in downtown Tehran, was a squat three-storey building fronting directly onto the sidewalk. Unlike the twenty-seven-acre U.S. embassy compound, whose lush grounds and classical architecture symbolized the special status Americans enjoyed in Tehran, the Canadian embassy was an inelegant, practical building with little more to distinguish it than the Canadian coat of arms at the main entrance.

Not so the new ambassador. Naturally gregarious, Taylor was a good fit for Tehran, and he knew it. "To me, this wasn't a scholarly post in Tehran. I'm sure there were other avenues, but I wasn't necessarily well suited to them, nor was I inclined to pursue them." Because he had come out of Trade and Commerce, Taylor was already on a first-name basis with the trade commissioners of all the Middle Eastern countries. It was obvious to his superiors at External Affairs that he had the talent and drive for promoting Canadian business in Iran. "I got a good response from Ottawa," Taylor said of his appointment. "We'd had our wars between the departments [External Affairs, and Trade and Commerce], but everyone was now fully behind a trade-oriented push. My predecessor hadn't pursued that, so in a program sense we knew we would have a different emphasis."[19] It was the great irony of Ken Taylor's foreign-service career that he should be sent to a virtually unknown corner of the world to flog Canadian exports and end up instead the most celebrated Canadian diplomat since Lester Pearson. It still makes him smile.

From the outset, Taylor was well liked by those who worked with him. "Mr. Taylor was the best boss I ever had," his secretary in Tehran, Laverna Dollimore, later recalled. Starting with her first posting to Egypt in 1955, Dollimore had spent most of her adult life working in Canada's embassies abroad, almost always as secretary to the Canadian HOM. Her "bosses" had included Ambassador Robert Ford in Moscow and General Stewart Cooper of the International Commission of Control and Supervision (ICCS) in Laos. Recalling Taylor's take-charge attitude during the Iranian revolution and the hostage crisis, Dollimore surmised that it was the Americans' good luck that they had somebody at the Canadian embassy who was not cut from the typical diplomatic cloth. "I don't think anyone else would have acted first and informed Ottawa later," said Dollimore. "And if they had gone by the book, nothing would ever have happened."[20]

Dollimore is exactly right. Though charming and affable, Taylor brought other qualities to the ambassador's office that would prove at least as important to his management of the myriad crises he encountered in Iran. Three character traits stand out. The first is what then undersecretary of state for external affairs Allan Gotlieb identified as shrewdness. "[Taylor] is so cool he is difficult to read," wrote Gotlieb in his book *The Washington Diaries*. "There is this vacant air about him, this sort of aw-shucks, Li'l Abner quality that makes him very appealing and makes people interested in knowing what is going on beneath the surface. One mustn't be deceived. He is very shrewd."[21]

The second is courage. Like many foreign-service officers, Taylor is cool under pressure. He evinces not simply the fortitude to stand tall in the face of threats or imminent danger, but the courage of his convictions. The cable traffic between Taylor and Ottawa during his thirty months in Tehran reveals a man utterly confident in his own ability to anticipate events, analyze them thoroughly and navigate his way around this most foreign of locales, even when it was spiralling into chaos. More than once, Taylor knowingly broke the chain of command back in Ottawa—sometimes even acting against the direct orders of the Canadian prime minister. He took matters into his own hands in the knowledge that he and his colleagues in Tehran knew better than their superiors in Canada what was happening on the ground. Yet rather than precipitating a painful breach with his political masters—the fate of his friend U.S. ambassador William Sullivan after he challenged the orders of President Carter—Taylor's solid judgment won him the support of his colleagues at External Affairs, who more than once had to run interference for him against the PMO.

As ambassador, Taylor was eminently capable of consultation. His door was always open, say those who worked with him in Tehran, and he was a good listener. He welcomed contrarian views and judged the contributions of his subordinates on their merits. But this willingness to collaborate, combined with his "aw-shucks" personal style, to borrow Gotlieb's phrase, belied the third and most important personal attribute that Taylor brought to the job: decisiveness. Taylor gave his co-workers ample opportunity to state their views, but rarely did he delegate decision-making powers to them. And never did he allow his colleagues, some of whom were also friends, to challenge his authority when command decisions had to be made.

~ ~ ~

The Iran that welcomed Ken Taylor in 1977 was a dynamic mix of the fourteenth and twentieth centuries. Foreign travellers remarked on Iran's breathtaking antiquities—the Bastan archaeological museum and Iranian Crown jewels—and the miles of vaulted streets that made up the Tehran bazaar. They remarked as well on the geography of the city's class structure, the rich, including the shah, comfortably ensconced in the city's cool, mountainous north; the poor, in the hot, dense south. Tehran's nightlife had become equally legendary, with its discos filling in at about midnight and churning until dawn. "It didn't matter if I was out every night until two o'clock," Taylor later recalled. "Tehran was a wide-open city. There were times when I had two drivers because they just got too tired. We'd start early, and then there'd be parties and dinners. I don't remember sleeping too much from the time I arrived in Tehran until I left, for good reasons or bad!"[22]

Ken Taylor's friend CBC journalist Joe Schlesinger, recalled Tehran in those days as a boom town, a place where "just about every snake-oil salesman in the world had come through town trying to pick up a few crumbs from Iran's hoard of billions of petro dollars."[23] The most noteworthy feature of daily life in Tehran, then as now, was the traffic. "Tehran has one million cars and most of them seem to be making a U-turn at full speed," wrote one breathless Canadian travel reporter. "Tehran is often described as one huge traffic jam, but it's far worse than that—it's more like one vast head-on collision."[24]

Ken Taylor, ushered into the Niavaran Palace to present his credentials, along with several other newly posted foreign ambassadors, quickly gauged that the ceremony was going to exceed even his own expectations. He had already been through two dress rehearsals. The palace was "resplendent with pomp and circumstance," he later recalled of his initiation into the shah's inner sanctum. The shah appeared in white military dress, his field marshal's uniform adorned with a gold, red and blue sash. Officials of the Imperial Court, including Minister of Court Amir Abbas Hoveyda, wore gold-braided diplomatic attire. "It put the British to shame," Taylor later recalled of the ninety-minute ceremony. "I'd been in London, and I'd been in Buckingham Palace. Buckingham Palace looked positively threadbare in relation to the shah's palace. Here, you had the most beautiful carpets ever woven, and artwork worthy of the Louvre."[25] The presentation concluded with a meeting between the shah and the newly accredited ambassador.

Along with the shah and Hoveyda, Taylor's first round of get-acquainted visits included talks with Prime Minister Amuzegar and top officials from Iran's economic ministries. Although Taylor was by his own admission somewhat star-struck by the heady atmospherics of these first visits, they did not prevent him from coldly assessing what he saw as systemic weaknesses in the Iranian economy. "The cost of Iran's search for immediate and evident industrial maturity is appalling," he cabled Ottawa after his first meeting with the shah. "A veneer of managerial capability exists, massive projects often threaten to topple fragile infrastructure and [Iran's] inexhaustible appetite for modern weaponry has priority."[26] On one point he found himself in agreement with his Iranian hosts, however. Both Amuzegar and Hoveyda had extended invitations for Prime Minister Pierre Trudeau to come to Iran, even indicating that they had set aside a week in March 1978 for a state visit. Taylor endorsed the idea. "The visit of the prime minister," he told his superiors, "would underline Canada's determination to achieve an important new relationship with Iran."[27]

Within days of presenting his credentials, Taylor began lobbying Ottawa for a "Canada Week" trade fair in Tehran, topped off with a visit by Trudeau. He was particularly bullish on defence equipment. Iran needed aircraft simulators, tank transporters, naval supply ships and even frigates. Canada should redouble its efforts to "seize Iranian interest," Taylor urged Ottawa, which really meant courting the Iranian general in charge of procurement, Hasan Toufanian. "A high level visit from Canadian Forces would be of great assistance in this respect."[28]

When External officials met to discuss Taylor's "Canada Week" proposal, it became clear that "only a few of Ambassador Taylor's proposals are likely to be acceptable." With a federal election looming in Canada, there was almost no chance of even a ministerial-level visit, let alone a visit from Trudeau. "Lack of funds" was also a problem.[29] Taylor took this lukewarm reaction in stride but knew that Ottawa had missed a great opportunity. "A visit by Trudeau would really have put the Iranian–Canadian relationship on the map," he later said. "It would have meant a big commercial relationship. We were looking for dollars, exports. I started this because I saw what the Americans and the British were doing. I said, we've got to change this. Trudeau had been to Iran before, and the Iranians liked him."[30]

~ ~ ~

As Ken Taylor settled into his new role as Canada's pre-eminent booster in the Imperial State of Iran, he could not help but notice that beneath the gilded facade of the shah's absolute authority seethed political dissidence on a vast scale. Ottawa noticed it too. "We would be grateful for a brief assessment from you on the prospects of the Iranian regime staying in power," External Affairs queried the new ambassador. "We realize the difficulties of such crystal ball gazing, but would appreciate it if you would get out on a limb and tell us what you see."[31] Taylor responded with a prognosis typical of virtually every Western Iran-watcher in those days. "Within the obvious limits of 'crystal ball gazing' we would register optimism about the long run stability of the Iranian regime," the ambassador informed his superiors. "With the exercise of reasonable political judgement, change should prove evolutionary rather than revolutionary."[32]

Ambassador Taylor's optimism would not survive his first winter in Tehran. For before long, there would be little room for "reasonable political judgment" on either side of Iran's great political divide.

Chapter 2
A TOAST TO THE SHAH

Ambassador Taylor was correct about the predominance of the Americans and the British in postwar Iran. Their influence was pervasive. The Anglo-American allies had helped plan and execute the 1953 coup that had made the shah the unrivalled master of Iran. And in the twenty-five years that followed, the shah had reciprocated by making Iran the bastion of Western strength in the Middle East. One of the Ottawa mandarins to visit Taylor in Tehran early in his tenure described Iranian society as "very *ancien régime*."[1] Decades of autocratic rule underwritten by British and American largesse had led to profligate corruption, decadence and waste. Just below the surface of imperial stability lay economic and social pressures that, by the late 1970s, could be contained only by the worst sort of repression.

William Daugherty, retired CIA officer, former hostage and the author of one of the finest books on the hostage crisis, *In the Shadow of the Ayatollah*, has described Iran as "a fish between two cats."[2] Both as ancient Persia and as modern Iran (the name was changed officially in

1935), it has been the country's geopolitical fate to be coveted by rival foreign empires. In the mid-twentieth century those imperial centres were London and Moscow. Thrown together as allies after the German invasion of Russia in June 1941, Britain and the Soviet Union occupied Iran during World War II in order to protect the vital shipping route through Iran to the USSR. They deposed the reigning monarch, Reza Shah, ostensibly for his Nazi sympathies, and replaced him on the throne with his own son, Mohammad Reza Pahlavi.

It was inevitable that Iran would end up a flashpoint for the Cold War rivalry between the United States and the Soviet Union. For one thing, it shared a 1,500-mile border with the USSR (the territory that became Turkmenistan after 1991). For another, Iran's southern coast runs along the entirety of the Persian Gulf, the Strait of Hormuz and the Gulf of Oman—the waterway through which roughly half of the world's crude-oil supply was shipped after World War II. The Red Army pulled out of Iran in 1946, but this did not assuage American Cold Warriors at the embassy in Tehran. They believed that the Soviets would invade Iran on the slightest pretext. The CIA took a different view, advising President Harry S. Truman that the Russians were far more likely to act clandestinely in Iran. Truman agreed. In 1951, he authorized U.S. covert operations against the Soviets in Iran while simultaneously using American funds to prop up the Iranian government. Over the next six years, Iran would receive $60 million in American economic and military assistance.[3]

Meanwhile, the continuing presence of the British, symbolized by the British-controlled Anglo-Iranian Oil Company (AIOC), inspired fierce antagonisms in Iran. By early 1951, Iranian nationalists led by Mohammad Mossadeq had turned the nationalization of the AIOC into a highly popular crusade against Western imperialism more generally. Mossadeq was a European-educated aristocrat and scholar who had first served in the Iranian Majlis in 1920. He had no love for the shah, and even less for the British. Yet unlike many of the left-leaning anti-colonial leaders then stepping onto the world stage, he remained a democrat. Seeing that Mossadeq enjoyed massive support from the Majlis and from the Iranian people, the shah reluctantly appointed him prime minister on April 19, 1951. Mossadeq moved immediately to nationalize the AIOC, promising that one-quarter of the company's revenues would be used to compensate the British. This was not good enough for AIOC executives, who promptly withdrew their refinery employees and imposed a blockade on Iranian oil. Iran's petroleum revenues dropped by more than half, precipitating a national economic crisis.

Mass strikes and demonstrations followed. Iranians' support for Mossadeq began to waver, and his behaviour became increasingly eccentric. He took to meeting foreign dignitaries in his pyjamas. Both the Truman and later the Eisenhower administrations, watching from the sidelines, were anxious about Mossadeq's continuing refusal to work out his differences with the British. The Iranian prime minister was no communist, all could agree, but the mounting political instability caused by his policies played to the advantage of the Soviets. Mossadeq might, in desperation, turn to the communist Tudeh party to shore up his government, which in turn might precipitate a Soviet-sponsored coup. In the intensely anti-Soviet Cold War climate of the early 1950s, this was a scenario Washington could not abide, in Iran or anywhere else.

In April 1953, Eisenhower's director of central intelligence (DCI) Allen Dulles authorized the CIA to work with British intelligence to remove Mossadeq from office. Kermit "Kim" Roosevelt, head of the Near East (NE) Division of the CIA's Clandestine Service, was put in charge of coup operations, code-named "TPAjax," with a budget of $1 million. Roosevelt wooed the reluctant young shah into backing the coup, offering him both real power in Iran and an ironclad alliance with the United States. Thugs were paid to lead anti-Mossadeq demonstrations. Iranian military officers were enlisted. The shah went to Rome to await the outcome of the uprising as chaos engulfed the streets of Tehran.

Finally, on August 19, 1953, tanks commanded by army officers loyal to the shah shelled the prime minister's residence. Mossadeq fled and went into hiding. From Washington, the coup was pronounced a resounding success. The shah returned to Iran three days later, accompanied on his royal jet by CIA chief Allen Dulles. The shah immediately worked out a new royalty-sharing agreement with British and American oil companies and began building the promised alliance with the Unites States. Mossadeq surrendered and was later tried for high treason, imprisoned for three years and then placed under house arrest, where he died in 1967. Tudeh party members who had supported Mossadeq were arrested by the thousands. For the remainder of his term as president, Eisenhower would reward the shah's loyalty with aid and military assistance to Iran totalling over a billion dollars.[4]

A view apparently widely held within the United States foreign-policy elite is that Iranians did not harbour hard feelings about the 1953 coup until the late 1970s, when it gave them a useful grievance against the United States.[5] In truth, there is a good deal of evidence to suggest that Iranians were deeply affronted by Mossadeq's over-throw and that they carried this grudge directly into both the revolution and the hostage-taking of November 1979. The revolution-ary leader Sadegh Ghotbzadeh, for example, later recalled sitting at Mossadeq's feet after his release from prison, where he fully imbibed the old man's nationalist distrust of the West.[6] Many of the students who would later occupy the U.S. embassy spoke of similar formative experiences. One American who correctly gauged Iranians' resent-ment was Richard Cottam, political officer at the U.S. embassy in Tehran between 1956 and 1958 and later an adviser to the Carter White House. "The widespread awareness of the American role in aborting nationalist leadership is the basis for the distrust of U.S.

policy in Iran today," Cottam wrote in 1979.[7] Tim Weiner drew the same conclusion in *Legacy of Ashes,* his history of the CIA (a book that is loathed at Langley). "The taking of the hostages was an 'act of vengeance' for the CIA's 1953 coup in Iran," Weiner writes. "A blaze of glory for the covert operators of the CIA's greatest generation became a tragic conflagration for their heirs."[8]

~ ~ ~

In the wake of the coup, the shah fashioned policies custom-made for American approval. He adopted an aggressively anti-Soviet foreign and defence policy, and he launched a crash modernization program in the Western image. He put himself at the centre of Iranian politics and life, adopting the titles "Shahanshah" and "Light of the Aryans."

The shah's program of reforms came to be known as the White Revolution—to distinguish it from anything influenced by the communist Reds. Land was redistributed, education and health care were enlarged and the rights of women were extended. Such a program was by definition Western and secular. It challenged Iran's Muslim elites on many levels, thus providing fuel for the clerical dissidents who were rising to prominence after the 1953 coup. The White Revolution was also accompanied by corruption on a vast scale, and by the heavy-handed stifling of political dissent. The students who seized the U.S. embassy compound in November 1979 called it "a colossal scheme for enriching the royal family and its cronies."[9]

The year 1963 was a decisive turning point in the rise of domestic opposition to the shah, for it brought to the forefront of the dissident movement the Ayatollah Ruhollah Khomeini, the shah's nemesis and the man who would literally personify the revolution that was to drive the shah from power. Born in 1902, Khomeini was a direct descendant of the prophet Mohammed. Both his father and grandfather had been ayatollahs. Ruhollah studied Islam in the Iranian cities of Isfahan and Qom. He began teaching philosophy at the age of twenty-seven, earning a reputation as a devout Shiite Muslim and a courageous Iranian nationalist. In 1941, he wrote a book challenging the "dictatorial state of Reza Shah."[10] In 1953, the year of the coup, Khomeini won fame throughout Iran as the man who would not rise and bow in the presence of the shah. "The king is a usurper," said Khomeini then. "Any respect for him is an anti-religious act."[11] In 1960 Khomeini became an ayatollah himself, an elite designation within Shiite Islam that confers not merely religious status but social standing. The ayatollahs' authority was so widely revered within Iran, and their status so elevated, that they were all but untouchable politically. As the only opposition group the shah was unwilling to crush mercilessly, the clergy led by Khomeini would emerge as the natural rallying point for virtually all of the dissidents arrayed against the regime. As the *New York Times'* Nicholas Gage observed, "Denied the outlets of free newspapers, political parties, student organization or free speech, the opponents of the shah gravitated toward the only forum that remained open to them: approximately 80,000 mosques and holy shrines, under the supervision of an estimated 180,000 mullahs.'"[12]

In July 1963, Ayatollah Khomeini made a bold anti-shah speech before 100,000 people at a mosque in Qom, after which he was arrested and imprisoned. He was not physically abused but he was reportedly made to listen to recordings of other prisoners being tortured. Released from jail a few months later, an unrepentant Khomeini openly criticized the Majlis for passing a bill exempting American military personnel from the jurisdiction of Iranian courts. "If an Iranian kills an American's dog," said Khomeini, "he goes before a court. But if an American shoots the Shah, we cannot try him."[13] In October 1964, Khomeini gave another major speech, this time fusing

---

* Muslim clerics

Islam to Iranian nationalism and appealing to Iranians to fight for a clerical form of government. "If the religious leaders have influence," he said, "they will not permit this nation to be the slaves of Britain one day, and America the next. . . . Let the American president know that in the eyes of the Iranian people he is the most repulsive member of the human race."[14] For these remarks Khomeini was again arrested. This time the shah had him exiled, first to Turkey and then to the southern Iraqi city of Najaf. For the next fourteen years, while Khomeini himself lived in relative seclusion in Iraq, hundreds of thousands of cassette tapes of his sermons were circulated covertly throughout the network of mosques of Iran, building the revolutionary movement that would later bring down the shah.[15]

~ ~ ~

Practically from the day of his return to Iran after the 1953 coup, Shah Mohammad Reza Pahlavi pursued an iron-fisted security policy, which meant surveilling threats to Iran and also to his own authority. In 1955, with the help of the CIA and the Israeli intelligence agency, Mossad, he created the Sazman-e Ettela'at Va Amniyat-e Keshvar (SAVAK), a vast intelligence and security organization that operated unchecked in Iran for the next twenty-four years. By 1977, when Ken Taylor arrived in Tehran, SAVAK had approximately 5,300 employees, 55,000 informers and an annual budget of $225 million.[16] "No matter which town, village or city I went to," Taylor later recalled, "there was always a local SAVAK official there who was seen to be at the same level as the local administrator. They were *everywhere*."[17]

The scale of SAVAK's human-rights atrocities in the 1970s remains almost unfathomable. To the dominant liberal-democratic sensibility in Canada—where a single tortured Canadian today inspires public outrage, a judicial inquiry and generous compensation—the apparatus of state-sanctioned torture and murder in imperial Iran seems a world away. Yet this apparatus is the starting point for any serious understanding of the Iranian revolution, of Iranians' devotion to Ayatollah Khomeini, of their seething hatred for the shah and his U.S. protectors, and even of their willingness to take American hostages to extort the shah's return to Iran to face justice.

Plausible estimates of the number of political prisoners jailed in Iran in the 1970s range from 25,000 to 100,000. (Iran's population, according to the 1976 national census, was 33.7 million—roughly the same as Canada's population today.) In 1980, the Pakistani journalist Eqbal Ahmed estimated that the number of Iranians killed under torture or execution since the 1953 coup totalled 125,000. "Iranians believe it was 150,000 or more," wrote Ahmed, "but God only knows. Iran's best poets died under torture. Iran's finest writers lived in prisons."[18] Writing in 1979, the Iranian-born history professor Ervand Abrahamian asserted that "[o]ver 90 per cent of the victims have been members of the intelligentsia—teachers, engineers, office employees, and undergraduates and high school students."[19]

Illuminating SAVAK atrocities put Amnesty International on the map in the 1970s, which in turn helped to make human rights "the idea of our time."[20] "The shah of Iran retains his benevolent image despite the highest rate of death penalties in the world, no valid system of civilian courts, and a history of torture which is beyond belief," wrote Amnesty's Martin Ennals in 1975 after talking to hundreds of SAVAK's victims.[21] Among the cruelties listed in Ennals' groundbreaking report were "whipping and beating, electric shocks, the extraction of nails and teeth, boiling water pumped into the rectum, heavy weights hung on the testicles, tying prisoners to a metal table heated to a white heat, inserting broken bottles in the anus, and rape."[22] Iranian poet Reza Baraheni later recounted to William J. Butler, a New York lawyer who investigated SAVAK for the International Commission of Jurists, how he had been imprisoned by SAVAK for 102 days in

1973. "They hang you upside down," said Baraheni, "and then some-one beats you with a mace on your legs or on your genitals, or they lower you down, pull your pants up and then one of them tries to rape you while you are still hanging upside down." Baraheni was released only when he agreed to make a televised confession denouncing com-munism. "I was told that if I didn't confess," he said, "my wife and 13-year-old daughter would be raped in front of my eyes."[23]

In an interview for *60 Minutes* in October 1976, one year after the explosive Amnesty International revelations, the shah denied that torture took place in Iran—"torture in the old sense of torturing people—twisting their arms and doing this and that. But there are intelligent ways of questioning now."[24] Two years later he was again questioned on television about torture, this time by a French journal-ist. "Well, this is a question that was put to me more than once," he replied in English, "and which I don't like at all. We don't have to tor-ture people. This is the way that unsophisticated organizations were doing things. We are as sophisticated as you are now."

Some American officials, including former U.S. ambassador to Iran Richard Helms, speculated that the shah did not know about SAVAK's methods. "In suppressing dissidence and active resistance to the Shah's rule, SAVAK, the Iranian security and intelligence service, inflicted its power ruthlessly," Helms wrote in his 2003 memoir. "I was never sure whether the Shah knew the extent of SAVAK's brutality."[25] American historian Nikki R. Keddie rejects such claims. "It is not credible," she wrote of the shah in 2006, "that he did not know of the tortures he often denied."[26] In 1979, former SAVAK officers Bahman Naderipour and Fereidoun Tavangari testi-fied in a revolutionary court that the shah had given them explicit orders four years earlier to hide evidence of torture. "Don't take any prisoners," the shah had said, "kill them."[27] Naderipour described taking nine political prisoners out of their Evin Prison cells, blindfolding them and machine-gunning them. Tavangari confirmed that he and Naderipour had also killed other prisoners in their cells, telling medical examiners that they had died resisting arrest.

The shah's opponents would later charge the United States with training and equipping SAVAK and with educating its officers in the ways of torture. A delegation of Americans was invited to Tehran in February 1980, for example, the fourth month of the hostage crisis, and given a tour by one of the hostage-takers, Massoumeh Ebtekar. "They even met some imprisoned SAVAK members," Ebtekar later wrote, "who explained how they had been trained in Israel by Mossad specialists in torture methods while in close 'professional' cooperation with the CIA."[28] There was a kernel of truth in such charges. Until 1961, the FBI and CIA had trained SAVAK officers, in the belief that the Soviets had never relinquished their designs on Iran and maintained an ever-present clandestine force there. But after 1961 Mossad alone had coached SAVAK. When the CIA's four officers at the U.S. embassy were taken hostage on November 4, 1979, they were specifically accused of training SAVAK in torture. "There was no truth to this," William Daugherty later wrote. "As I repeated many times to my captors, not only is systematic torture not a part of the American tradition, certainly no one needed to teach Iranians how to torture; they had long been masters of the art."[29]

The charge levelled by Iranians like Massoumeh Ebtekar that does ring true is that Washington had done little to criticize the shah's human-rights abuses, and even less to curtail them. Appearing before a congressional committee reviewing Iranian human-rights abuses in October 1976, Alfred L. Atherton, assistant secretary for Near Eastern and South Asian affairs, summarized U.S. policy in Iran after 1953. "[W]e believe that the administration of Iranian judicial and penal systems is above all a matter of internal Iranian responsibility and that one sovereign country should not interfere lightly in another's domestic affairs," he said.[30] Henry Kissinger agreed. "I hold the strong view that human rights are not appropriate for discussion in a foreign policy context," Kissinger said flatly in 1975, when he was President Gerald Ford's secretary of state.[31] Four years later, in February 1979, when the Iranian revolution was in full flame, Kissinger told *The Economist* that President Carter's flirtation with human rights had been a disaster in Iran. "If we attempt to take the curse off our geo-political necessities by placating our human rights advocates in the middle of [a] crisis we make a catastrophe inevitable," he said. "In Iran our human rights policy has contributed to instability."[32]

~ ~ ~

Like most Westerners, Canadians were appalled by the revelations of SAVAK's brutality, by the shah's reputed complicity in it and by the Americans' apparent indifference toward it. "The Canadian media does indeed seem to follow the general fashion of making Iran rather a *bête-noir*," wrote one External Affairs official to the Canadian embassy in Tehran in early 1977.[33] When Ayatollah Khomeini appeared on the world stage the following year, denouncing the shah and demanding that Iran be returned to the Iranian people, Canadians who knew little about his politics and even less about his faith understood implicitly that he was taking a stand against tyranny. Such sentiments persisted until well after the shah's overthrow and, in some quarters, even into the period of the hostage crisis. The Canadian-born scholar Jim Cockcroft put the case this way in a published "letter from Tehran" in February 1980: "The demand for the return of the ex-Shah and his stolen wealth needs to be understood—in the context of Iran's highly moralistic atmosphere and the students' idealism—as more than a desire for personal revenge or destruction of the dynastic claim. Rather, it expresses the desire of Iranians that the world know what happened under the Shah and how it was made possible by U.S. support. The criminality and corruption of the Shah's regime go beyond most people's imagination, and Iranians feel the world must know 'so that it should never happen again, anywhere.'"[34]

Ambassador Ken Taylor had not been in Tehran a month before he had taken the measure of the shah's repressive security apparatus and what it meant for the diplomatic corps in Iran. "SAVAK was an evil presence," Taylor later recalled, "but it had become a way of life." On a personal level, Taylor was a proponent of what would later be called "constructive engagement": "I thought that the further Iran integrated itself into the international community, the more the regime would see that it was in its interests to improve its record on human rights." Yet as a professional diplomat, Taylor was very much a man of his times. Like Henry Kissinger and other Cold War practitioners of *realpolitik*, he believed that if human-rights talk was allowed to dilute a clear conception of the national interest, the results could be disastrous. "Everybody talked about SAVAK with distaste and abhorrence," he said, "but nobody really saw it as a plank in their relationship with Iran."[35]

Asked recently whether as ambassador he had been in any position to advance human-rights reforms in Iran, Taylor insisted that the culture of international diplomacy mitigated against it. "I don't think it was the mood in Ottawa, and it was not the mandate of our embassy. If Ottawa had sent me something saying, go and see the highest official you can and pursue this issue of human rights, I would have been astonished. It simply was not something that Canada pursued internationally with respect to bilateral relations. It was fine to support the UN refugees program—it was fine to adopt some sort of principle or measure at the UN—but in terms of implementing it on a bilateral basis, I don't think it was in anybody's letter of instruction."[36]

~ ~ ~

The biggest riddle of the Iran hostage crisis is why U.S. president Jimmy Carter—the man credited with putting human rights on the U.S. foreign-policy agenda—adopted his predecessors' policy of massive support for the shah and, in so doing, made himself an object of loathing for the Iranian people.

The answer to this riddle lay in Carter's inheritance from Richard Nixon. In the wake of Vietnam, Nixon and Kissinger decreed a new strategic orientation for the United States, the Nixon Doctrine. The United States could no longer afford to pursue a policy of global anti-communism, they asserted, if this meant confronting insurgency in every corner of the world. Henceforth, the United States would pick its fights. It would disengage from the zero-sum game of containment unless its national interests were directly threatened. This new, downsized Cold War strategy was perfectly suited to the shah, whose aspirations to establish Iran as a regional superpower were limitless.[37] But it was a disaster for the U.S. in Iran. "The Nixon years crystallized the U.S. government's relationship with the shah at the expense of the Iranian nation as a whole," William Daugherty has explained "From then until the end of Mohammad Reza Pahlavi's rule, U.S. national security policies in the Middle East were predicated on him and his retention of power."[38]

In May 1972, President Nixon visited the shah and agreed to an arms deal that would give Iran almost unlimited access to America's non-nuclear arsenal. Over the protestations of the Pentagon, Nixon even promised the shah F-15 fighter jets—planes so new that they were not yet in use by the U.S. Air Force. As Jimmy Carter's secretary of state Cyrus Vance later observed, nobody knew when this deal was inked that within a year the OPEC oil crisis would give the shah the money to commence "a military build-up of abnormal proportions."[39] By 1977, the shah's generals had placed orders for an astounding $30 billion in new armaments from the United States, making Iran the Americans' largest weapons export market by far. Ken Taylor's friend Michael Shenstone visited Iran in February 1978 and could hardly believe what he saw. "I remember going out with

Ken to Isfahan," said Shenstone. "We landed at Isfahan airport, and on the other side of the airport was a huge field—it looked like a square mile—of military helicopters that the shah had bought from the U.S. Helicopters as far as the eye could see. For what? You could see there the conspicuous waste. What was he defending himself against?"[40]

Many American policy-makers who later tried to figure out what went wrong in Iran highlighted the divergent views of Cyrus Vance and National Security Advisor Zbigniew Brzezinski, as though President Carter was incapable of reconciling their competing conceptions of America's strategic interests. Carter's DCI, Stansfield Turner, for example, believed that the "Brzezinski–Vance schism . . . badly hurt the President's foreign policy."[41] Yet even at the worst moments of the hostage crisis the president never concurred in this view. "Zbig is a little too competitive and incisive," Carter confided to his diary in February 1979. "Cy is too easy on his subordinates. And the news media constantly aggravate the inevitable differences and competition between the two groups. I hardly know the desk officers and others at State, but work very closely with the NSC people. . . . [W]e've never had any problems between the groups."[42]

Vance and Brzezinski disagreed on many things, but not on the necessity of maintaining the Nixon Doctrine, especially in Iran. While Vance would be called the dove of the Carter administration, there was nothing dovish about his hard-nosed assessment of the shah's importance to American national interests. "Iran was a reliable supplier of oil to the West," Vance observed, "and its exports were crucial to our NATO allies and Japan. The shah had refused to join the 1973 Arab oil embargo or to use oil as a political weapon. He was also Israel's primary external source of oil."[43] The hawkish Brzezinski agreed completely. Iran was, he noted, "our major strategic asset" in the Middle East.[44] President Carter did not have to be convinced. Academic studies of Carter's human-rights speeches show that, as president, "he went out of his way to exempt the shah from harsh criticism allotted to strategically less important countries."[45]

What did set Carter apart from Nixon and Kissinger was his belief that quiet diplomacy was the best means of advancing human-rights reforms in Iran. This would turn out to be the fatal flaw in Carter's Iran policy. In May 1977, the president sent Cyrus Vance to Tehran to "put our human rights and arms sales policies in proper perspective."[46] As expected, the secretary of state found the shah anxious about the new human-rights orientation of U.S. foreign policy and disheartened about all of the bad press he was getting in the United States. Vance quickly put him at ease, extending a personal invitation from the president to visit the White House in November 1977. He also agreed to sell the shah new F-16 fighters and AWACS aircraft. When they got around to the subject of human rights, their discussion was cordial. Vance reminded the shah that "the president was committed to reaffirming the primacy of human rights as a national goal."[47] The shah replied that his regime was "under attack from within by Communists and assorted other fellow travelers and that there were limits on how far he could go in restraining his security forces."[48]

This was good enough for the secretary of state. "We applauded and supported the measures the shah was beginning to take to improve human rights," Vance later wrote. "He already had begun to curb SAVAK in its use of extralegal measures to control subversion, and he was working to strengthen judicial and police procedures for dealing with political opponents."[49]

~ ~ ~

The cracks started to appear in President Carter's quiet diplomacy in November 1977, the month that Ambassador Taylor presented his credentials at the palace. Since Carter's inauguration the previous

January, a group of leading non-communist Iranians had organized themselves into the Committee for the Defense of Human Rights and Liberty. They openly lobbied the shah for human-rights reforms in the belief that the Carter White House would prod the regime in the same direction.[50] For a time, their instincts proved correct. Over the summer and fall of 1977, the shah did permit "a degree of mild dissident activity," as a confidential cable from the Canadian embassy to Ottawa noted. "These moves were seen as reflecting the shah's sensitivity to or uncertainty about President Carter's human rights posture."[51] Then, on November 15, 1977, the shah made his promised state visit to Washington. The expectation in Iran was that Carter would use the occasion to leverage further human-rights reforms. As the visit unfolded, however, it became clear that this was not going to happen.

The shah's appearance at the White House would later be recalled by almost everyone connected with the hostage crisis as an omen of the disaster to come. At 10:30 a.m., President Carter, the shah and their wives assembled together for a welcoming ceremony on the lawn of the White House. Meanwhile, in the Ellipse, to the south of the White House, pro- and anti-shah demonstrators got into a brawl. DC police had to break up the melee using tear gas, clouds of which then drifted into the White House garden. As the television cameras rolled, the two heads of state, their wives and various officials began to cough and dab their eyes. "I stood and wept," President Carter later recalled. "Tears were streaming down the faces of more than two hundred members of the press. It was a memorable moment."[52]

If the optics of the two leaders weeping on the White House lawn were bad, Carter's warm personal rapport with the shah was worse. "The Shah was a likable man," the president had discovered, "erect without being pompous, seemingly calm and self-assured in spite of the tear-gas incident, and surprisingly modest in demeanor."[53] In a private meeting in the White House Cabinet

Room, attended by Vance and Brzezinski, Carter and the shah amicably discussed world politics and the many complicated problems afflicting the Middle East. After this session, Carter requested a private meeting with the shah so he could impart his thoughts about Iran without embarrassing his guest. "You have heard of my statements about human rights," Carter told the shah. "A growing number of your own citizens are claiming that these rights are not always honored in Iran." He then asked specifically about the mounting protests of Iranian religious leaders and students. "Iran's reputation in the world is being damaged by their complaints," said Carter. "Is there anything that can be done to alleviate this problem by closer consultation with the dissident groups and by easing off on some of the strict police policies?"[54]

The shah paused to gather his thoughts and then gave an answer that would have surprised none of Carter's predecessors. "No, there is nothing I can do," he said. "I must enforce the Iranian laws, which are designed to combat communism. This is a very real and dangerous problem for Iran—and, indeed, for the other countries in my area and the Western world. It may be that when this serious menace is removed, the laws can be changed, but that will not be soon. In any case, the complaints and recent disturbances originate among the very troublemakers against whom the laws have been designed to protect our country. They are really just a tiny minority, and have no support among the vast majority of Iranian people."[55]

This was good enough for Carter, as it had been for Vance. The state visit was pronounced a success, and the two leaders parted in "good spirits," as Carter himself put it.[56]

It was not long before the grim consequences of Carter's personal diplomacy were resonating in the jails of Tehran. The moment the shah returned home from Washington, he returned to his hardline stand against political dissidence, freeing SAVAK to undertake the worst repression Iran had seen in a year.

From the vantage point of the White House, the shah's state visit had served to placate a key ally. Cyrus Vance later recalled happily that "we received from the embassy in Tehran glowing reports of [the shah's] new mood of confidence."[57] The view from beyond the U.S. embassy compound in Tehran was not nearly as sanguine, however. "The consequent crackdown immediately following the shah's return from Washington DC," the Canadian embassy cabled Ottawa, "fuelled speculation that ... President Carter adopted a relatively soft posture on human rights in deference to oil considerations and Iran's strategic importance."[58] Ayatollah Khomeini drew precisely the same conclusion. From his revolutionary headquarters in suburban Paris, he promptly issued a fatwa against the shah, calling him a "usurper" and urging Iranians not to obey his laws or pay their taxes. In issuing this decree, Khomeini referred to himself for the first time as Imam, a salutation reserved for Shiite leaders believed to be divinely inspired.[59]

Carter's reciprocal state visit to Iran occurred over New Year's Eve 1978, a one-night stop on a nine-day tour of the Middle East. The president's critics liked to say that he had a knack for bringing trouble down on himself, and on this occasion they were dead right. During a lavish banquet for the president, the shah introduced Carter by speaking of Americans' "high ideals of right and justice, moral beliefs in human values."[60] Ignoring his advisers' suggestion that he respond with understatement, Carter answered with an equally obsequious speech. "Iran, because of the great leadership of the shah," said Carter, "is an island of stability in one of the more troubled parts of the world. This is a great tribute to you, your majesty, and to your leadership, and to the respect and admiration and love which your people give to you."[61] Broadcast throughout Iran and around the world, the president's body language conveyed at least as much as his words. Speaking extemporaneously, his face intensely sincere, one hand in his suit-coat pocket, the president turned and faced the shah directly when he spoke of the love of the Iranian people. Coming from a man renowned for his monotonous speeches and his southern Baptist reserve, it was unexpected, unscripted and heartfelt.

It was, in short, a bombshell. And in Iran it changed everything.

~ ~ ~

Ken Taylor was not invited to the shah's New Year's fete, but he recognized immediately the significance of President Carter's speech. "Everybody knew the toast by heart in Tehran," the Canadian ambassador later recalled drily.[62] From that moment on, the Iranians' brewing resentment of the shah would be tinted by an equally intense anti-Americanism. "To the Iranians in the streets [Carter's] speech was tantamount to an irreversible breach of faith," William Daugherty later wrote, "the final proof to millions of Iranians who had counted on the president to bring human rights to the oppressed. Feeling abjectly betrayed, the Iranians lost faith in President Carter and, with the viciousness of the scorned, came to loathe him with a personal intensity."[63] "Death to Carter!" would now be chanted in the streets of Tehran along with "Death to the shah!"

For Ambassador Taylor, Carter's New Year's toast marked the beginning of the end of everything he had been sent to Iran to accomplish. From that moment on, his dispatches to Ottawa would centre not on trade fairs and export contracts, but on the steadily mounting chaos in the streets of Tehran and the equally steady erosion of the shah's authority. "[T]he recent pattern of dissent activity escalates the risk of a future convergence of leftist and rightist elements," the Canadian embassy informed Ottawa in its confidential monthly report for February 1978. "Should the various ideologies in fact converge . . . one can expect the greatest threat to the Shah's regime since the Mossadegh coup to develop."[64] By March 1978, seven months before the CIA even acknowledged the possibility that the shah might fall, the Canadians in Tehran knew that they were witnessing the origins of a full-blown revolution.

Posted to Iran to drum up exports and to manage Canadian trade, Ken Taylor's appointment as ambassador had been a strictly status quo, business-as-usual affair. Only two months had passed between his presentation of credentials and Carter's New Year's toast, and yet already the ground was shifting beneath his feet.

Fortunately for the Canadians in Iran, and especially for their American friends, the rookie ambassador was not a status quo, business-as-usual sort of man.

PART TWO
REVOLUTION

Chapter 3
THE DOWNWARD SPIRAL

Ken Taylor and his colleagues at the Canadian embassy spent most of 1978 watching from the sidelines as the shah's regime self-destructed, along with Iran's strategic alliance with the United States. Canada's diplomats were astute observers of the deteriorating political scene in Tehran. Their voluminous cables to Ottawa were peppered with detailed analyses of the shah's efforts to retain power and the work of his enemies to thwart them. By the time the shah fled Iran, in January 1979, few people anywhere had a better understanding of the complex mechanics of the Iranian revolution, or of the approximately forty dissident groups that had rallied behind Khomeini to triumph over the shah.

The shah's ability to manage events in Iran unravelled just days after Jimmy Carter's New Year's toast. On January 7, 1978, an article was published in Tehran claiming that Ayatollah Khomeini was a traitor and a homosexual. Such a libel would never have appeared in print without the shah's authorization, Iranians reasoned. The

following day, protesters loyal to Khomeini staged a massive demonstration in Qom. They were met with an overwhelming show of
force. A riot ensued, police fired on the crowds and several demonstrators were killed. Over the following months, protests and rioting
spread to the industrial city of Tabriz, and from there to Isfahan and
Tehran. By the summer of 1978, mass demonstrations accompanied by crippling strikes threatened to paralyze the country. The same
scenario repeated itself time and again in the streets of Iran's seething
cities. Poorly trained and zealous police clashed with equally zealous
protesters who were prepared to become martyrs in the fight against
the shah's tyranny.

The shah appeared not to know how to cope with the new reality. He was, as Cyrus Vance later recalled, "under intense pressure
from military hawks and civilian advisers alike to discontinue his
policy of political liberalization and crush the demonstrations with
unrestrained force."[1] For a time the shah opted for carrots as well as
sticks. In a televised address to the nation on August 5, he announced
a program of political reforms that included freedom of speech, of
the press and of assembly. Iran would also have a free parliamentary
election the following summer, he said. In an effort to thwart corruption and nepotism, the shah decreed that his own family would
henceforth be prohibited from participating in public-sector projects. He also made a significant symbolic step in the direction of
human-rights reform, recalling Nematollah Nassiri, the notorious
former head of SAVAK, from his ambassadorial posting in Pakistan
to face torture charges before a military tribunal. It was all too little
too late for his critics. They were emboldened rather than appeased
by his unprecedented concessions. The street violence escalated.

On the evening of Saturday, August 19, arsonists set the Rex
Theatre in the Iranian port city of Abadan ablaze, killing 377 people,
most of them children. Local police told the press that "entire families were wiped out."[2] The massacre was made worse by the theatre's

policy of locking the exit doors, a common anti-terrorism strategy in Iran at the time. Within 24 hours, as new victims succumbed to their burns, the death toll rose to 430, making the fire one of the world's worst ever in a place of entertainment. Virtually every sector of Iranian society, including opposition leaders and prominent Shiite clergy, condemned the attack and mourned its victims. Yet instead of using the tragedy to rally the country's sympathies, the shah stoked political tensions by blaming "communists and conservative religious fanatics" for the blaze.[3] Another round of massive street demonstrations followed.

Washington's view of the mounting political violence in Iran was polarized. American diplomats in Tehran, led by Ambassador Bill Sullivan, implored their colleagues at the State Department and the White House to hedge their options in Iran and make contact with the shah's opponents, including Khomeini. "[T]he embassy continued to expand its network of contacts among the dissidents and to gain their confidence," Ambassador Sullivan later recalled of his activities in the spring and summer of 1978. "Many of them were genuinely surprised to discover that we were intellectually sympathetic with them."[4] Although Cyrus Vance was personally ambivalent, the idea that the shah should forge a coalition with the Iranian opposition was gaining ground at the State Department. The hawks in the Carter cabinet took a contrary view. They believed that an "iron fist" from the shah would cool the street protests and restore the status quo. Zbigniew Brzezinski was categorical in his advice to Carter. The president had to make it easy for the shah to be "tough."[5] Carter, who was preoccupied with other foreign-policy concerns—the Camp David summit on the Middle East, strategic arms limitation talks with the Soviets, normalization talks with China—tacitly followed a middle path on Iran. He urged the shah to take a stronger stand against the dissidents while simultaneously pressing for human-rights and democratic reforms.

Brzezinski would later say that Carter's mixed messages to the shah at this critical juncture were the undoing of his Iran policy and ultimately of his presidency.[6]

~ ~ ~

If the view from the White House was fractious, the view from Langley was myopic. The CIA's inability to gauge the strength of the forces building against the shah is now widely regarded as one of the agency's worst intelligence failures prior to September 11. "We did not understand who Khomeini was and the support his movement had," said DCI Stansfield Turner. "We were just plain asleep."[7]

There were several reasons for this intelligence failure. The most obvious was the assumption—shared by virtually everyone in Washington until well into 1978—that although the shah had to contend with a determined opposition, it posed no serious threat to his regime. "The Shah will be an active participant in Iranian life well into the 1980s," stated an internal CIA report on Iran in August 1977.[8] One year later, in August 1978, the CIA produced its now-famous National Intelligence Estimate (NIE) on Iran, asserting that the country "is not in a revolutionary or even a prerevolutionary situation."[9] Not until the following month did the agency begin to temper its optimism. "The political unrest that has occurred during 1978 has raised for the first time in many years the serious possibility that the Shah may be forced from power," said a second NIE on Iran, written in September 1978.[10] It wasn't until early November that President Carter was fully apprised of the shah's precarious grip on power.

The second reason for this intelligence breakdown was that both the State Department and the CIA had long since stopped gathering their own intelligence from within Iran. SAVAK dutifully shared its domestic intelligence with Langley; thus as long as the shah remained in power, there was little rationale for the Americans themselves to spy on his opponents. The shah never fully trusted the Americans not to make common cause with his enemies, moreover, which meant that an active covert intelligence program in Iran might actually have undermined the U.S. strategic alliance with Iran. CIA officer William Daugherty later observed that by 1978 almost no one in the U.S. embassy in Tehran spoke Persian or understood Iranian culture.[11] Back in Washington, neither the State Department nor the National Security Council had an Iran expert on staff in the 1970s, which meant that intelligence analysis was weak. And even if they had, it is apparent that they would have had little to analyze, since the raw intelligence coming out of Iran was so flawed.

Nothing in the experience of Washington's Cold Warriors, in fact, had readied them for the possibility that subversion of the shah would come from Islamic militants rather than from the communists. SAVAK's fierce reprisals against the Soviet-allied Tudeh party and other Marxist organizations in Iran reinforced this bias. For decades the Americans had been far more interested in collecting intelligence on the Soviet Union, which bordered Iran, than on Iran itself. The CIA had, since the 1950s, been eavesdropping on the Soviets by means of secret signals-intelligence (SIGINT) sites on the Iran–USSR border. Of the seven listening posts built by the Americans in Iran, the two most important were code-named "Tacksman"—one in the mountains near the town of Behshahr, the other near Kabkan. The latter was only 650 miles from the Baikonur missile base in Kazakhstan, where the Soviets tested new ICBM designs by launching them toward Kamchatka. Tacksman surveillance was thus able to capture essential information about the weight, trajectory and speed of new weapons in the Soviet nuclear arsenal. This intelligence in turn directly affected the Cold War balance of power by giving the United States an ironclad means of verifying Soviet claims about arms reductions. (Not until the Tacksman project was declassified in the early 1990s did America's strategic debt to the shah become apparent. As Cyrus Vance observed, the Americans' loss of the Tacksman sites after the Iranian revolution put them at a serious disadvantage vis-à-vis the Soviets during the SALT II ratification process.[12] Late in 1979 Zbigniew Brzezinski and Deng Xiaoping secretly negotiated the construction of U.S. eavesdropping sites in China to replace the Tacksman installations in Iran.)[13]

Seen in retrospect, the CIA's intelligence failure was symptomatic of a broader pattern of official American ignorance about Iran. In 1979, there were six thousand political scientists with doctorates working in the United States, but fewer than ten specialized in contemporary Iran.[14] Not one anticipated the rise to political power of Iran's Muslim clergy. This ignorance extended to the American diplomatic corps and beyond, according to James A. Bill, a professor of international studies. "The American diplomatic and intelligence mission in Tehran, one of whose tasks it is to remain *au courant* with things Iranian, has had a most undistinguished record for many years," Bill stated bluntly in *Foreign Affairs* in 1979. "The ambassadors and chiefs of mission have, until very recently, been more concerned with confirming Washington's stereotype of Iran than encouraging their diplomats to develop a true understanding of Iranian society."[15]

~ ~ ~

One of the CIA's greatest assets when it came to maintaining American power abroad during the first three decades of the Cold War was its own mystique. The CIA could not actually *be* everywhere at once doing the covert bidding of an imperial U.S. presidency, but the *appearance* that it could gave the United States an enormous psychological advantage against its nominal enemies, particularly in the developing world. That myth is now in tatters, owing mainly to the work of the Senate Select Committee on Intelligence Activities (SSCIA), which in the mid-1970s exposed many of the CIA's coup plots, assassination schemes and other "dirty tricks."[16] Poison pens, private armies, biological weapons, secret deals with mafia hitmen—no stone was left unturned or unexploited by committee chairman Frank Church and his colleagues. In November 1975, the Church Committee, as it became known, published the document that would recast the CIA in the popular imagination as the "rogue elephant" that Senator Church himself said it was. Entitled *Alleged Assassination Plots Involving Foreign Leaders,* this book-length report revealed to Americans that their government had tried and failed to murder Cuba's Fidel Castro and Congo's Patrice Lumumba, and that it was implicated in the killing of the Dominican Republic's Rafael Leónidas Trujillo and South Vietnam's Ngo Dinh Diem.

Even prior to the revelations of the Church Committee, the myth of CIA omnipotence was alive and well in Iran, directly informing the rise of anti-Americanism there. As noted earlier, the agency's role in the 1953 coup and its presence at the founding of SAVAK were two historical realities, the impact of which many Americans never fully understood. After the publication in 1975 of *Alleged Assassination Plots,* however, Iranian conspiracy theories went into overdrive. With some 54,000 Americans in Iran by that time—2,000 of them posted to the U.S. embassy in Tehran and another 10,000 working as military advisers—it was entirely plausible to many ordinary Iranians that their country was precisely what the shah's enemies said it was: a vast network of American spies who collaborated with SAVAK and propped up the lackey shah. With the declassification of Soviet archives, it is now known that the KGB and its agents in Iran took every opportunity to inflame this paranoia, running sophisticated misinformation campaigns and covert "active measures."[17] Even the shah had suspicions that the CIA was plotting against him.

Commenting on Iranians' belief that the CIA was a ubiquitous and insidious presence in the shah's Iran, former American spies like William Daugherty would later emphasize just how limited the U.S. intelligence capability actually was. Yet seen in hindsight, it was the Americans themselves, far more even than the Soviets, who had unwittingly fuelled Iranians' conspiracy theories. The key moment came in 1973 when President Nixon appointed Richard Helms as U.S. ambassador to Iran, before he had even retired as director of central intelligence. ("We hear the Americans are sending their Number One spy to Iran," the Soviet ambassador Vladimir Yerofeyev reportedly said to Prime Minister Hoveyda when he heard about the Helms appointment. "The Americans are our friends," Hoveyda replied. "At least they don't send us their Number Ten spy."[18]) Henry Precht, in 1973 a political officer in Tehran and during the hostage crisis the director of Iranian affairs in the State Department, understood the symbolism of the appointment, even if President Nixon did not. "We were amazed that the White House would send a man who, after all, had such associations with the CIA, which was deemed by every Iranian to be responsible for the fall of Mossadeq," said Precht. "It seemed to us to abandon any pretense of a sort of a neutral America and to confirm that the shah was our puppet."[19]

Helms served as ambassador to Iran from March 1973 until December 1976. He had known the shah since 1957, however, when he was part of the CIA team sent to Iran to negotiate the terms of the Tacksman program. From then until 1961, Helms had enjoyed almost unequalled access to the shah. "We always met *tête-à-tête*," Helms later wrote in his memoirs, "with no note-takers or advisors."[20] As ambassador, Helms' relationship with the shah remained a close one. He wrote, "My relationship prospered in part because the Shah had always been well impressed by the quality of the CIA people he had met through the years."[21] During his ambassadorial tenure, Helms was recalled to Washington fourteen times to testify before the Church Committee, becoming its main villain in the process. Yet never does it appear to have occurred to anyone at the Nixon White House to have him recalled. Less than a year after his retirement, in December 1976, Helms was indicted by the Justice Department on charges that he had lied about the CIA's involvement in Chile. One year later, he was convicted of failing to testify "fully and completely" before a congressional committee.[22]

When the shah was admitted to the United States in the fall of 1979 for cancer treatment, Richard Helms visited him in the hospital, confirming for conspiracy minded Iranians that the CIA's loyalty to the deposed tyrant had known no bounds. They did not need the student hostage-takers to tell them that the U.S. embassy compound was a nest of spies.

~ ~ ~

In early September 1978, clashes between the shah's regime and Iranian dissidents again burst into full flame. Massive demonstrations were organized in Tehran on September 4, following which the shah decreed a ban on public gatherings. Undaunted, on September 7, Iranians once again took to the streets, where they were subdued with tear gas. The following day, September 8, immortalized in Iran as "Black Friday," the shah imposed martial law. Demonstrators clashed with the Iranian army in Tehran's Jaleh Square, and hundreds, perhaps thousands, were killed by machine-gun fire. Many more were injured. Much of downtown Tehran, including banks, cinemas, gas stations and department stores, was torched and reduced to ashes. By nightfall, the shah's security forces had rounded up hundreds of opposition leaders. Under martial law, the official decree cited "the inability of the clergy to impose constraint on religiously motivated manifestations and involvement of 'armed subversives financed by foreigners.'"[23] Among those Iranians caught in the dragnet were journalists now regarded by state authorities as subversive. Freedom of the press disappeared.

U.S. ambassador Bill Sullivan reported to Cyrus Vance that the shah appeared to be immobilized by Black Friday, in part because a rumour was circulating in Tehran that the United States and various opposition groups were plotting a coup against him. Vance and Brzezinski together suggested to President Carter that he telephone the shah in person to affirm Washington's unequivocal support. Carter obliged, calling the shah the morning of September 10 to express his continuing personal friendship and to wish him luck on implementing his political reforms. Again the shah disappointed the hawks in the White House by adopting an appeasement strategy rather than an iron fist. "It was clear that the Shah felt that our human-rights policy had aided his opponents," lamented Brzezinski, "and that he was not certain of American support."[24] In October, the shah went so far as to announce that he was scaling back his military purchases in order to finance extensive reforms in housing, education and agriculture. Again, his concessions only fuelled the opposition. Demonstrations and strikes grew in intensity and effectiveness. Iran's oil exports dropped from six million barrels a day to one million, its once limitless supply of petrodollars slowing to a trickle and strangling the Iranian economy.

Watching and stoking the shah's contortions was the exiled Ayatollah Khomeini. He, his entourage and hundreds of journalists had arrived in the Paris suburb of Neauphle-le-Château on October 6, 1978, after the shah had persuaded Iraqi strongman Saddam Hussein to have Khomeini deported from Najaf. Little did the shah realize that Khomeini's ability to harness the international media to the cause of his revolution would be vastly greater in Europe than it had been in isolated Iraq. The ayatollah now gave interviews daily from his Paris refuge. Positioning himself as Iran's political heir apparent, Khomeini had by this time abandoned his strident anti-Americanism in favour of a conciliatory tone toward the United States. This was part of a broader strategy to make him look statesmanlike. "The American president should quickly realize," the ayatollah told *Al Mostakbal*, a Paris-based Arabic newspaper, "that his protection of the shah served neither the Iranian people nor the United States."[25]

Carole Jerome, a CBC correspondent who had begun a torrid love affair with Khomeini loyalist Sadegh Ghotbzadeh in Paris, was in a unique position to take the measure of Khomeini and his entourage at this critical moment in the consolidation of the revolution. The day after Khomeini's arrival in Paris, on October 7, Jerome interviewed the holy man. Her first impression of him was intense. "As the black-robed Khomeini approached," she later recalled, "I watched him intently. His facial expression betrayed no emotion, and his eyes seemed like black holes. I had a sudden sense of foreboding, a feeling that I was looking into the face of evil."[26] Jerome also got an unrivalled glimpse into Khomeini's inner circle as it functioned in France. His key advisers, Sadegh Ghotbzadeh, Abolhassan Bani-Sadr and Ibrahim Yazdi, she called "a *magi*—a trio of wise men."[27] Western-educated and fluent in French and English as well as their native Persian, they wrote Khomeini's speeches, stage-managed his public appearances and, more generally, articulated his vision of an Islamic republic to the Western world. "Khomeini emerged from Bani-Sadr's nervous lips," Jerome observed, "as an apostle of social democracy; from Yazdi's he sprang forward as an inexorable force of Islamic destiny and democratic will; from Sadegh's mouth he was an ambitious apostle of life, liberty and hellfire."[28]

On November 6, 1978, the shah abandoned any pretence that he could maintain order in Iran and established a military government. Desperate for scapegoats, he had former prime minister Amir Abbas Hoveyda arrested and thrown into Tehran's infamous Evin Prison. Hoveyda had resigned as the shah's minister of court early in September over the shah's imposition of martial law. This was a courageous stand, inspiring nine opposition members of Iran's Majlis to resign and another eighteen to walk out in protest. The shah had three of Hoveyda's former cabinet ministers arrested on corruption charges in September, along with several lesser officials and Iranian businessmen, but he had left the popular Hoveyda alone. Now, however, in November, he decided that the former prime minister was expendable. Hoveyda was one of sixty former government officials arrested on charges of corruption and abuse of power. Hundreds were eventually jailed in the purge.[29]

With Iran in chaos and the shah's regime now plainly desperate, Ambassador Sullivan sent Washington a cable entitled "Thinking the Unthinkable." The United States, he wrote, should begin thinking about Iran without the shah. True to form, Zbigniew Brzezinski rejected any such equivocation in favour of a coup. Resentful of what he saw as Sullivan's increasing insubordination, Brzezinski had taken to phoning the shah directly in an attempt to shore up his resolve—a tactic that infuriated Cyrus Vance and appeared only to add to the shah's confusion. Faced with a divided cabinet and a menu of apparently hopeless policy options, President Carter took the path of least resistance. "It was becoming increasingly evident that the shah was no longer functioning as a strong leader," he acknowledged. "There was no question in my mind that he deserved our unequivocal support. We knew little about the forces contending against him, but their anti-American slogans and statements were enough in themselves to strengthen our resolve to support the Shah as he struggled for survival."[30]

How far Carter's support actually extended became clear in late December 1978, when the shah asked him to support "a policy of brutal repression."[31] The United States would back a military government to "end bloodshed," Carter replied, "but not to apply the iron fist to retain his throne."[32]

There would be no repeat of 1953 while he was president, Carter was signalling, whatever the consequences to his ally.

~ ~ ~

In general, Ken Taylor cleaved to the views of his friend Ambassador Sullivan, partly because the two HOMs had a common responsibility to protect the lives of their nationals in Iran, but also because Taylor shared Sullivan's view that the diplomats on the ground in Tehran knew better how to manoeuvre in revolutionary Iran than did their superiors back in Washington or Ottawa. Unlike Sullivan, of course, Taylor had few strategic national interests to protect, beyond the relatively minor one of safeguarding Iranian oil exports to Canada.[33] Certainly, he had no one like Zbigniew Brzezinski or even Cyrus Vance breathing down his neck. Seldom did Taylor or his Canadian colleagues face the bitter hatred many ordinary Iranians had come to feel toward American officials in their country. Never were they accused of being CIA, and never were they targeted for physical abuse or assassination. Not once while he was in Tehran did Taylor hear the phrase "Death to Canada!"

For the first few months of 1978, there was an occasional semblance of business as usual in Ambassador Taylor's personal exchanges with the shah. The two met on April 9, for example, to review a proposal Taylor had been putting together since his arrival in Tehran. It envisaged a Canadian consortium that would design and build a 2,000-megawatt thermal generating station in Iran, at a projected cost of C$1.2 billion. The shah liked Taylor's plan, calling it "a forceful and complete proposal in the face of potential European competition."[34] Though he was well aware of the political challenges facing the shah, then and later, Taylor was optimistic about the prospects for this project. After all, Iranians would need electricity no matter who was running the country. "This thermal power loomed very large," he later recalled. "It was combustion engineering. It was one of our chief priorities."[35] The ambassador also persisted in some of his earlier efforts to stimulate trade, pressing for export contracts for Canadian firms and monitoring the progress of the massive Stadler Herter project on the Caspian. In May 1978, Taylor even persuaded the shah to attend the formal opening of Stadler Herter's giant Gilan pulp mill—another highly symbolic milestone since the revolution would before long "obliterate" Gilan and bankrupt Stadler Herter.[36]

Not surprisingly, the bulk of the correspondence between the Canadian embassy and Ottawa prior to Black Friday concerned Tehran's volatile political landscape and the rising violence that accompanied it. Shifting alliances within the Rastakhiz party—as of 1974 the only legal political party in Iran—were followed closely, as liberals like Abdol Majid Majidi attempted to use the shah's summer reforms to open up the political process. The shah's failing efforts to keep the dissident opposition divided were analyzed minutely, since it was obvious to everyone that a united front against the regime would be formidable. By August 1978, the month the CIA told President Carter that Iran was not in a revolutionary or pre-revolutionary state, the Canadians could see the writing on the wall. "The sustained widespread violence and the failure of government action to pacify the dissidents by responding to their demands as well as the conspicuous absence of the Shah from public life for the past month may mean that a major shakeup of the political system is in the offing," they told Ottawa. "Regardless of what actions the Shah decides to take, one can expect Iran to undergo a relatively turbulent transition during the next year."[37]

~ ~ ~

Into the midst of this turbulence, in July 1978, arrived Ken Taylor's wife, Pat, and their only child, Douglas. Pat Taylor is a fourth-generation Australian of Chinese descent. Petite and pretty, with a youthful appearance that has always belied her age, she is known to her friends as "the energizer," a reference to the indefatigable zest for life she has in common with her husband. After earning two science degrees at the University of Queensland in Australia in the 1950s, Pat completed her PhD in bacteriology at the University of California, Berkeley, in 1963, while living and working in Guatemala. It was while she was at

Berkeley that she met Ken, who was there studying for his MBA. Pat's doctoral dissertation, "The Inter-relationship Between Nutrition and Infection," established her as a rising star in the field of virology and epidemiology, a vocation that she would pursue without interruption for the next four decades, producing scores of scholarly articles and receiving some of the world's most prestigious research appointments and awards. Pat Taylor's avocations are equally impressive. In the 1960s and 1970s, she performed as a violinist with the University of California symphony orchestra, and as a ballet dancer with the Oakland (California) Light Opera Ballet Company and the Guatemalan National Ballet.

In 1960, the year Ken and Pat Taylor were married, spouses of foreign-service officers were forbidden to accept paid work abroad. (This stricture would remain on the books until the early 1980s, when it was removed by officials at External Affairs.) Unwilling to sacrifice her research aspirations simply because she had married a Canadian diplomat, Pat quietly took matters into her own hands. "Prior to going on a posting," she later recalled, "I would search the literature, talk to colleagues and determine what suitable research institutes were in the country to which we were going. Then I would write to the director of the institute, include my résumé and any other pertinent materials, and ask if there was a position that I could fill for three to four years. Luckily, I always received positive responses, often positions that were made to accommodate me." Once Pat arranged for a foreign research appointment, Ken, always a solid supporter of his wife's career aspirations, would formally request the permission of his superiors required for her to accept it. "Luckily," said Pat, "there was always concurrence. It wasn't an easy business at that time, but well worth the effort since it allowed me to pursue my career without pause."[38]

Pat Taylor remained in Ottawa for the first eight months of Ken's posting to Iran, missing out on much of Tehran's high-flying nightlife before the imposition of martial law in 1978. She had been working since 1976 on a major research project at the Health Protection Branch of the Department of National Health and Welfare. Not wanting to abandon her work, Pat opted to finish out her stint in Ottawa, visiting her husband in Tehran at Christmas 1977 and Easter 1978. Her son, Douglas, then fourteen years of age and a student at the prestigious Lycée Claudel in Ottawa, accompanied her on these visits, relocating permanently to Tehran with his mother in July 1978.

Despite the mounting chaos in the streets, Pat and Douglas adjusted quickly to life in Tehran, settling into the daily routines at the Canadian ambassador's residence. Pat accepted a full-time position as a research scientist in epidemiology at Tehran's National Blood Transfusion Service. She also worked as a consultant to the Pasteur Institute and an occasional lecturer to postgraduate medical students at the University of Tehran. Douglas enrolled at the French lycée in Tehran, commencing his classes in September. Both would come to count among their closest acquaintances some of the Iranians they got to know over these first few months in the country. Pat immersed herself in her research but was also happy in the role of ambassador's spouse. "Her life had two dimensions," Ambassador Taylor later recalled. "During the day she was a virologist in a scientist's white lab coat, and at night she was the hostess of an elegant embassy reception."[39] This was nothing new to Pat. She had learned how to balance the competing demands on her time during Ken's previous postings to Guatemala City, Detroit, Karachi and London. "I loved entertaining, being entertained and participating in all of the other activities that accompany a diplomat's position," she said.[40]

In contrast with both the Canadian embassy and the ambassador's residence, which were located in "tranquil" North Tehran, as Ken Taylor put it, the Blood Transfusion Service was in the city's south end, the scene of the many violent confrontations between the shah's forces and his opponents. From the moment Pat Taylor started her new job, she thus found herself face to face with the street violence that was engulfing the city's downtown core. "Pat was the one from the embassy who was out in the field, so to speak," Ken Taylor later recalled. "Those of us at the embassy had our patterns. We travelled between our homes and the embassy, and then maybe went out to a restaurant nearby. But Pat was out pretty well every day."[41] Unbeknownst to Ken, each morning before his wife left the ambassador's residence, she would pack what she called a "hostage kit" along with her lunch. "I had a big handbag," said Pat. "People used to ask me what on earth I carried in it, and I told them—shampoo, a change of clothes, toothbrush, hypertension pills, all sorts of things. Every day I went to work I carried it with me, and they asked what it was. I said, 'That's my personal hostage kit.' And of course they laughed."[42]

Ambassador Taylor later recounted an anecdote that encapsulated his wife's day-to-day existence in Tehran. "During the revolution, of course, blood was a necessary commodity," he said. "The revolutionaries wanted it, and the Iranian army wanted it. Yet even at the height of the hostilities, in 1978, the Blood Transfusion Service had to remain neutral. They were supplying blood to the soldiers *and* the rebels. One time the rebels came running into the centre with the troops following close behind. Pat wasn't necessarily sympathetic to either group. But she said, 'For the moment, put on one of these white coats.'"[43] The wife of the Canadian ambassador thus concealed the revolutionaries from the inquiring soldiers when they arrived, saving Iranian lives in the process.

For his part, Douglas Taylor settled into his academic life at the Tehran lycée much as any teenager might, making friends and enjoying the social life of the school. Since the academic term coincided with the escalating violence of Black Friday and its aftermath, Douglas and his peers grew accustomed to periodic school closures. Finally, in late October 1978, most of the schools in Tehran, including Douglas's lycée and the other international schools, shut down permanently. Douglas later recalled the cancellation of classes as a welcome holiday.

"When you're that age," he said, "the fact that you have school closed isn't such a bad thing. That's how I looked at it." He and his classmates were nonchalant about the closure of their school due to the threat of violence. "It was much like it can be in any other city. You can have a snow day, except in Tehran it's a demonstration day."[44]

Ken Taylor was asked recently whether he, Pat and Douglas were afraid for their lives during the revolution. "It wasn't necessarily fear," he replied. "There was that element, but there was really a total lack of predictability, in the absence of any type of law and order or judicial process. There just wasn't any. In Tehran you've got eight million people in the middle of a revolution, and there's no recourse, there's no justice. You're pretty much on your own."[45]

In September 1978 Ambassador Taylor was also joined in Tehran by the person who would become his right-hand man during the revolution and the hostage crisis, First Secretary Roger Lucy. "I got to Iran about a week before they declared martial law," Lucy later recalled with a wry smile. "I was number two in the political section. Paul Thibeault was political officer, and I sort of backed him up. I did things like reporting on the oil industry. I did such cultural work as they liked to do, though that was steadily diminishing."[46]

Thirty-one years of age, single, outgoing, adventurous and fanatical about Middle Eastern history, Lucy was a natural for Tehran in the late 1970s. Like Taylor, in fact, he had requested the posting, calling in a few favours at External Affairs to haggle his way out of an assignment in Iraq. For his habit of wearing fatigues and his fascination with military insignia, some of his colleagues thought Lucy eccentric. But he possessed three qualities that would serve him and Ken Taylor extremely well in Tehran: courage, a chess master's mind for strategy and a historian's eye for minutiae. Lucy's grasp of the dynamics of the Iranian revolution were second to none in the Canadian embassy, the product of his close study of Iranian politics, culture and language. When he discovered that he could not fully acculturate to life in Iran without knowing Persian, he simply taught himself to read Persian script, a daunting task as it is based on the Arabic rather than the Western alphabet. Little did he know in the fall of 1978 that his ability to read Persian would literally change the course of the hostage crisis a year and a half later.

~ ~ ~

In late October 1978, Ambassador Taylor sent an unusual (for him) slice-of-life cable to Ottawa, setting out the new reality in Iran under martial law. The first thing the arriving visitor would encounter, he wrote, is a deserted airport, since only diplomats and incoming passengers were permitted to enter the premises. En route into Tehran one could not help but notice Chieftain tanks "not discreetly parked" here and there. The hotels were overbooked as usual, the Hilton having been "buffeted by a two-day strike last week with the bar and luxury restaurant occupied by strikers casually enjoying the hotel's supply of pistachio nuts." Traffic, always chaotic, was now "aggravated by troop movements." Meetings with government officials were still being held, but internal unrest was causing the "semi-paralysis" of the government bureaucracy. Strikes in banking, customs and transit were confounding the daily rhythms of Iranians. "Tehran by night begins early with restaurants and discotheques open and relatively busy by 7:30 rather than the traditional 11:00."

All told, concluded the ambassador, "although there is disruption, there is currently little reason for a visitor, on pleasure or business, to postpone his or her trip for reasons of security. A philosophical approach to sudden and frustrating changes in situation (notably to unexpected strikes and/or shortages) is, however, a distinct asset to the foreign traveler."[47]

Chapter 4

THE OVERTHROW OF THE SHAH

On November 4, 1978, less than two weeks after Taylor penned his slice-of-life cable, Iranian soldiers fired on student demonstrators at the University of Tehran, killing ten. Angry crowds then took to the streets, "in scenes of unprecedented violence," as one Canadian embassy staffer put it.[1] Banks, cinemas, airline offices, stores and buses were torched and destroyed. "The Canadian embassy was somewhat to the north of the area affected," Roger Lucy wrote a few days later in a letter to his parents. "We had a good view of the fires. The burning of the National Iranian Gas Company's building was particularly spectacular."[2] Marie Mercer of Stephenville, Newfoundland, was one of the Canadians caught up in the chaos. She was trapped in a Tehran hotel room with her husband, an employee of a Canadian company operating in the Iranian capital. "We were watching from the hotel window," she said. "They were breaking windows in furniture stores and liquor stores and pouring the liquor over the beautiful furniture and setting fire to it." Afraid for their lives, Mercer and her husband locked themselves in their room and lay on the floor holding hands. "Well, we're both going together," they thought.[3] Not only did the Mercers survive the riot, but once the dust had settled they decided to stay on in Tehran.

The gravest responsibility that falls to an ambassador caught up in any kind of local insurrection is that of protecting his country's citizens. Ken Taylor recognized immediately that the violence of November 4 had altered the security status of the approximately two thousand Canadians known to be residing in Iran. "Disturbances have not as yet directly affected Canadians," he told Ottawa, but "Canadian residents in Tehran are increasingly nervous."[4] From this point on, Taylor made the safety of Canadians in Iran his top priority, starting with his own staff. Until then, embassy security had been provided by unarmed commissionaires. After November 4, Taylor had six Canadian Forces military police (MPs) assigned to guard the embassy. "We needed six so they could stand guard in rotation," Roger Lucy later explained. "They were attachés—they had diplomatic status. It was a dangerous time. We scaled up security and downsized the embassy."[5]

On December 1, Ambassador Taylor received an ominous note from Michael Shenstone in Ottawa. "Our assessment is that Iran faces several months at least of tension and disorder," it read, "whether or not the shah and his regime succeed in staying on." Anticipating the "total collapse of government authority," Shenstone asked Taylor for his thoughts on a contingency plan for the evacuation of Canadians from Iran, including "non-essential personnel" at the embassy itself. Shenstone's short list of scenarios that might necessitate an evacuation included the fall of the shah, the return of Ayatollah Khomeini to Iran and any other provocation to civil war. The Canadian embassy should also be ready to act if there were "credible threats directed against Canadians." Shenstone advised Taylor to remain in daily contact with other Western embassies in Tehran. "Grateful your views by return tel," he signed off as usual.[6]

Taylor replied immediately. He agreed entirely with Shenstone's sense of the escalating crisis, and had already begun to confer with other Western diplomats. (After meeting with their counterparts at the U.S. embassy to discuss contingency planning, the Canadians astutely noted that the Americans' "political assessment remains more optimistic than that of other Western embassies.") What Shenstone had not fully appreciated, however, was that the question of whether or when to evacuate foreign nationals from Iran had serious political implications. "When do you evacuate? When do you bring in the planes?" Taylor later explained. "We got into quite an argument with the Europeans. The American ambassador, Bill Sullivan, and myself said, 'We're moving our planes in early.' And the other ambassadors said, 'Well, you can't do that—you're compromising the integrity of Iran. By bringing in your planes and evacuating people, you have officially said you've given up on the government.' And then it was the Iranian government saying, 'Whatever you do, don't bring in your planes prematurely to evacuate people.'"[7]

While Taylor and Shenstone were working out their evacuation strategy, the violence in Tehran escalated yet again. Over the night of December 2–3, demonstrations racked the city. For the first time they were concentrated in the northern area where most of the Canadians lived. Embassy staff were clearly unnerved by this new development, telling Ottawa that some of the protests "took place literally in front of the chancery and were dispersed by troops firing."[8] Meanwhile, Iranians and foreigners alike had begun stampeding out of Iran, according to the local press, in the expectation that the shah and his opponents were preparing "a bloody showdown." Officials at Tehran's Mehrabad International Airport reported "utter chaos," as thousands of people scrambled for airline tickets out.[9] Among them were eight hundred Canadians who had decided they had seen enough. They left on their own steam.

By December 6, Ottawa's evacuation planning was complete. If commercial aircraft were not available to airlift the remaining 1,200 Canadians out of Iran's various airfields, the Department of National Defence would provide six C-130 Hercules to do the job. Turkey, one of Canada's NATO allies, had already granted permission for the Canadian flights to land at Ankara. "Prime responsibility to recommend a formal warning to Canadians to leave, and implementation of evacuation plans, rests with Ambassador Taylor in Tehran," it was agreed. "If consultation with Ottawa is impossible he is authorized to act on his own."[10] Undersecretary Allan Gotlieb informed External Affairs Minister Don Jamieson of the plan in a "Canadian Eyes Only" memo. Gotlieb underscored the need for secrecy, presumably because of the political delicacy of the situation seen from both Tehran and Washington. "The fact that such joint planning is taking place is being kept strictly confidential by all concerned," he told the minister.[11]

The Canadians remained at their highest state of alert through the weekend of December 9–10, in the knowledge that massive demonstrations were planned for Tehran on December 11 and 12. As expected, vast street marches immobilized the city. An estimated one million Iranians participated, chanting "Our leader is Khomeini!" and "Death to the shah!" To the astonishment and relief of everyone, however, the demonstrations in Tehran were peaceful. Only in Isfahan were there clashes between the army and the protestors, with loss of life. As the U.S. embassy later reported, the shah's security forces had struck a "gentleman's agreement" with opposition organizers on condition that they maintain discipline. The army sealed off North Tehran from the south using tanks and roadblocks, and then they stood aside. Muslim clergy and National Front leaders announced a seventeen-point program calling for the return of Khomeini, an end to the shah's regime and the institution of a democratic Islamic republic.[12]

Ken Taylor was impressed. He thought the demonstrations so well managed and free of violence that it would now be safe to have the Hercules "stand down," in light of the high cost of keeping them on standby.[13]

For the moment, the crisis seemed to have passed.

~ ~ ~

On December 11, 1978, Amnesty International published a new report accusing Iranian authorities of "systematic torture of political prisoners." The new document flatly contradicted claims that the shah had decreed an end to torture as part of his liberalization reforms. Some people had been tortured to extract information or confessions, others merely as a punishment for political activities. Among the methods described were "whipping with wire, beatings on the soles of the feet, kicking, punching, burning with cigarettes, long periods of solitary confinement and prevention of sleep."[14] One week after the publication of Amnesty's findings, Ayatollah Khomeini called for a general strike in Iran. He took the opportunity to criticize President Carter's human-rights policy. "Does not the universal declaration of human rights to which Mr. Carter so often refers admit the right of all peoples to determine their own destiny?" Khomeini asked. "Or is Iran an exception because of its strategic importance to the United States and because of the interests which they hold there?"[15]

Iran's peaceful and well-managed demonstrations ended on Christmas Day. Rioting again brought Tehran to a standstill. Vehicles were torched, buildings ransacked or defaced. Protests in the southern Iranian city of Shiraz took a decidedly anti-American tone when demonstrators firebombed the Iranian–U.S. cultural centre there. On December 28, troops fired into crowds of demonstrators in the northeastern city of Mashed, killing seven hundred. Enraged mobs then turned on local authorities, hanging several SAVAK agents and secret police. In Tehran, mobs also gutted a SAVAK building, later displaying the numerous instruments of torture they had found, along with a collection of severed human limbs they claimed had been stored on-site.[16]

On New Year's Eve, after a series of meetings with U.S. ambassador Sullivan, Shah Mohammad Reza Pahlavi made the dramatic announcement that he would be leaving Iran temporarily, so as to remove the "obvious focus of popular discontent."[17] The same day he designated Shapour Bakhtiar as prime minister, an appointment obviously intended to appease his critics. Bakhtiar was a lawyer who had served as deputy minister of labour under Mossadeq in the early 1950s. He had been jailed several times for his criticism of the regime. He was a courageous and popular figure in Iranian politics, but the gamble he took in allowing himself to govern as the shah's prime minister, with the monarchy intact, was ill fated. When his appointment was announced, he was immediately expelled from the National Front, where he had long served as deputy leader. His former comrades called him a traitor.[18] Bakhtiar's fervent belief that Muslim clergy had no place in Iranian politics also put him on the wrong side of Ayatollah Khomeini. As the Canadian embassy reported to Ottawa, even Bakhtiar's cabinet, "mostly civil servants and technocrats," would likely work against him.[19]

~ ~ ~

With the violence escalating once again, Western diplomats met to implement what Ken Taylor called "a coordinated approach to our problems." A consensus quickly emerged. All foreign nationals should be encouraged to get out of Iran while commercial flights were still available. "In the light of the prevailing economic situation in Iran," stated the official embassy press release, "the Canadian Ambassador recommends that Canadians take steps to arrange departure from Iran for themselves and their dependants at the earliest opportunity unless there are compelling reasons to remain."[20] The hope that all Canadians could get out of Tehran on commercial flights proved optimistic, so Taylor redirected two of the six Canadian Hercules transports to the Iranian capital. The remaining four would fly to the military airbase at Rasht, as planned, where roughly one thousand foreign nationals, half of them Canadian, would be airlifted out. Working closely with Stadler Herter project director Robert McCullough, Taylor agreed to send one of his staff to help in the evacuation. There was never any question about who would go. It would be Roger Lucy.

"I'm not really looking forward to going up to Rasht to face 350 cold, hungry and puzzled Canadians," Lucy wrote his parents on January 2.[21] The next two days were a blur for the young political officer. Lucy worked from 6 a.m. on January 2 until 4 p.m. on January 3, preparing flight clearances for the Canadian planes and then driving up to the Caspian himself to lead the Canadians down to Rasht in a convoy of buses. Greta Murray, one of the evacuees, later recalled that the school bus in which she, her husband and their three children were riding, from the navy base to the Rasht airport, was fired on by Iranian commandos. "To get off the base," she said, "we had to lie on the floor of the bus. We had to go through a barricade of gunfire."[22] Two other buses were stoned by angry mobs as they made their way to the airport. All of the Canadians' homes were ransacked by Iranians after they were abandoned. A rumour later circulated through Iran that the fleeing Canadians had taken with them $6 billion in gold and jewellery. It was far from true. Some of the evacuees had had the foresight to convert their worthless Iranian currency into portable valuables, but most lost everything they had accumulated in Iran, many of them over many years. "We packed everything we owned into crates," said Kathy Storch, one of the evacuees, "but we don't know if we'll ever see it again."[23] They would not.

Among the Canadians to leave Iran at this time was Douglas Taylor, though not as an evacuee. Douglas's lycée had closed in the fall and, like most of Tehran's teenaged students, he had been happy to have the holiday. By Christmas, however, he was bored at the ambassador's residence. Without any prospect of the lycée reopening, he was also at risk of losing his school year. Douglas and his parents agreed, therefore, that after the Christmas holiday he should leave Tehran for France, where he could easily resume his studies at the start of the winter term. "The view was," said Douglas, "that France was closer to Tehran than going back to Canada."[24] Douglas flew out of Iran on a commercial flight to Switzerland just after New Year's Day. He stayed in Berne with Canadian friends, one of whom was a foreign-service officer and former colleague of Ken's, and spent several days skiing. From there, Douglas went to the Centre International de Valbonne, a lycée in Sophia Antipolis, a small town near Cannes.

The evacuation of Canadian nationals from Iran began on January 3 and took three days, the last of the evacuees arriving in Ankara on January 5. All told, roughly 1,200 Canadians and another 400 foreigners were airlifted to safety courtesy of the Canadian embassy and the Department of National Defence. "We muddled through very successfully and no-one got left behind, despite the stickiness of Iranian Customs," Roger Lucy later wrote. "It was an excellent operation, exhausting but exciting, and we really achieved something worthwhile."[25] Ken Taylor, Roger Lucy and their colleagues at the Canadian embassy were the toast of Ottawa, their reputations for courage and leadership cemented by their almost flawless execution of the evacuation plan.

On January 4, the first of the Canadian evacuees arrived back in Canada, tired and cold but also relieved. They had been flown directly from Ankara, Turkey, to Ottawa on a Canadian Forces Boeing 707. "We're happy to be home," said evacuee Gary Goldstein when he arrived at CFB Uplands Airport in Ottawa. "The feeling we had when we saw the Canadian Forces plane come to pick us up is indescribable, a very emotional feeling. We're glad to be out."[26] The returning Canadians reported that they had seen little of the violence that had been tearing Iran apart, until the last week, when they had been targeted by angry crowds shouting insults and throwing rocks. They had always been treated well by the Iranians, most of the evacuees reported, but as anti-Americanism reached fever pitch, the Canadians were occasionally targeted by mistake. "We were very afraid at what was happening," commented Bruce Allain, another evacuee. "At one time my wife was caught in the middle of riots between pro- and anti-Shah supporters. It was very scary."[27]

The last of the Canadian civilians to leave Iran would be airlifted out of the country on February 6, 1979, along with some straggling Americans and Europeans. They were taken to Mehrabad Airport in buses guarded by Iranian soldiers, and flown out on the last of the Hercules "freedom flights," as the airlifts were now known.[28]

Only 130 Canadians now remained in Iran. Roughly half were embassy personnel and their families.

~ ~ ~

Just as Ken Taylor's star was rising in Ottawa, his friend Bill Sullivan, the U.S. ambassador to Iran, was becoming *non grata* in Washington. By January 1979, Sullivan was convinced that the Americans' only remaining option in Iran was to broker a deal between the Iranian army and Khomeini. He was by this time telling Washington in no uncertain terms that when the shah left Iran for his "holiday," the Pahlavi dynasty would be finished. His cables had grown more and more frantic and less and less diplomatic. "I became increasingly troubled by the attitude of Ambassador Sullivan," Jimmy Carter later recalled, "who seemed obsessed with the need for the shah to abdicate without further delay."[29] Khomeini, now clearly enjoying the upper hand, announced from Paris that he intended to establish a secular government that would be directed and shaped—but not run—by Muslim clergy. Cyrus Vance read this as a good sign and urged Carter to speak directly to the ayatollah. The president rejected his advice, believing that such a move would undermine the already shaky Bakhtiar government. This was the time, Carter reasoned, to show the shah, Bakhtiar and the Iranian military "consistent American support."[30]

Distrusting Sullivan, Carter dispatched General Robert "Dutch" Huyser, deputy commander of U.S. forces in Europe, to Iran. His orders reflected the ambivalence that now pervaded U.S. policy in Iran. According to Cyrus Vance, Huyser was "to do everything possible to induce the Iranian military to support a pro-Western civilian government capable of restoring order and economic production. However, if the government were on the verge of collapse, we would understand the need for contingency plans and actions to end the disorder, bloodshed, and violence."[31] Brzezinski, on the other hand, understood military "contingency planning" to be Huyser's pre-eminent concern. "I publicly stressed firm U.S. support for the Bakhtiar government," Brzezinski later wrote, "but I also stressed that Huyser should prepare the Iranian military for a coup in the likely event that Bakhtiar should fail."[32] (A frustrated Brzezinski actually said to President Carter, in a quiet moment, "World politics is not a kindergarten and we [have] to consider what will be the longer-range costs if the military fail[s] to act."[33])

Huyser's efforts were doomed from the start. Iranians knew that his official mission was to rally the generals' support for Bakhtiar, but they saw his presence as yet another instance of American meddling in Iranian affairs. Many suspected that he would be Jimmy Carter's point man for a repeat of the 1953 coup. Given Brzezinski's efforts to achieve just such an outcome, their suspicions were not unwarranted. "Death to Huyser!" was quickly added to the lexicon of Iranian street protesters.

Bakhtiar, meanwhile, forged ahead with what Ken Taylor called a "conciliatory" agenda. He moved the curfew from 9 to 11 p.m., ended press censorship, promised a gradual end to martial law, proposed the dissolution of SAVAK and spoke of leading Iran toward social democracy.[34] None of these overtures appeased Khomeini, who called

Bakhtiar's government "illegal" and Bakhtiar himself a "creature of Satan."[35] No one at the Canadian embassy—or anywhere else for that matter—held out much hope for the new prime minister. "The life expectancy of the Bakhtiar government can probably be reckoned in days," the Canadians told Ottawa bluntly.[36] On January 9, Bakhtiar announced that he had persuaded the shah to leave the country and create an eight-member regency council to govern Iran in his absence. The same day, the shah himself announced that he would turn over hundred of millions of dollars from his royal fortune to the people of Iran and amnesty 266 political prisoners. Such last-ditch concessions proved counterproductive. The very next day, massive demonstrations again swept the country, this time with "considerable loss of life."[37] Rumours of coup plots in the Iranian military were rife.

~ ~ ~

On January 16, 1979, Shah Mohammad Reza Pahlavi and his entourage left Iran for Egypt. Wearing a dark suit and a winter coat, and accompanied by Empress Farah in furs, the shah was described as "ashen-faced and fighting back tears" as he climbed the steps into his jumbo jet.[38] The shah and the empress were the last of the royal family to leave, their four children and various other relatives having already flown to the United States. The royal couple departed Tehran in two planes, one carrying their possessions, the other the shah's many advisers, servants and guards. The shah himself piloted the 707 carrying his loyal retinue. As the news spread throughout Tehran that the shah had cleared Iranian airspace, people poured into the streets, shouting *"Shah raft! Shah raft!"* ("The shah is gone!").[39] At Tehran University students chanted, "We got rid of the king. Now America will be next!"[40]

President Carter publicly invited the shah to take refuge in the United States, evidence not only of his sense of obligation to the Iranian monarch but of his sense that no harm would come of it. Had the shah flown directly to the U.S. on January 16, the outcry in Iran would have been considerable, but it would not likely have inspired anyone to take American diplomats hostage to compel his return. Ayatollah Khomeini was still in Paris, his "Islamic republic" still lay in the future and the political factions that would tear Iran apart over the following year were still unified behind their common objective of overthrowing the shah. Anti-Americanism was on the rise in Iran but it was not yet militant. Moderate Islamic politicians, many of them extremely close to Khomeini, still appeared to have the upper hand. They envisaged a democratic Iran and they understood the need for some kind of continuing military alliance with the United States to keep the Soviets at bay. They also understood the enormous risk to Iran's standing in the world if it were to become an outlaw state. In November 1979, when Islamic militants stormed the U.S. embassy compound and took American diplomats hostage, the rudderless Iranian revolution badly needed a rallying point, a pretext to purify the revolution and purge its rivals. In January 1979, this was not true.

Jimmy Carter thought the shah's departure "curiously anti-climactic," but this was not the view of Canada's diplomats in Tehran.[41] They described the Iranians' reaction to the news as "euphoria."[42] The day after the shah fled, Ambassador Taylor assessed Iran's future for the benefit of his colleagues in Ottawa. With the shah gone and Khomeini promising to return home, he wrote, Bakhtiar would simply have to "bow to the inevitable and resign."[43] In his typically terse but perceptive manner, Taylor summarized the ayatollah's probable impact on Iran in one sentence: "The new government will impose a more rigorous Islamic way of life on Iranians, relics of the old regime particularly will be expunged and many leading government, military and commercial figures will be purged or exiled." On one aspect of Iran's future the ambassador's instincts were dead on. "Having achieved the unifying goal of expelling the shah," he wrote, "factional dissension seems almost inevitable." [44]

The day the shah left Iran, Pat Taylor found herself again caught up in the chaos of the moment. "The Blood Transfusion Service almost never closed, because the revolutionaries *and* the military needed blood for wounded people," she later recalled. "But it closed early the day the shah left. So this friend of mine said, 'Pat, it's going to be awful outside, so I'll take you home and you'll be safe with me.' He'd been to Harvard, and he looked *very* American. He was tall, and he had a shock of grey hair, and he always wore a duffel coat and heavy-rimmed glasses. So we were walking to his car and this group of revolutionaries surrounded us, and started yelling insults. I noticed that they were really focusing on him. They didn't say anything to me. So when we were reunited at my friend's house he said, 'What happened to you?' And I said, 'What happened to *you?*' He said, they were calling me all these terrible names in Farsi, so I answered and gave it all back to them!"[45]

~ ~ ~

On January 18, 1979, two days after the flight of the shah into exile, one and a half million Iranians assembled in the streets of Tehran for the largest demonstration in Iranian history. A ten-point statement was read by Muslim clerics and their political allies. To the delight of the roaring crowd, they declared the shah deposed and the Bakhtiar government illegal. They asked that the current Majlis resign and that the Iranian armed forces declare themselves loyal to the revolution. "We reject the reactionary system of Shahenshahi [monarchy]," they said, "and demand the establishment of a liberal Islamic republic in Iran, which shall be installed by popular vote and shall conduct the affairs of the nation on the basis of the invigorating teachings of Islam."[46]

A banner in the crowd was addressed to President Carter. "Jimmy boy, run, run, run. The people of Iran are picking up the gun."[47]

Chapter 5
AYATOLLAH KHOMEINI IN POWER

The imam, Ayatollah Ruhollah Khomeini, arrived in Tehran at 9 a.m. local time on February 1, 1979, after a five-and-a-half-hour flight from Paris. Seventy-six years old, white-haired and slow-moving, he had not set foot in his native Iran in fourteen years. He returned not only as a conquering hero to millions of his Iranian compatriots but as a divinely inspired leader to Shiite Muslims worldwide.

Khomeini kept the crowds at Mehrabad Airport waiting forty minutes before he appeared at the door of his Air France 747. He made his way down the long flight of steps assisted by the plane's pilot, surrounded by his Paris entourage and followed by a large group of journalists. A Mercedes sedan drove him to the airport's VIP lounge. From there he was taken by Jeep first to Behesht Zahra Cemetery, where the martyred bodies of many of his followers were buried, and then to a former girls' school in downtown Tehran where he intended to set up his office. The streets of Tehran filled with three million Iranians, once estimated to be the largest mass gathering in human history. "Praise to Allah!" shouted the adoring crowds as they crushed toward the vehicle to get a glimpse of Khomeini. "I was mesmerized by the spectacle," recalled Canadian journalist Carole Jerome, who had been on the Air France flight along with her lover, Sadegh Ghotbzadeh. "We were in the middle of one of the great historic events of the twentieth century, and we knew it. It was exhilarating beyond all measure, even for jaded journalists."[1]

~ ~ ~

The ayatollah wasted no time establishing his political agenda. Calling his organization the Muslim National Movement, he demanded that the Bakhtiar government "step down and hand over power."[2] As Bakhtiar knew, Khomeini now had momentum on his side. Over the last week of January 1979, the prime minister had tried to assert his authority, ordering the Iranian army to post tanks around Mehrabad Airport to prevent the ayatollah's plane from landing. Violent clashes in the streets of Tehran followed. At least forty people were killed in two days of rioting, and over five hundred were wounded, making the melee the worst for bloodshed in the new year. On Saturday, January 27, to quell the mayhem, Bakhtiar announced his willingness to negotiate with Khomeini, even asking the ayatollah for a meeting in Paris. "I have said repeatedly that the deposed Shah was illegal, the parliament was illegal and the Bakhtiar Government is illegal," Khomeini replied. "I will not receive that illegal man."[3]

With the ayatollah now in Iran, Bakhtiar tried again to initiate a dialogue. Again he was rebuffed. Worse, the Iranian army refused to prevent Khomeini from establishing his own parallel government, despite the fact that Bakhtiar had threatened to arrest anyone appointed by him. At a February 3 press conference, the ayatollah stated that he would proceed immediately with the creation of an

Islamic republic in Iran. He would appoint a provisional government and introduce a new constitution. He would open talks with the Iranian army and win the allegiance of its 430,000 soldiers.[4] Bakhtiar resigned himself to the inevitable. He publicly likened Khomeini's provisional government to a shadow cabinet in a liberal democracy, and continued to press forward with his own agenda. He pulled Iran out of CENTO (the twenty-year-old Central Treaty Organization that bound Iran to Pakistan, Turkey, the United States and Britain), and he pushed a bill through a heavily guarded session of the Iranian Majlis to abolish SAVAK.[5] Ken Taylor grasped the prime minister's fate immediately. "Bakhtiar seems the right man in the wrong place at the wrong time," he said.[6]

On February 4, Khomeini appointed Mehdi Bazargan as his provisional prime minister. It was a brilliant political appointment, for Bazargan's credentials mirrored Bakhtiar's almost exactly. Both men had served in the government of Mohammed Mossadeq prior to the 1953 coup, and they had been comrades for the next twenty-five years in the National Front. Bazargan was known to Western leaders as "an educated, secular man," and within Iran as a courageous Islamic nationalist and defender of human rights.[7] Most of the diplomatic corps in Iran, including the Canadians, thought him "moderate and pragmatic," which came as a great relief since they had assumed that Khomeini would appoint a militant.[8] "Bazargan was a good guy," Ken Taylor later recalled. "He gave his life for his country."[9]

Khomeini had not been in Iran a week before the country again exploded into violence. Rival factions fought in the streets. The Iranian armed forces, as President Carter himself put it, "simply disintegrated."[10] Soldiers outside Tehran declared themselves loyal to Khomeini and began fighting openly with units of the Imperial Guard. Before long, there were defections from within the Guard itself. In cities traditionally dominated by the Muslim clergy, including Isfahan and Qom, directives from the Bakhtiar government were ignored. Curfews were ended, alcohol outlawed, and women made to wear the full-length chador. Civil servants were told to take their orders from the mullahs or leave. Young militants wearing armbands took over policing duties. Courts of law were replaced by revolution-ary courts. Mosques took over the provision of basic social services.

Over February 10 and 11, more than five hundred people were killed and another two thousand wounded in the worst two days of civil bloodshed Iran had seen since the 1953 coup. Civil war seemed imminent. Then, to the jubilant cries of Iranians in the streets every-where, the last of the Imperial Guard holdouts announced their decision to withdraw their support for Bakhtiar. The prime minister resigned and, fearing for his life, went into hiding. The shah, watch-ing his loyal troops capitulate from the relative safety of a borrowed palace in Egypt, was said to be "a confused and bitter man."[11] He had been gone only twenty-six days. In mid-March 1979, Bakhtiar would surface in Paris, warning of a "new dictatorship" under Khomeini.[12]

Now Iran's unrivalled secular leader, Bazargan moved into the prime minister's residence and announced his government's pro-gram. All power would be surrendered to his provisional government, a new parliament as well as a constituent assembly would be elected and a referendum would be held to decide the future of the country. Bazargan knew that the greatest strategic threats to Iran came from Iraq and the Soviet Union, as they always had. He thus announced that his government would maintain diplomatic relations with the United States. "The cooperative attitude of Bazargan's government," Cyrus Vance later observed, "was indicative of the political moder-ates' strong desire to continue a military relationship with the United States and their healthy concern for Iran's external security."[13] Jimmy Carter doubted that Bazargan's ability to govern revolutionary Iran was any better than Bakhtiar's, but he agreed that the United States should now make its best efforts to cooperate with him. The U.S. for-mally recognized Iran's new government on February 14.

Two days later, Canada's external affairs minister, Don Jamieson, followed the American lead and extended diplomatic recognition. Prime Minister Trudeau sent Bazargan a telegram wishing him every success and expressing the hope that "the existing good relations between our two countries [would] continue to develop."[14] Ambassador Taylor reported back to Ottawa that Iranian authorities were appreciative of this "good news" from Canada.[15]

~ ~ ~

With Khomeini in charge, Bazargan installed, Bakhtiar in hiding and the shah obviously gone for good, Iranian militants turned their wrath on the collaborators who had kept the shah in power. In every major Iranian city, mobs went after former agents of the hated SAVAK, beating them to death or subjecting them to public execution by disembowelling or hanging. In a Tehran suburb, revolutionaries broke into the home of a former colonel in SAVAK and discovered there a torture chamber complete with bone-crushing machines and electrical rods.[16] On February 12, in one of the defining moments of the Iranian revolution, seventy-one-year-old General Nematollah Nassiri, the former head of SAVAK, was dragged through the streets of Tehran with a rope around his neck and later subjected to a televised interview with revolutionaries and journalists. "What did my children do to you that you killed them?" asked one of his inquisitors, the father of four young rebels SAVAK had imprisoned and killed. "Why did you torture them so much? Why did you pull out all their fingernails?" The beleaguered Nassiri offered a Nuremberg-style defence. "I just did the office work," he said.[17] Three days later, Nassiri and four other SAVAK generals were executed on the roof of Khomeini's military headquarters with pistol shots to the back of the head. Twenty more SAVAK officers were executed by machine-gun fire the next day, after having been found guilty by a hastily convened "people's court" of "torture, tyranny and dishonesty."[18] Photographs of the corpses were published in Iranian newspapers.

The execution of the generals was a turning point in the evolution of Iran's fledgling Islamic republic. Just two days earlier, Khomeini had said, "We will not repeat the evils of the Pahlavi dynasty. These people must be arrested by the people and in due course they will be brought before properly constituted Islamic courts where they will be tried for their crimes."[19] But now the ayatollah had conceded vigilante justice to the mobs. Prime Minister Bazargan was reportedly "furious" that Khomeini had condoned such summary executions, but, in truth, vigilantism was but a symptom of two trends in Iranian politics that had already begun to overtake the prime minister.[20] The first, the explosion of sectarian violence, had been widely expected. The second, the creation of a secretive, unelected "Revolutionary Council" that would govern alongside Bazargan and ultimately usurp him, was not. Both of these developments would gain momentum over the course of 1979, transform Khomeini's revolution and culminate in the hostage crisis.

The movement to rid Iran of the "criminal shah" had united political dissidents of every stripe. Khomeini's gift was to speak in vague generalizations about what his Islamic republic would look like while espousing a general anti-capitalist and anti-imperialist policy orientation that virtually all of the shah's opponents could support. He spoke of nationalizing Iran's resources, limiting private property, redistributing wealth and establishing Iran internationally as a non-aligned state. Beyond that, he said little. With the shah's defeat and exile, everything changed. For the front-line troops in the war against the shah—the men and women who had been mangled and killed by the thousands for opposing the dictatorship—the sacrifices of the struggle translated into a strong desire for power. Within weeks of Khomeini's return, roughly fifteen opposition organizations had already appeared, some of them well organized and functioning as parties. They ranged from the neo-Nazi Pan-Iranist party on the right, through the centrist National Front and Iran Nationalist parties, to the Society of Iranian Socialists on the left.

Two groups of guerrilla fighters in particular had been crucial to the overthrow of the shah, the Mujahidin Kalq (Holy Warriors) and the Fedayeen Kalq (Self-sacrificers). The Mujahidin Kalq were "Islamic Marxists" inspired mainly by the Islamic wing of the National Front. They had launched as a political movement in the early 1960s and commenced paramilitary operations in Iran in 1971. The Fedayeen Kalq began at roughly the same time but evolved out of the communist Tudeh party and the Marxist wing of the National Front. Both groups envisaged a revolution in Iran that would end Western imperialism, overturn Iran's dependence on foreign capital and usher in a classless society. The only way to shatter the "atmosphere of terror" in imperial Iran, they believed, was through "heroic acts of violence."[21] The shah's regime had gone after them with every resource SAVAK could muster. Hundreds, possibly thousands, were killed in battle or executed under torture. The guerrillas, wrote the Iranian historian Ervand Abrahamian in 1980, "had gained not only armed experience but also a mystique of revolutionary heroism," and were thus ready after the fall of the shah "to move into action and take advantage of the revolutionary situation."[22]

Other dissident organizations followed. One was a group of disillusioned clerics, including the popular ayatollahs Kazem Shariatmadari and Mahmoud Taleghani, who had backed Khomeini in exile but who came to oppose his increasingly autocratic rule. Also unleashed by the overthrow of the shah were the aspirations of Iran's ethnic and linguistic minorities. These included the approximately two million Kurds living in Iran, half a million Turkomans and a large number of Shiite Arabs living in the Iranian province of Khuzestan. All of these groups challenged Khomeini's conception of an Islamic republic, many of them by the same violent means they had used against the shah. Thus as soon as the initial euphoria of the ayatollah's return to Iran wore off, the country was again plagued by sectarian violence—this time over the very character of the revolution. Khomeini and his loyalists responded with tactics the shah himself would have approved. Mobs of Khomeini loyalists fought the guerrillas in the cities. In the Iranian hinterland, home to Iran's ethnic minorities, the army was sent in to "wipe out and destroy all counter-revolutionary elements," as Deputy Prime Minister Abbas Amir Entezam put it in March 1979.[23]

The second development to colour Iranian politics throughout 1979 was equally Machiavellian but even more shadowy. As the Canadian embassy reported from Tehran on February 21, just three weeks after Khomeini's return, power was already moving from Bazargan's provisional government to an elite group of militants loyal to the mullahs. "The government is theoretically controlled by PM Bazargan," Ambassador Taylor told Ottawa, "but in effect it is the Revolutionary Council headed by Khomeini and of unknown composition which directs all major policy."[24] This Revolutionary Council was a group of fifteen or so men hand-picked by Khomeini himself, some of them clergy, some not. It included Prime Minister Bazargan, Sadegh Ghotbzadeh, Abolhassan Bani-Sadr, Ayatollah Mohammad Beheshti and mullah Hashemi Rafsanjani. The council ostensibly controlled the so-called Islamic tribunals, but Khomeini had in fact delegated responsibility for trials and executions directly to Sadegh Khalkhali, a man known to Westerners as "Judge Blood" and the "Hanging Ayatollah."[25] The Revolutionary Council also oversaw the Revolutionary Guards, or Pasdaran-e Engheleb-e Islami, bands of armed militants that had emerged from local *komitehs* entrusted with protecting the clerics. Throughout 1979, a frustrated Prime Minister Bazargan would repeatedly offer Khomeini his resignation, saying that he could not govern if real power was concentrated in the Council.

Taken together, the mobilization of Khomeini loyalists against dissidents and the consolidation of power in the Revolutionary Council embodied a process of *purification,* the term used by militants of every stripe to bring the revolution closer to "the line of the Imam."

~ ~ ~

For the handful of Canadians stuck in Iran after Khomeini's return from exile, life became even more harrowing. Janette Orr, a thirty-year-old married to an American working in Abadan, was one of several Canadians whose name appeared on a local "death list." Because of what she called "a bureaucratic tangle," she had been unable to get an exit visa from Iranian authorities. She and her husband thus took a 16-hour bus ride from Abadan to Tehran in order to flee Iran on one of Ken Taylor's emergency evacuation flights, "a Canadian Armed Forces mercy flight to freedom," she later called it.[26]

Rising anti-foreign sentiment in Iran became a looming preoccupation for the ambassador. Taylor reported to Ottawa that Western embassies had not yet escalated their warning level, but that he and his colleagues were in the process of contacting all Canadians still in Iran, updating their records and advising them on contingency planning. He made a point of informing his superiors that the American embassy had offered to reserve emergency seats for him and the other Canadian embassy staff on C-141 Starlifter cargo aircraft, which were still flying daily into Mehrabad Airport.[27]

By now, everything Taylor had worked for since arriving in Iran in 1977 lay in ruins. "Time ran out on us," he later observed.[28] Virtually all of the resident Canadians excepting his own staff and the spouses of Iranian nationals had been evacuated; virtually all of the Canadian business deals he had helped to promote were dead. Canada's Economic Development Council reported that $400 million in Iranian–Canadian joint ventures had ground to a halt, Stadler Herter alone accounting for $280 million. The negotiations for a $1.2 billion thermal power station that Taylor had initiated had broken down. The Iranian plan to build an oil refinery at Come By Chance, Newfoundland, another $200 million project, was shelved. Canadian banks had closed their Tehran branches. (The only bright spot for Canadian financial institutions was that they represented a safe haven for a good deal of the capital that wealthy Iranians were moving offshore.[29]) The scene at the Canadian mission, meanwhile, had grown "chaotic," as Taylor himself later put it, "with two hundred people out in the street trying to break down the embassy door to get exit visas. There was no law and order."[30] By the spring of 1979, the number of Iranian applications for emigration visas to Canada would exceed six thousand and would require additional embassy staff to process them.

~ ~ ~

Into this tempest came a most extraordinary request. If it was not too much trouble, Ottawa queried Ambassador Taylor, would he mind if the Canadian embassy represented Israel's interests in Iran?

Publicly, Iranians and Israelis evince mutual hostility, and have done so since the founding of the state of Israel in 1948. During the Cold War, however, they shared strategic interests and even a similar world view. Iranians and Israelis saw themselves as proud heirs to ancient civilizations and believed themselves to be superior to their Sunni Arab neighbours. Both were allies of the United States; both loathed the Soviets and distrusted Arab flirtations with communism.[31] Shah Mohammad Reza Pahlavi understood the strategic importance to Iran of an alliance with Israel, and managed it deftly. Although the two countries never formally recognized each other, it was an open secret that they had achieved an entente. A pipeline was built to carry Iranian oil into Israel. In return, Israelis shared their expertise in agriculture and irrigation. Israeli intelligence officers reportedly trained the shah's secret police, Mossad assisting SAVAK in the interrogation of dissidents throughout the 1978 revolution.[32] The Israeli Trade Mission functioned as a de facto embassy in Tehran, enjoying all of the attendant diplomatic protections—immunity, tax exemptions, licence plates, courier privileges and access to coded cable services. By 1978, Iran–Israeli trade was estimated at $300 million, with 70 per cent of Israel's petroleum imports coming from Iran.[33]

But Ayatollah Khomeini had no love for Israel. When it became known early in 1979 that he was allying his movement with Yasser Arafat's PLO, the Israeli government had little choice but to accelerate its contingency planning for a complete diplomatic break with Iran. Israel's worry was that Khomeini would not only make common cause with the Arabs in the region but would make available to them all of the military hardware that the Americans had been providing the shah over the years.[34] As part of his government's contingency planning, Israeli prime minister Menachem Begin asked Prime Minister Trudeau whether Canada might consider representing Israeli interests in Iran. "Subsequently, we were asked for observations and implications about the Israeli request," Ambassador Taylor later recalled. "It was a domestic political issue. If anything ever came out, the Canadian prime minister wouldn't want to be seen as turning down the Israelis."[35]

Taylor had been following Israeli activities in Tehran since his arrival in 1977. In anticipation of Canada's assuming Israeli interests, he began meeting with the Israeli HOM in Iran, Uri Lubrani. "We used to meet at the French bistro in the Hilton hotel," said Taylor. "We discussed the transfer of Israeli interests to Canada all the time." Taylor fully expected that revolutionary Iran would sever diplomatic relations with Israel, expel its diplomats, cut off its oil supply and terminate El Al's landing rights. He knew about Project Flower, the ultra-secret weapons-development program designed to create an Iranian missile system using Israeli technology, but was never told anything officially. "You know, they'd say, well, there's a lot more going on between the Iranians and the Israelis than you think," Taylor recalled recently of Project Flower. "But I assumed that it was under the U.S. umbrella."[36] In fact, the deal was put together by Uri Lubrani and Iranian general Hasan Toufanian and never included the United States. "What was most astonishing about the project," writes Trita Parsi, a leading scholar on Iranian–Israeli relations, "was that both countries went to great lengths to keep the Americans in the dark."[37]

On January 5, 1979, a "Secret Canadian Eyes Only" cable arrived in Ottawa from the Canadian embassy in Tel Aviv. If Canada agreed to represent Israeli interests in Iran, cautioned the telex, it would also end up representing "the Jewish community of Iran, [which] is frightened and suffers from great anxiety."[38] Ambassador Taylor was copied on the Tel Aviv cable and recognized immediately what it meant: potentially far greater insecurity for Canadians in Tehran. "The decision on our part to represent Israel could push Canada into the limelight of the central foreign policy issue of the Middle East," Taylor wrote Ottawa two days later, "with all of the political ramifications that might involve."[39] Taylor was not reluctant to list the many reasons why he thought the idea of Canada taking on Israeli interests was wrong-headed. "With both the USA and Israel as the most visible scapegoats for the Iranian opposition," he cabled Ottawa, "Canada could become caught in a slipstream and become a secondary focus for popular dissatisfaction should we choose to represent Israel."[40]

"We gave Ottawa a thoughtful piece," Taylor later recalled with a chuckle, but he knew the decision had already been made.[41] "Would you please meet with the Israeli head of mission as soon as possible to assume Israeli interests?" was Ottawa's reply.[42]

On February 18, right in the middle of Canada's negotiation of Israeli interests, PLO leader Yasser Arafat arrived in Tehran for meetings with Khomeini, accompanied by fifty-nine PLO officials. The PLO had trained many of the guerrillas who had confronted the shah's army, so Khomeini was to some extent beholden to Arafat. In a bold gesture on the day of Arafat's arrival, the ayatollah announced the expulsion of all Israelis from Iran and the recall of all Iranian diplomats from Israel. According to the Israeli government, most of its nationals had already been evacuated. Only thirty-four Israelis remained, a mix of El Al employees, embassy personnel and Mossad officers. All had gone underground, in fact, and were living secretly in three apartments in Tehran.[43] Khomeini also announced that Iran would no longer sell petroleum to Israel, a blow cushioned by the fact that, unlike the CIA, Mossad had seen the Iranian revolution coming the previous summer and had advised the Israeli government to start diversifying its sources of oil.[44] On February 19, Iranian officials, including the ayatollah's son, Ahmad Seyyed Khomeini, attended the inauguration of the PLO office in the former Israeli mission. Ahmad rallied the crowd with a call for Iran and the PLO to work together to launch a worldwide Islamic revolution. "We will continue our struggle until we free all Islamic countries and hoist the Palestinian flag with ours," he cheered.[45]

At the end of February, the thirty-four Israelis hiding out in Tehran were exfiltrated. In a joint covert operation of the Israeli defence department and the CIA, they were flown out of Tehran on two commercial Pan Am flights, disguised as Americans.[46] The Canadian embassy appears to have had nothing to do with the logistics of this operation. Ambassador Taylor had discussed it beforehand with Ambassador Bill Sullivan, only to be told by his friend, in typically jocular fashion, "Well, now the Israelis are *your* business!"[47] The only Israelis left in Tehran after this exfiltration were an undisclosed number of deep-cover Mossad officers. Taylor knew about them, and wondered what would happen if they were discovered while Canada was representing Israeli interests.

Ambassador Taylor and Iranian foreign minister Karim Sanjabi signed the formal agreement on Israeli interests on February 24. "Sanjabi was one of Bazargan's people," Taylor later recalled. "He was from the old school."[48] Sanjabi liked the interests arrangement, but because of Khomeini's strong commitment to the Palestinian cause, he said there could be no formal acknowledgment of it from Tehran. He understood that an announcement might be necessary in Canada but asked that the Canadians keep the deal quiet in Iran.[49] At the same meeting Taylor met, for the first time, Ibrahim Yazdi, then serving as deputy foreign minister and well known as one of Khomeini's closest advisers. Taylor's first impression of Yazdi was positive. "He had advanced degrees from the U.S., very articulate, very much part of the entourage," said the ambassador. "I met him and told him, according to protocol, that Canada was assuming responsibility for Israeli interests in Tehran. He looked at me and said, 'Are you out of your mind?'"[50]

Canada formally assumed Israeli interests on March 1, 1979. External Affairs went to a great deal of trouble to couch the agreement in the language of diplomatic neutrality, in part to placate anxious Canadian diplomats in Arab countries. A press release was issued, but the North American media paid virtually no attention to it.[51] As promised, nothing was announced in Iran. Taylor and his colleagues feared a backlash but, strangely, it never came.

One question remained: What was Canada's obligation to the deep-cover Mossad officers left behind in Iran? Led by Avraham Geffen, this group was running a daring clandestine program called Operation Laid Table, through which a total of approximately 40,000 of Iran's 100,000 Jews would ultimately be rescued from the revolution. Using bogus passports and birth certificates they had printed themselves, Geffen and his comrades personally supervised the Jews' passage through Mehrabad Airport, normally six or seven at a time. It appears that Taylor and his colleagues never had to run interference for Geffen or his men. "We didn't know what to expect," Taylor later recalled. "What if the Iranians had arrested an Israeli, and they claimed he was a Mossad agent? Then the Israelis would have said, no, no, he's an El Al employee. We were prepared to do something if they got into trouble."[52]

Roger Lucy told the same story. "Mossad agents never showed up," he said. "Presumably they went underground. The only thing respecting Israeli interests that came onto our radar screen was an Israeli who had overstayed his visa. He ended up in jail, and he finally got out with the help of the Red Cross."[53] Avraham Geffen was not so lucky. In March or April 1980, after the Canadians themselves had fled Iran, he would be captured by the Revolutionary Guard, imprisoned, tortured and starved. He was released on payment of a $150,000 ransom raised by Iranian Jews, and only because no one in Iran believed he could actually be Mossad.

In 2006, Ken Taylor was invited to a commemorative service in Tel Aviv organized by Skylink, an aviation company whose board he sits on. Taylor knew he would be asked to plant a ceremonial tree, but he had no idea of the surprise introduction that had been planned for him. "After I planted the tree, the host Israeli, with tears in his eyes, admitted that he had been a Mossad officer and he had been in Iran in 1979. He said, 'We were told that if we got into any trouble at all we should go and see Taylor.' I had a sense that we were the place of last resort, but clearly they took it very seriously. Hotel Canada—the ambassadorial residence—was already overbooked, but we could have accommodated them!"[54]

~ ~ ~

At roughly 4 a.m. Ottawa time on February 14, 1979, the night staff at the Pearson Building received the first of four flash cables from the Canadian embassy in Tehran, along with a request that the information it contained be forwarded to the State Department Operations Center ("Ops Center") in Washington. "The U.S. Embassy came under attack presumably by communist terrorists late a.m. local time," it read. "Fate of embassy personnel unknown."[55] A second telex arrived less than two hours later, informing Ottawa that Ambassador

Sullivan and Major General Philip Gast, chief of the U.S. military mission to Iran, were now "prisoners of the communists." "Mullahs and pro-Khomeini irregulars appear to have arrived at the embassy to assist," it said, "but are receiving heavy fire from inside the embassy compound."[56] A third cable arrived an hour later and described the denouement of the siege. "We have confirmation by radio from the embassy compound that the embassy is now being protected by Khomeini militia."[57] A fourth and final cable followed shortly after that, relaying word from the rescued American diplomats that the occupation had ended and they were taking stock of their battered embassy.

Only days later did Ottawa get the full story of the Valentine's Day siege. A unit of roughly seventy-five well-armed Fedayeen Kalq guerrillas had crashed through the embassy gates and attempted to occupy the main chancery building by force. ("It looks like the Reds are trying to make a play for a takeover before Khomeini's lot get too strong," Roger Lucy observed at the time.[58]) After destroying all of the classified documents that remained on hand, Ambassador Sullivan had calmly ordered the Marine guard and his embassy staff to surrender to the invaders. Seventy Americans were handcuffed, hooded and led out of the chancery building. Some of them, including Sullivan, were beaten. Ibrahim Yazdi and a squad of "Islamic police" loyal to Khomeini arrived in short order to evict the guerrillas and return the embassy to its American owners, as required by diplomatic protocol. A firefight between the guard and the guerrillas ensued. Several Iranians were reported killed, but there were no serious American casualties. (The U.S. embassy in Kabul, Afghanistan, did not fare so well, however. Hearing that the Tehran embassy had been overrun, some Afghan rebels decided to kidnap the American ambassador, Adolph "Spike" Dubs. When the Afghan government tried to rescue Dubs by force, his kidnappers murdered him.)

Ken Taylor had been in periodic telephone contact with his friends at the U.S. embassy during the Valentine's Day siege, hence the series of cryptic, real-time telexes that had flowed from the Canadian embassy to Ottawa. The ambassador knew instinctively that the occupation marked a watershed for diplomats posted to Tehran. "My first thought was, from now on, only in our imaginations could we count upon a veneer of diplomatic immunity," he said. "As from today, protocol is out the window, and we make and play by our own rules. Sophistication is out and guile is in."[59]

After the February 14 attack, American civilians in Iran were instructed to leave the country immediately. "We cannot protect American lives in Iran," Ambassador Sullivan announced in a directive to U.S. nationals. "We strongly recommend evacuation."[60] Prime Minister Bazargan ordered safe passage for the estimated five thousand Westerners who wanted to leave, but worried that the same guerrillas who had stormed the embassy would ambush the buses carrying fleeing Americans. The opportunity now existed to close the U.S. embassy altogether. Hal Saunders, Assistant Secretary of State for Near Eastern and South Asian Affairs, later reflected on the dilemma facing Washington. "This is a familiar choice in dangerous situations," he wrote. "In the end policymakers usually decide, if the country is an important one, that it is more consistent with American interests to be present than to be absent."[61] Since there was never any doubt about Iran's strategic importance to the United States, President Carter decided to reduce embassy staff to sixty but also to redouble American efforts to work with Iran's provisional government. Security at the U.S. embassy compound was enhanced. Grills were welded to windows, steel doors replaced wooden ones, electronic access devices were installed, windows were fitted with bulletproof glass. Files that might compromise U.S. operations in Iran were shipped to Washington.

Ambassador Taylor followed the American lead and ordered security at his own embassy enhanced. Each day hundreds of impatient, often unruly, Iranians seeking visas or immigration permits crowded around the Canadian chancery, creating an atmosphere of "constant chaos," as the ambassador himself put it.[62] The Canadian Forces MPs posted to the embassy six weeks earlier had been designated "military attachés" and were thus unarmed. Taylor now directed that weapons be brought into Iran for their use, including 9 mm Browning high-power pistols and 9 mm Sterling C1 submachine guns. Transporting arms through Mehrabad Airport was a risky operation, since the Revolutionary Guards periodically confiscated diplomatic bags. After consulting with his colleagues in Ottawa, Taylor decided that it would be best to fully disclose his plans to Iranian foreign ministry officials. At his second meeting with Minister Sanjabi and Deputy Minister Yazdi, the ambassador stated that he had no choice, given the pandemonium at the gates of his embassy, but to arm his security detail. Cringing, the two Iranians reluctantly concurred. "I could almost read their minds," Taylor later recalled. "'What is it with these Canadians—first Israeli interests, and now guns?'"[63]

~ ~ ~

DCI Stansfield Turner would later recall that the Carter administration neglected to convert the lessons of the February 14 siege into a blueprint for future embassy occupations. "No one mentioned it," he wrote, "but we had been so glad to put the Valentine's Day problem behind us that we had never discussed what we would do if the embassy were taken again. We had no contingency plans."[64] Turner and his colleagues did, however, begin thinking seriously about the consequences of allowing the exiled shah into the United States. A study done by embassy staffers in Tehran concluded that "if the shah were permitted to come to the United States, it would be seen by most Iranians as an indication that we intended to restore him to the throne and overturn the revolution."[65]

Ayatollah Khomeini's view of the Valentine's Day attack on the U.S. embassy was unambiguous. He turned resolutely against the myriad Iranian leftists who had once been integral to his revolutionary coalition. The guerrillas were nothing but "anti-Islamic opportunists," he said flatly.[66] Thereafter, clashes between protesters carrying hammer-and-sickle banners and those carrying pictures of Khomeini became commonplace in Tehran.

As for Ambassador Taylor, he sent Ottawa a typically terse but accurate assessment of the new reality in post-shah Iran. "The situation in Tehran," he wrote, "is one of de facto anarchy."[67]

Chapter 6
FATEFUL DECISIONS

During the wee hours of March 15, 1979, Amir Abbas Hoveyda was hauled out of his Qasr Prison cell to stand trial before a revolutionary tribunal. The charges against him included spying for the United States, heroin smuggling, interfering in elections and "entering into battle against God and his emissaries."[1] The prosecutor demanded the death penalty. Prime Minister Bazargan was appalled when he got word of Hoveyda's secret trial, publicly calling the revolutionary courts and their summary executions a disgrace to Iran. Ayatollah Khomeini decreed a halt to the executions on March 16, bringing Hoveyda a temporary reprieve. Three weeks later, however, the midnight trials and executions resumed under powerful new guidelines giving a "religious judge" and a five-man revolutionary court the authority to try enemies of the state without provisions for their defence or the right of appeal.[2] All sentences now had to be carried out within twenty-four hours of sentencing.

Ken Taylor received a telex from Ottawa on March 27 informing him that Prime Minister Trudeau, who had befriended Hoveyda during his 1974 visit to Ottawa, was concerned about the fate of the former Iranian prime minister. "If Hoveyda's life is still in danger," the cable read, "or if at any time he should be put on trial again with a possibility of the death sentence, you should inform us immediately so that representations may be considered."[3] Taylor replied that, to the best of his knowledge, Hoveyda's trial had been suspended after Khomeini's decree. He urged External Affairs to recommend that Trudeau not send a personal message until Hoveyda's legal status could be verified.

On April 4, it was announced that Hoveyda's trial would resume the following week. Bazargan wanted an "open official trial," but Khomeini's Revolutionary Council was pressing for a closed session.[4] Prime Minister Trudeau again made it clear to External Affairs that if Hoveyda's life were in danger, he wanted to send a personal message to Bazargan. On April 5, Taylor received from Ottawa the text of a letter from Trudeau, which he was instructed to present to Bazargan either when a death sentence was pronounced or, if he judged that there would be too little time to do so between the sentence and the execution, at the beginning of the trial. "Canada values its relations with Iran and with your government," said the letter. "I am particularly impressed at the way in which you personally have, through the most difficult times, shown concern for human rights and the development of national reconciliation in Iran. A show of mercy to former prime minister Hoveyda, in this spirit, would be warmly welcomed by Iran's friends all over the world. Yours sincerely, Pierre Elliott Trudeau."[5]

Taylor's view—one widely shared within Tehran's diplomatic corps—was that a personal message seeking clemency for Hoveyda would be tantamount to triggering a summary execution. He proposed, therefore, that Trudeau send a more generalized appeal for adherence to international standards of justice, coupled with an expression of concern about reports that people were being executed in Iran for political offences. Trudeau could mention Hoveyda's case specifically in this context. Taylor's superiors at External Affairs supported this strategy.

Two days later, however, on April 7, after a six-hour closed trial, Hoveyda was sentenced to death by Ayatollah Khalkhali and executed immediately. Khalkhali reportedly asked for the pistol with which Hoveyda had been killed, to keep as a souvenir. The following day, several Western nations, including the United States, registered official protests. Iranian state radio, now headed by Sadegh Ghotbzadeh, mocked Washington's response to the execution. "The U.S. State Department, clinging to the excuse of human rights, has expressed its regret over the revolutionary punishment of Amir Abbas Hoveyda, their lackey and slavish mercenary in Iran," it said.[6] Ottawa cabled Ambassador Taylor immediately. "Was the PM's message to Bazargan delivered to anyone?"[7] he was asked. "The PM's message was not delivered, as news of execution was received at the same time (2200 HRS 7 April) as news that the trial resumed," Taylor replied.[8]

With this exchange of notes, a tsunami of recrimination began to roll through External Affairs. The Clerk of the Privy Council, Michael Pitfield, was Trudeau's point man on the Hoveyda file. He expressed in no uncertain terms the prime minister's displeasure that Taylor had not registered his protest with Bazargan. "I can understand the difficulties faced by External in this case," Pitfield scribbled in the margins of a May 1 memo, "but conclude that the department certainly did not distinguish itself in a matter of considerable importance to the p.m. I intend to say so to A.E.G. [Allan Gotlieb]," which he did.[9] Gotlieb tried to assuage Pitfield. "In the abnormal circumstances prevailing in Iran," he replied, "one can understand why the ambassador thought it best not to deliver a message urging clemency when, as far as he or anyone else knew, the trial had not even been resumed and the Iranians were showing some sensitivity about foreign intervention in their judicial process. This does not make it any the less regrettable that the Prime Minister's wishes were not carried out."[10]

Taylor believes that he and his superiors were unfairly criticized over the Hoveyda imbroglio. "In the middle of a bloody revolution," he has said, "you hope to make sense out of chaos and base human nature. Very rarely does anything unfold as planned or anticipated. Tehran at that time was a lawless society. The chief executioner, Ayatollah Khalkhali, was vengeful and totally intolerant of what he viewed as Western influence and meddlesome preaching. Amir Hoveyda was my friend as well as the prime minister's. The morning after his execution, the *Tehran Journal* ran a photograph of Hoveyda on the front page, bare-chested and lying on a cement slab. The image is still with me today and will be tomorrow."[11]

~ ~ ~

On the last day of March 1979, Iran held its long-promised referendum on the question "Are you for the replacement of the monarchy with an Islamic Republic, the constitution of which will be approved—yes or no?"[12] Opposition groups challenged the vagueness of the wording, among them a growing chorus of women's groups. Khomeini's order that Iranian women must wear the chador had had the unintended effect of mobilizing Iranian feminists against his Islamic republic. On March 12, twenty thousand women converged on the television studio of Iran's national broadcaster to protest the decree. They were dispersed by armed revolutionaries firing shots into the air.[13] Khomeini's apparent endorsement of the stoning of a youth convicted of rape also raised doubts about his proposed Islamic republic in the days leading up to the referendum.[14] Like most Western observers in Iran, Canadian embassy staff were wary of what they called "Khomeini's implacable resolve to create an Islamic state."[15] The ayatollah in power was turning out to be far more doctrinaire and authoritarian than his statements from Paris had ever implied. "Responsible Iranians," Ambassador Taylor told Ottawa, "are unable to envisage or describe the form such a government will take, and vague pronouncements of Khomeini and his advisors Yazdi, Ghotb-zadeh and Bani-Sadr provide small comfort or elucidation."[16]

The ayatollah proclaimed his Islamic republic on April 1, 1979, even before the referendum votes were counted. "This is the first day of God's government in Iran," he said.[17] Throughout Iran, crowds of Iranians chanted *"Allah-o akbar!"* ("God is the greatest that can be conceived!") and fired their weapons into the sky well into the night. According to the Iranian ministry of the interior, when the votes were counted the next day they showed a 97 per cent turnout and a 97 per cent vote in favour of an Islamic republic. Khomeini moved immediately to implement the draft constitution he had car-ried with him from Paris. After several false starts and an election that went "smoothly if not exactly honestly," in the words of Roger Lucy, a 75-man Assembly of Experts was elected to review the 151 articles contained in the final draft.[18] The document's defining clause had been inserted after the ayatollah's return to Iran, and was inter-preted by his critics as evidence that he had never been serious about bringing democracy to Iran. It allocated "supreme spiritual and pol-itical power" to Iran's ranking cleric, Khomeini himself.[19]

~ ~ ~

In the wake of the Valentine's Day attack on the U.S. embassy, the Bazargan government issued a decree confiscating all of the shah's assets, valued at about $4 billion. (Estimates of the value of the shah's foreign investments ranged up to $20 billion.) It also directed Iran's embassies in the West to press foreign governments for information on the shah's offshore real estate holdings. At the same time, Kho-meini began calling publicly for the return of the shah to face justice in Iran, promising to try him in absentia for "crimes against the Iranian people" if he did not return. Privately, the ayatollah dispatched assassins—the "Islamic Avengers"—to kill the shah.[20] Rumours circulated that the exiled monarch was buying property in British Columbia and negotiating through a third party for admission to Canada.[21]

The shah had indeed become a fugitive. After a short stay in Egypt, he had gone to Morocco, then to the Bahamas, then to Mexico, each stop either not to his own liking or unacceptable to his hosts. In April, he decided that he would join his family in the United States, putting Jimmy Carter in an awkward position. The president had invited the shah to come to the United States in January, it was true, but times had changed. Welcoming him now would endanger the lives of Americans in Iran. As Carter confided sardonically to his personal diary, "I don't have any feelings that the Shah or we would be better off with him playing tennis several hours a day in California instead of Acapulco."[22] Cyrus Vance was of two minds on the matter but finally advised the president to say no—"one of the most distasteful recommendations I ever had to make to the president," he later admitted.[23] Aggravating Carter's dilemma was the considerable (and very public) pressure he faced from Henry Kissinger, David Rockefeller and other prominent Americans who believed that denying the shah admission to the United States was beneath American dignity. "[W]e should not be influenced by threats from a third-rate regime," Zbigniew Brzezinski himself declared in a meeting with Carter and Vance. "[A]t stake are our traditions and national honor."[24]

"Fuck the shah," a frustrated Jimmy Carter reportedly told his advisers in July.[25] There would be no offer of admission for now.

~ ~ ~

Summary executions in Iran continued throughout the spring, steadily broadening to include leaders of the country's ethnic and religious minorities. Ayatollah Khomeini himself was unhappy with this widening persecution. On May 12 he issued a decree limiting executions to cases of murder and imposing the death penalty against anyone found to be carrying out executions in violation of this order.[26] Whether Ayatollah Khalkhali would acquiesce in the decree or whether Khomeini would even keep to it himself were open questions as far as Western diplomats in Tehran were concerned, including Ken Taylor. The Canadian ambassador was instructed explicitly by Ottawa to again call on the Iranian foreign minister to express Canadians' concerns about summary trials and executions.[27]

Two days after Khomeini's decree, Khalkhali announced that his revolutionary courts had passed death sentences on the shah, members of his immediate family and a long list of officials, including former prime minister Shapour Bakhtiar and former ambassador to the United States Ardeshir Zahedi. "Whoever carrie[s] out this sentence," Khalkhali said, "would be considered a court executioner and will be absolved of their blood."[28] The Iranian press ran advertisements the same week stating that the person who murdered the shah would win a free trip to Mecca.[29] Meanwhile, back in Canada, one of the favoured territories for wealthy Iranian expatriates hoping to set up new lives and businesses, the prospect of Iranian "death squads" roaming the streets of Canadian cities brought additional headaches for immigration authorities.[30] In mid-May, nine Iranians living with the exiled shah on Paradise Island in the Bahamas approached External Affairs about the possibility of coming to Canada to set up businesses in Toronto. Together their net worth was estimated to be in the $3 billion range. "It is being studied now," observed an unnamed Canadian immigration official, "and before we give an answer there are lots of questions that need to be answered. We'd want to be quite certain that the assets are legitimate—that they haven't been plundered from their country."[31]

On May 17, U.S. senator Jacob Javits sponsored a Senate resolution expressing Americans' "abhorrence of summary executions

without due process" in Iran.[32] He warned that human-rights violations endangered U.S.–Iranian relations, to which an irate Ayatollah
Khomeini replied, "Well, we hope to God that they are endangered.
What do we want with the United States?"[33] Javits's wife, Marion, had
been a Washington lobbyist for Iran Air during the shah's reign and
remained a close friend of the shah's sister, Ashraf. Senator Javits's
resolution thus incensed the Iranians on every level. The ayatollah
retaliated against the United States by refusing to accept the credentials of the man appointed to replace Bill Sullivan as U.S. ambassador, Walter Cutler. Popular anti-Americanism, smouldering in Iran
since President Carter's New Year's toast, burst into full flame. One
Canadian who witnessed Iranians' wrath first-hand was the freelance
journalist Linda McQuaig, who had arrived in Tehran in April 1979.
"Iranians react bitterly to charges by foreign lawyers and activists that
human rights are being violated in Iran," she wrote in a feature for
the *Globe and Mail*. "Where were these critics when the shah was vio-
lating human rights? is the common retort." McQuaig interviewed
any number of SAVAK's torture victims, including *Omid Iran* editor
Ali Reza Nourizadeh and Professor Homa Nateq of the University of
Tehran. "Torture stories are endless," wrote McQuaig. "One almost
becomes hardened to them after a while."[34]

The United States now became the preferred target of Iranian demonstrators, along with the "puppet shah." Mobs routinely
set American flags ablaze in front of the U.S. embassy and chanted
"Marg bar Carter!" ("Death to Carter!"). Iranian newspapers published exposés of senior Carter administration officials' connections
to the shah, including National Security Advisor Zbigniew Brzezinski
and DCI Stansfield Turner. In mid-July the trial of a former minister of the shah revealed that each time Henry Kissinger had visited
imperial Iran, between $720,000 and $850,000 was spent to entertain
him.[35] The lesson for ordinary Iranians was obvious: the shah had
been squandering the national wealth.

Seen in retrospect, Senator Javits's resolution was not merely inflammatory but counterproductive, for it handed Iran's clerics new ammunition to use against the provisional government. Prime Minister Bazargan told the French newspaper *Le Monde* in May that "furious disagreements had sprung up within the revolutionary courts about whether political executions should continue."[36] Bazargan himself had come out in favour of a general amnesty in Iran, which would allow the government some breathing room to start addressing the country's mounting economic problems.[37] Foreign Minister Ibrahim Yazdi and Deputy Prime Minister Abbas Amir Entezam agreed, taking direct aim at the mullahs. "Mr. Khalkhali is not head of the revolutionary tribunals and he is not even a member of the courts," Yazdi told the foreign press. "So we are very sorry that the Senate issued a declaration based upon an unconfirmed report."[38]

~ ~ ~

L. Bruce Laingen became U.S. chargé d'affaires in Iran on June 18, 1979. A youthful fifty-eight years old, soft-spoken, bright and personable, Laingen had first served in Tehran for two years before the 1953 coup that toppled Mossadeq. He later recalled that his return to Iran was tinted by his earlier infatuation with the country and its people. "I had been enamored by the stark beauty of its landscape and the translucent blue of its skies," he wrote. "I had come to understand how the starkness of the Persian landscape was relieved by the rich color and form of Persian carpets and architecture, above all by the majestic mosques with the special appeal of blue so evident in their intricate tile work and mosaics—mosques that also spoke of the role of Islam in Iran's history and in the fabric of life for every Iranian."[39] Laingen was extremely popular among his own staff and within the Western diplomatic corps. CIA officer William

Daugherty admired him as gracious and helpful, calling him and the head of the U.S. Military Assistance Advisory Group (MAAG) at the time, Major General Philip Gast, "exceptional gentlemen."[40] Ken Taylor thought equally highly of the new American chargé, and would continue to do so during the hostage crisis, when their lives became intimately intertwined. "Bruce Laingen was quite remarkable," says Taylor, who remains close friends with Laingen to this day. "He handled the crisis well, and he has handled it well since."[41]

The immediate goal of Chargé Laingen and his staff was to stabilize U.S. relations as much as possible with the Bazargan government. A secondary aim, over which they had admittedly very little control, was to see that secular leaders like Bazargan and Yazdi remained strong in the face of the growing power of the Islamic hard-liners. With Laingen's arrival, U.S. consular services resumed. Embassy staffers began clearing the backlog of visa applications from the many young Iranians who wanted to study in the United States. One of Laingen's first requests of the Iranian government was that it remove a *komiteh* that had been squatting within the embassy compound since the Valentine's Day occupation. This small paramilitary unit was composed for the most part of undisciplined young men whose activities included roaming around the compound and torturing prisoners in their guardroom.[42] According to diplomatic protocol, the host country is responsible for the safety of foreign diplomats serving on its soil. What Laingen needed was a professional unit like the one that had driven out the guerrillas on Valentine's Day.

The day after Bruce Laingen took charge of the U.S. embassy, Ken Taylor met with Iranian foreign minister Ibrahim Yazdi. A former chemistry professor and medical researcher who had spent many years in the United States, Yazdi was virtually the only man in Khomeini's inner circle with the talent and savvy to advance the ayatollah's agenda, on the one hand, and to safeguard Iran's international obligations and strategic alliances, on the other. At this meeting, Taylor learned for the first time that "Ayatollah Khomeini and his supporters were astounded by the rapid and total collapse of the shah and his army. They had anticipated years of struggle and counted on more time to introduce and form a government in exile during a lengthy transitional period."[43] Yazdi told Taylor that his government was prepared to acknowledge the international protests against summary executions in Iran, but added that "three hundred executions were a comparatively low revolutionary cost for transforming a country from dictatorship to republic."[44] By the end of their talk, Taylor had taken the full measure of the challenges facing the foreign minister. "Yazdi is currently, outside the clergy and the prime minister, the most influential political figure in Iran," he reported to Ottawa. "He alone publicly takes issue with radical ayatollahs and yet apparently continues to benefit from Ayatollah Khomeini's total confidence. Yazdi will be a key figure during the move from provisional government to elected assembly."[45]

~ ~ ~

"On the first day of October 1979," Jimmy Carter later recalled, "I heard about the Shah's illness."[46] Cyrus Vance had heard about it two days earlier, calling the news "a virtual bombshell."[47]

The shah had been diagnosed with lymphoma in 1978, but he had held the secret so closely that even his doctors in Mexico had no idea how sick he was. It was David Rockefeller's personal physician, in fact, who had examined the shah in Mexico. In light of the shah's visible decline—severe weight loss, jaundice—State Department Medical Director Dr. Eben Dustin recommended that he be brought to the Cornell University Medical Center in New York for diagnosis and treatment. As Vance later recalled, "we were faced squarely with a decision in which common decency and humanity had to be weighed against possible harm to our embassy personnel in Tehran."[48]

Jimmy Carter would undoubtedly like to have taken some time to ponder the matter of the shah's health, but time was not on his side. On October 3, during a session of the UN General Assembly in New York, Ibrahim Yazdi met in person with Cyrus Vance and his aides. As Assistant Secretary of State Hal Saunders later recalled, during these talks Yazdi returned repeatedly to "the theme of American culpability for all that Iranians had suffered under the regime of the shah."[49] Vance tried to reassure Yazdi that the United States was not interested in destabilizing the Bazargan government. "I told him that we recognized and accepted both the revolution and the new government," he said. "I told him that we were prepared to deal with Iran in the future on the basis of friendship and mutual respect."[50] Yazdi asked Vance point-blank if Carter intended to allow the shah into the United States. The secretary of state replied that the matter was under consideration.

On Friday, October 19, Carter put the question to his foreign-policy advisers. Some, like Director of Iranian Affairs in the State Department Henry Precht, argued strongly against the shah's admission. "[I]f we are going to establish a relationship with the new revolutionary Iran," Precht said, "we can't maintain our old ties and our personal obligations to a man who worked with us for decades."[51] Bruce Laingen agreed. "I thought that until the revolution had put its own institutions of government in place," said the chargé, "and until we had put an ambassador in place, and thus signaled in that way our acceptance of the revolution, that it would be dangerous to proceed with his admission. That could trigger demonstrations, it might even be a repeat of the February 14 attack."[52] Vance, however, had by this time overcome his own reservations, reluctantly agreeing with Brzezinski that the shah should be allowed into the United States on compassionate grounds. President Carter was under no illusions. "I asked my advisers what course they would recommend to me if the Americans in Iran were seized or killed," he later wrote.[53] No one answered.

Carter and Vance directed Laingen to talk to Bazargan and Yazdi about a possible decision to admit the shah. The chargé was to stress that the admission of the shah would constitute not a political act but merely a humanitarian gesture. He also asked the Iranian government explicitly for its guarantee that U.S. nationals in Iran would be protected. Anticipating that the Iranian people would see the shah's illness as a ruse, Yazdi asked Laingen if Washington would agree to allow an Iranian physician to examine him. The chargé was instructed by the White House to say no. Both told Laingen that they feared Iranians would react with hostility to the decision to admit the shah. It is commonly believed that the Iranians committed themselves to the protection of the embassy and its personnel at this time, but the declassified cable traffic between Laingen and the State Department demonstrates the opposite. Neither Bazargan nor Yazdi believed the embassy could be protected.[54]

On October 20, the White House received an update on the shah's condition from Deputy Secretary of State Warren Christopher. "We have now learned," it read, "the Shah's illness is malignant lymphoma compounded by a possible internal blockage which has resulted in severe jaundice."[55] Mexican doctors lacked "essential diagnostic tests which are necessary to establish proper diagnosis," added Christopher.[56] The recommendation of the attending physicians was, therefore, that the shah be transferred to the United States for diagnosis and treatment. Sloan-Kettering hospital in New York City was thought to be a suitable facility.

Jimmy Carter then made the most fateful decision of his presidency. "I told Brzezinski to permit the Shah to go to New York for medical treatment, and just inform our embassy in Tehran that this would occur," he wrote in his personal diary.[57] Bazargan and Yazdi were notified, but the United States sought neither their approval nor their permission.

The shah arrived in New York on Monday, October 22, 1979, on a plane bearing a tail number registered to the CIA.[58] He underwent surgery to remove his gall bladder and a lymph node two days later. For the first week or so, Iranian reaction to the news that the shah was in the United States was muted. Carter and his advisers at the State Department interpreted this initial response as evidence that Iranians understood that the shah was terminally ill and that there was nothing more to his admission than a humanitarian gesture toward a dying man. This turned out to be far too optimistic. By October 30, Iranians' anger about the decision to admit the shah had crystallized, and street protests of up to a million people engulfed Tehran. The main target of these rallies was the U.S. embassy compound, where irate crowds burned effigies and shouted anti-shah and anti-American slogans. Ayatollah Khomeini inflamed the mobs, releasing anti-American statements and demanding the return of the shah. Ayatollah Khalkhali went even further, exhorting his sympathizers in New York to take matters into their own hands. "I order all students and Muslims in the United States, including Africans, Filipinos and Palestinians, to drag [the shah] out of the hospital and dismember him," he reportedly said.[59]

As the street protests escalated, Mehdi Bazargan and Ibrahim Yazdi flew off to Algiers to participate in that country's independence celebrations. While they were there, the two Iranian leaders met privately with Zbigniew Brzezinski, who was attending the same ceremony on behalf of the United States. It was the Iranians, not the national security adviser, who asked for the meeting and who took the upper hand. They demanded of Brzezinski that the United States promise not to destabilize the new regime, that it continue providing military aid to Iran and that it cooperate in the Iranians' investigation into the shah's wealth. Cyrus Vance knew nothing of the meeting until after the fact, but he recognized immediately that the optics would be catastrophic. Bazargan and Yazdi had made themselves "vulnerable to attack by extremists who wanted to purge the government of its secular and sometimes pro-Western elements," he observed.[60]

What Vance did not say but what he almost certainly understood was that Brzezinski's private meeting with the heads of the Iranian government could mean only one thing to the men and women in the streets of Tehran: the Americans were planning another coup.

~ ~ ~

Ambassador Taylor cabled Ottawa on October 29, 1979, a terse and pessimistic synopsis of the scene in Tehran. "Prospects for the establishment of a coherent progressive government by the early 1980s are diminishing," he said. "Evidence of the mullahs' influence abounds. The draft constitution is theocratic, justice is cavalierly meted out by the sinister Ayatollah Khalkhali, millions demonstrate in response to exhortations from the mosque, and Ayatollah Khomeini's pronouncements legislate." As for the diplomatic corps in Iran, Taylor reported that everyone was waiting and watching. "The majority of foreign governments are acting judiciously until the situation clarifies and the temper of the ayatollahs is determined."[61]

Meanwhile, at the Aryamehr University of Technology in Tehran, engineering student Ibrahim Asgharzadeh and some of his friends were drawing the obvious conclusion about Brzezinski's meeting with Bazargan and Yazdi in Algiers: the United States was conspiring with Iran's provisional government to overthrow the revolution. "The Americans were obviously looking to make history repeat itself," said Asgharzadeh, "and we had to deliver a blow to them to make them come to their senses."[62]

The simplest plans were always the best, the students agreed. They would seize the U.S. embassy.

PART THREE
HOSTAGES AND HOUSEGUESTS

Chapter 7
MARG BAR AMRIKA!

n the fall of 1979, the U.S. embassy compound in Tehran looked
much like an ivy-league university campus. Twenty-seven acres of
arching old-growth trees and winding roads linked the chancery
(the mission's main office building) with the ambassador's residence
and various outbuildings. Fortified by a ten foot brick wall on all
sides, the property was affectionately known as "Fort Apache" to the
diplomats who worked there. The wall containing the main gate ran
for six hundred feet along Taleghani Avenue to the south (formerly
Takht-e-Jamshid Street) and remains, even now, instantly recognizable
as the main site of the Iranians' massive anti-U.S. street demonstrations. Until the hostage crisis, the lush grounds of the embassy stood
in such marked contrast to the urban sprawl outside that some called
it an oasis. This was not how U.S. chargé d'affaires Bruce Laingen saw
it. The compound had come to symbolize everything that had "gone
wrong" in Iran, he later wrote. "Too large and too centrally located,
its scattered buildings were almost impossible to defend; it was also a

chancery devoid of aesthetic appeal. For Iran's revolutionaries during the shah's later years, it had symbolized what was wrong in terms of a visual presence and influence propping up a hated regime, just as the similarly large compounds of the British and Soviet embassies had symbolized perceived wrongs in earlier Iranian history."[1]

On the morning of November 4, 1979, a Sunday, the first day of the Iranian workweek, Tehran was overcast and drizzly. Starting at about 9 a.m., crowds chanting *"Allah-o akbar! Marg bar Amrika!"* assumed their positions outside the compound gates as usual. For U.S. embassy personnel, the day's routines also began in typical fashion. Bruce Laingen chaired a short meeting of the embassy's department heads, as he did every week, then headed off with two colleagues to an appointment at the Iranian foreign ministry. His staff of eighty Americans, living and working in a vast enclave that was once home to over two thousand, settled into their workday, coffee cups close at hand, post-weekend chitchat in the air. Shah Mohammad Reza Pahlavi had by now been in the United States almost two weeks. Although there had been several large street demonstrations in Tehran over the preceding week, the weekend (Friday and Saturday) had been so calm as to suggest to the American diplomats that any serious threat to their security had passed. For the first time in many weeks, the anxious atmosphere at the embassy had eased.

Only one person in the American sphere appears to have known that a group of university students was hatching a plot to take over the U.S. embassy: Somchai (Sam) Sriweawnetr, an unassuming young Thai national who had been working for many months as a cook and odd-jobs person for several of the U.S. diplomats. On Thursday, November 1, Sriweawnetr had been shopping in a Tehran market when he ran into an Iranian friend. "He told me, maybe tomorrow the embassy will be taken over by students," Sriweawnetr later recalled.[2] Upon hearing this, Sriweawnetr went directly from the market to the Tehran office of the Iran–America Society (known by the acronym

ICA because its two directors, Kathryn Koob and Bill Royer, were also officers in the International Communications Agency). He told a nonchalant Royer what he had heard. "Bill said no, don't believe that. He said to me, it's okay. Then I heard the embassy took over by students. I say to Bill Royer, this has come true."[3]

Not for the last time would Sam Sriweawnetr, one of the unsung heroes of the Iran hostage crisis, play the role of Cassandra to the luckless Americans. Bill Royer did not alert Bruce Laingen or anyone else about the rumoured student occupation. "The only warning we had about a possible attack," Marine Sergeant Jimmy Lopez later recalled, "was our own misgivings. There was no official warning from anyone higher up."[4] Every American posted to the Tehran mission would be taken completely by surprise by the events that enveloped them on that wet November day. Not even the CIA knew what was coming.

~ ~ ~

Much of what is known about the young Iranians who planned and perpetrated the takeover of the U.S. embassy compound comes from the recent memoir of Massoumeh Ebtekar, the young American-educated Iranian student christened "Tehran Mary" during the hostage crisis. Ebtekar joined the embassy occupation on November 7, when the occupiers discovered that they needed a fluent English-speaker to liaise with foreign media. Then nineteen years old, she emerged as a leading figure in the 444-day hostage drama, despised in the United States, venerated in Iran. She would go on to marry one of the student militants she met during the siege. She would also surprise many conservative Iranians and Americans alike by participating in the reformist "Tehran spring" under Mohammad Khatami, president of Iran between 1997 and 2005.

The students were compelled to seize the U.S. embassy on November 4, 1979, because they feared a repeat of the 1953 coup, according to Ebtekar. "A strong sense of devotion and love for the values of the revolution, and for Iran as the homeland of a free people, filled our minds and hearts," she wrote. "Our reading of our own history told us that we had to act quickly. The stubborn and bullying attitude of the American government as it confronted the Islamic Revolution made it clear that we had few alternatives left to consider. Action was our only choice."[5] Ayatollah Khomeini was not asked directly for his blessing on the takeover plan, but the students believed they would be advancing his cause. They named their group "Muslim Students Following the Line of the Imam." By apparent coincidence, the ayatollah had issued a statement to all Iranian students on November 2, when the takeover plan was gestating. "It is incumbent upon students in the secondary schools, the universities and the theology schools to expand their attacks against America and Israel," Khomeini exhorted. "Thus America will be forced to return the criminal, deposed shah."[6]

The students who initially organized the assault on the embassy compound were drawn from the Muslim Students Association, and were devoutly loyal to Khomeini. A five-man "Central Committee," representing the five Tehran universities involved in the planning, was established. A detailed list of the student participants was drawn up, in part to ensure that no militant leftist groups had infiltrated the movement and also to identify anyone martyred during the action. Arm bands bearing the slogan *Allah-o Akbar* were issued, as were five-by-seven-inch pictures of Khomeini that could be pinned to clothing. The Central Committee decided that the students would storm the embassy compound in five groups, each one responsible for occupying one of the compound's five major buildings. In contrast with the Fedayeen Kalq guerrillas who had attempted to take the chancery building by force on Valentine's Day, the students opted for a non-military occupation. The success of the action would depend not on the force of arms, they believed, but on the force of their convictions. The students surveilled the embassy grounds extensively for days beforehand. Some prepared food and other provisions to see them through what they expected would be a three-day "set-in."

The students arrived at the embassy's front gates as planned at about 9:50 a.m. Iranian police standing post at the entrance did nothing to impede them—a lapse of security that the Americans immediately recognized as collusion. Designated individuals began scaling the walls of the embassy at 10 a.m. Young women were prominent in the first wave of occupiers—a shrewd strategy on the part of the planners, for as they well knew, the Marine guard would be loathe to fire on unarmed females. Some of the women carried bolt-cutters under their chadors. The locks on the embassy gate were cut from the inside. Hundreds of young men and women then poured into the compound, cheering wildly and hoisting large posters of Ayatollah Khomeini. "They're coming over the wall!" shouted incredulous Americans like press attaché Barry Rosen, who happened to have a south-facing office. The students moved directly across the large motor pool, fanning out toward the ambassador's residence, the chancery and other targeted buildings. Once all of the assailants were inside the compound—a number the Americans estimated at between three and five hundred—they bolted the embassy gate from the inside using padlocks they had brought themselves. The feeds from embassy security cameras were cut.

The ambassador's residence was easy to conquer, but the students knew that the nerve centre of the U.S. embassy compound, the chancery, would be a far more formidable challenge. A long, three-storey office building, the chancery contained the offices of all State Department officials and CIA officers in Tehran. It also housed the embassy's communication equipment and all of the vaults containing sensitive intelligence files. Persistently checking all access points for weakness, the students caught a lucky break. They found a first-floor window grate unbolted and unguarded, and slipped through it easily.

Having watched the students charging into the car pool, most of the chancery staff had already congregated on the second floor, barricaded behind the newly installed bulletproof glass and heavy steel doors. After the February 14 attack, a new security plan had been developed, in which the upper floors of the chancery would serve as a refuge for embassy personnel for as long as was needed to defuse a crisis. Unfortunately for the Americans, things did not go according to the new plan. When the students showed up at the second-floor entrance demanding that the officials inside surrender, security officer Al Golacinski stepped out to try to reason with them. He was immediately taken hostage and threatened with death if the students were not allowed to enter the second floor of the chancery. A second officer, John Limbert, tried the same strategy to win Golacinski's freedom and was himself taken hostage.

With two captives now in hand, the occupiers had the leverage they needed to force the surrender of the building.

~ ~ ~

Deputy Secretary of State Warren Christopher wrote in 1985 that little was known of the true identities of the student occupiers, and that little may ever be known. "It seems quite plausible to me," he observed, "that they were not initially controlled by the government but were seen by it as a dangerous element that had to be treated gingerly and then co-opted."[7] DCI Stansfield Turner also recalled that Washington's intelligence on the hostage-takers was paltry. "[W]e were embarrassingly dependent on press stories," he said, "almost all based on communiqués released by the gang that had seized the embassy."[8] American author Mark Bowden has asserted more recently that the occupation was the brainchild of three young Iranians—Ibrahim Asgharzadeh, Mohsen Mirdamadi and Habibullah Bitaraf—each of them genuine university students, politically non-affiliated and professing loyalty only to the ideals of Ayatollah Khomeini.[9] Massoumeh Ebtekar's memoir resolutely paints the same portrait. From beginning to end, according to Ebtekar, the occupation was an independent student action, and one that was guarded jealously against outside interference or infiltration.

There are at least three problems with this characterization of the occupiers as idealistic student amateurs. The first concerns the sophistication of the planning. Virtually every American at the embassy with military or intelligence training agrees that the plot was not the work of amateurs but of professionals with a keen sense of operational strategy likely born of prior training and experience. The longer the hostage crisis persisted, the more obvious became the occupiers' paramilitary command structure, and their administrative competence and discipline.

The second problem is evidence to the contrary. In mid-November 1979, Ken Taylor reported to Ottawa that the takeover was widely acknowledged within Iran to have been "organized by an orthodox clerical group within the Revolutionary Council in order to dismantle the secular cabinet of Bazargan."[10] The Canadian journalist Carole Jerome, who got her information directly from Sadegh Ghotbzadeh, wrote bluntly in her 1987 memoir that "the PLO was, in fact, in cahoots with the students."[11] Some of the occupiers had been trained in PLO camps; others were recognized as guerrillas from South Lebanon by foreign journalists covering the hostage-taking. It is now known that Ayatollah Khomeini had been developing ties with Palestinians and Lebanese in the years before the Iranian revolution, and that both of his sons, Mustafa and Ahmad, had undergone military training in guerrilla camps near Beirut. For fighting alongside guerrillas loyal to Yasser Arafat in Lebanon, Ahmad Khomeini had been named an "honourary member of Fatah (the main political faction of the PLO)."[12] A core group of seven hundred Khomeini loyalists, who would later form and lead the Revolutionary Guards, were also trained by the PLO in Lebanon on Arafat's orders. Israeli intelligence, and hence the CIA, knew as early as 1975 that Fatah had also been training members of the Mujahidin Kalq, a group they came to believe had a hand in the embassy takeover. Charlie Beckwith, the Green Beret in charge of the Eagle Claw rescue mission, later recalled that the premise of intelligence experts in Washington was that students were not working alone. "The analysts assumed the student militants who were holding the hostages were receiving assistance from the Palestinians or the SAVAMA [successor to SAVAK]."[13]

The third and most compelling reason to question Ebtekar's characterization of the takeover as a conspiracy of pious young men and women from Tehran's university classrooms was the viciousness of the hostage-takers' threats and the cruelty of their interrogation methods. The contrast between the myth of the hostage-taking as non-violent and the reality of its brutality is not incidental to the story of Ken Taylor's activities during the crisis. It is central to any understanding of what he and his Canadian colleagues did on the hostages' behalf. Asked recently when he reckoned the hostages were being abused, Taylor replied, "From day one."[14] Not for a moment did Taylor labour under the impression that the hostages were, as their captors repeatedly claimed, well treated. Never did he buy into the occupiers' staged hostage "interviews," in which captive Americans were filmed attesting to the civility of their jailers. It was "pure propaganda," says Taylor. "I never ruled out the possibility that they would be executed. I never saw any benevolence."[15]

Massoumeh Ebtekar is unflagging in her assertion that the entire 444-day hostage crisis was conducted with the utmost humanity and respect for the lives of the hostages. It is possible that she actually believes this version of the crisis to be true, which indicates that her assigned role as spokesperson for the students may have been so compartmentalized that she was not privy to the violence that accompanied the action. As noted above, she was not recruited to the occupiers' inner circle until the third day of the crisis, by which time concealing violence against the hostages had become a central element in the occupiers' media strategy to win world sympathy. It is also possible that the role of non-students in the occupation was underestimated by Ebtekar, or that their later infiltration of the student ranks was unknown to her. Lastly, it is possible, even likely, that Ebtekar believed so fervently in the right-eousness of her cause that she was deluded. Even when confronted with the reality that she had participated in the imprisonment and even the interrogation of U.S. government officials, she and her university friends persisted in their hope that they could win the affections of their hostages. "[W]e somehow expected them to agree with us gladly," she later mused.[16]

Whatever the reason, Ebtekar's apparently sincere belief that the entire drama was played out without violence is not consistent with the historical record. Ebtekar asserts, for example, that the students' original plan—to seize the embassy without the use of arms—was strictly enforced and ultimately successful. "It is possible," she wrote, "that a handful of students may have entered the embassy prem-ises with arms in violation of our plan of action. But if any arms were present during the takeover they were never used, never even shown. The Americans surrendered for other reasons. They were at first stunned, then overwhelmed by the swift, forceful, disciplined, non-violent action of the students."[17] Her description of the students' action against the Americans they found within the chancery makes a similar claim. "In order to avoid any possible conflict, they tied the hands of the captives and blindfolded them," she wrote. "All the while, the Melli University students' representative kept reminding the students that they must treat their captives humanely and avoid violence unless it became absolutely necessary. This was not only our principle throughout the initial phase of the occupation; it was one we respected to the end."[18]

In truth, the occupiers did not remain unarmed for long. At least ten of the invaders were armed with pistols.[19] Physical violence and the threat of torture and execution began within the first hour of the storming of the embassy and never ceased. Even before the chancery had been surrendered, for example, Alan Golacinski had had a pistol stuck to the back of his head and a flaming magazine shoved in his blindfolded face. Other hostages were similarly threatened—paraded or ordered around the compound with pistols held to their heads. At least two Americans, Rick Kupke and CIA station chief Tom Ahern, were subjected to vicious beatings the moment they fell into the occupiers' hands, Kupke's so bad that he thought his jaw was broken. To coerce their captives, the hostage-takers pointed guns in their faces, and threatened that their eyes would be gouged out or their feet put into pots of boiling oil.

"I'm tired of seeing those bastards holding our people referred to as 'students,'" a frustrated President Carter told his National Security Council in the first days of the crisis. "They should be referred to as 'terrorists,' or 'captors,' or something that accurately describes what they are."[20] Seen in retrospect, there was as much instinct as invective in the president's outburst. Not all of the hostage-takers were abusive, and not all hostages experienced violence equally. Starting the first week of the crisis, in fact, the occupiers allowed Red Crescent doctors to periodically visit with groups of ten or twelve selected hostages. The visits had the desired effect, the doctors invariably reporting that the hostages they saw were in good health.[21] But the fact remains: not until the last few weeks of the hostage crisis, when it appeared that the Americans would be freed, did the occupiers relent in their threats of violence or their arbitrary abuse of their prisoners. And never did anyone privy to inside information on the conditions of their 444-day captivity, including Ambassador Ken Taylor, believe for a moment the occupiers' claims about their good intentions and non-violent ideals.

~ ~ ~

Just after 3 a.m. Washington time on November 4, the first call from
the U.S. embassy in Tehran came in to the State Department Operations Center in Washington, DC. The Ops Center operated on a
round-the-clock basis on the seventh floor of the State Department
building, in suites adjacent to the office of the Secretary of State. It
was a scene of continuous communication between Washington and
American diplomats abroad, with telephones constantly ringing and
telexes constantly clacking out their uppercase cables. Calling from
the second floor of the besieged chancery was Ann Swift, the forty-
year-old chief of the embassy's political section. Calm and unflappable, Swift reported that a large group of Iranian militants had
stormed the embassy compound and broken into all of the buildings,
including the chancery. Her call was immediately patched through to
the homes of three senior State officials, including Hal Saunders. For
the next two hours, Swift and her colleagues in Washington would
keep a conference line open.

From the moment he took Ann Swift's call, Hal Saunders took
charge of the State Department's Iran Working Group, reporting
directly to Cyrus Vance and Warren Christopher, and through them
to the president. Saunders had distinguished himself in 1978 with
his work on the Camp David Accords and had become a favourite
of Jimmy Carter. Though he could hardly have imagined it then,
Saunders' working group would run for fifteen months continuously, making it the longest-running in State Department history.
(Uniquely, it would include a special section to maintain contact
with the families of the hostages. FLAG, the Family Liaison Action
Group, was founded by Penne Laingen, the wife of Chargé Bruce
Laingen, and given office space at the State Department.) Hal Saunders' principal deputy was Peter Constable, a young career diplomat
who had risen quickly through the ranks of the State Department

after serving as deputy ambassador to Pakistan. Constable would, among other things, be the State Department's main liaison during the hostage crisis with Canada's ambassador to the United States, Peter Towe.

Quickly surmising that the student occupation of the embassy was serious, Saunders gave the order to awaken senior White House officials. National Security Advisor Zbigniew Brzezinski was the first to get the call, just after 4 a.m. It was Brzezinski who notified President Carter by phone of the takeover of the embassy, and Vance with whom the president first consulted in person. "We were deeply disturbed," said Carter, "but reasonably confident that the Iranians would soon remove the attackers from the embassy compound and release our people."[22] Vance was not so sure. "We all prayed they would be able to withstand the mob until help came from the Iranian government," the secretary of state said of his besieged colleagues. "We knew that no embassy could hold out for long without help from the host government."[23] DCI Stansfield Turner was awakened at 5:30 a.m. Washington time with the news. The crisis-management machinery of the United States government then lurched into action. The Pentagon began contingency planning for various military scenarios. Officials at the State Department started sketching out various permutations of the crisis, including the worst-case scenario: the killing of some or all of the hostages. The National Security Council began analyzing the strategic implication of the takeover, including possible Soviet responses to the crisis, uncertainties about U.S. oil imports, the security of Iranian diplomats and citizens in the United States, the export of U.S. arms and spare parts to Iran and the status of Iranian financial assets in American banks.

Not everyone in Washington—or even Tehran, for that matter— thought the occupation all that serious. "We expected that it would be a replay of Valentine's Day," Ken Taylor later recalled of the general reaction to the news that the U.S. embassy had been stormed. "On the

Sunday night, November 4, there was a big party—Soviet national unity day—and we were all there. And everybody said, 'Oh, it will all be over tomorrow.'"[24] Those like Taylor who had been present during the Valentine's Day attack on the U.S. embassy had every expectation that the Iranian government would again evict the occupying force. Indeed, because this new occupation was thought to be the work of unarmed students, it seemed far less worrisome than the guerrilla attack in February.

It is a measure of how casually Jimmy Carter's White House staffers took the news of the embassy occupation that they later recalled being far more preoccupied with Senator Ted Kennedy's nationally televised interview with journalist Roger Mudd the evening of November 4. Kennedy had not yet announced his intention to challenge Carter for the Democratic presidential nomination in 1980, but it was widely known that he would run. Carter's chief of staff, Hamilton Jordan, later wrote that the mood in the Monday morning staff meeting on November 5 was not sombre but "cheerful." Kennedy had stumbled badly during the interview, particularly on the subject of Chappaquiddick, the 1969 scandal in which Washington secretary Mary Jo Kopechne had drowned in an automobile accident and Kennedy, the driver of the car, had fled the scene. Carter's campaign team was savouring the moment. When the question of the hostage-taking came up, Jordan confidently told his staff that there were no casualties and thus there was nothing to worry about. "Don't forget," he said, "this same thing happened last February. We're talking to our diplomats at the embassy and Foreign Minister Ibrahim Yazdi and Prime Minister Mehdi Bazargan at the Foreign Ministry. As soon as the government gets its act together, they'll free our people."[25]

President Carter himself seems to have been of two minds about the crisis on November 4. "I spent most of the day, every spare moment, trying to decide what to do," the president later confided to his diary.[26] Yet, much to Zbigniew Brzezinski's enduring astonishment,

Carter would not assemble his top advisers to discuss the hostage-taking until the morning of November 5, more than twenty-four hours after Ann Swift had placed her fateful call to Washington.

~ ~ ~

Chargé d'Affaires Bruce Laingen and his two confrères, Political Counsellor Vic Tomseth and Security Officer Mike Howland, were at the Iranian foreign ministry office when the students went over the wall. They had just concluded a short meeting with ministry officials on the question of diplomatic immunity for American military personnel. The half-hour talk went well. "We had the traditional Iranian cup of tea and parted with the usual Iranian cordiality and hospitality," Laingen later recalled.[27]

The meeting over, Laingen and Tomseth proceeded to their car, where Howland was waiting for them. Howland was listening intently to his "lunchbox" radio, a walkie-talkie-type device about the size of a standard lunchbox that had been issued to all U.S. embassy personnel as part of their "escape and evasion network" ("E&E net"). He had just received a transmission from Alan Golacinski. "There was a bit of a dust up at the embassy," Howland informed Laingen.[28] All that was known was that roughly five hundred demonstrators had breached the front gates of the compound and were scattering across the motor pool.

The three Americans got in their car to return to the U.S. embassy compound, but before they had gone even a few hundred yards, Golacinski radioed Howland again, urging them to stay put. "The situation looked very serious indeed," Laingen said. "They advised us to go back to the foreign ministry to seek assistance from the government of Iran."[29]

Returning to the ministry building, Laingen requested that Iranian chief of protocol Ali Shokouhian and Deputy Foreign Minister Kamal Kharrazi take immediate action to remove the attackers and reinforce embassy security. "We didn't care whether those were national police, or revolutionary guards, or various of the paramilitary forces that were then in Tehran," Vic Tomseth later observed, "but some kind of help had to be got to them as quickly as possible."[30] Laingen also requested several dedicated phone lines. "We had contact by radio, of course," said Tomseth, "but we wanted the more secure contact of a telephone connection, to call Washington and let them know what was up. Those requests were readily granted."[31] Sequestered in the large office of Foreign Minister Ibrahim Yazdi, Laingen and Tomseth opened lines with several local American government offices, the State Department and the U.S. military command in Germany, which was responsible for American security in the Middle East.

As for Yazdi himself, he was en route from Mehrabad Airport back to his office, having just returned from his meetings in Algiers. When he got to his office at the foreign ministry, just before noon Tehran time, he was confronted by a visibly anxious Bruce Laingen, who insisted that he remove the occupiers as he had on February 14. Yazdi apologized for the students' attack on the embassy and told Laingen that he would do everything in his power to rectify the situation. He would not, however, be going to the embassy in person. Laingen understood immediately that Yazdi was no longer confident in his ability to remove the occupiers, a sign that his authority—and the authority of the Bazargan government more generally—was diminishing. Nothing in Yazdi's response suggested to Laingen that he had any sympathy for the occupiers. "He was cordial throughout," Laingen said of the foreign minister on that stressful day. "We always had a cordial relationship."[32]

Laingen's own gut response to the student occupation was not fear but frustration. As he later put it, with typical understatement, "My capacity to function as the chargé of that mission was clearly limited by the fact that my embassy was stolen."[33] Laingen would urge Yazdi repeatedly to take responsibility for the situation at the U.S. embassy, in accordance with international law. But it was precisely the minister's inability to act, Laingen observed, "that made the Iranian example of terrorism so unique. The embassy was well protected, with all of the devices that we'd put in place after the February 14 attack. But all of that is useless if you don't have the assurance from the government to which you are accredited, that they would provide security assistance for you."[34] Some sense of how the crisis affected Laingen on a personal level can be gleaned from a letter he wrote to his son five days after the embassy was taken. "I have *no* trouble in standing up to this," he wrote, "however sad it is and however reprehensible it is what happened to all those now hostage in the embassy compound. It will haunt me all the rest of my life."[35]

Unbeknownst to Laingen, Yazdi had problems of his own on November 4. That very morning, the Iranian press had published photos showing him and Prime Minister Bazargan shaking hands with Zbigniew Brzezinski in Algiers the day before. As Hal Saunders observed, pictures of leading government officials talking in private with the U.S. national security adviser were evidence in the minds of the Iranian radicals of near-traitorous behaviour. "Those photos dramatized to the Islamic purists in the revolution," said Saunders, "the realization of their worst fears—renewal by government leaders of a closer relationship with the United States."[36] Ironically, the opposite was true. It was Bazargan who had requested the meeting with Brzezinski, and Brzezinski who had made concessions. "I made the point," the national security adviser later said of the meeting, "that the United States was not engaged in, nor would it encourage, conspiracies against the new Iranian regime and that 'we are prepared for any relationship you want.'"[37]

~ ~ ~

Almost as soon as they had turned their car around and returned to the Iranian foreign ministry, Vic Tomseth suggested to Bruce Laingen that he order the destruction of sensitive materials in the vaults of the chancery building. The chargé hesitated. "He preferred to wait a bit," Tomseth said later, "having in mind our experience of the attack in February, when it took literally weeks to put the embassy back together following that attack because of the extensive destruction of material and equipment that we carried out."[38] Tomseth maintained an open line with Ann Swift throughout the morning, interrupting Laingen's continuous call with Washington occasionally to report on new developments at the embassy. At one point, Swift told Tomseth that the students outside were threatening to kill Golacinski and Limbert. "You tell Laingen I said to open the goddamn door *now!*" a frantic Limbert could be heard yelling from the other side of the door.[39] That was enough for Tomseth and Laingen. "We instructed the people to stall off as long as they could in order to complete the destruction program in the vault," said Tomseth. "When they reported that they had done that, we told them to go ahead and surrender to the people who were outside the vault door."[40]

The students' angry threats notwithstanding, the Americans who surrendered the chancery believed, like President Carter, that the occupation would be short-lived. "Our whole thought," Ann Swift later said, "was to give up peacefully so we could be released peacefully."[41] At noon local time (5 a.m. EST), acting on Laingen's orders, Swift opened the door to the militants, surrendering herself and her staff. Now fully at the mercy of the occupiers, the Americans were blindfolded with broad white strips of linen, their hands bound with nylon cord. Television cameras recorded the scene as the hostages were led in single file out of the front doors of the chancery. The crowd beyond the embassy gates had grown to a seething mass as word of the takeover spread. Some of the hostages later said that they were at least as worried about the mobs as they were about their captors. The crisis would be resolved before long, they believed—but would the end come before the mobs got to them?

Their set-in a resounding success, the triumphant students released the first of their many communiqués. They were occupying the

U.S. embassy to protest the U.S. decision to grant asylum to the shah, they announced, and to advance the struggle of the Iranian people for freedom. Sixty-two Americans and thirty-six non-Americans from the "nest of spies" were now in their custody, they said.[42]

At the foreign ministry, Bruce Laingen informed Ibrahim Yazdi that he had ordered the surrender of the chancery and urged him again to take action. Distressed that a student demonstration was now threatening to blow into an international incident, Yazdi drove to Qom to talk to Khomeini in person. The ayatollah told him to throw the students out of the embassy as he had the previous February. Yet by the time Yazdi returned to Tehran, Khomeini had already made a public address applauding the student occupation, a reversal that came as no surprise to the foreign minister, who knew well the imam's tendency to vacillate. For the remainder of the afternoon and into the evening, Yazdi, Laingen, Tomseth and Howland remained holed up in Yazdi's office. "We had not given up on a possibility of the cavalry arriving, and we continued to press for that," Tomseth later recalled. "However, by early evening I think we had concluded that it was not likely that something was going to happen that day."[43]

As night fell on Tehran, Laingen, Tomseth and Howland were escorted to the third floor of the Iranian foreign ministry building, to a suite of rooms that were normally used for diplomatic receptions. It included a large vaulted ballroom, Tomseth later recalled, with some "very gorgeous Persian carpets on the floor and furniture scattered about."[44]

Though they could hardly have imagined it that first night, the three American diplomats would be held prisoner in this gilded cage for over a year.

Chapter 8
ON THE RUN

Directly northeast of the chancery building, less than a short city block away, stood the newly renovated American consulate. This was a sturdy two-storey office building with state-of-the-art security, built not to deter illegal occupations but rather to control the steady flow of Iranians seeking exit visas. The main entrance to the consular building fronted directly onto Bist Metri Street, to the north. Its secondary door faced south onto a small gated courtyard within the embassy compound.

Emerging at the consulate, alongside the hostage-taking at the chancery on November 4, 1979, was a second and even more extraordinary human drama, one that would draw Ken Taylor and his Canadian colleagues more deeply into the Iran hostage crisis than any other group of diplomats except the Americans themselves. Inside the consular building that morning, going about their business as usual, were fourteen American diplomats and their twenty-five Iranian staff. Another sixty or so Iranian civilians were already queued up, visa applications in hand, hopeful for the fresh start that would come with emigration to the United States. The chief of the consular section was Dick Morefield, a heavy-set middle-aged man with hair greying at the temples and bright, intelligent eyes. Bob Anders, a handsome fifty-four-year-old with charcoal hair, bushy sideburns, piercing grey-blue eyes and a broad smile, was the head of the immigrant visa section. Other officers working at the consulate that day included Bob Ode, a retiree drawn back into service in Iran to help with the backlog of visa applicants, and Vice Consul Richard Queen, a quiet twenty-eight-year-old rookie.

Consular officers Joe Stafford and Mark Lijek, both quiet, serious twenty-nine-year-olds, were also at their desks the morning of November 4. So, too, were their wives, consular assistants working under Dick Morefield's supervision (and the only two spouses of U.S. diplomatic personnel approved for employment in Iran). Kathy Stafford, a pretty twenty-eight-year-old with a ruddy complexion and a friendly demeanour, stood several inches taller than her husband, Joe. Mark Lijek's wife, Cora, twenty-five, bore the rounded facial features of her Japanese-American heritage, along with an infectious smile and sense of humour. The sole Marine guard stationed within the consulate was Sergeant James Lopez, a courageous and brash twenty-two-year-old known to everyone as Jimmy. A scruffy twenty-six-year-old American tourist named Kim King also happened to be at the consular building, conferring with Mark Lijek because he had overstayed his visa and run out of money.

At 10 a.m. the morning of November 4, most of the staff in the consulate were doing what they considered drudge work—keying data into a new global data-management system for visa applications to the United States. "It began as a normal day," Anders later recalled. "There was the usual bunch of demonstrators outside in the street— several thousand. We didn't pay a whole lot of attention to that. It was part of the normal routine."[1] The consular officers were no more prepared than their chancery colleagues for the wave of students that suddenly came rolling over the grounds of the compound. Keeping to the plan they had hatched in their university dorms, the students responsible for occupying the consulate moved quickly and purposefully into place, bypassing the chancery, surrounding the consular building. "We first learned of the attack when two local staff came rushing back from a cookie-buying trip," Mark Lijek later recalled. "They breathlessly informed us that the motor-pool gate had been breached and that they had been chased from their car to the court-yard gate."[2] The staff inside the consulate were taken completely by surprise. "It happened so fast," said Jimmy Lopez, "that as soon as I heard the [radio] transmission about people being over the walls, there were already people running on the compound."[3]

As the students closed in on the building entrances, Morefield and Lopez directed everybody to head up to the second floor. Standard procedure for any sort of security breach was to lock down the building, with the staff safe inside, and wait for the host government to send in police or the army to expel the assailants. Because the students had the element of surprise on their side, even this simple exercise was a challenge. Sergeant Lopez later recalled having to scramble to shoulder his shotgun and gas grenades, and then to secure the doors and windows. Because the main-floor entrances had solid double doors with electronic locks, the students tried to gain entry via the second floor. Armed and battle-ready, Lopez had begun doing circuits around the interior of the building to check and recheck all of the points of entry. On one of his passes he entered the second-floor washroom to find a student pressing his way through the window from a ladder below. Lopez pushed the ladder away, along with the student. He fired tear gas into the crowd below to discourage them from trying again, and then he and Dick Morefield locked the window with coat hangers. About an hour after they arrived, the students cut the power to the consular building from the outside.

Ann Swift, in the chancery, had a phone line open to the consular office, relaying information from both the State Department and Bruce Laingen. When it became clear that the student occupation was serious, Swift forwarded Hal Saunders' order to destroy the consulate's visa plates, lest the occupiers capture them and start printing out "genuine" U.S. visas. Dick Morefield asked Richard Queen to remove the plates from the consular vault. Jimmy Lopez then smashed them into pieces using a retaining bar from a filing cabinet. Mark Lijek suggested that they also shred consular documents that might incriminate Iranians. "Any name the militants found," Lijek said, "they presumed the person was some kind of spy."[4] To his later regret, Morefield told him it was not necessary.[5]

Laingen, meanwhile, gave Sergeant Lopez—the only armed person in the consulate—a direct order not to open fire on the attackers. Despite the commotion, Morefield later recalled that the scene in the darkened consulate was calm. "I can honestly say that, until the very end, there was no indication of even serious concern among either the Iranians who were there for business or my Iranian employees, and certainly not the Americans."[6] They all believed, erroneously, that the Iranian government had told Chargé Laingen just a few days earlier that it would defend the embassy compound by force of arms if necessary. "I figured it would only be a matter of minutes, or an hour at most," said Morefield, "until the government itself came to do what they had an obligation to do under international law, which was to provide protection and control for our area."[7]

At 10:30, Mark Lijek received a call from the Tehran police asking whether he and his colleagues needed help. He answered in the affirmative, but no one was sent. By noon, it became clear that the Iranian authorities were not going to evict the occupiers. Morefield, Anders and Lopez conferred. They agreed that, instead of giving themselves up, the better option would simply be to make their way inconspicuously out of the consulate and onto Bist Metri

Street. As the Americans and Iranians made their way down the stairs and toward the bulletproof glass door, Lopez continued his security checks throughout the building. Morefield decided that the Americans should exit in small groups, and that he and Lopez would be the last to leave. He allowed the Iranian visa applicants to exit first. They were followed by Iranian consular staff and finally by the Americans. Morefield and Lopez closed and padlocked the consulate door behind them. They expected to have to run a gauntlet of militants en route out of the building, but the protesters who had congregated outside the main entrance suddenly bolted away to the chancery— presumably because they had learned via the E&E net that it had now been conquered. Instead, the Americans encountered only a few Tehran police. "Richard Queen had made a habit of chatting up the cops and knew some of them," Mark Lijek observed, "including one of the ones outside our door. He told them that we were planning to leave the building and they said okay."[8] Kim King later recalled that when he and the others left, there seemed no threat to them at all. "We didn't feel any need to run," he said.[9]

It was pouring rain when they emerged from the consulate. "I remember thinking that I would look silly walking in the rain wearing a nice suit but with no umbrella or overcoat," Mark Lijek later said. The Americans decided to break into two groups and to make their way to other foreign diplomatic missions in Tehran—standard procedure in a crisis. The closest of these was a large office building that housed offices of the Swedish and Austrian missions, but getting there would have required walking south and west, right into the mass demonstration that had engulfed the south wall of the embassy compound. Bob Anders, the Staffords, the Lijeks, Kim King and a young woman named Lorraine were the first to leave. They decided to take their chances crossing the main thoroughfare, Taleghani Avenue, and make their way southbound through back streets in the direction of the British embassy. "It is pretty much standard practice to turn to the British embassy almost anywhere in the world," Anders reasoned. "They're certainly one of our closest allies and we generally cooperate with them everywhere."[10] Kim King decided that he would break away from the group and make his way alone.

The five diplomats and Lorraine got within a block of the British embassy and saw immediately that it was having its own problems containing a demonstration in the streets. "We got out of the way where people couldn't see us," recalled Cora Lijek, "and talked for a few minutes trying to decide what to do. We were not going to fight our way through the demonstration to get to the British embassy!"[11] They decided that the safest place to wait out the crisis was Anders' own apartment, which was only three blocks from the U.S. embassy compound. They made their way through the back streets to Anders' building and managed to get inside as directly as possible. "We were still operating with the assumption that this whole thing would blow over, maybe even later that day," said Mark Lijek. "So all we had to do was find a place to hang out, for an hour, or maybe a day at the most."[12] Lorraine had come to the consulate that day to confer with Bob Anders about getting her Iranian husband a U.S. visa. From his apartment, she attempted to call her husband repeatedly, but to no avail.

Richard Queen, Dick Morefield, Jimmy Lopez, Robert Ode and two other Americans made up the second fugitive group. Lopez had disarmed and had cast off his Marine uniform in a makeshift attempt to look like a civilian, borrowing a coat from a consulate staffer named Ismail. Lopez and Morefield agreed that they should try to make their way toward Morefield's residence, which was close by. Morefield had just moved into the house. He reasoned that it would be a good place to hide out because there was not yet a paper trail at the chancery containing his home address for the militants to follow. Before the Americans had gone a block, a group of eight or nine Iranian militia ran up to them, apparently on the instructions of their comrades within the embassy compound. The Iranians had only one automatic weapon among them. They fired it into the air, yelling, "Stop, CIA, stop!" Their leader said to Morefield, "You're a hostage!" An angry Morefield replied, "Hostage? That's stupid. Hostage for what?"[13]

Surrounded and unarmed, the Americans had little choice but to give themselves up. As Iranian film cameras rolled, the militiamen stripped them of their briefcases and other goods, and walked the six captives through a delivery gate and back into the embassy compound. There Lopez, Morefield and the others suffered the same humiliating fate as the Americans taken hostage at the chancery. "We were blindfolded," Lopez said. "We were not allowed to talk. We were barely allowed to move. I was in a very uncomfortable position and should I shift my shoulders because part of my back would go to sleep, some little sawed off bastard sitting behind me would actually step on my hand."[14]

~ ~ ~

Bob Anders, the Lijeks and the Staffords spent the rest of that first day at Anders' apartment, eavesdropping on events at the U.S. embassy on their lunchbox radio. "We could hear what was going on in the chancery," said Cora Lijek, "because even though the students had gotten in, the staff were behind secure doors. The students hadn't reached them yet."[15] Anders feared the worst. "More and more voices on the radio were speaking in Farsi and not in English, so it was pretty obvious that the whole place was gradually being taken over."[16] The phone at Anders' apartment was functional and apparently untapped, so the fugitives felt free to call friends. Still believing that the crisis would be solved in short order, they were not much concerned about their own security. They did not call any embassies, or give any serious consideration to going into hiding. "About 4:00," said Mark Lijek, "we heard [communications specialist] Charles Jones inform Washington on the radio net that he was going to open the door to the communications vault because they were threatening to kill someone if he didn't. This represented the final surrender of the chancery."[17] At 7 p.m., Lorraine's husband showed up. He offered to take all of the Americans into his care but they declined. He and Lorraine went out to get the others dinner—lamb kebab, the Iranian national dish—and then left them on their own. The Americans later learned that Lorraine's husband was executed as a counterrevolutionary.

Among the friends the five Americans called from Anders' apartment was Kathryn Koob, whom everyone knew as Kate. Forty-two, single, a devout Catholic and a dedicated liberal internationalist, Koob was the executive director of the Iran–America Society (known as the ICA) in Tehran. In the evening, when it became clear that the occupation was not going to be resolved quickly, Koob asked the group hiding out at Anders' apartment if they could do a shift at the ICA so that she and her colleague Bill Royer could get some sleep. She sent two of her Iranian staffers to Anders' place at about 11 p.m. to fetch the five in her Citroën Deux Chevaux. Because there was room enough for only six people in the car, Anders decided that he would stay behind to purge his personal papers—a sensible precaution in the likely event that the militants would figure out where the diplomats lived and ransack their residences.

Koob and Royer were delighted and relieved to see the Staffords and the Lijeks when they showed up at about midnight. "Our night watchmen let them in and they came back into the room in the area where we were working," Koob said. "It was really good, of course, to see them and to know that there was somebody else out there who was as concerned as we were, and who was willing to work."[18] Catching up with her friends, Koob explained how she had got word of the storming of the embassy after leaving Bruce Laingen's morning staff meeting. "When I hadn't had any instructions or any word after a couple of hours," she told them, "I phoned the embassy. That's when

I found out the situation had deteriorated so badly that the students were in charge of the switchboard." Koob then used a second line to call the people who were busily destroying documents in the chancery vault. She asked Charles Jones if there was anything she could do. "Charlie said yes," she later recalled. "Call the State Department and tell them that nobody has been harmed or injured. So I did that. And the State Department then said, don't hang up. So then we were sort of a link between the men in the vault and the State Department, relaying questions."[19]

By the time the Staffords and the Lijeks showed up at the ICA, Koob and Royer had been on the phone with the State Department for more than ten hours straight. Their visitors agreed to maintain the ICA's open phone lines to Washington and other sites in Tehran, just as Koob had. "The important thing," Koob later recalled of these marathon phone sessions, "is to keep voice flow going. Otherwise, you'll lose your line. So they were pressed into service keeping that line open. We trusted them, we knew everything was in good hands."[20] Koob and Royer immediately headed for couches in their office library, where they tried to get some much-needed sleep.

They awakened at about 5:30 a.m. the next day, Monday, and immediately resumed their work on the phones. The Staffords and the Lijeks left the ICA about half an hour later—"reluctantly," as Koob later recalled, but in the knowledge that if Iranian militants discovered fugitive American diplomats there, it would do nobody any good.[21] They were driven by the same two ICA employees to the Staffords' apartment, with a brief stop at the Lijeks' to pick up some clothes and food. Bob Anders had planned to head over to the ICA office himself that morning, but before he left his apartment he got a call from Mark Lijek on the radio advising him to stay put. Koob had radioed Lijek to tell him that the phone lines from the ICA office had been compromised, leading her to suspect that the militants were on their way over to search for more American "spies." The Lijeks and the Staffords spent

Monday, November 5, holed up at the Staffords' apartment, increasingly anxious about their own security. "I worried about people discovering the embassy housing records and visiting all the residences," Mark Lijek later recalled. "I figured it was only a matter of time before somebody came to that house to look for Americans who might have gotten away."[22]

At 1:30 that afternoon, just as Koob had anticipated, militants from the embassy showed up at the ICA office. "We could hear feet scurrying around the building as I suppose there were about twenty men who came looking for the Americans," Koob said. She, Royer and their American secretary executed their own evacuation plan. The Germans in charge of the Goethe Institute around the corner had agreed to provide ICA personnel with sanctuary if their office was ever attacked. When the militants showed up at the front door of the ICA, the three Americans slipped out the back door, climbed into the secretary's car and drove the three blocks to the Goethe Institute. Their Iranian staffers were at no risk, so they stayed behind at the office. The Americans' German hosts met them at the front door. "The Germans were absolutely fantastic," Koob later said. "They not only provided us with refuge immediately but were quite willing— and offered, as a matter of fact—to take us into their homes if we needed deep cover or we needed a really good hiding place."[23] Koob believes that just about anybody in the diplomatic corps in Tehran would have made the same sort of provision for fugitive Americans, but she retains a deep sentimental attachment to the Germans of the Goethe Institute. "They were my Canadians," she says.[24]

If Koob and her ICA colleagues had remained with their German friends, it is likely that they would have joined the other fugitive diplomats and been saved the anguish of becoming hostages. As it was, however, they asked two institute staffers if they would mind walking down to the ICA office to see what had become of the twenty or so Iranians. The Germans reported that the Iranians had left. Everything was quiet and back to normal. "So we talked it over," said Koob, "and decided that we should go back and get back on those phones and continue with our work. So we went back."[25] Within hours, the Iranian militants returned to the ICA, but this time they surrounded the building and barricaded all of the exits. They barged into the office and demanded that Koob accompany them out. She did so, telling her terrified Iranian employees to "carry on." The students pushed her into a car, and there she found that Bill Royer and another of her American employees, a young woman, had already been captured. "We were all hauled off to the embassy,"[26] she said.

Koob's fate was to become one of only two women, along with Ann Swift, to be held captive for the 444-day duration of the hostage crisis. Bruce Laingen was nonplussed when he heard, in early January 1980, that the Iranians thought Koob worked for the CIA. "Kate Koob, as warmhearted a person as ever walked the earth, picked up at her Iran-America Society as a spy!" he exclaimed.[27] Koob's faith and her strength of character made a deep impression on some of her jailers, but not enough that they let her go free. Never would they accept that she was not part of U.S. intelligence in Iran, or that the ICA was anything other than a CIA front. And never would Koob stop denying their charges. "There just simply is no connection between the CIA and the work that I do and the work my agency does," she said. "We're in the business of public affairs, press and media and educational and cultural exchange."[28]

~ ~ ~

The person on the other end of Kathryn Koob's ICA phone line when she was seized by the Iranians was Vic Tomseth, now in his second day of isolation at the Iranian foreign ministry building. "Kate came to the phone," Tomseth later recalled. "She said the militants from the embassy had just arrived, about five minutes before, and that [the

Americans] were being taken to the embassy compound to join the other hostages there."[29] For Tomseth, this move against ICA person-nel signalled an escalation of the militants' terror campaign. He and Laingen agreed that the need to find refuge for the fugitives from the consulate was now urgent. "We realized we had to do something about the other five who at that point had gone back to their apart-ments," said Tomseth. "So I set about to see if I could make some arrangements to get them to a safer location."[30]

On Tuesday morning, Vic Tomseth called some friends at the British embassy, who agreed to help in whatever way they could. At 1 p.m. he called the Staffords' apartment, telling the Lijeks and the Staffords that the British had invited them to stay at their residential compound in North Tehran, known as Golhak Gardens. It seemed as safe a place as any, and certainly safer than any apartment registered to an American. Mark Lijek called Anders, telling him, for security reasons, only that somebody would pick him up at his apartment immediately. "I didn't know who was coming to pick me up or why," said Anders, "and I wasn't entirely sure if it was perhaps somebody holding a gun to Mark's head." Being alone and only three blocks from the mobs at the U.S. embassy, Anders decided it was worth the risk to sit tight and hope that the offer of safe haven was genuine.

The Lijeks, the Staffords and Anders waited anxiously for their British escorts, but they did not arrive as planned. The Americans wondered whether something had gone badly wrong. Joe Stafford called the chargé d'affaires at the British embassy only to have the conversation cut short when the chargé exclaimed, "The bastards are coming over the wall!" A second embassy, it appeared, was in the process of being taken over. At 6:15 p.m., the two young men from the British embassy finally showed up. They knew that their own embassy had been attacked but because the militants had shown no interest in the Golhak residence, which was many blocks from the embassy, they persuaded the Americans to keep to Tomseth's plan.

Accompanied by their British escorts, the fugitives walked several blocks from the Staffords' apartment to the waiting cars. "I was wearing Bob Anders' bright yellow sweater," Mark Lijek later recalled, "and felt as if it were neon. Even when we were safely ensconced in the autos, I still felt very conspicuous in that sweater."[31] The Lijeks and Joe Stafford went directly to the residence in a car driven by one of the Brits. Kathy Stafford accompanied the other in a second car and picked Anders up at his apartment. "We had to try to appear to be nonchalant, as if we were just a normal part of the scenery," Anders said of the nerve-racking car ride through downtown Tehran.[32] "We were stuck in bumper to bumper traffic most of the time," said Mark Lijek, "so I was a little nervous—just because when you're moving that slowly people can see into the car. They were all looking at us."[33]

When the five Americans finally made their way onto the grounds at Golhak Gardens, a lush, tree-lined compound surrounded by high stone walls, they were welcomed warmly and offered a house of their own. They unpacked, dined on fish and chips that evening at the home of an English diplomat, Mike Connor, and settled into their new refuge, happy and relieved that they would be riding out the storm as guests of the British.

~ ~ ~

The morning of November 5, Ayatollah Khomeini's son Ahmad showed up at the U.S. embassy compound and praised the students' actions. "This is not an occupation," he told the crowd of five thousand. "In fact, we have thrown the occupiers out!"[34] From that moment on, the ayatollah himself endorsed the takeover, hitching the hostage-taking to his grand design for Iran. "What is the point in holding the Americans hostage?" an incredulous Abolhassan Bani-Sadr asked the ayatollah.[35] "Our regime is consolidating itself," Khomeini replied. "We can use the hostages to get the constitution passed, then to get a president and a legislative assembly elected. Once we have done all that, we can think again. Our internal enemies will have been unable to move because to do so would expose them to the charge of being traitors."[36] Khomeini had decided that "he wanted to rule, not reign," as the Canadian journalist Joe Schlesinger aptly put it. The takeover of the U.S. embassy "would become the Ayatollah's road to absolute power."[37]

With sixty-six hostages locked down in the chancery, Bruce Laingen and his colleagues prisoners at the Iranian foreign ministry and the fugitives from the consulate in hiding with the British, little remained of President Carter's hope that the crisis would blow over. "The first week of November 1979 marked the beginning of the most difficult period of my life," Carter later said. "The safety and well-being of the American hostages became a constant concern for me, no matter what other duties I was performing as President. I would walk in the White House gardens early in the morning and lie awake at night, trying to think of additional steps I could take to gain their freedom without sacrificing the honor and security of our nation. I listened to every proposal, no matter how preposterous, all the way from delivering the Shah for trial as the revolutionaries demanded to dropping an atomic bomb on Tehran."[38]

The forced confinement of accredited foreign diplomats was plainly a violation of international law and established diplomatic convention. It breached both the 1961 Vienna Convention on Diplomatic Relations and the 1963 Vienna Convention on Consular Relations. *New York Times* columnist James Reston spoke for many Americans (and other Westerners) who were as baffled by Iran's behaviour as they were incensed. "The niceties of normal diplomatic procedure are not working in Tehran because this is not a rational conflict between sovereign states but a hijacking," wrote Reston. "It has been established for generations that an embassy is not only a symbol but a physical part of a nation's sovereign territory. Even in the ugliest phase of the Cold War, embassies were respected."[39] As the

Pakistani journalist Eqbal Ahmed observed, however, quiet approval for the hostage-taking could be discerned in the developing world. "The Iranian taking of hostages is deplored by every Third World *government*," observed Ahmed. "But I will add that the Iranians are admired by the *people* of the Third World for one bad reason: they feel some pride that, for once, the weak, the poor, the oppressed have openly violated international law—the law of the powerful against the weak."[40]

~ ~ ~

Before the hostage crisis had entered its third day, it was already clear that the irresistible force of Iranians' hatred for the shah had collided with the immovable object that was the Americans' refusal to evict a friend under threat. President Carter took some comfort in the knowledge that, on the basis of prior hostage-taking incidents at least, with each passing hour and each passing day, the hostages were less and less likely to be executed. Yet as the stand-off hardened, and as the United States appeared to forfeit its prerogative to defend its national honour with some sort of decisive military action, it seemed to many that neither President Carter nor the Bazargan government nor even the student militants any longer had the situation in hand.

The ball was now in Ayatollah Khomeini's court, and his alone. The looming question—for President Carter, and for the likes of Bruce Laingen and Ken Taylor on the ground in Tehran—was what to do about it.

Chapter 9

DIPLOMATIC MANOEUVRES

On November 6, backbench Conservative MP Bob Corbett unexpectedly stood up in the Canadian House of Commons and moved that Parliament protest the "criminal aggression" of the Iranian government against U.S. diplomats. Introducing his motion, he spoke of the "contemptible attitude of the Ayatollah Khomeini of Iran towards the civil liberties and rights not only of his countrymen, but those of legitimate aliens domiciled within Iran's borders."[1] Canadian parliamentarians required no convincing. The motion passed with the unanimous consent of the House. Up the street at the Pearson Building, Corbett's initiative took External Affairs officials by surprise. There had been no official Canadian statement on the hostage-taking prior to that point. And if there had, as Michael Shenstone told Ken Taylor, it would not have used the "polemical language" of the parliamentary resolution.[2]

Corbett had correctly gauged the public mood. Most Canadians were appalled by the hostage-taking, particularly after Ayatollah

Khomeini endorsed it. "Even by the standards of what is becoming an age of mass terrorism, this is a bizarre episode," said one of many like-minded newspaper editorials in Canada. "The kidnappers act on the authority of the head of state, committing odious crimes in the name of holiness, and demanding that a former ruler be returned to face the 'justice' of a country that has constituted itself a lynch mob."[3]

Odious though it was, state-sanctioned hostage-taking was also turning out to be complicated. The crisis could have far-reaching implications for Canada's alliances, for its interests in the Middle East and especially for the security of Canadian diplomatic personnel in Iran. Coming up with an official Canadian position that balanced these interests while making a strong statement of outrage against the occupiers was not easy. Would Canada be willing to intervene to help resolve the crisis? Would it back a military response from the United States? Alternatively, would it fall in behind American trade sanctions or a naval blockade of Iran? And if Canada did offer its support to the Carter White House, would this aggravate the crisis? Would it put Canadians in Tehran in harm's way? Parliament's censure of Iran accelerated this debate in Ottawa. No sooner had Bob Corbett's motion passed than Shenstone cabled Taylor with advice on how to spin it in Tehran. "It reflects the spontaneous reaction of MPs' concern at the absence of effective protection (required by international law) for foreign embassy personnel," he wrote. "You could emphasize that the wording of the resolution was not chosen by the government and should not be read as a government statement of policy."[4]

If Shenstone thought the motion might have overplayed Taylor's hand, he need not have worried. The ambassador's position on the hostage-taking was categorical from the moment he heard that Khomeini had given it his blessing. "This was a war with no holds barred," he said. "I couldn't care less about convention, about the protocols, about the righteousness. Iran had taken those people prisoner. They were not only doing irreparable damage to the whole functioning of diplomacy, they were ruining their own reputation."[5]

Everything that Ken Taylor said or did in his capacity as Canada's ambassador to Iran, from that moment on, followed from this conviction. He would act the diplomat when called upon to do so—and, indeed, spearheading a diplomatic response to the crisis would absorb vast amounts of his time and energy. But he was not prepared to stand idly by while the very foundations of his profession—diplomatic convention, international law, even common decency—were ravaged by an outlaw state. The Iran hostage crisis was, at bottom, a diplomatic crisis, and Taylor was Canada's top diplomat in Iran. All of the Americans taken hostage or in hiding were his comrades in the diplomatic corps, and some, like Bruce Laingen, were his friends. For Taylor, this was personal as well as professional.

As his steadily expanding cable traffic with Ottawa attested, the Canadian ambassador believed that Ayatollah Khomeini was driven by two obsessions. The first was "to ruthlessly avenge himself on the shah regardless of cost." The second was "to establish a theocracy in Iran." Khomeini would pursue these goals recklessly if need be, Taylor believed, and without regard for Iran's standing internationally. "Iran as a nation is of no import to Khomeini," he said flatly.[6]

Diplomacy was one thing, Taylor reasoned, and it was important. But this—this was something else again.

~ ~ ~

By Monday morning, November 5, when he first assembled his top advisers to discuss the attack on the embassy, Jimmy Carter felt the full weight of the hostage-taking upon him. His hopes for a quick resolution dashed, he ordered that the crisis be managed through a Special Coordinating Committee (SCC) chaired by National Security Advisor Zbigniew Brzezinski. Working in parallel to Hal Saunders' Working

Group at the State Department, this committee would include the secretaries of state and defence, their deputies, the chairperson of the Joint Chiefs of Staff, and the director of central intelligence (DCI). One consequence of institutionalizing decision-making in the SCC was that it compartmentalized the work of the various government departments. "The State Department's Iran Working Group performed heroically over the fourteen month period," Warren Christopher later lamented, "but it had little opportunity to affect planning or execution in the phases of the crisis being managed by other departments."[7] The great advantage of compartmentalization, however, as Ambassador Taylor would come to know, was that it preserved secrecy where it was most needed and put everyone in Washington connected with the hostage crisis on a need-to-know footing.

The White House and State Department crisis teams agreed to a two-track diplomatic strategy on Iran, one they hoped would free the hostages without compromising American national honour. The first track envisaged America's diplomats abroad pressing for "a broad international outcry" against Iran.[8] The second track was to pressure the Iranian government itself to free the hostages. On the essentials of the plan, Vance, Brzezinski and Carter concurred. As Vance put it, "We would not return the shah to Iran, offer any apology for past American policies or actions, or permit the hostages to be tried."[9] Brzezinski thought that the United States should consider punishing Iran's diplomats in the United States "in some reciprocal fashion."[10] This idea was so appalling to Vance that it was dropped immediately. ("Cy was clearly motivated by a personal sense of responsibility for his imprisoned colleagues," Brzezinski later wrote, "and his compassionate feelings were stirred by meetings with their families. I deliberately decided to avoid such meetings in order not to be swayed by emotions."[11])

In Iran, the militants at the U.S. embassy compound warned the United States against a retaliatory response. "If America takes any military action," they said in a communiqué, "we will kill them all."[12] (Ken Taylor reported to Ottawa that, in fact, the students had said they would "annihilate" the hostages, a threat he took seriously.)[13] President Carter preferred to negotiate an end to the crisis, but he knew that he must also prepare for the worst. Meeting with the Joint Chiefs of Staff in secret on the third day of the crisis, he began considering military options. Of the three scenarios proposed by the Pentagon—invasion, blockade and rescue mission—only a rescue attempt was compatible with Carter's goal of saving the hostages' lives. The joint chiefs' view of a rescue mission was so "pessimistic," however, that the president shelved the idea of a military solution for the moment.[14] This did not stop Republicans in the United States, including presidential hopeful George H. W. Bush, from publicly urging military action.[15] Nor did it dampen many ordinary Americans' enthusiasm for a fight, especially after the media began reporting that an elite U.S. commando squad led by former Green Beret Charlie Beckwith was on standby in North Carolina, waiting for orders to go to Iran.[16]

On November 6, while Carter was weighing his options, Iranian prime minister Mehdi Bazargan made the dramatic announcement that he was resigning. "Outside opposition" made it impossible for him to govern, he said vaguely.[17] Ayatollah Khomeini had rejected Bazargan's letters of resignation many times over the previous ten months, believing that the prime minister's principled opposition to midnight tribunals and summary executions could be assuaged. Not this time. "I have assigned the Revolutionary Council to run the affairs of the country," the ayatollah told Iranians.[18] Ibrahim Yazdi had little choice but to follow Bazargan's example. He resigned as foreign minister and accepted an appointment as Khomeini's adviser on relations with ethnic minorities. Abolhassan Bani-Sadr was named Iran's new foreign minister. Bazargan joined the Revolutionary Council.

The resignation of the secular government was seen by most Westerners as a clear victory for the Islamic militants in Iran—those occupying the embassy and those in the Revolutionary Council. "Although Bazargan's government was considered weak and transitional," Ken Taylor observed, "there was a comforting element that the group of moderate nationalistic Iranians composing his cabinet acted occasionally to modify the radicalism of the Ayatollah. The country is now confronted with the absolute supremacy of the clergy."[19]

Uncertain as to who, apart from the ayatollah himself, actually held power in Iran, Carter and Vance decided to send former attorney general Ramsay Clark and former foreign-service officer William Miller on a secret mission to Tehran to make direct contact with Khomeini. Clark was chosen for his leftist politics and his public sympathy for the Iranians who had opposed the shah, Miller because he had served in Iran in the early 1960s, had many close friends there and spoke Persian. The afternoon of November 6, President Carter briefed the two envoys and sent them off with a personal letter addressed to the ayatollah. "In the name of the American people," it read, "I ask that you release unharmed all Americans presently detained in Iran and those held with them and allow them to leave your country safely and without delay."[20]

In a pattern that would be repeated over the course of the crisis, the secret mission was exposed by the American press even before Clark and Miller had left U.S. airspace. Adamant that they not be seen acquiescing to Washington, even moderate Iranians immediately distanced themselves from the initiative. On Wednesday, November 7, Khomeini decreed that Clark and Miller were not welcome in Iran. The two envoys waited in Istanbul for a week and then returned to Washington, Carter's unopened letter in hand. For Vic Tomseth, stuck at the Iranian foreign ministry building, the news that their mission had fizzled came as a cold shot. "At that point," he later recalled, "I think we began to think that we were there for a longer stay."[21] The only other promising offer to mediate the crisis came from the PLO. Distasteful as the prospect seemed, DCI

Stansfield Turner advised President Carter to accept. "CIA analysts believed Arafat had good access to Khomeini and might be willing to use it to improve his standing with the United States," he told the president.[22] Vance opposed the idea, fearing that Yasser Arafat was simply trying to leverage U.S. recognition of the PLO. He thanked the PLO for any efforts it might make to improve communications between the United States and Iran, but was not surprised when this initiative fizzled as well.

By the fifth day of the crisis, Stansfield Turner later wrote, "we in the Carter administration were willing to try almost anything rather than look impotent."[23] His military options limited and his efforts at dialogue stillborn, Jimmy Carter had little choice but to act unilaterally. He suspended all shipments of military equipment and spare parts to Iran—a harsh tactic since the Iranian armed forces had been built on U.S. technology and could not adequately defend the country without it. The president directed his attorney general, Benjamin R. Civiletti, to start deportation hearings against "any Iranian students in the United States who are not in compliance with the terms of their entry visas."[24] He also forbade anti-American demonstrations by Iranians in front of the White House. "American citizens—including the President—were in no mood to watch Iranian 'students' denouncing our country," he said later.[25] On November 10, Carter took the advice of his wife, Rosalynn, and announced that the United States would no longer import Iranian oil.

President Carter had been scheduled to visit Canada on November 8 but in light of the hostage crisis he decided to postpone. "Staying close to Washington quickly became standard policy," he later wrote.[26] Canadians up to and including External Affairs Minister Flora MacDonald understood why the president's preoccupations might keep him in Washington, but in the United States his timing was suspect. The week the hostages were taken, the Democratic campaign for the presidential elections of 1980 kicked off, with California governor

Jerry Brown and Senator Edward Kennedy announcing their candidacy for the Democratic nomination. Carter's stay-at-home stance came to be known as his "Rose Garden strategy," named after the White House rose garden, where he was now almost exclusively seen. The president later observed that he was happy with allowing others to worry about his electoral prospects for him. "After the American hostages were seized," he wrote, "I did not ignore the Democratic primary contests, but depended on Fritz [Walter Mondale], Rosalynn, and others to do the campaigning while I concentrated on Iran and my many other duties."[27]

In truth, the hostage crisis put Carter in a terrible bind domestically, since there was little he could do publicly to assuage Americans' anger without putting the hostages in greater jeopardy. This dilemma alone made Carter look far weaker than he actually was. Fearing that Khomeini's "irrational" behaviour, as he put it, might provoke reprisals against the hostages, the president was at pains never to use abusive language when discussing the crisis. He appealed to Congress and even the media to follow his example. "The President knows that no matter how deeply we may feel," Press Secretary Jody Powell told a media scrum, "none of us would want do anything that would worsen the danger in which our fellow Americans have been placed. He calls on all Americans, public officials and private citizens alike, to exercise restraint."[28]

Meanwhile, in Tehran, there was little rhetorical restraint emanating from the ranks of the militants. On November 8, the *Toronto Star* reported on a telephone interview it had conducted with some of the embassy occupiers. "The American doctors must cure [the shah]," said a pensive young man in heavily accented English. "Then he must be sent back to Iran. Then we can kill him."[29]

~ ~ ~

Having followed the downward spiral of Iranian–American relations for two years, Ambassador Ken Taylor was not surprised when the students' set-in at the U.S. embassy exploded into a full-blown international incident. "The occupation of the U.S. embassy compound," he wrote Ottawa on the third day of the crisis, "and the brief takeover last night of the British grounds are a further reflection of Iran's current state of disorder. These events are also a culmination of Ayatollah Khomeini's recent exhortations to Iranian youth to 'march forward bravely and deal with devilish American power.'"[30] Taylor was not worried about his own embassy being overrun. "There are no indications that other embassies will be attacked," he told Ottawa. "However we have rechecked security procedures, the disposition of files and the consular list." Taylor secured the embassy as best he could. He ordered embassy staff to destroy all but the most essential documents and prepare contingency plans. Non-essential personnel were evacuated, whittling the total number of staff down to sixteen.[31] Back in Ottawa, Iranian chargé d'affaires Mohammad Adeli reassured Michael Shenstone that Taylor's embassy would continue to enjoy the protection of the Iranian government. When informed of this, Taylor cabled back in his usual terse manner. "Contrary to Chargé Adeli's assurances," he wrote, "no embassies are currently receiving security from Iranians nor with the exception of the USA have they since last December."[32]

One of the earliest and most important efforts Ken Taylor made on the Americans' behalf was to fill the information vacuum left when the U.S. embassy, which included the Tehran CIA station, was taken over. By day three of the crisis, the Canadian embassy in Washington was being copied on all of Taylor's correspondence with Ottawa, and duly forwarded it to the State Department and the White House. The Carter administration was "extremely grateful for our offer to assist on a contingency basis with communications," reported Canada's ambassador in Washington, Peter Towe.[33] When he heard this, Taylor immediately began to expand the number and length of his cables. Two weeks later, State Department officials reiterated that they had "no information beyond that contained in media reports" and thus were indebted to receive the Canadians' "excellent" cables.[34] It was Taylor's connections, and his willingness to ferret out information, that proved of greatest value. One example among many was his effort to get to the bottom of a rumour that the hostages were going to be moved to Tehran's notorious Evin Prison. Taylor first consulted with the Swedish ambassador, whose office overlooked the U.S. embassy compound. He told Taylor that he thought the hostages might already have been transferred. Taylor then contacted some Iranians who knew guards at Evin, and they confirmed that some of the hostages had indeed shown up there.[35]

Ambassador Taylor's primary responsibility as Canada's top diplomat in Iran was to represent the views of the Canadian government. In this endeavour he was tireless, expressing Canadians' abhorrence of the hostage-taking practically daily. But Taylor also worked assiduously behind the scenes to push the full diplomatic corps in Tehran toward some kind of unified protest. In doing so, he knew that he was acting on the wishes not only of his superiors at External Affairs, but of Prime Minister Joe Clark and External Affairs Minister Flora MacDonald, both of whom were under considerable public pressure to lead the international outcry against Iran. "I didn't have to receive instructions from Ottawa to take a stand," he acknowledged. "That was our policy."[36] Taylor also knew that he was advancing President Carter's agenda. Despite his mounting frustration with the lack of resolve in the ranks of Tehran's foreign diplomats, pressing for a diplomatic solution to the hostage crisis was a job Taylor took extremely seriously.

There were roughly seventy-five ambassadors in the diplomatic corps in Iran. The dean of the group, by virtue of seniority, was the Czech ambassador, Vladimir Polacek, a man who cleaved to the Soviet line and dragged his feet even on the simple expedient of sending a *démarche* (letter of protest) to Ayatollah Khomeini.[37] One week after the seizure of the embassy, a clearly exasperated Taylor told Ottawa that "the entire diplomatic corps with the exception of the eastern bloc is extremely dissatisfied with the performance of the dean."[38] What Taylor did not say but what he later confided privately to Bruce Laingen was that Polacek was "faithfully responding to Soviet pressure behind the scenes to ensure that no [unanimous appeal from the diplomatic corps] was possible."[39] Eastern-bloc intransigence became so frustrating in Ottawa that Allan Gotlieb advised Flora MacDonald to "convey to the Czechoslovak and Soviet Ambassadors Canada's keen disappointment that these countries have not seen fit to cooperate fully with other members of the Diplomatic Corps in Tehran in conveying collective disapproval and concern to the Iranian authorities."[40]

Despite such obstructionism, Taylor and other like-minded diplomats met repeatedly to hammer out a *démarche* that the entire corps could present to Foreign Minister Abolhassan Bani-Sadr. One such meeting was supposed to have been held at the residence of the Turkish ambassador, but when Taylor arrived he found the front gate chained and padlocked, the ambassador incommunicado and one of his guards saying simply that the meeting had been cancelled. "The momentum now appears to be lost," Taylor cabled Shenstone dejectedly.[41] When the session reconvened, this time at the Danish embassy, it became clear that nothing resembling a united front would be possible. "It was inevitable," said Taylor. "We broke up into groups—the Soviet bloc, the Latin Americans, the European Community. The Chinese kept to themselves, they didn't come to any meetings. That left a group of twelve—Australia, New Zealand, Spain, the Scandinavian countries, Canada, Greece—but even within this twelve there were differences." Taylor liked to share the credit for keeping this broad diplomatic offensive alive, particularly with his fellow ambassadors Chris Beeby of New Zealand and Troels Munk of Denmark, but he was clearly one of the most assertive. "I certainly was outspoken about it," he concedes. "I didn't mince any words."[42]

Not until November 13, at a meeting that was boycotted by the twelve Soviet-bloc ambassadors, did the corps finally table a draft *démarche* for Bani-Sadr. "We emphasize that the inviolability of diplomatic personnel and missions is to be respected in all cases, in accordance with internationally accepted norms," it read. "We would ask that your Excellency convey as soon as possible to His Eminence Imam Khomeini, as the leader of the Iranian people, whom we hold in highest respect, our appeal, which is based on humanitarian grounds, that he use his influence with the people of Iran to secure the safety and release of the diplomatic personnel now being held in this country."[43] Taylor and his allies did what they could to build a consensus around the document, but of the fifty-nine countries in attendance only forty-seven voted in favour of it. Among those that refused to sign off was the PLO delegation. The meeting broke up with nothing accomplished.

Four days later, a smaller group of "angry and frustrated" ambassadors again met to "table a unified document," as Taylor put it.[44] By this time, the Canadian ambassador despaired of the diplomats' ability either to mount a unified protest or, more to the point, to influence Khomeini or the Revolutionary Council even if they could. Over the following months he never entirely abandoned the project of rallying the diplomatic corps—that remained his official mandate, after all. But by the end of November, he was conceding secretly to Ottawa that the only outcome of all of his efforts, and those of his allies in the diplomatic corps, was "frustration and despair." "It is ironic," he wrote Shenstone on November 26, "that we find ourselves using accepted and proven practices of negotiation with a leadership whose actions seriously place in question the historic principles of diplomacy itself."[45] Taylor was outraged when some of the ambassadors in Tehran proposed expressing their gratitude to Bani-Sadr for allowing some of their nationals out of the U.S. embassy compound, where they had been taken hostage along with the Americans. "This strikes me as if one from his hospital bed expressed to his attacker that he was grateful he only broke one of his legs instead of two," he commented to Shenstone.[46]

Taylor never entirely lost his faith in diplomacy, but with only a handful of exceptions, he had lost his faith in diplomats.

Chapter 10
COMING IN FROM THE COLD

For the first forty-eight hours of their captivity at the Iranian foreign ministry, Bruce Laingen, Vic Tomseth and Mike Howland faced a dilemma of their own. Should they tell their Iranian counterparts—most of whom had no sympathy for the student hostage-takers—that there were American diplomats in hiding in Tehran? They decided that they should, delegating to Tomseth, the only Persian speaker among them, the duty of informing ministry officials. Seen in retrospect, this was a fateful decision not only for the fugitives but also for so-called moderates at the Iranian foreign ministry who had to pretend that they did not know about the embassy staff who had got away. Tomseth later explained the rationale for revealing the secret. "We hoped that the [crisis] would be resolved fairly shortly and we didn't want the fact of the existence of these people to come as a surprise to the government at the time we reached a resolution," he said. "We decided that we did have to tell the foreign ministry about these people and I got in touch with one of the officials on the phone and did that. I said, in effect, that you should be aware that several people who were not caught by the student militants are presently in Tehran. That was the end of the message. We had no intention of telling them where they were."[1]

Bruce Laingen later recounted his own rationale for the decision. "At the time we were still dealing with the provisional government that was in power," he said. "It assured us of its intention to provide security for us, and it was seeking to resolve the crisis as soon as possible. So, we felt that it was in our interest to inform and then to seek their help and get [the fugitives] out of the city, as rapidly as possible."[2] Laingen was not particularly confident about this strategy, which explained his refusal—then and later—to discuss the precise whereabouts of the fugitive diplomats. "We didn't tell them where they were," he said. "We didn't do anything more than say, 'Look, we've got this problem. We need your help in it. You are trying to resolve the crisis. Let's at least get rid of this aspect of it by getting them out of the city.'"[3] What lay behind Laingen's gambit, of course, was his continuing belief that the time-honoured rights and responsibilities of host governments toward foreign diplomats still applied in Iran.

Chargé Laingen was cagey in the aftermath of the crisis about which Iranians were informed about the fugitives' existence. Ibrahim Yazdi does not appear to have been told directly, but Chief of Protocol Ali Shokouhian was among those who were. When Laingen's secret Tehran journal was published as a book in 1992, he praised Shokouhian as "a diplomat of the old school and the epitome of Persian courtesy [who] will forever be my friend."[4] Ken Taylor was another diplomat to hold the chief of protocol in high esteem. Shokouhian's secret reports to Taylor were among the most important the Canadians relayed to Washington, in fact, since they kept the State Department abreast of Laingen's conditions of captivity and his state of mind. Four days into the hostage crisis, Taylor reported that Shokouhian had told him that Laingen was "well and secure," and that the chief of protocol had himself moved into the foreign ministry "in quarters adjacent to those of Laingen."[5] It was Shokouhian who lobbied Khomeini directly in the first weeks of the crisis to allow Taylor and other Western diplomats to visit Laingen at the foreign ministry. At one point, Shokouhian even intervened personally to prevent Revolutionary Guards at Mehrabad Airport from intercepting the New Zealand embassy's diplomatic bag.[6]

Vic Tomseth later acknowledged that he and Laingen were well aware of their captors' lack of sympathy with the actions of the hostage-takers, and that they were not above exploiting it. "We never passed up an opportunity to play upon the feelings of guilt that a lot of professional staff in the foreign ministry had, about the conditions under which the people at the embassy were being held," said Tomseth. "Everyone knew about it and emphasized in particular the inhumanity of depriving these people of all contact with the outside world. I think that those efforts very clearly had an effect on the people in the foreign ministry but the real problem was that they had no influence with the student militants at the embassy."[7]

Taylor knew that Laingen had informed Shokouhian about the existence of the American fugitives. It was a calculated gamble on Laingen's part and Taylor thought he played it well, at least in the sense of divulging very little specific information and making it easy for officials in the provisional government to obscure what they knew and when. "I think they just wanted to forget about it," Taylor later said of the Iranian officials who knew the secret. "I think their lives were complicated enough. I didn't think they would seek favour with the so-called students." Asked recently whether he ever confided in anyone at the Iranian foreign ministry, Taylor's reply was an emphatic no. "I wouldn't tell them my second name! There was no one in the Iranian apparatus I would have told."[8]

In mid-November, Kim King, the American tourist who had fled the U.S. consulate with Bob Anders' group, blurted out in an interview with CBS News that eight American diplomats were still at large in Tehran. Iranian radio and television picked up on the remark immediately. In Washington, State Department officials told Ambassador Towe that they were "displeased" by King's recklessness but added that "the Iranians had always been aware that some American staff were missing and had already been looking for them."[9] "Although I am not overly troubled by this statement," Ken Taylor later wrote Michael Shenstone about King's unguarded comments, "I would appreciate clarification in the event that it receives further coverage in the press."[10]

For weeks Iranian media continued to report that some U.S. diplomats had gone underground in Tehran. The existence of the fugitives thus became an open secret, as Vic Tomseth later observed. "During the first couple of days, there were a number of people who knew about the existence of several Americans, not necessarily six, who had not been captured by the student militants. There were a number of Iranian employees at the Iran-America Society where four of the five from the consular section had gone the first night, who were certainly aware of their existence. We had also talked to several Iranian friends about help in moving them from one place to another. So it's possible that twenty, thirty, maybe even more people knew."[11]

~ ~ ~

Bob Anders, the Lijeks and the Staffords spent a restful night at the British residential compound in North Tehran but awakened the morning of Wednesday, November 7, to find that they could not stay. "We were somewhat surprised and perhaps even a little shocked at this," said Anders, "because we felt that this was a good place to be and a place to wait out the whole thing."[12] They were told by their British hosts that Iranian militants had overrun their embassy the previous day and were threatening further action. (It turned out that the occupiers were protesting against the British in the belief that former prime minister Shapour Bakhtiar was in hiding in London. They left when they received confirmation that he was, in fact, in Paris.) As Anders himself acknowledged, "the situation was just too hot."[13] Bruce Laingen and Vic Tomseth agreed. "The British felt themselves to be under a great deal of pressure," Tomseth said. "In a subsequent conversation with the chargé d'affaires, he suggested that it might not be safe to keep the five people that they had in their housing compound much longer, and asked me to think about alternative arrangements."[14]

The same morning, November 7, Chief of Protocol Ali Shokouhian told Tomseth and Laingen in a private moment that they should perhaps make fewer local phone calls. This kind word the Americans interpreted to mean that their calls were being monitored. How to continue advising Anders' group on logistics without betraying their location thus presented a new challenge. "In order to minimize the risk of our plans to move these people, of being compromised," Tomseth reasoned, "we thought to do it in a language that hopefully the Iranians would not understand."[15] Between them, Laingen, Tomseth and Howland spoke English, German, French and Persian—all languages in common usage at the Iranian foreign ministry. Tomseth, however, also happened to speak Thai, which he had learned during a previous posting to Thailand. Knowing that his Iranian keepers were not likely to speak Thai, Tomseth placed a call to Sam Sriweawnetr. Speaking in Thai, well within earshot of Iranian foreign ministry officials, Tomseth asked Sriweawnetr to do him a favour. "Victor Tomseth told me they got five American diplomats, still outside of the embassy," Sriweawnetr later recalled. "Stay in British embassy at the time. He told me to look [for] a place for five people, where they can stay."[16]

Sriweawnetr reminded Tomseth that his wife worked in the home of John Graves, one of the American embassy officers who had been taken hostage. Graves' house was set off the street and thus afforded a fair degree of privacy. Assuming that the militants at the embassy were not likely to figure out who among their captives lived where, Tomseth and Sriweawnetr agreed that Graves' house would be as good a sanctuary as any for the five diplomats. "It was a good move to go to Graves' house," said Anders later, "because it was a reasonably good place to stay and at this point certainly no one felt that the demonstrators down at the American embassy compound were able to make a detailed check for the location of the residences of embassy officers."[17] The fugitives were driven after dark to Graves' house by the same British drivers who had taken them to Golhak. "Mike Connor gave me a dark green rain jacket to cover my neon yellow sweater," Mark Lijek recalled, "for which I was very grateful."[18] Sam Sriweawnetr met Anders, the Lijeks and the Staffords at Graves' house. "The five Americans ran to the house," said Sriweawnetr, "then I come back to pick up all the bags and put in the house, then come to say goodbye to the driver from the British embassy. Then he left."[19]

Mark and Cora Lijek had not initially been convinced that John Graves' house was any more secure than the British residential compound. Cora became far more comfortable with the idea of hiding at Graves' place once she met the two Thai women who worked there—Sriweawnetr's wife and an elderly housekeeper named Neet. "We felt that this was a reasonably good arrangement," said Cora, "because we would have people to take care of us and go outside and do shopping. It would allow us to stay in the house and stay hidden all the time, which was the main thing we needed."[20] Mark, however, thought that only a site completely unconnected with the U.S. presence in Tehran was truly safe. "For me," he said, "going to [Graves'] house was a step backwards because we were again in a house that was leased by the embassy and consequently one which could be traced from records that were at the embassy and at that time already in the custody of the students. So it didn't make me feel particularly secure knowing that once they got around to researching those records they could find all the addresses of those houses and would, I thought, check them out."[21]

The five Americans spent one relatively restful night in Graves' house. They passed the next day playing poker, watching Iranian television broadcasts and reading newspapers. "One humorous moment," Mark Lijek later observed, "occurred when we found a 16 mm film and projector, so decided we'd watch the one movie we could find. It turned out to be film of the shah's coronation. That provoked some gallows humour, as we joked how the militants would tell the world that we so loved the shah that we passed our time in hiding watching his coronation."[22] On Thursday, November 8, the fugitives learned from Vic Tomseth that Iranian foreign ministry officials would no longer allow him or Bruce Laingen to make local calls. "We were on our own and good luck," Anders remembers.[23] Laingen would be permitted to place direct phone calls to Washington from time to time, and to meet occasionally with other foreign diplomats in Tehran—evidence that, like their counterparts at the U.S. State Department, Iranian officials knew the wisdom of maintaining at least one medium of direct communication. The chargé was also allowed to use the foreign ministry telex machine to send messages to the State Department, knowing, of course, that all such cable traffic would be monitored by his captors. "Obviously we couldn't discuss anything very sensitive in that channel," Tomseth later recalled. "Those messages tended to be rather anodyne except in instances where we were trying to convey a specific message to the Iranians and not to Washington."[24] As for the five fugitives, Anders was correct: they were now on their own. Anything they would hear from this point on about their imprisoned colleagues they would get second-hand, and almost exclusively from Ken Taylor.

The same day they lost their phone link to Laingen, the fugitives were informed by Sam Sriweawnetr that the militants were rumoured to be rounding up U.S. government personnel in Tehran. "For some reason," said Mark Lijek, "Sam was convinced the *komiteh* would come that night, and he developed a plan that had us going out the back door, around the side of the house and then to Kate's place at the other end of the block. Joe and I stayed up virtually the entire night, listening to shortwave broadcasts from all over as well as every local sound that might signal the arrival of the *komiteh* men."[25] Meanwhile, Neet, who had worked at the Graves residence for years, had grown increasingly distraught about the possibility that the Americans would be discovered there and she would be arrested as an accomplice. "We used to be like a family," Sriweawnetr said to Cora Lijek, "and now she won't even talk to us."[26] The Americans understood that the house was no longer secure or hospitable, and agreed that they should start planning another move.

Sriweawnetr knew that Kathryn Koob had been taken hostage and that her house, just a few blocks from Graves', was now empty. He suggested to the five Americans that they hide at Koob's place. They agreed to check it out. An Iranian friend of Sriweawnetr's drove them to the residence in his taxi. The moment they let themselves in, they knew that they would not be safe there. The house had large picture windows that fronted directly onto the street. "We could not go into the kitchen without risking being seen by any person walking down the sidewalk," Mark Lijek observed. "I think we decided within a few minutes of our arrival that this was just not an acceptable hiding place."[27] Bob Anders called a friend at the Australian embassy, Bob Conkey, who kindly offered to share his Tehran apartment with him. Anders declined, saying that he was one of five and that the group preferred to stick together. Again it was Sam Sriweawnetr who presented an alternative. "Vic Tomseth told me before," said Sriweawnetr, "if you got problems with the five people here, call to the Canadian embassy. This is what I tell Bob. To call the Canadians, give him the telephone number and talk to Mr. Taylor, the ambassador."[28]

Anders made the call.

~ ~ ~

In November 1979, John Sheardown was the head of the immigration section at the Canadian embassy in Tehran. Fifty-five years old, heavy-set, ruddy-faced with a full white beard and moustache, the pipe-smoking Sheardown had a grandfatherly appeal that endeared him to many of his younger colleagues. A veteran of World War II, he exuded the sort of quiet but unyielding resolve that made him a natural leader in a crisis. His wife, Zena Sheardown, was roughly ten years younger, her bobbed black hair, broad face and pretty smile giving her an even more youthful air. As Flora MacDonald later recalled, although Zena was the spouse of a Canadian consular officer, she did not have diplomatic immunity in Iran. "She was born in British Guiana," said MacDonald, "and never had the opportunity to stay in Canada to become a Canadian citizen."[29] The Sheardowns had arrived in Iran at the end of June 1978, almost a year after Ambassador Taylor, and were plunged directly into the chaos of the revolution. They moved into a house in the city's north end where the outgoing Canadian military attaché had lived, and immediately began receiving death threats that appear to have been meant for him. Zena Sheardown did not take paid employment in Tehran, and thus spent most of her time sequestered in the residential part of the city. This isolation undoubtedly heightened her justifiable feeling of vulnerability.

John Sheardown knew, possibly as early as the day the U.S. embassy was attacked, that Bob Anders had not been taken hostage. How he came by this information he has never said. "He heard it through the grapevine," Zena recalled recently, with a smile. The Sheardowns were close to Anders, who was in Tehran without his wife. "He was John's counterpart at the U.S. embassy," Zena later recalled. "He came over a couple of times to our house." Knowing that Anders might be in need of refuge, John and Zena decided that they would open their home to him regardless of what Canada's official policy might be. "We knew the situation, how dire it was," said Zena. "We knew there would be very few people, volunteers, willing to stick their necks out for the Americans. We decided that should he call and ask for help, we would take him in. It was just between the two of us."[30]

Anders' call to the Canadian embassy the evening of November 8 was taken by one of the young Canadian MPs and immediately transferred to Sergeant Jim Edward, the head of embassy security. "It came as quite a surprise to me that anybody from the U.S. embassy had actually escaped after the Iranian takeover," said Edward.[31] He gave Anders the Sheardowns' home number, and Anders immediately called John. "Bob advised me that he had other people with him," John later said of this first conversation. "I said, 'Well, we've got lots of room, Bob, bring them along.'"[32] The two men agreed that if there came a point when the five fugitives had to flee John Graves' house, they would make their way immediately to the Sheardowns'.

John Sheardown knew that he did not have the authority to make an official commitment to Anders and the others, but he had no doubt that Ambassador Taylor would sanction his plan the moment he was informed about it. After Anders' call, Sheardown met with Taylor and brought him up to date on the precarious situation of the fugitive U.S. diplomats. Taylor knew nothing of the fugitive Americans until that point, but he did not equivocate for a moment. He agreed with Sheardown that they—and by extension Canada—should do everything in their power to help. The two men immediately started working out the logistics of bringing the Americans in from the cold. They eliminated the embassy building as a possible refuge—it contained no living quarters and was, in any case, a high-visibility, high-traffic site. Taylor volunteered his ambassador's residence, since it had the dual advantage of distance from the U.S. embassy compound and proximity to other ambassadors' residences if they were ever needed. Knowing that he had Zena's prior approval, Sheardown offered his own residence as well. The two men agreed that the appearance of North Americans would strike their Iranian housekeeping staffs as unusual, possibly even suspicious, so they opted for a simple arrangement requiring little outright deception.

They would identify their visitors simply as houseguests.

~ ~ ~

Having devised what they thought was a good rescue plan, Taylor and Sheardown immediately drafted a flash cable for their superiors at External Affairs. The telex expressed the two men's strong conviction that they should offer the five Americans refuge. It was not, however, presented to Ottawa as a *fait accompli*. At this point, the Anders group had not yet relocated, nor even confirmed the necessity of vacating the Graves residence. The flash cable was received at the Pearson Building early in the morning of Thursday, November 8, where it was promptly distributed to senior members of the department, including Allan Gotlieb and Michael Shenstone. These officials immediately concurred with Taylor and Sheardown's judgment that harbouring the fugitive Americans was the right thing for Canada to do. They agreed to seek the approval of the external affairs minister and the prime minister to fast-track the implementation of their rescue plan. At no point did anyone equivocate.

As it happened, Flora MacDonald did not hear about the plan to harbour the five fugitives until the next day, Friday, November 9. She had been so busy trying to "unscramble" all of the arrangements for President Carter's abortive state visit, as she later put it, that she could not make the time for any serious consideration of the hostage crisis until then. Her advisers understood this. They called her from the Pearson Building first thing in the morning to propose that they meet her at her parliamentary office. "I thought, that's fine," she said later. "It would not be unusual because it was a Friday morning and I'd be going into the House at eleven to answer questions. So it might be something I was going to face in Question Period."[33] Michael Shenstone led the delegation to MacDonald's office and broke the news to her. "What we need is to have your approval to have these people stay with our embassy people in Tehran," she recalls Shenstone saying.[34] Allan Gotlieb was just as adamant. "I recommend that we urgently authorize the Ambassador to accommodate these people," he wrote in a memo for MacDonald the same day. "There would be a certain risk to our premises and personnel. . . . This possible risk, however, is outweighed in my view by the very serious danger in which these U.S. personnel find themselves. I think that in all conscience, we have no alternative but to concur."[35]

MacDonald knew that initiating a plan of refuge for Americans in Iran required an executive decision. "I gladly give you my approval," she told her advisers, "but I really believe that I should check it with the prime minister."[36] Since she was literally en route to the House of Commons, where she knew she would see Joe Clark, she decided to broach the subject with him then and there. She would have to do so discreetly, of course, for the issue of the houseguests had to be handled with the utmost secrecy. Already the U.S. State Department had politely requested that MacDonald keep her remarks on Canada's role in the hostage crisis to vague generalities. "USA DOES NOT WANT US TO BE MORE SPECIFIC," read her briefing notes for November 9.[37]

At 11 o'clock, MacDonald took her seat next to Prime Minister Joe Clark in the House of Commons for Question Period, quietly requesting that he remain in his seat afterwards. "I said to Joe," she later recalled, "when Question Period is over there is something very urgent I have to talk to you about."[38]

As expected, the Liberals immediately took her to task over her handling of the hostage crisis.

"Can the minister tell us whether she has personally been in touch with our ambassador in Iran in order to ascertain that there is no danger to Canadians who are presently in Iran, and that there is no danger of an interruption of oil supplies from Iran to Canada in the months to come?" asked Liberal veteran Marc Lalonde.[39]

"I can assure the honourable member that at the present time there is no real cause for concern," replied MacDonald. "That information has been conveyed to us both by our ambassador in Iran and also by the chargé d'affaires of the Iranian embassy here in Ottawa."[40]

Lalonde fired back with his follow-up question. Had the minister been in touch with Imperial Oil and other petroleum companies to ensure the supply of Iranian oil to Canada? Before he could finish, he was cut off by Minister of Finance John Crosbie, who said, "You are a jerk."[41] Minister of Energy, Mines and Resources Ray Hnatyshyn then told Lalonde that it was his understanding that minor disruptions in Iran had not hurt the international supply of petroleum.

Just after noon, with Question Period over, Flora MacDonald informed Joe Clark that Ambassador Taylor had requested the government's permission to provide refuge for five fugitive American diplomats who had escaped the U.S. embassy takeover. "I told him the whole story, and of course, Joe gave his approval immediately," said MacDonald.[42] "We agreed, literally on the spot in the House," Joe Clark later recalled, "that she would communicate back through Canadians officials in External Affairs to our embassy in Tehran, conveying our approval."[43]

At three o'clock the same day, Michael Shenstone cabled Ken Taylor. "You are authorized by the SSEA [Secretary of State for External Affairs] to accommodate USA embassy staff," he wrote. "We leave the location to your judgment, depending on the circumstances. But we believe that the official residence might be best because of its location and the fact that like the chancery (but unlike staff quarters) it enjoys full diplomatic immunity."[44] In a separate telex, Shenstone added that "there is concern at the topmost levels here about possible implications for our embassy staff and other Canadians if and when accommodation is given to USA embassy members." Canadian staff should "take all feasible precautions," he advised.[45]

~ ~ ~

When Ambassador Taylor got to his Tehran office on the morning of Saturday, November 10, Shenstone's cables were waiting on his desk. He was extremely pleased to see them. "I had sent a memo to Joe Clark," he later recalled, "saying this is what we proposed to do, and it came back immediately, saying, do what you have to do. They didn't take it to Cabinet. Flora and Joe decided."[46]

Shenstone's missive had arrived not a moment too soon. At one o'clock that afternoon, the expected call from Bob Anders came to the Sheardown house. "I answered the phone and it was Bob," Zena recalls, "and he said the time is now. I said, do you need transportation. He said no, but he needed directions."[47] Anders had arranged to be driven, along with the Lijeks and the Staffords, by the same British embassy staffers who had taxied them around earlier in the week. As before, they travelled in two cars. Zena called John, who had gone to the Canadian embassy just in case Anders' call had come in there, and was relieved when he arrived back home ahead of the Americans. The five houseguests arrived at the Sheardown residence to find John nonchalantly watering his front sidewalk—a common practice in Iran because of constantly accumulating dust. He greeted them with a friendly wave and ushered their cars directly into his garage. The Americans wore clothing intended to hide their identities, the women's heads covered with scarves, the men huddled in high-collared jackets. When the garage door closed behind them, they climbed out and introduced themselves to their host. Sheardown welcomed Anders warmly. "We were very, very happy to be there," Anders later recalled of their reunion.[48]

To get from the Sheardowns' detached garage to their house required walking outdoors in full view of the street, a risky but unavoidable passage. "Next door to us," Zena explained, "there was an unfinished building, and there were a lot of young men hanging around there. We also had a man in front of our house watching us."[49] Once they were all safely inside the house, Anders introduced the Lijeks and Staffords to Zena. They were also introduced to a Canadian named Mr. Taylor, who had just driven up in his two-seater Volvo. "I was embarrassed," said Mark Lijek, "because I asked John whether his ambassador knew that we were there. To this point we did not know whether this was John acting on his own or an official decision by the government. We had been introduced to Ken by name, not title, so we all laughed when John informed me that, yes, the ambassador knew, and, by the way, he's sitting next to you."[50] Ambassador Taylor was greeted by the Americans with expressions of sincere gratitude. "The fact that it was a government that was protecting us was reassuring," recalled Cora Lijek.[51] Mark agreed. "I think Ken also said that the prime minister had personally approved our being there," he recalled. "We had found the obvious good hiding place. If there was one in Tehran, this was it."[52]

Ken Taylor recognized immediately that Bob Anders' maturity and cool demeanour made him the natural leader of the fugitive group. "Bob was very much the father figure," said Taylor. "He was the oldest, unassuming, nice—a very solid individual, gregarious and with a great sense of humour."[53] Because Anders had been a regular guest at the Sheardown residence prior to the hostage crisis, there was never any question of trying to pass him off as a visitor from abroad. The Sheardowns' maid, Lolita, a Filipina, took one look at the Americans when they entered the house and said to Zena, "Ma'am, we can't do this!" Zena replied, "They have nowhere else to go. It will only be for a week."[54]

Also present at the Sheardown house that first morning was Tricia Otto, the daughter of the former Canadian military attaché in Tehran, and a friend of Zena's. The wisdom of allowing this young woman in on their secret was immediately questioned by the houseguests, not least because she had an Iranian boyfriend. Anders was generous in his assessment of the risk the two outsiders represented. "I don't think it was any real problem because, of course, there were many Iranians at that point whom we felt were still very much pro-Western and pro-American," he said. "So we felt that if Tricia was a trusted member of the group and she trusted her boyfriend, there was no real problem there at all."[55] The others were not convinced.

The houseguests and their hosts relaxed in the Sheardowns' spacious living room, exchanging information and fleshing out their new living arrangements with the Canadians. It was agreed that the Lijeks and Anders would stay with the Sheardowns and that the Staffords would go to Ken Taylor's residence. "We wanted to stay together," said Mark Lijek, "but we accepted Ken's logic that from both a logistical and political standpoint, one couple should be at the residence."[56] Just before noon, the Staffords climbed into Taylor's car, the three of them abreast across two bucket seats, and drove off with him to the ambassador's residence. There they met Pat Taylor for the first time, as well as the residence's eight servants. Ken was able to place a call to Bruce Laingen at the Iranian foreign ministry, telling him, in code, that the houseguests were now safe with the Canadians. "That was a matter of great relief for us," Laingen said, "because we did not perceive that the embassy of Canada was suspect or in a place of particular threat from the Iranians."[57] Later in the week, Taylor would meet Laingen at the foreign ministry for the first time, and there bring him up to date on the houseguests' situation. "Thus began a time of very close and concerned association between us and Ambassador Taylor," Laingen later wrote.[58]

The evening of November 10, the day they welcomed the houseguests into their homes, the Taylors and the Sheardowns attended a reception hosted by a senior member of the Iranian foreign ministry. "Ambassador Taylor, his wife, Zena and I found ourselves in a very odd and very strange situation," John Sheardown later recalled, "in that we were harbouring fugitives in our home and accepting hospitality from this senior Iranian diplomat." While they were at the diplomat's home, the assembled guests listened to the BCC's radio coverage of the hostage crisis. At one point, John Sheardown asked his host point-blank whether he thought the militants at the embassy would follow through on their threats against the hostages. "Iranians are basically very kind people," was the reply.[59]

The houseguests settled quickly into their new lives as refugees, relieved finally to be beyond the reach of the Iranian militants and their relentless search for American diplomatic personnel. "The key decision in the whole process was the decision to take us in," Mark Lijek observed. "Once we were safely under John's roof—or Taylor's roof, in the case of the Staffords—I figured we would get out of Iran safely. I quit worrying about it. There were intense moments from time to time, but basically, that was it."[60] No sooner were the houseguests installed in the Taylor and Sheardown residences than they began seeing the televised coverage of the embassy occupation. Cora Lijek recalls being spooked by the parade of bound hostages being led out of the chancery. "The fact that they were blindfolded was pretty scary," she said. "We were actually pretty close to a lot of people at the embassy. Hearing something is one thing but actually seeing it on TV was just a little bit too difficult to watch."[61] "Before John's TV died," added her husband, Mark, "we were able to watch an Iranian TV program detailing some of the evidence of espionage activities found at the embassy. While some things were damaging, such as Tom Ahern's multiple passports, others were more symbolic of the ignorance of the militants and their intended audience. For example, they displayed an office Dictaphone and called it spying equipment."[62]

The Americans' odyssey had ended well, it seemed, but Sam Sriweawnetr's was just beginning. As Mark Lijek had anticipated, Iranian militants had compiled lists of Tehran residences leased by U.S. embassy personnel and were now methodically staking them out—Bill Royer's, John Graves' and Kathryn Koob's houses among them. Sriweawnetr happened to be at Koob's house the afternoon of November 8 when some of the students from the embassy showed up. "One of the guy they put the gun on my stomach," he later recalled. "Then they say, 'Where is the American? Where is the American?' I say, 'No, I don't have American. I work with the American but my boss is at the embassy already. There is no American around here. I am cook.'"[63] Sriweawnetr was spooked. He went directly to the Thai embassy, where he hoped he could hide from the militants. "If they find out I hide the American people and help the American people," Sriweawnetr reasoned, "they will kill me."[64] The Thai embassy refused him entry, saying that his activities on the Americans' behalf had placed them, too, in jeopardy.

Sriweawnetr saw no alternative but to go underground himself. He lived in the basement of a Filipino friend for several months, then moved to a Korean friend's house and finally ended up with a Thai family. Although he was not bitter about it, Sriweawnetr was disappointed that while he was on the run the Americans stopped paying him. Asked later how he was able to survive without working, Sriweawnetr said that Victor Tomseth's wife sent him a monthly stipend of $200 from the United States, and that his friends in Tehran pitched in with food and cigarettes. After eighteen months on the run, by which time all of the American houseguests and hostages had returned to the United States, Sriweawnetr was advised by Vic Tomseth to get out of

Iran. Tomseth cabled money to the Swiss embassy in Tehran to pay for Sriweawnetr's airline ticket to Bangkok. He flew to Thailand and took a job at the U.S. embassy in Bangkok. Later, he emigrated to the United States, where he worked for the Sheraton hotel chain.

~ ~ ~

By mid-November 1979, the American and Iranian positions on the hostage crisis had hardened against each other. Frustrated with Ayatollah Khomeini's refusal even to talk about the stand-off, President Carter announced on November 14 that he was freezing all Iranian government assets in the United States in the interests of "national security."[65] This was a risky move, for it was sure to mean headaches for American financial institutions and possibly even squabbles with U.S. allies. "I hesitated," the president said of the new measures, "only because such action was likely to reflect adversely on us as a reliable trading partner and might frighten other major depositors and investors into a massive transfer of their funds to other countries."[66] Two days later, Carter gave a major speech denouncing the Iranians as terrorists. "Ours is not a country that responds or ever will respond to intimidation or blackmail," he said. "We will not honor in any possible way the threats or actions of terrorists."[67]

Resolute though he was in public, in private President Carter remained insistent that some channel of communication with the Iranians be found. Ramsay Clark, now operating strictly as a private citizen, was working to establish a back channel for negotiations. So was Secretary-General of the United Nations Kurt Waldheim, who even managed to persuade Secretary of State Cyrus Vance to meet secretly with Iranian foreign minister Abolhassan Bani-Sadr. It was Bani-Sadr who scuttled Waldheim's mediation efforts, apparently because he faced intense pressure from the Revolutionary Council to take a hard line against Washington. As Ken Taylor observed,

Bani-Sadr's overriding priority was self-preservation. "He genuinely wanted a resolution of the hostage crisis early on," said Taylor, "but on the other hand, he had to keep his place within the revolutionary cadre. And to do that he had to roll with the tide."[68]

The question of a mediated settlement became moot when Ayatollah Khomeini himself joined the war of words. On November 12, Khomeini gave a major speech in response to President Carter's economic sanctions against Iran. "We are a nation of 35 million and many of these people are looking forward to martyrdom," said the ayatollah. "We will move with the 35 million. After they have all been martyred, then they can do what they want with Iran. We are not afraid of these threats. We are fighters."[69] Four days later, the Iranian government released an even more explosive communiqué written by Khomeini in the aftermath of Pope John Paul's failed bid on November 11 to mediate the crisis. The Church had had fifty years to intervene against the shah and his American backers, wrote the ayatollah, but "never did it occur to the Great Pope to defend the rights of this impoverished people."[70] The embassy takeover was inspired by an understandable reaction to the brutality and corruption of the shah, said Khomeini. "He is the same person who killed our youths, who roasted our young people in frying pans, who charred them on fire and who cut their limbs. We demand that you surrender this person to us, so that we may give him a fair trial."[71]

Newly sequestered in the homes of the Canadian ambassador and the head of the Canadian immigration service, the five American houseguests recognized that the escalating war of words between Washington and Tehran did not bode well either for them or for their comrades held hostage at the U.S. embassy.

For the houseguests, the hardening stand-off meant that they would have to impose on their Canadian hosts for longer than originally planned, possibly much longer. For their hosts, it meant escalation of a different kind.

Chapter 11

WALKING LAPS IN THE BALLROOM

On the fifth day of the hostage crisis, before the houseguests had even moved into his house, Ken Taylor was asked by the U.S. State Department if he could arrange a personal visit with Bruce Laingen at the Iranian foreign ministry. "If this proves possible," read the official request, "the Canadian ambassador should take the opportunity to brief the chargé on the situation, including his latest diplomatic initiatives, and to reassure him that the hostages remain unharmed."[1]

Taylor was only too happy to oblige. He tried to see Laingen for the first time on Saturday, November 10—the day he and the Sheardowns took in the houseguests—but he was turned away by a group of what he called "rag-tag militiamen."[2] Frustrated by his lack of access to his American counterpart, Taylor appealed to Chief of Protocol Shokouhian, who quietly arranged for a meeting with Laingen five days later. As Taylor discovered the moment he was reunited with his friend, Laingen was beside himself. In the first forty-eight hours of the crisis he had spoken with almost every ranking Iranian government official other than the prime minister himself. Now, with Mehdi Bazargan and Ibrahim Yazdi gone, he was completely cut off.

After greeting each other warmly, Taylor and Laingen devised a strategy for conferring in confidence. They walked laps together around the large foreign ministry ballroom, speaking in whispers, while Mike Howland and Vic Tomseth made a pretence of listening to the radio at high volume. In this way, Taylor's conversation with Laingen could not be overheard, or bugged, above the din of Iranian radio programming—a pattern the two HOMs would repeat on every subsequent visit. On this reunion visit, Taylor and Laingen spent much of their time together discussing the "severe mental and psychological strain and stress" to which the hostages were being subjected, as Laingen put it.[3] They also explored possible avenues of protest available to the diplomatic corps and even to Laingen himself. "We are outraged, angry, frustrated, and bored, in roughly that order," Laingen complained.[4] After bidding his friend adieu, and promising to visit the next day, Taylor cabled Ottawa. "All are in good health," he said of the three captive Americans, "but Laingen particularly is angry and frustrated about the treatment of the hostages and his own inability to either enhance their welfare or contribute to a resolution of the crisis."[5]

As promised, Taylor returned the next day with clothes and books for the three. He also smuggled in some Scotch in aftershave bottles— a brief and welcome exposure to "the corruptibility of the West," as Laingen later joked.[6] Taylor was a most welcome visitor, the chargé later recalled, "because of the kind of cheerful, positive nature that he always demonstrates. It was always a shot in the arm for Ken to come in to see us. He would bring us greetings as well from his lovely wife, Pat, who was equally cheerful and positive in everything she did. So those visits were exceedingly welcome."[7] Vic Tomseth agreed. "Ken Taylor came in to see us several times during the first two and a half months that we were there," said Tomseth. "We knew that he was one of the most active among the diplomatic corps, and even at that stage one of the most daring in the sense that he very clearly was prepared to put his embassy and his staff in some risk in order to help the Americans that he was sheltering."[8]

Chief of Protocol Shokouhian also arranged for visits to Laingen from the Swedish, Dutch and Syrian ambassadors, as well as the French and Algerian chargés. Such visits tended to take the form of social calls. (The Dutch ambassador, who brought Droste Haarlem chocolate, Laingen described as "jolly.") The Canadian ambassador, on the other hand, and later Swiss ambassador Erik Lang, were secretly enlisted to carry sensitive information between the State Department and the chargé. Once it became known in Washington that Taylor and Laingen were able to confer privately during their indoor walks, the State Department began sending Taylor questions to put to Laingen. Some concerned the prosaic matters of the captives' day-to-day existence, or basic information on U.S. citizens in Iran. Others, however, concerned intelligence. "Can you describe in general terms any of the kinds of documents you believe may have fallen into students' hands?" Taylor was requested to ask the chargé on November 20. "Is Laingen able to tell us the contents of a specific safe or container not destroyed during the attack?"[9]

Taylor was happy to serve as Laingen's conduit. "Would the USA have any other messages other than that conveyed in your telex?"[10] he cabled Michael Shenstone on November 25. The State Department answered in the affirmative. "Would Ambassador Taylor please ask Bruce Laingen in the strictest confidence whether Laingen has any reason to believe that students or other revolutionary groups outside the compound have a precise knowledge of how many embassy employees are confined in the [foreign] ministry? When the final release is achieved, will the students expect only three Americans to leave the ministry premises?"[11] Taylor answered the next day. "My impression," he wrote, "is that revolutionary groups are fairly certain that three employees are confined in the ministry."[12]

When Taylor next met with Laingen, on the evening of December 1, he was confronted by a new and unnerving situation: sixty Iranian soldiers surrounded the foreign ministry and also posted within it. According to Shokouhian, the troops were there to protect the three Americans from possible incursions by the embassy occupiers or leftist militants. Laingen told Taylor that he was pressing Shokouhian for a meeting with the Iranian foreign minister, but neither man was optimistic that it would happen. (It never did.) "Laingen himself appears somewhat more drawn each week but this is not surprising," Taylor reported to Ottawa and Washington. "The deplorable condition of the hostages is understandably upper-most in Laingen's mind." It happened that December 1 was the birthday of the chargé's wife, Penne Laingen. "If by slight chance mention of this occasion slipped by," Taylor added, "I am sure he would welcome his best wishes being conveyed."[13]

In mid-December 1979, the Iranian press discovered that Taylor had been meeting privately with Laingen. The militants at the U.S. embassy reacted angrily to the report, as Taylor had known they would, but he planned simply to ignore them. "If my 'no comment' position becomes absolutely untenable," he wrote Shenstone, "I will merely mention that my visits were on the basis of straight-forward humanitarian concerns."[14] For a time Laingen's friends were refused admission to the foreign ministry, apparently because the occupiers had lobbied Ayatollah Khomeini to have the visits terminated.[15] In less than two weeks, however, the storm died down, the visits resumed and Taylor once again did what he could to move information between Laingen and Washington. Ambassador Towe reported regularly from the Canadian embassy in Washington that State Department officials thought Taylor's analyses of the complex political and diplomatic situation in Tehran brilliant—a measure of their growing confidence in both his judgment and his discretion. Yet all that was known publicly was what Taylor was willing to tell Canadian journalists, and that was not much. "We have been helping the Americans in a small way whenever we can," Taylor told *Toronto Star* reporter Haroon Siddiqui, who was writing a series of features from Iran. "We are not officially designated as the American government's representative, but since we are so very close to the American people and their government, we are doing our bit."[16]

Already Taylor had begun to deploy his affable "aw shucks" persona as a smokescreen to conceal his increasing indispensability to the Americans in Tehran.

~ ~ ~

On November 15, President Carter sent a letter to Prime Minister Joe Clark and other heads of state asking that they express "the strongest possible remonstration" against Iran. If they could not recall all of their diplomatic staff from their Tehran missions, said Carter, they could at least cut their staffs. "I hope I can count on you to join with us in setting ourselves firmly against any inclination to continue business as usual with the Government of Iran should the hostage situation continue to remain unresolved," he wrote.[17]

A personal letter from the president of the United States is taken seriously at every level of the Ottawa bureaucracy, up to and including the Prime Minister's Office. Carter's request had no sooner arrived at External Affairs than Michael Shenstone and Ken Taylor were exchanging cables as quickly as their communicators could fire them off, working through various downsizing scenarios for the Canadian embassy. None seemed viable. "The strong inclination at the official level in this department," Shenstone wrote, "is to recommend no reduction on grounds that reduction on a scale likely to

impress the Iranians would greatly handicap your efforts to be helpful diplomatically as well as making it difficult or impossible to continue to shelter your American guests."[18] Taylor agreed. It was hardly
in the Americans' interests to have the Canadian ambassador recalled
and the mission closed. A reply letter bearing Joe Clark's signature
was dispatched to President Carter a few days later. It expressed
Canada's "whole-hearted support" for efforts to secure the release of
the hostages but insisted that any reduction in Canadian diplomatic
staff in Iran would be counterproductive.[19] Publicly, Clark issued a
strongly worded statement calling for a common declaration against
the hostage-taking from all Western heads of state. "It would carry
one step further to the heads-of-government level the initiatives that
Canada has already taken in Iran," said Clark.[20]

"It soon became apparent," President Carter later lamented, "that
even our closest allies in Europe were not going to expose themselves
to potential oil boycotts, or endanger their diplomatic arrangements
for the sake of American hostages, and would be very cautious in
their public statements and actions."[21] Not so Canada. Officials from
the Iran Working Group continued to express their "warm appreciation" for the assistance the Canadian diplomats in Tehran were
providing the Americans there. "They are fantastic!" said one State
Department official.[22] National Security Advisor Zbigniew Brzezinski echoed this sentiment, telling Ambassador Towe in a private
meeting that the Carter administration was "genuinely appreciative"
of Canada. "When the time [is] ripe to talk publicly about support
the USA had received from others, Canadian efforts would be given
rightful prominence," said Brzezinski. "Canada had done more than
other friends of the USA and what was particularly satisfying was the
fact that many of the actions Canada had taken were taken at [its]
own initiative and without prompting from the USA."[23]

~ ~ ~

Although the State Department had requested that Ken Taylor assuage Bruce Laingen about the welfare of the hostages, the truth is that American officials knew almost nothing about the conditions of their captivity for the first two weeks of the crisis. Iranian students like Massoumeh Ebtekar claimed that the hostages were being well treated by their captors, but the hostages themselves tell a different story. They were subjected to physical and psychological abuse from the outset, the worst of it taking place during the first three weeks of the crisis, usually in the form of individual interrogations. Not all hostages were interrogated brutally, but all suffered severe privations day to day, all lived with the fear that they might be tried and executed as spies, and many were subjected to periodic torments—mock executions and Russian roulette, for example—that kept them in a state of high anxiety.

Not surprisingly, the three captured CIA officers were singled out for special treatment. Before the end of the first day of the occupation, William Daugherty had been separated out from the other hostages and questioned at gunpoint. During his initial two-week interrogation session, Daugherty was beaten severely, once on the palms of his hands with a rubber hose, which he later recalled as the worst pain he had ever experienced.[24] CIA station chief Tom Ahern got the same rubber-hose treatment on his hands repeatedly, and was threatened with beatings on the soles of his feet. (Ahern later told author Mark Bowden that he was so unsettled by the prospect of being subjected to a public trial and execution that he developed a contingency plan for suicide.)[25]

Even the American hostages who were not savagely beaten were kept in near-total isolation, in violation of the Geneva Convention, and forbidden access to newspapers or other sources of news about the outside world. One of the more insidious forms of abuse they suffered was disinformation, both political and personal. In the case of hostages Chuck Scott, David Roeder and presumably others, the Iranians made explicit threats against their families back home in the United States. Roeder was told, for example, that the occupiers knew his son's school-bus route, and that if he did not cooperate with them, they would kidnap the boy and send pieces of him to his wife.[26] The hostages were also moved regularly and without warning, a dislocating and sometimes violent experience. Within days of the embassy seizure, for instance, Dick Morefield was transferred off the embassy grounds, presumably to give the militants some leverage in the event of an American invasion or rescue mission. Blindfolded the entire time, he was taken to a grim basement cell somewhere in Tehran, told to lie face down over a floor drain, had a rifle placed on the back of head and heard the click of the empty chamber.[27] Other hostages experienced similar torments, either as part of their interrogations or simply for the amusement of their captors.

Disinclined to dwell upon his own suffering in his book *In the Shadow of the Ayatollah*, William Daugherty was asked recently about the extent of the abuse he and others suffered at the hands of his captors:

> I think it's probably fair to say—without diminishing the awful experiences of any of our colleagues in any way— that Ahern and I were interrogated more severely and treated worse, overall, than anyone else. Not only did we, as CIA officers, possess numerous secrets (as of course did Chuck Scott and the defence attaché officers), the Iranians had an obvious quest for revenge against the CIA that they didn't have for the U.S. military. In that respect, Tom and I were surrogates for the CIA of 1953; unable to punish those involved in the 1953 coup, the Iranians took out their anger on us.
>
> For openers, Ahern went into solitary on day 18 and I went into solitary on day 19, and we remained in solitary for the rest of the time (425 and 426 straight days in solitary); no one else came close (I think Mal Kalp was something like

385 days), and it was solely because we were CIA. There were also some colleagues who were put into solitary, or who were beaten at times, only because they deliberately pissed off the Iranians by trying to escape or attacking the guards. And our senior military officers were also harshly interrogated and at times put into solitary for lengthy periods. But only Tom and I were in solitary on a permanent basis. That said, Chuck was something of a special case for the Iranians, because in addition to being a senior military officer, he was the head of the MAAG [Military Assistance Advisory Group] and he did speak Farsi. I think being a Farsi-speaker made the Iranians even more suspicious of Chuck; they probably assumed he was CIA or closely associated with CIA, and that would not have made them very happy.[28]

Both Scott and Daugherty, veterans of many combat missions in Vietnam, later acknowledged that their military training had been crucial to their survival strategies as hostages. Each man gauged his capacity to resist his interrogators against the legendary courage of the American POWs in Vietnam. Other hostages to demonstrate grit in the face of their tormentors included political officer Michael Metrinko. For shouting insults about Ayatollah Khomeini during one of his many interrogation sessions, Metrinko was handcuffed for two weeks straight without relief, even when eating, sleeping or using the toilet.[29]

Starting the day of the embassy takeover, the occupiers made a priority of capturing classified documents from "the den of spies," documents they believed would expose the intrigues of the CIA during the shah's regime. William Daugherty later recalled thinking that he should have tossed a match into the pile of shredded paper he left in the CIA vault before being ordered to surrender. He had opted not to, reasoning that the Iranian authorities would show up before long to end the crisis.[30] No such luck. Once the vault was surrendered, the students imposed a strict rule that it was not to be disturbed in any way. They then resolved to catalogue and reassemble all of the shredded strips by hand. Teams of up to twenty volunteers, most of them high school students, worked for the next six years recombining the tangled contents of the shredders. In 1985, their work was complete: 2,300 files (a total of 3,000 pages) were published in 85 volumes. Many U.S. intelligence documents on the Iranian revolution available to researchers today are those that were painstakingly reconstituted from quarter-inch shredder strips.

Whether the reassembled documents had genuine intelligence value is a matter of debate. According to Israeli author Ronen Bergman, the captured files were damning. They showed that the CIA had had five thousand Iranians on the payroll, from all walks of life, and they revealed Mossad's extensive complicity with the shah's regime.[31] Certainly the militants believed that they had unearthed all of the evidence they needed to confirm their worst suspicions of U.S. plots. "A vast spectrum of intelligence sources and spies were identified in sensitive positions such as government offices and the military," said Massoumeh Ebtekar. "Several espionage networks, including a full-fledged coup d'état plot, were discovered and foiled."[32] American intelligence officers, including William Daugherty, scoff at such claims, asserting that the Iranians wasted a vast amount of time and energy to reveal practically nothing. Jimmy Carter took the same view. "I went over an assessment of the embassy documents that had fallen into the hands of the militants," he said, "and found that they were not damaging."[33]

In mid-November 1979, Abolhassan Bani-Sadr requested of Ayatollah Khomeini that the students hand over any captured documents to the Revolutionary Council. According to Massoumeh Ebtekar, the students believed that he was trying to cover up his own secret contacts with U.S. embassy personnel.[34] Khomeini replied publicly that the documents should remain in the students' hands and that they should publish everything they find. "Even if you find something against me," said the ayatollah, "publish it!"[35] The documents did reveal that an intelligence officer posing as an American businessman named Rutherford had attempted to establish a relationship with Bani-Sadr, whom he code-named "SD-Lure." Because the militants thought Bani-Sadr "one of our most spiteful critics" and a traitor to his country, they took extra care in tracing every detail of his relationship with Rutherford.[36] Tom Ahern told them during his interrogation that the CIA had sought to employ Bani-Sadr on a $100-per-month retainer but that Bani-Sadr never understood this as anything other than a legitimate consultant's fee.[37] Other revolutionaries charged with spying as a direct result of the documents published by the occupiers included Abbas Amir Entezam, the former deputy prime minister in the Bazargan government.[38] As Ken Taylor observed, Entezam's arrest in mid-December 1979 "unsettles those Iranians who had good relations for what may well have been totally innocent reasons with the USA."[39]

On November 18 and 19, thirteen of the American hostages, all of them women or African Americans, were unexpectedly released by the militants and allowed safe passage out of Iran. The occupiers claimed in several communiqués that women and blacks in the United States were victims of American imperialism and that they should, therefore, be sympathetic to "the sufferings and inflictions that the shah has brought upon our nation."[40] The thirteen freed diplomats were flown to the U.S. Air Force hospital in Wiesbaden, West Germany, and then on to Washington. Their release was accompanied by a threat. If the United States took military action against Iran, said the militants, they would execute all of the remaining hostages, blow up the U.S. embassy and seize all other Americans in Iran, whom they estimated to number three hundred.[41] (They also advocated "Nuremburg-type" trials for Jimmy Carter and Richard Helms.)[42] Ayatollah Khomeini backed the militants' threats. "Our youth have announced that if such a thing [an attack] happened they would destroy all the hostages together with the embassy," he said. "We would not be able to restrain our youth because of an upsurge of their feelings. Let [the Americans] try and we shall wipe them out. We shall die but we shall kill them as well."[43]

The day after Khomeini's chilling pronouncement, November 23, Jimmy Carter met with his top advisers at Camp David. The president himself proposed measures that might be taken against Iran if the hostages were harmed, including mining the country's harbours and imposing a naval blockade. Carter also committed himself to "a direct military attack on Iran" should any of the hostages be executed.[44] Because the White House still had no direct communication with Khomeini, Carter sent a secret message via "several of our friends" to Abolhassan Bani-Sadr. It stated that "any harm done to any hostage would result in direct retaliatory action."[45] Some officials in Washington later credited Carter's warning with attenuating Iranian threats to try the hostages as spies. "If the hostages had been put on trial, if some of them had been executed," Henry Precht later reflected, "that would have meant war. I don't think President Carter would have hesitated a minute before sending in the planes."[46]

The return to the United States of the thirteen black and women hostages on Thanksgiving morning gave American officials their first solid information on the conditions in which the hostages were being held. Stansfield Turner later described what he learned from these debriefings as "appalling."[47] Even those hostages with no connection to U.S. intelligence suffered long periods of immobilization, sleep deprivation and solitary confinement. "It is clear that they were subjected to very sophisticated and subtle techniques and their treatment at the very least has been somewhat more harsh than previously reported," said White House press secretary Jody Powell. "It's very reminiscent of some of the more sophisticated techniques used to break down prisoners in the past, including almost total isolation, no communication with fellow hostages and attempts to prove through forged documents and other things that their government had abandoned them."[48] An unnamed U.S. official told the press that the captors were "highly sophisticated" and "meticulously trained"—evidence that if students had been the original occupiers, they had been supplanted by professionals. "Their knowledge of interrogation techniques certainly goes beyond being a freshman in university," he said.[49]

None of this surprised Ken Taylor or Michael Shenstone, both of whom had for weeks been "greatly concerned about reports of harsh treatment of hostages in their confinement."[50] On November 28, Taylor and eleven other Western ambassadors met with Abolhassan Bani-Sadr, pressing him to act forcefully to improve the conditions of the hostages' captivity. "We noted that they were receiving worse treatment than prisoners of war," said Taylor.[51] Bani-Sadr insisted that the hostage-taking was the "will of the people" but promised to discuss the ambassadors' concerns with Ayatollah Khomeini the same afternoon. "When pressed about the possibility of a trial," an exasperated Taylor later wrote Shenstone, "he said you worry too much."

Taylor signed off with a cold shot at the acting foreign minister. "In summary, Bani-Sadr moved from realism to fantasy."[52]

Chapter 12
STALEMATE

Abolhassan Bani-Sadr resigned as Iran's acting foreign minister just hours after meeting with Ken Taylor and the other Western diplomats. Sadegh Ghotbzadeh was appointed in his place, while Bani-Sadr retained the finance portfolio. The forty-two-year-old Ghotbzadeh, who had attended university in Washington, DC, and Nelson, BC, and spoke English fluently, immediately became the most recognizable Iranian official connected with the hostage crisis. "Tall and massive, with black hair and soft eyes," journalist Carole Jerome later wrote of Ghotbzadeh, "he looked like an elegant bear in a light cashmere coat."[1] Ken Taylor's first impression was equally strong. "He was almost Hollywood-cast as an underworld figure," said Taylor. "He was never exactly clean-shaven. He was that way before it became an Iranian way of appearance. There was so much speculation about how he financed himself and how he got so close to Khomeini, which side was he really on and how did he make a living. His past was really murky. His dress was really Western, not flashy, but he was one of the few who was well set out."[2]

Ghotbzadeh became acting foreign minister at a critical time. On the one hand, despite the chaos in Iran, Ayatollah Khomeini was deftly consolidating his theocratic state. A new Iranian constitution was approved in a national referendum held on December 2. Unlike the "democratic" version that Khomeini's inner circle had drafted in Paris, it contained a provision on *velayat-e faqih*, giving the imam the divine right to rule and the power to disqualify candidates for the office of president, among other powers.[3] On the other hand, the hostage crisis was deadlocked. The few promising channels for resolving it—from the PLO and various private interventions to the United Nations—had turned out to be dead ends. Officials in the Carter administration hoped that Ghotbzadeh would give them access to those in power in Tehran. "We had been told," said Hal Saunders, "that Khomeini treated Ghotbzadeh like his own son. We knew we had to find access to the group around Khomeini, and Ghotbzadeh seemed to have the double advantage of that entrée and of holding the position of Foreign Minister."[4]

Just days after his appointment, Ghotbzadeh created a stir in Tehran and Washington by announcing that Bruce Laingen, Vic Tomseth and Mike Howland were free to leave the foreign ministry any time they liked but that he could not guarantee their safety. "How can you hold hostages who are of clerical level under charges of espionage and yet at the same time allow the most senior officer at the embassy to depart freely?" an incredulous Ken Taylor cabled Ottawa when he heard Ghotbzadeh's statement.[5] The militants at the U.S. embassy were no more enamoured of Ghotbzadeh than they were of Bani-Sadr, and they used his statement as an occasion to assert their own authority. "The spying chargé d'affaires of the USA and his colleagues who are staying in that ministry are the hostages of the Iranian people," they announced in a communiqué.[6] Ambassador Taylor immediately grasped the significance of the students' challenge. "Foreign Minister Ghotbzadeh is recognized as an opportunist," he said, "but at least he can comprehend Western concepts. Total rejection of his statements by the occupiers, five times this week to be precise, does not bode well for his tenure. His successor is likely to wear a turban."[7]

The atmosphere in Washington was little better than in Tehran. The day that Ghotbzadeh replaced Bani-Sadr, the White House learned that the shah was now well enough to leave the United States. He had been expected to return to Mexico, but the Mexicans had inexplicably refused his re-entry, saying that his visa was no longer valid. "I was outraged," said President Carter. "The Mexicans had no diplomatic personnel in Iran, had moved all their people out of the country, and did not need Iranian oil."[8] Egypt's Anwar Sadat, who had a great deal more to lose, offered to take the shah in again, but Carter did not want to burden him with this responsibility. "For days," Hal Saunders later complained, "all our energies were absorbed not in trying to work out a [release] scenario with the Iranians but in finding a new home for the shah."[9] In the end, President Carter dispatched White House chief of staff Hamilton Jordan to Panama, where he met in person with General Omar Torrijos and asked that Panama take in the shah. Torrijos agreed to do so, as a favour to Carter. The shah flew to Panama City on December 15.

At 9 p.m. on November 28, a visibly exhausted Jimmy Carter held a televised press conference on the hostage crisis. "The actions of Iran have shocked the civilized world," he said. "For a government to applaud mob violence and terrorism, for a government to actually support and, in effect, participate in the taking and holding of hostages is unprecedented in human history." For the first time in a public statement, Carter spoke explicitly of the hostages' plight. "We are deeply concerned about the inhuman and degrading conditions imposed on the hostages," he said. "The Government of Iran must recognize the gravity of the situation, which it has itself created, and the grave consequences which will result if harm comes to any of the hostages." At the end of the prepared speech, the president invited questions from journalists. One quoted Khomeini's taunt to the effect that Carter lacked the guts to use military force against Iran. The president ducked. "It would not be advisable for me to explore publicly all of the options open to our country," he said. He was then asked if he regretted his decision to allow the shah into the United States. "No," Carter replied. "I took the right decision. I have no regrets about it nor apologies to make."[10]

Publicly, the Carter administration spent early December pressing its case against Iran at the UN and the International Court of Justice (ICJ). On December 4, Resolution 457 passed in the UN Security Council, calling for the release of the hostages and the peaceful resolution of issues between Iran and the United States. Eleven days later, the ICJ ruled that the hostages should be freed and the U.S. embassy returned. Iran ignored both rulings, claiming that international law had been corrupted to serve the interests of the United States.

Behind the scenes, Zbigniew Brzezinski resuscitated his idea of a covert operation against Iran along the lines of the 1953 coup. This time he was even able to persuade Cyrus Vance to consider it. When Stansfield Turner at the CIA learned of the proposal, however, he stated categorically that Brzezinski was deluded. "What made this new idea naïve," he said, "was that the situation in Iran in 1979 was so different from that in 1953. Covert actions to overthrow governments work best when the situation is unstable and only a small push is needed to change it, as was true with Mossadegh. Covert action is far less likely to bring about the reorientation of a government that enjoys wide support, as did Khomeini's."[11] Brzezinski tried to press American allies into support for his plan but failed. Seeing that Turner could not be won over, Brzezinski set up his own steering group at the National Security Council to work on covert planning. Turner, in turn, dismissed everything that came out of this group as unrealistic. "Most were feats of derring-do, such as sabotaging public facilities in Iran, though there was little hope that any such action would seriously affect Iran, let alone achieve the release of the hostages."[12]

~ ~ ~

In Ottawa, meanwhile, the opposition Liberals were doing everything in their power to confound the government's efforts to keep a lid on Canada's role in the hostage crisis. Day after day, Pierre Trudeau and his lieutenants attacked Prime Minister Joe Clark and External Affairs Minister Flora MacDonald for doing too little for the United States. And every day their top foreign-affairs advisers kept them abreast of Canada's ever-deepening involvement. "The fact that we have given sanctuary to houseguests and represent Israel in Iran are two points of specifically Canadian vulnerability," wrote Allan Gotlieb in a "Canadian Eyes Only" memo dated December 4, 1979. "The discovery of the first and recollection of the latter could lead to our premises and personnel becoming instant targets."[13] Joe Clark left much of the day-to-day handling of the crisis to MacDonald, and was thus spared at least some of his minister's worry. MacDonald later recalled being acutely anxious throughout the hostage crisis because she feared that she might inadvertently betray the secrets she bore.

Ambassador Taylor, on the other hand, was insulated from the political fallout from the crisis by Michael Shenstone and Allan Gotlieb, and also, implicitly, by the prime minister. "I really didn't have much to do with Joe Clark," said the ambassador, "because everything was through Shenstone."[14] Asked recently whether he knew that Clark was making things easy for him in Tehran, Taylor was emphatic. "I never, at any time, had anything other than support for what I was doing from Joe Clark. There was never any second-guessing. They said, look, for better or worse we've got this guy in Tehran, and we hope that he can pull it off!"[15]

The Liberals' attacks on the government were led by Marc Lalonde and Allan MacEachen, who demanded that Joe Clark take the lead in rallying Canada's allies in a multilateral protest against Iran. Pierre Trudeau entered the fray on November 21, addressing himself to the prime minister in the House of Commons. "I hope he will ... tell the world that in this case it is not a matter of supporting the United States alone," said Trudeau, "but it is a matter of supporting the concept of civilized international law without which all order in the world would end."[16] Clark thanked the former prime minister for his wise counsel. "I can assure the House that the Government of Canada has acted on a wide range of fronts to make exactly that point known to the authorities of Iran," he said.[17]

Trudeau kept up the attack, demanding repeatedly that the government be more aggressive in protesting the hostage-taking. On November 26, after one of Trudeau's many speeches on the subject, Clark decided that he would simply take the former prime minister into his confidence. In the middle of Question Period, as the television cameras rolled, Clark got up from his seat, walked across the floor of the House of Commons, sat down beside Trudeau and told him that the Canadian government had authorized Ambassador Taylor to provide sanctuary to the fugitive Americans in Tehran. "I think I told him quite starkly what had happened," Clark later recalled. "We were trying to hold this as closely as we could to avoid some kind of leak."[18]

To Clark's astonishment, Trudeau behaved subsequently as if nothing had been disclosed at all. The very next day, in fact, November 27, Trudeau berated Flora MacDonald in the House for her government's supposed aloofness. "We are condemning the actions of the government of Iran in not taking firm steps to set free the hostages," Trudeau exhorted, "but we will soon be condemning this government if it continues to take such stand-offish attitudes."[19] MacDonald could hardly contain her anger. "I am sure that the former prime minister recognizes that the Prime Minister has made statements on this subject, and that he has been staunch in his support of the United States throughout the last 24 long days through actions many of which cannot be publicly conveyed, and of which the honourable member should be aware are taking place in everything that we do."[20] Trudeau, unrepentant, again confronted MacDonald, demanding "collective action" from the Canadian government.[21] "What got me," Flora MacDonald later said of Trudeau's performance, "was that Clark had briefed him in the House of Commons, yet he kept asking questions as to why we weren't doing more. That really upset me."[22]

Ken Taylor was not impressed by Trudeau's behaviour either. "Trudeau was playing a dangerous game, suggesting that we weren't doing enough. You'd assume that he would be prepared to just let it rest."[23] It remains a mystery to the former ambassador why Trudeau would reduce himself to scoring cheap political points when lives hung in the balance. He is not alone in this view.

~ ~ ~

After moving into the Sheardown and Taylor residences, the houseguests fell into the monotonous routines that would characterize their many weeks underground. They listened to the radio, watched television and read newspapers voraciously. As an antidote to their near-total isolation, they played board games and engaged their hosts in lengthy conversations about their own situation, the progress of efforts to resolve the crisis, and the state of their colleagues at the embassy compound and foreign ministry.

Boredom was now the houseguests' worst enemy. "Each day is the same, and you have no control over the situation," Cora Lijek said of her time in hiding at the Sheardowns'. "There's really nothing much you can do."[24] Zena Sheardown sympathized. "They had to be suffering from cabin fever because they had to stay indoors and out of sight for so much of the time."[25] Occasionally, as on Thanksgiving Day and Christmas, all of the houseguests would reunite at the Sheardown residence, where they would enjoy some holiday cheer with the handful of Canadians who knew their secret. "On special occasions," said Mark Lijek, "John would also invite people from other diplomatic missions who knew about us, especially Australians, New Zealanders and the Danish ambassador."[26] At other times, the houseguests' confinement got the better of them. "I think everyone was very restless, not knowing when they could come out," Pat Taylor later observed. "They wanted to go out to celebrate New Year's. I said to Ken, 'They've got to wait, because if anything happens on the way, or coming home   if the car breaks down—they're stuck.' I know they were very keen to get out and party, but they stayed put."[27]

Both the Sheardowns and the Taylors got along well with the houseguests, which helped to alleviate some of the tension that inevitably arose from their precarious situation. Of the four hosts, only Zena Sheardown spent her days at home with the houseguests, which may explain why she felt the insecurity of the arrangement most intensely. "I don't think I had a moment's peace for the entire time," she said. "I don't think any Canadian—living in Canada—can appreciate what it was like for us. We were a very small foreign community, and there was a lot of hostility to foreigners there. They had just had a revolution, and they didn't want foreigners there because there was always fear of a counterrevolution. So we had to be very circumspect. We had to keep a very low profile at all times. Even getting from one part of the city to the next was fraught with all sorts of dangers. I think people forget what it was like then."[28]

Secrecy and discretion were also paramount in the Taylor household. "There were lots of questions," Pat recalled. "The servants would say, 'They never go out!'"[29] One evening Ken's friend Peter Jennings, then an ABC News correspondent in Tehran, went to dinner at the

Taylors' house. For the entire visit the Staffords remained out of sight, hidden in a second-floor bedroom. (When Jennings found out later that Taylor had been withholding the scoop of a lifetime, he playfully chastised the ambassador.) On another occasion, in early January 1980, the phone at the Taylors' residence rang, Pat answered it and a man who would not identify himself asked to speak to Joe Stafford. "I don't know who you are talking about," replied Pat. "There is no one by that name here." She later observed that because the voice was that of an English-speaking North American, without any hint of an Iranian accent, neither she nor Ken was overly concerned about the incident. "Ken told me that the real worry," she said, "was that the media had the story."[30]

Ken Taylor's embassy colleague Roger Lucy was one of the house-guests' regular visitors. Lucy had been on holiday in Europe when the U.S. embassy was taken over on November 4. He later recalled that the news of the Americans being hidden by Canadian diplomats very nearly leaked in mid-November. "I was visiting friends in Switzerland and later Belgium," said Lucy. "A friend posted at NATO in Brussels showed me a summary of all of the interesting diplomatic cables, and there was a reference to the houseguests. It was the first I'd heard of it. It's really a miracle that it never slipped out." Once he was back in Tehran, Lucy was happy to serve as the houseguests' part-time pro-tector. "A couple of times I had to take the ones from Sheardown's place over to my place because the Sheardowns' landlord wanted to show the place to prospective tenants," he said. "So I packed them into my car and drove them over to my apartment." Lucy was casual about moving the Americans through Tehran by car from time to time but admits that there were some tense moments. "One day it was snowing. We got stuck in the driveway and some Iranians had to push us out."[31]

The morning of November 21, Ken Taylor got an unexpected call from Kaj Sundberg, Sweden's ambassador to Iran. He was calling to tell his Canadian counterpart that a U.S. agricultural attaché named

Henry Lee Schatz had been in hiding at the home of one of his staffers since November 4.

"I don't mean to be facetious," Sundberg told Taylor, "but you know that you and the Americans are one and the same in terms of the Iranian perception. We just can't go on harbouring this diplomat."

"Well, it really doesn't matter that much," Taylor replied. "What's the difference between five and six?"

"What do you mean, you have five?" a dumbfounded Sundberg asked Taylor. He had had no idea that any other American diplomats had evaded the militants.[32]

Lee Schatz was a lanky thirty-one-year-old Midwesterner with a gregarious, sometimes mischievous demeanour. He worked out of a leased office in a building occupied by the Swedes, which happened to overlook the U.S. embassy compound. The morning of November 4, he watched from his office window as the students poured through the main gate and scattered to the various buildings inside. He also eavesdropped on all of the radio net traffic, since he had been given a standard-issue "lunchbox" like the others. Early in the afternoon, Bruce Laingen directed him to lock up his documents and leave the building. On his way out, he bumped into some Swedish diplomats, who welcomed him into their offices to wait out the occupation. He remained that first night in the Swedish embassy. The next day, the Swedes got word that Schatz's name was on the occupiers' list of wanted Americans. They agreed to move him immediately to the apartment of Swiss consular officer Cecilia Lithander, where he ended up staying for over two weeks. ("Cecilia was his babysitter," Roger Lucy later joked. "She basically took him home. She was a great cook. I don't think he was terribly happy to be separated from her.")[33] Schatz kept in close telephone contact with the other houseguests, particularly Joe Stafford, but for security reasons they never divulged to each other where they were hiding. "I was just as surprised as anyone when it turned out to be the Canadians that had been taking care of everyone," Schatz said.[34]

The day after Kaj Sundberg told Ken Taylor about Schatz, John Sheardown appeared at Cecilia Lithander's apartment building. Nobody had told the young American that he was going to be moved, so Sheardown used the opportunity to play a practical joke on him. Without introducing himself, he escorted Schatz out of the building and ordered him brusquely into a waiting car. Schatz assumed that his mysterious driver was from the CIA, and imagined that he was about to be spirited out of Tehran. "I was pretty paranoid," he later recalled.[35] Only after they had been in the car for a while did Sheardown break a grin and introduce himself. The two had a good laugh, stopped at the Canadian embassy to pick up some clothing for the other houseguests and then drove on to Sheardown's house. There Schatz was reunited with Bob Anders and the Lijeks. He was the last of the fugitive American diplomats to be brought in from the cold.

Only three Western HOMs other than Bruce Laingen knew about the houseguests' existence: ambassadors Troels Munk of Denmark, Chris Beeby of New Zealand and Sir John Graham of the UK. Ken Taylor later recalled how Munk and Beeby in particular went well beyond their official mandates to assist in sheltering the six Americans. "They were caught in a box," said Taylor. "Iran was New Zealand's largest customer for lamb, and it was a big market for the Danes' dairy products. So although both governments were very supportive of Canadian efforts, the two ambassadors had to quietly go beyond any [formal] instructions, quite understandably, because their countries didn't want to jeopardize a very valuable market by being complicit in what the Iranians would have seen as some destructive espionage ring. Both of the ambassadors were very careful not to jeopardize their countries' position, but at the same time—I can say this thirty years later—they went considerably beyond their mandate. They'd do anything almost. They were just extraordinarily helpful."[36] Ambassador Beeby visited the Sheardown home regularly, playing chess with Bob Anders and bringing "little delicacies" that added variety to the houseguests' menu, as John Sheardown put it.[37]

Douglas Taylor was another person to befriend the houseguests, if only for a short period. The ambassador's son had left Iran after New Year's 1979 to attend school in France. He had returned to Tehran for summer vacation, and planned to do so again at Christmas break, little knowing that his parents and the Sheardowns were playing host to six fugitive Americans. Douglas has recalled recently that neither he nor his parents were particularly anxious about his returning to Tehran during the hostage crisis. "Anybody would know that if you are going back to Tehran for Christmas," he said, "it's not going to be a fun place to go for a couple of weeks. You knew that there had been a revolution. You knew that it had been bloody. You knew that everything had shut down and that there was a hostage crisis ongoing. I don't think anyone would say, 'Hey, I'm off to Tehran and I'm going to have a great time.'" Not until two days before Christmas, in fact, when Douglas was en route to the ambassador's residence from Mehrabad Airport, did his parents inform him of the presence of the houseguests. "I was certainly surprised," he later recalled. "It was a little unusual. I was never sworn to secrecy, but it was suggested that I keep this to myself. It was obvious that I was not going to go around and share that information with anybody else."[38]

As soon as he arrived at the ambassador's residence, Douglas was introduced to Joe and Kathy Stafford. The couple recognized immediately that their presence in the house might be stressful for a youth of fifteen and sought to put him at ease. "They were very friendly and easygoing," said Douglas of the Staffords. "With me, they were trying to be straightforward and reasonably relaxed. It might be that they were more relaxed when I was there than at other times, given that I was younger. There wasn't any tension in the house." His memories of Christmas 1979 are those of a typical North American teenager, betraying more anxiety about boredom than danger. "It was just like any other Christmas," he said. "I remember it being bad weather most of the time, grey skies. When I had gone back in the summer, the political instability could be felt everywhere, but not everything had been shut down. Whereas, in winter, there were fewer things to do even if things were open, and you add to that that everything had been shut down, then you are spending a lot more time in the house. You really were somewhat confined."[39]

One way Douglas and the Staffords broke the monotony of their Tehran Christmas was by playing cards and board games, by this time the salvation of all of the houseguests' sanity. They grew particularly adept at a game called Persepolis, an Iranian variation on Monopoly complete with oil rigs in place of Boardwalk and Park Place. In one of his last visits with Shah Pahlavi, the monarch had presented Ambassador Taylor with a special gift, a Persepolis board in handcrafted leather with solid gold game pieces. Douglas and the Staffords whiled away hours on that game over the Christmas holiday, Ken later recalled. When Douglas left Iran for France and the start of a new school term, just after New Year's Day 1980, he did so in the knowledge that, however limited his own horizons had been in cold, grey Tehran, he had brought a great deal of joy to his parents, and more than a little to his new American friends.

"The six Americans were like guests who had come to dinner and would not leave," Stansfield Turner later remarked. "Although the Canadians were standing staunchly by us, there was concern that our people would be found while in hiding or while attempting to escape. If the Canadians became implicated in our hostage problem, their diplomats might end up being hostages too."[40] The houseguests themselves knew, of course, that their hosts' necks were on the block along with their own. "I think that we assumed—and the Canadians assumed—that if we were ever found, we would all end up in the same place together," Cora Lijek recalled. "They took a great risk."[41]

Bored and anxious though they sometimes were, the houseguests did not for a moment forget that the plight of their imprisoned colleagues was vastly worse. With every passing week, they knew how fortunate they were to have escaped the embassy takeover. So did their Canadian hosts. Together they played countless games of chess and Scrabble and Persepolis, drained what was left of the Canadians' reserves of contraband alcohol and plotted their escape from Tehran.

~ ~ ~

When the Iranian students stormed the U.S. embassy compound on November 4, nobody could have imagined that the standoff would drag into Christmas. In the United States, the hostage crisis cast a pall over the holiday season, especially for President Carter. Instead of observing the usual tradition of lighting the White House Christmas tree before hundreds of festive onlookers, he instructed that the tree be left darkened—to signify, as Carter himself put it, "our sorrow about the hostages' loss of freedom."[42] It would be lit, he said, when the hostages came home.

Now, eight weeks into the standoff, Ken Taylor's emotions were decidedly mixed. "There is little joy in Tehran this Christmas Eve," he wrote in an unusually gloomy missive to Ottawa on December 24. "In Tehran this exceptional crisis is entering its 52nd day to the tiresome echoes of government announcements and chants from the streets and the mosques. There are signs of battle fatigue on all sides with implications therein: diplomats display progressively greater despair; journalistic horizons reach far beyond reasonable expectations; occupiers seek, in unpredictable fashion, new avenues to broadcast their message and exploit their hostages."[43] Later on Christmas Eve, however, Taylor met up with Roger Lucy. After sharing some seasonal libations, they dashed off a telex to Michael Shenstone:

AERIAL INFILTRATOR—IRANIAN AIR FORCE REPORTS INTER-
CEPTION 2300 24DEC OF FLYING OBJECT OF HITHERTO
UNKNOWN DESIGN. AIRCRAFT WAS FORCED DOWN OVER

PROHIBITED QOM AIRSPACE. PILOT IDENTIFIED AS NICHO-
LAS MYRA CARRIED NO/NO IDENTIFICATION PAPERS. HE IS
BEING HELD PENDING TRIAL BY REVOLUTIONARY COURT ON
CHARGES OF OVERFLIGHT WITHOUT PERMISSION, ILLEGAL
ENTRY, SMUGGLING AND IMPORTING REINDEER WITHOUT
PROPER VETERINARY CLEARANCES. MERRY CHRISTMAS
FROM TEHRAN.

A seeming bright spot in this otherwise dismal Christmas in
Tehran came when the militants announced that they would allow
three American clergy to visit the hostages. The clerics would be the
first people other than their jailers to see the captives since the occupation began, thus expectations ran high—too high, as it turned out.
One of the clergymen, Reverend William Sloane Coffin of New York,
had once been a CIA officer and thus seemed wise to the fact that he
was being asked to participate in a Potemkin Christmas. The others,
William Howard and Thomas Gumbleton, were not. The entire scene
was carefully scripted and controlled by the militants. Small groups of
hostages met the clerics in short intervals over Christmas Day, never
out of the sight of their jailers. Many of the captive Americans understood the event as a propaganda exercise. Some refused to attend. One
participant did manage to tell Coffin in confidence that the whole
event was being staged for the benefit of the TV cameras and that,
in fact, the hostages were all being treated appallingly. The evening
of December 28, U.S. television networks broadcast the occupiers'
footage of the hostages' Christmas. Americans were incensed at the
spectacle. "There was a tremendous amount of manipulation going
on," said Ken Taylor. "There was a lot of role playing, and everybody
was being exploited. It was really distressing to me. That was one of
the low points."[44]

Hal Saunders' main recollection of the Christmas period was
the great stress it brought the State Department because it focused

Americans' attention on the number of hostages. Until then, Washington had been cagey about the exact head count in order to conceal the existence of the houseguests. The visiting clergymen, however, had counted only forty-three hostages, a number that even the State Department knew to be low. Sadegh Ghotbzadeh, who was aware that some American diplomats were hiding in Tehran, complicated things by stating publicly that he did not know how many hostages there were. The State Department had little choice but to adopt an obfuscation strategy, discouraging "pessimistic speculation" and "maintaining their count at 50."[45] When Peter Towe, Canada's ambassador in Washington, asked privately about the numbers, he was told that the fifty did not include either the houseguests or the three men being held at the foreign ministry.

Christmas in Washington was also complicated by the Soviet invasion of Afghanistan on December 27, which signalled a new and unexpected escalation of the Cold War. "The brutality of the act was bad enough," said President Carter, "but the threat of this Soviet invasion to the rest of the region was very clear—and had grim consequences. A successful takeover of Afghanistan would give the Soviets a deep penetration between Iran and Pakistan, and pose a threat to the rich oil fields of the Persian Gulf area and to the crucial waterways through which so much of the world's energy supplies had to pass."[46] How the Soviets' bold move into Afghanistan bore on the hostage crisis in neighbouring Iran was immediately apparent to Zbigniew Brzezinski. The United States had little choice but to "mobilize Islamic resistance against the Soviets," he acknowledged, "and that dictated avoiding anything which might split Islamic opposition to Soviet expansionism. In turn, it was more important than before to avoid an Iranian–American military confrontation."[47]

~ ~ ~

Battered by the myriad foreign-policy crises afflicting the United States, the Carter administration decided to ratchet up the diplomatic pressure on Iran. On Monday, December 31, the UN Security Council passed Resolution 461, a first step toward imposing economic sanctions on Iran. The same day, UN secretary-general Kurt Waldheim went, uninvited, to Tehran. Iranians saw Waldheim's presence as an affront, and they let him know it. Even before he arrived in Tehran, the national press had dredged up old pictures of Waldheim fawning over the shah and his sister. Once the secretary-general was in Iran, he was harassed by hostile mobs everywhere he went. "It was a travesty," Ken Taylor later said. "It was sad, very sad."[48] A dejected Waldheim met privately with Jimmy Carter and Cyrus Vance on Sunday, January 6. "He spent the first hour with me in a very emotional and excited recitation of his horrible experiences there," Carter later recalled, "at times with tears in his eyes. Waldheim believed his life had been in danger on three different occasions, and that he was lucky to be alive."[49] Sanctions would do nothing to free the hostages, said Waldheim. He thus urged Carter to delay the Security Council vote on economic sanctions to allow time for a possible diplomatic solution.

One aspect of the secretary-general's visit seemed promising. Sadegh Ghotbzadeh, working quietly with Iranian chief of protocol Ali Shokouhian, had arranged a meeting between Waldheim and Laingen at the foreign ministry. Ghotbzadeh was reportedly at pains "to demonstrate proper treatment of the three USA officials" because, as the Americans later learned through a back channel, he disdained communism and was deeply concerned about the Soviet invasion of Afghanistan.[50] He was not alone. In early January, a "senior Islamic statesman" visited Washington secretly to discuss the prospects of a mediated deal on the hostage crisis.[51] The visitor informed the White House that Ayatollah Khomeini's refusal to talk directly with the U.S. meant that the only remaining option was to work through a third-party mediator. What was needed was a connection to an

Iranian who had access to Khomeini but who also understood the West. The visitor thought Abolhassan Bani-Sadr or Ayatollah Mohammad Beheshti were the Americans' best bets.

Whether coincidentally or not, Ken Taylor had drawn the same conclusion. Fed up with trying to mobilize the diplomatic corps, the Canadian ambassador proposed to work with New Zealand ambassador Chris Beeby to establish a "negotiating link" to Ayatollah Beheshti. In a flurry of cables among Tehran, Ottawa and Washington, it was agreed that such a link would be used "only for substantive USA content rather than simply to reiterate USA positions taken in public."[52] Unfortunately, Taylor's meetings with Beheshti yielded only "very vague stuff."[53] Like Ayatollah Khomeini, Beheshti was still talking about possible spy trials or an international investigation of the shah—measures wholly unacceptable to the United States. When Peter Constable of the Iran Working Group heard about Taylor's back-channel overture to Beheshti, on January 14, his response was lukewarm. "Constable thanked us for the proposal," the Canadian embassy in Washington told Ottawa, "but left us with the impression that the USA did not feel any particular concern about channels. We doubt whether our suggestion for a negotiating link will be followed up in the near future."[54] The initiative died then and there. Taylor never mentioned it again.

Meanwhile, the Carter administration had opened what they hoped was a truly effective back channel. Two Paris lawyers, Christian Bourguet and Hector Villalon, told Hamilton Jordan early in the new year that they had good contacts within the Iranian government and would be pleased to try to broker a deal on the hostage crisis. On January 19, Jordan and Hal Saunders flew secretly (and in disguise) to London to meet the two Frenchmen. There they agreed to pursue a new dialogue.[55] Villalon and Bourguet demonstrated that they had direct access to Sadegh Ghotbzadeh, but the Americans were never sure whether this translated into access to Khomeini. Cyrus Vance later recalled being "skeptical" about just how much the Frenchmen could deliver.[56] Ken Taylor was even more skeptical.

Saunders, Jordan and the French lawyers worked for weeks on what they called "the scenario"—a carefully scripted quid pro quo that would allow the hostages' release on terms agreeable to both Iran and the United States. The scenario envisaged Kurt Waldheim sending a commission of inquiry to Tehran to allow the Iranians to air their grievances against the shah and the United States. The commissioners would then meet the hostages and report to the Revolutionary Council that they were being kept in inhumane conditions. The Council would order the hostages transferred from the occupiers' control to a Tehran hospital. The commission would then issue its report to the UN, and the Iranians would pardon and deport the hostages.[57] On January 28, Saunders and Vance flew to New York to brief Waldheim on the scenario.

President Carter approved the terms of the scenario but continued to pursue alternative avenues as well. On January 12, the Soviets vetoed a UN Security Council vote to impose sanctions on Iran. Carter therefore decided to apply sanctions unilaterally, and urged U.S. allies to follow suit. He was disappointed but not surprised when most of them declined. He and Cyrus Vance also drafted a new statement of terms on which they were willing to see the hostage crisis resolved. On January 13, Kurt Waldheim delivered it to the Iranians. The six-point statement was predicated on "the safe and immediate release from Iran of all Americans held hostage," as expected. But it also expressed sympathy for the Iranians' concerns about "the practices of the former regime" and a willingness to "work out in advance firm understandings on a forum in which those grievances might subsequently be aired." After the release of the hostages, the United States would unfreeze Iranian assets, confer with the Iranian government on "the current threat posed by the Soviet invasion of Afghanistan" and resume the shipment of military parts to Iran. The president also agreed to "make a statement at an appropriate moment that it understood the grievances felt by the people of Iran and that [the United States] respected the integrity of Iran and the right of the people of Iran to choose their own form of government."[58]

These were generous concessions from Jimmy Carter—politically because they smacked of appeasement; personally, because they cut directly across his hardening sense of outrage. On January 16, the president made the following entry in his personal diary: "I got a letter from one of the hostages which remarkably was mailed in Iran and had not been censored. It was written the day after Christmas. He pointed out that they were denied basic human rights; confined in a semi-darkened room without sunshine or fresh air; were given no news of any kind; hands kept tied day and night; bright lights burning in the room all night long; constant noise so they are unable to sleep properly; not permitted to speak to another American, even those in the same room. He slept on a hard floor for 33 out of the 53 nights. Has been given only three brief periods of exercise outdoors in the 53 days. His personal mail is being withheld. He points out that he's not been visited by any representative of the U.S. government, apparently not understanding that we have not been able to visit him. That he's seen no friendly diplomatic representative of any other country."[59]

The letter was from Robert Ode, one of the immigration officials captured while fleeing the U.S. consulate on November 4. Coming directly from a hostage, and written in his own words, the letter had a dramatic impact on the president. "I was sickened and additionally alarmed to hear about the bestiality of the Iranian captors," he later reflected. "How could any decent human beings, and particularly leaders of a nation, treat innocent people like this— week after week?"[60]

~ ~ ~

Ken Taylor's sentiments mirrored the president's exactly. "I passed the USA embassy compound yesterday and what a desolate, forlorn and bitter site it is," Taylor wrote Michael Shenstone on January 15. "Much has been said concerning the psychological hardship and deprivation that the American embassy staff face after 73 days of imprisonment but the advent of winter with its cold dreary presence must add to their physical discomfort which is already considerable."[61]

For seventy-three days the Canadian ambassador had followed the machinations of the Iran–U.S. standoff more intently than any other third-party observer. He had played a decisive role in the effort to achieve a diplomatic solution to what was, after all, a crisis of diplomacy. Despite his best efforts, he had failed in this endeavour, his counterparts in the diplomatic corps fragmenting into impotent factions, their political masters unwilling even to put their names to a united *démarche*. Taylor could take heart in the unparalleled efforts he and his Canadian colleagues had made on behalf of the houseguests and the three U.S. diplomats imprisoned at the Iranian foreign ministry, but he knew as well that there were limits to President Carter's capacity to stand idly by while a handful of Iranian militants thumbed their noses at the United States.

Ayatollah Khomeini's tough talk about Iranians' willingness to perish in a fight to the death with the United States gave an air of unreality to the crisis, but Taylor believed that time was not on Tehran's side. "The U.S. was going to do something, and heaven help if they bombed Iran," he thought. "If the hostages were shot, even inadvertently, it would bring some sort of retaliation of that nature. A far better response was some sort of raid, as ill fated as it could be, to at least surgically remove these people. And how were they going to plan for that?"[62]

When the Americans went looking for some help in preparing just such a rescue mission, Ken Taylor did not have to think twice.

PART FOUR
INTELLIGENCE

Chapter 13
THIS IS WAR

In addition to the Special Coordinating Committee (SCC) created at the outset of the hostage crisis, National Security Adviser Zbigniew Brzezinski formed "a small and highly secret group" dubbed the "mini-SCC," which he chaired.[1] Its membership was limited to Secretary of Defense Harold Brown and Chairman of the Joint Chiefs of Staff (JCS) General David Jones. Its mandate was to develop military options for the crisis, but only in the utmost secrecy. "I feared the pattern of massive leakage in the U.S. government, the endless multiplication of papers, the rather loose enforcement of limited access to restricted information, as well as the unavoidable penetration by hostile agents, would compromise our mission," Brzezinski later recalled. "The specter that haunted me was that at the critical juncture the Iranians would be forewarned, probably by the Soviets, and the mission would be destroyed because it lacked the essential elements of surprise and secrecy."[2] Brzezinski's handwritten notes on these mini-SCC meetings constitute the only documentary record that they even existed. They likely will never be declassified.

~ ~ ~

The first session of the mini-SCC took place on Monday, November 5, after a three-hour meeting of President Carter and his top advisers. From the beginning, the president approved extensive military contingency planning for Iran and followed it closely. Like Brzezinski, he wanted to be able to act quickly if the hostages were killed. Carter ordered the mini-SCC to begin work on three military scenarios: a rescue operation, a retaliatory response to the killing of some or all of the hostages and a plan to seize Iran's oil fields should the country fall into complete political chaos.[3] By mid-November, a short list of targets in Iran was drawn up and the U.S. armed forces placed on a two-day standby. Brzezinski took seriously the Iranians' threats that the hostages might be tried as spies and executed. He believed that a rescue mission under such circumstances would be "a moral as well as a political obligation."[4] Carter agreed. On Tuesday, November 6, just hours after Ayatollah Khomeini escalated the hostage crisis by extending his support to the occupiers, Brzezinski and Brown again met with Carter in the Oval Office. "I want to punish them as soon as our people have been released," Carter told them, "really hit them hard. They must know they cannot fool around with us."[5]

The November 8 meeting of the mini-SCC took place in the White House Situation Room. Aerial photographs of the U.S. embassy compound were studied closely, and a rescue plan began taking shape. A helicopter assault on the U.S. embassy compound by a specially trained team of commandos would extricate the hostages, fly them to a Tehran airfield and whisk them out of the country. The scenario had two obvious problems. The first was logistical—how to get American helicopters through vast deserts and into the middle of a large, hostile and densely populated city. The second, according to Brzezinski himself, was "inadequate intelligence regarding the disposition of the hostages."[6] At this point, Brzezinski, alone among the president's top advisers, believed that a rescue mission should be accompanied by a retaliatory strike on Iran. He reasoned that if the rescue mission failed, the attack would at least salvage American national honour. This option would remain on the table until April, when it would also be urged upon the president by Harold Brown and Stansfield Turner. Never could Secretary of State Cyrus Vance be persuaded to sanction a wider military intervention. What Carter thought of this combined rescue/invasion plan is not clear, but the fact that it remained on the table for months suggests that he had not decided categorically against it.

On November 11, on his way out of a regular SCC meeting, Stansfield Turner happened to overhear Brzezinski's secretary remind him of a meeting with President Carter. This was Turner's first inkling that military planning was taking place and that he was being kept in the dark. He confronted Brzezinski angrily. If the CIA was excluded from planning, he pressed the national security adviser, what in the world would he be using for intelligence? Brzezinski replied that the Defense Intelligence Agency (DIA) had the matter in hand. "I was livid," Turner later recalled.[7] He reminded Brzezinski that, as well as heading up the CIA, the job of director of central intelligence was to marshal all intelligence-gathering within federal agencies and to serve the president by always presenting that intelligence impartially. Brzezinski conceded the point and agreed to bring Turner into the loop. Presumably he would have done so sooner or later, since it was already apparent by November 11 that the rescue mission would depend upon CIA intelligence-gathering and covert action.

Later on November 11, Turner was invited into a conference call with Harold Brown and David Jones. They told the DCI that they were working on a highly secret rescue plan code-named "Rice Bowl."

(The moniker Rice Bowl was itself a diversion, meant to evoke an operation in Asia. It would be rechristened "Eagle Claw" in March 1980.) The plan required the CIA to clandestinely place forty to sixty Special Forces soldiers in Tehran and to hide them there for up to twenty-four hours. The next day, at an in-person meeting at Brzezinski's White House office, Turner learned that this was one of two military rescue scenarios being plotted. The other was a variation that would see the commandos dropped outside Tehran to work their way overland toward the embassy compound.

From the moment military planning began, it was agreed that Delta Force would be the key operational unit. Delta was, and remains, the army's elite counterterrorism outfit, commissioned in October 1977 with Colonel Charles ("Chargin' Charlie") Beckwith, an Army Ranger with a distinguished combat record, as its founding commander. Eagle Claw would be Delta's first mission, and Beckwith, a tough, chain-smoking forty-nine-year-old, would lead it. To expedite planning, Beckwith sent one of his closest comrades, Major Lewis "Bucky" Barruss, to Washington to serve as his liaison with the Joint Chiefs. Major Richard (Dick) J. Meadows, a highly decorated former Green Beret, was also involved in military planning from the beginning, serving as a "civilian adviser" to Beckwith and his small cell of Pentagon planners.[8] So, too, was General Samuel V. Wilson of the DIA, who had worked closely with Delta Force in the two years since its inception. Wilson's close personal relationship with Beckwith, and Carter's and Brzezinski's obsessions with secrecy, help to explain why Stansfield Turner was left out of the planning at the outset.

The person selected to head up rescue planning at the Pentagon was Major General James B. Vaught, reporting directly (and only) to JCS chairman General Jones to safeguard the secrecy of the mission. On November 11, U.S. Air Force special operations commander Colonel James H. Kyle was brought in to oversee the airborne components of rescue planning. Like Bucky Barruss, he

immediately joined the joint task force created by Vaught to cen-
tralize rescue planning.

For reasons unknown, Vaught did not meet Turner in person
to discuss rescue planning until November 30, twenty-six days after
the embassy was seized. By this time, the Eagle Claw rescue plan
had taken its final form. It called for eight helicopters to rendezvous
in the Iranian desert with three C-130 Hercules transport planes.
The choppers would be refuelled in the desert at a site code-named
"Desert One" and meet the Special Forces commandos there. They
would then fly to a secret staging site at Manzariyeh, fifty miles south
of Tehran, code-named "Desert Two." The Manzariyeh site was an
abandoned Iranian air force bombing range, and it included a paved
airstrip suitable for the takeoff and landing of large planes, including
the C-130s. The site was to be occupied and, if necessary, defended
against Iranian troops by a U.S. Army Ranger unit. After lying low
for a day, the commando squad led by Beckwith himself would be carried by trucks to the U.S. embassy compound in Tehran and to the
foreign ministry offices, where they would rescue all of the hostages.
The trucks were to be readied beforehand, presumably by intelligence
officers working covertly in Tehran. The hostages would be taken in the
same vehicles to a Tehran sports stadium. The choppers would then
ferry them back to Desert Two, where the Hercules would carry them
out of Iran and back home to safety. Everyone acknowledged that it
was an extremely complicated and risky plan, with almost no margin
of error and enormous potential to go badly wrong.

To the military planners' great surprise, President Carter
unexpectedly ordered an "all-stop" on rescue planning on November 22, the eighteenth day of the hostage crisis.[9] All planning, including intelligence-gathering, was simply to cease. Stansfield Turner was
not informed of this decision until almost a week later, on November 28, and was justifiably annoyed. "[A] typical lack of coordination"
is how he described the decision.[10] Turner was of two minds about

terminating rescue planning. He understood that the more undercover work the CIA was doing in Tehran, the greater the chance that it would be discovered and scuttle Vance's back-channel negotiations with the Iranians. On the other hand, Turner also knew that clandestine intelligence-gathering cannot be rushed. "We couldn't catch up by simply doing things faster," he wrote of the intelligence ops that Carter had suspended. "If clandestine operations are going to work, they must be done at a natural tempo lest they attract public attention." In the end, Turner ignored Carter's all-stop order and decided not to terminate intelligence operations in Tehran. "I knew I was sticking my neck out," he later recalled. But he also remembered Admiral Arleigh A. Burke's advice to him when he had been a naval officer. "No commanding officer is worth his salt, Turner," the admiral had said, "who does not occasionally exceed his authority."[11] In the end, Turner's instincts were vindicated. Before long, Brzezinski persuaded President Carter to resume intelligence-gathering operations in Tehran.

"The vital importance of good, sound intelligence cannot be stressed enough," Charlie Beckwith later wrote. "Without it there is nothing, with it there is something. It's the difference between failure and success, between humiliation and pride, between losing lives and saving them. Intelligence is to special operations as numbers are to a mathematician."[12] The intelligence required for Eagle Claw was extensive. According to U.S. Navy captain Paul B. Ryan, author of *The Iranian Rescue Mission,* it included the following:

> Find a remote desert site where the helicopters could re-fuel from air-dropped fuel bladders. When this proved infeasible, find a remote landing strip suitable for receiving six C-130 transport planes and eight helicopters.
>
> Insert secret agents into Tehran and arrange for their communication with Washington.
>
> Locate a hiding place within about two hours' driving

time from Tehran to shield the rescue force during fourteen hours of daylight.

Locate a suitable airfield in a friendly nation within flight distance of Iran both to serve as a launching point and, possibly, to receive the C-130s after the mission.

Locate an airstrip in a friendly nation near the Arabian Sea for refueling the C-130s.

Find out exactly, by agent reports and satellite photography, where the hostages were being held within the 27-acre embassy compound.

Transfer eight helicopters from the United States to an aircraft carrier in the Indian Ocean without arousing suspicion.[13]

This would have been a tall order under even the best of circumstances. But in mid-November 1979, the U.S. intelligence capability in Tehran was not merely reduced, it was non-existent. All of the official-cover CIA officers working out of the Tehran station (Ahern, Daugherty, Kalp and Ward) had been taken hostage. A clandestine network of five CIA officers, headed by Howard Hart, had also been operating in Tehran, but this group was recalled soon after the embassy takeover, apparently because there was so much heat on them that they were at risk of being captured.

The seizure of the official CIA station and the exodus of the unofficial network, in short, left Eagle Claw planners with no human intelligence in Tehran.

~ ~ ~

In late December, the CIA managed to place its one and only undercover officer in Tehran, a Cold War spy code-named "Bob" who had been called out of retirement personally by Stansfield Turner.

Bob has been described in various CIA histories as "short, compact and rugged looking."[14] In fact, according to some of those who worked closely with him in Tehran, he was tall and somewhat unkempt. This contradiction suggests that his true identity remains a closely held secret. What little is known about Bob has been cobbled together mainly from the memoirs of Eagle Claw participants and from a handful of declassified documents. Bob was a European who spoke several languages but he did not speak Persian. He entered Iran with a non-official cover as a European businessman who was starting up a construction company in Tehran. His normally long grey hair was closely cropped and dyed black. Accompanying Bob was an Iranian-born U.S. airman code-named "Fred," who had family in Iran.[15] Neither man had any trouble clearing Iranian customs when they entered via Tehran's Mehrabad Airport. Bob's central importance to Eagle Claw planning has been acknowledged by all of the key players in Washington, including President Carter. He was the only CIA officer active in Tehran after Howard Hart's clandestine group returned to Washington. And he appears to have remained alone in Tehran for the three months after his arrival in December, until Beckwith's undercover man, Dick Meadows, showed up for the first time.

Ever mindful of the need for total secrecy on rescue-mission planning, Jimmy Carter insisted on seeing raw intelligence as well as the processed work of intelligence analysts. "We had blueprints of our embassy buildings in Tehran," the president later wrote, "and we had talked to the black and female hostages who had been released before Christmas. . . . Much more important, we received information from someone (who cannot be identified) who was thoroughly familiar with the compound, knew where every American hostage was located, how many and what kind of guards were there at different times during the night, and the daily schedule of the hostages and their captors. This was the first time we knew the precise location of the Americans."[16] Stansfield Turner was explicit about the CIA's good fortune in being able to attract Bob out of retirement and into Tehran. "We looked desperately for CIA people whose cover would hold up under rigorous scrutiny," wrote Turner. "Most who went into Tehran in this period would not volunteer for a second shot because the chances of being recognized—and brutalized—were too great. We found Bob, though, a retired officer of foreign origin and irrepressible self-confidence. He was perfect for what had to be done. Fortunately, he was also willing. Bob traveled in and out of Tehran repeatedly during this period to make the necessary arrangements for Delta Force."[17] Turner's high opinion of his hand-picked intelligence officer never changed. "Because Bob took such risks, and his contribution was so important, when it was behind us, I took him to the Oval Office to receive thanks from the President."[18]

Charlie Beckwith's relationship with Bob has been the subject of divergent interpretations. Most of the authors who have written about Eagle Claw have suggested that Beckwith did not trust Bob's judgment, and some have gone so far as to say that at some point their professional antipathy became personal. The two men got on each other's wrong side, so the story goes, and they were never able to reconcile. Beckwith himself has challenged this interpretation directly, calling Bob's insertion into Tehran in December 1979 "a Christmas present" for Eagle Claw planners.[19] "I was introduced to him," Beckwith later recalled of Bob. "His mannerisms, the deliberate way he spoke, even his appearance, reminded me of Anthony Quinn playing Zorba the Greek. He was a very professional individual, and was prepared to do the job. He accepted all the risks and was confident he would succeed. I have since read that Bob and I were bitter enemies. I can't believe that. If we were, I didn't know it."[20] Even if Bob and Beckwith were not personally at odds, it is clear that there were disagreements about rescue-mission planning, and that some of them were conveyed in shouting matches. During the planning for Eagle Claw, Bob flew to Athens and Rome several times to attend meetings with the mission principals, including Beckwith. After one of these meetings, in January 1980, Bob returned to Tehran in a despondent mood because the State Department, the CIA and the military planners could not seem to agree on anything.

According to the interpretation of the story that has Bob and Beckwith at odds, Beckwith did not trust Bob's intelligence and thus insisted that the rescue planners get somebody he did trust into Tehran. Again, Beckwith's own words contradict this version of events. Beckwith credited Bob with singlehandedly pulling together such formidable intelligence on the U.S. embassy compound that the rescue planners were able to "frame a detailed assault plan."[21] Bob's raw data determined, for example, that the hostages were being held in a maximum of six, and more likely four, of the compound's fourteen buildings. Beckwith later wrote that, as of Saturday, January 5, he was very pleased with the intelligence that Bob was passing forward to him and the Pentagon. "The scheme appeared sound," said the commander of the plan to hide his Delta commandos in Tehran. "Its various threads were being slowly and carefully braided together."[22]

What Beckwith did worry about was the suitability of the arrangements made on behalf of the rescue team by Bob in Tehran, including the trucks and especially the hide-site. This was a legitimate concern, and Bob likely understood it as such. As Beckwith later observed, "[I]t was vital to Delta's success to look over all the arrangements and examine critical areas through Delta's eyes. I respected Bob, but of course he didn't know anything about Delta. I didn't want to risk the lives of about 120 guys to someone I didn't know."[23] Beckwith suggested several men from his own unit who he thought would be suitable for intelligence training and infiltration into Tehran, but in every case there were problems with the men's cover stories. One Delta man, according to Beckwith, would have been perfect for the job but because he looked like Robert Redford he could not blend into Iranian society. Beckwith was irate about one decision the CIA made, to bring Bob to Washington to meet Beckwith in person. "It was against all security rules," said Beckwith. "They should have known better."[24] Stansfield Turner later recalled that General Vaught had the same worries about intelligence-gathering as Beckwith. "It worried Jim," said Turner, "that Bob was neither American nor military."[25]

The person who volunteered to be Beckwith's inside man in Tehran was Dick Meadows, who had been working on Eagle Claw planning on Beckwith's behalf from the beginning. Decorated though Meadows was, the CIA thought him a weak choice. Beckwith appears to have agreed with this assessment but saw few alternatives. "I don't know why Dick volunteered to go to Iran," Beckwith said later, "but I suspect he thought, being a civilian, the mission would go off and leave him behind. After much arguing, the intelligence community reluctantly accepted Dick. They gave him the code name Esquire."[26] Meadows was not adequately trained in intelligence, and he had trouble learning enough Portuguese, the language required by his cover legend, to get him through Mehrabad Airport. There was too little time to make of Meadows what the CIA would have liked for such a key clandestine operative inside Tehran. Turner raised his own objections, presumably at the highest levels, but, extraordinarily, Meadows responded by threatening to go to Tehran even without the blessing of the CIA. Turner gave up. "Strictly speaking," historian John Prados has concluded bluntly, "the Meadows mission was an egregious security error."[27]

Meadows' first infiltration into Tehran would come in March 1980, three months after Bob's arrival and at least four months after the departure of Hart's clandestine CIA network. Meadows arrived bearing a bogus Irish passport courtesy of the CIA, his feigned Irish accent adequate to fool Iranian customs officers. He was accompanied by the Iranian-born U.S. airman code-named Fred. Two German-speaking Green Berets entered Tehran through Mehrabad on different flights the same day, posing as German businessmen. They would serve as Meadows' drivers. Meadows' mission was to review all of the arrangements made in Tehran by Bob. This, as Charlie Beckwith later wrote, was a tall order. "There was much that needed to be done and not much time to do it in. The trucks had to be moved, the warehouse where they were going to be stored needed watching, routes had to be gone over and memorized, alternate routes had to be found, someone had to man the radio and both targets—the embassy and Foreign Ministry Building—needed to be watched."[28]

Meadows' ability to move in and out of Iran at will gave the Eagle Claw planners a big boost. After his team's reconnaissance mission was completed, Meadows returned to Washington to report on all of the arrangements that Bob had made, including that of the hide-sites, trucks and other gear accumulated for the rescue mission. He returned to Tehran on April 21, 1980, to be one of the inside men during the rescue mission. He again met up with Fred and the two Green Berets, who had never left. Meadows sent a secret signal via satellite radio from Tehran to Washington in April 1980 to say that everything was in place for the rescue. After that, the Eagle Claw mission was a go.

One other source of human intelligence proved useful to the mission planners. In mid-April 1980, whether by design or coincidence, an American intelligence officer met a Pakistani cook on a plane en route from Tehran to Ankara, Turkey, and learned from him the precise location of the hostages within the chancery building. Yet as valuable as this intelligence windfall was, according to former CIA Near East (NE) chief Charles (Chuck) Cogan, "the military were skeptical of the information because it did not come from American eyes."[29]

Other than Bob, the CIA had no human intelligence of its own in Tehran prior to March 1980. For precisely this reason, Stansfield Turner redoubled the agency's efforts to collect intelligence from outside of Iran. Turner himself, for example, asked former Tehran station chief George W. Cave to head up a team to gather evidence from Iranians abroad—a largely fruitless enterprise that involved interviewing hundreds of Iranians living in Europe only to find that they could contribute almost nothing of value.[30] In *Charlie Wilson's War*, author George Crile claims that the CIA's Gust Avrakatos persuaded two Iranians to surveil the U.S. embassy compound just prior to the Eagle Claw mission.[31]

~ ~ ~

Ambassador Ken Taylor had been drawn steadily into the confidence of American intelligence officials since the embassy takeover, earning their trust and respect at every stage. He and John Sheardown had agreed to harbour the houseguests and to act as conduits for the movement of sensitive information between them and Washington. Taylor alone served as a crucial back channel for intelligence moving between Washington and Chargé Bruce Laingen starting in mid-November 1979. His connections in Tehran and his willingness to ferret out and analyze information useful to the United States impressed the Americans greatly, and they thanked him repeatedly for it. Whether the White House sought to establish similar arrangements with their other allies' representatives in Tehran is impossible to say. From what is known of the events of December 1979 and January 1980, it seems highly improbable. What is certain is that Ken Taylor's discretion, judgment and courage so impressed the Carter administration that they chose him for a role of singular importance.

What the Americans asked him to do amounted to nothing less than this: they asked him to gather the intelligence for them.

Chapter 14

A NEST OF SPIES

The Canadian role in intelligence-gathering for the Eagle Claw rescue mission has until now remained virtually unnoticed even by the most competent historians of American intelligence. President Jimmy Carter has never mentioned it. Neither Stansfield Turner or Zbigniew Brzezinski ever said anything specific about intelligence-gathering efforts made on behalf of the mini-SCC between November 8 and late February 1980, a fourteen-week gap. National-security historian John Prados has affirmed recently that planning for Eagle Claw was a daily obsession for both Carter and Brzezinski, which implies that intelligence-gathering was never far from their thoughts.[1] What Brzezinski did say in his memoirs is vague but insightful. "I have to note that some other countries were helpful to us in some aspects of the internal preparations in Iran for the execution of the mission, and we owe them a debt of gratitude which someday doubtless will be acknowledged."[2] In May 2008, Brzezinski was asked explicitly whether this debt of gratitude was directed toward Ken Taylor and the Canadians. "While I cannot comment on or confirm every one of your specific statements," he replied, "I can certainly affirm (with genuine gratitude) that the Canadians were truly and bravely helpful to our efforts to secure the freedom of the hostages."[3]

One reason the Canadian contribution has gone unsung stems from the commonsense premise that planning for Eagle Claw was secret—so secret that foreign countries, even close allies, would never have been consulted. Charlie Beckwith's *Delta Force* sheds an interesting light on this premise. Well before Bob was placed into Tehran, one of Beckwith's friends in the German counterterrorism unit GSG-9 offered to help gather intelligence for the Americans using a German television crew as a cover. Beckwith wanted to accept the offer, but Vaught vetoed it. "This is too sensitive," Vaught told Beckwith. "We can't work with a foreign government on this."[4] An even more obvious reason that the Canadian contribution remains unknown is that the top decision-makers on Eagle Claw deliberately obfuscated the historical record. Stansfield Turner, for example, wrote in his memoir that Bob was assisted only by "Iranians he had recruited to help him."[5] Historians have thus reconstructed the Eagle Claw story as if there were no foreign collaboration, but also as if there could not have been. This has produced a fundamental misunderstanding not only of how the intelligence was gathered but also of how it was transmitted, how much there was and how good it was.[6]

In truth, the human intelligence coming out of Tehran between late November 1979 and late January 1980 was excellent with respect to both quantity and quality. And all of it, even Bob's, was piped out to Ottawa, Washington and Langley directly from the Canadian embassy in Tehran courtesy of Ambassador Taylor and his staff.

~ ~ ~

The exact moment when Ken Taylor was approached officially to collect intelligence for the United States remains unknown, and is also difficult to deduce. This has something to do with the nature of intelligence-gathering. Diplomats and intelligence officers distinguish between two kinds of intelligence: that which can be gleaned and therefore communicated passively and that which is sought actively. All foreign diplomats are engaged in passive intelligence-gathering, at least in the sense that they provide information about their host countries to their own governments. So it was for Ken Taylor. On November 28, for example, the day Sadegh Ghotbzadeh took over from Abolhassan Bani-Sadr as Iranian foreign minister, Taylor sent a detailed report to Ottawa and Washington on three aspects of Iranian military preparedness that had obvious intelligence value. The first was that Chief of Staff General Valiollah Fallahi "has closed air space over Qom to all air traffic and is considering an emergency plan to mobilize all regular and irregular armed force," presumably as a defensive measure in the event of an American invasion of Iran. The second was that the militants occupying the U.S. embassy compound were reported to have planted explosives and mines around the buildings where the hostages were being kept. The third concerned the persistent rumours that some or all of the hostages had been moved to Evin Prison, notwithstanding Bani-Sadr's explicit claim that he knew nothing of any such relocation.[7]

Four days later, on December 2, Taylor reported that he had it "on good authority" that the Iranian air force had been placed on Stage I alert, an increase from Stage II the week before. The escalation, he explained, was occasioned by the loading of Phoenix missiles onto Iranian F-14 fighter planes, all of which had been purchased from the United States during the shah's regime.[8] In a separate cable the same day entitled "Options When Diplomacy Fails," Taylor offered his perspective on the viability of a U.S. military rescue mission to Tehran. "The application of a viable military option in the present case would be hard to achieve," he wrote. "It seems difficult to conceive of a military operation which could be mounted at short notice with sufficient strength and secrecy to have more than a slight chance of rescuing any of the hostages alive."[9] He did not state explicitly whether his pessimism was shared by Bruce Laingen, but because he had visited with the chargé the previous evening, it seems likely that he had taken his friend's views on the matter into account. It is certain that Taylor would not have offered his own analysis of a possible rescue mission had he not been asked for it.

On both occasions, November 30 and December 2, Taylor's information was transmitted in routine situation reports ("sitreps") that were classified "confidential" rather than "secret" and sent to Washington via Michael Shenstone's established contacts at the State Department. (In Canada, the classification "secret" implies both a significantly higher level of sensitivity and a far narrower distribution than "confidential." Canadians almost never use the classification "top secret.") These cables did not position Taylor as an active intelligence gatherer, but they clearly evinced his willingness to provide information and ponder questions that had military-intelligence value. On December 3, presumably at the suggestion of the State Department, Peter Towe, Canada's ambassador to Washington, recommended to Ottawa that the distribution of Taylor's more sensitive cables be limited. Only normal sitreps from the Canadian embassy in Tehran should continue with wide distribution, he advised.[10] It is easy to imagine that the State Department and possibly even the CIA, both of which had for weeks been receiving all of Taylor's cables, decided at this point that the time was right to ask whether he might consider *active* intelligence-gathering on Washington's behalf.

The official American request that Ambassador Taylor gather intelligence for the United States made its way via established channels at External Affairs after a meeting of senior department officials with Admiral John Rodocanachi, director-general of intelligence and security at the Department of National Defence, and his counterpart in the RCMP Intelligence Service, General Michael Dare. Taylor answered without hesitation in the affirmative, knowing that he had the support of his closest colleagues in Ottawa, the Canadian intelligence establishment, and the prime minister himself. From this moment on, the number of Canadians who knew that Taylor had agreed to collect and transmit intelligence to the United States never numbered more than a handful. Joe Clark, Flora MacDonald, Admiral Rodocanachi and General Dare knew. So did Michael Shenstone; E. P. "Pat" Black, assistant undersecretary for security and intelligence at External Affairs; and Louis Delvoie, director of the intelligence analysis division at External Affairs. The distribution list for Taylor's daily intel cables was, however, limited to only two people at External Affairs— Delvoie and Black—who reported their contents directly to Joe Clark and Flora MacDonald. In order to safeguard the secrecy of the operation, neither Delvoie's immediate boss, Bill Hooper, Director-General of the Bureau of Intelligence and Security, nor even Undersecretary Allan Gotlieb was privy to Taylor's intel cables. Remarkably, Defence Minister Allan McKinnon appears to have been excluded from the distribution list.

In Tehran, Ken Taylor's accomplice in intelligence-gathering was Sergeant Jim Edward. Prior to the occupation of the U.S. embassy, Edward was head of security at the Canadian embassy, a job that would fall to Sergeant Claude Gauthier once Edward was reassigned to intelligence-gathering on a full-time basis. Then in his mid-thirties, fair-haired, blue-eyed, broad-shouldered and six feet tall, Edward seemed an unlikely choice for a clandestine operative whose mission would require him to mingle inconspicuously with the crowds of Iranians outside the U.S. embassy compound and elsewhere. "Being a Canadian," Edward later remarked, "I stood out like a sore thumb amongst the Iranians. I am somewhat over 6 feet tall, fair skinned and of course, I didn't fit in well with the crowd and I did stand out quite a bit amongst the Iranian population."[12] Even so, Edward agreed to gather intelligence for the Americans because he understood that their options in Tehran were extremely limited. "When the U.S. government realized that most of the operatives in the Middle East at that time had been captured as a result of the embassy takeover," he later disclosed to Canadian filmmaker Les Harris, "they had to look around for other people who could provide them with the intelligence and the information for the rescue attempt. I happened to be the unfortunate individual who they chose."[13]

Although he had no prior intelligence training, Jim Edward had some experience doing surveillance. "My experience had been limited to police investigations," he said, "which involved a certain amount of surveillance. But insofar as intelligence activities are concerned, I had no background in that."[14] Edward nonetheless seemed to Ken Taylor, and also to American intelligence officials, to be well suited to his new assignment—soft-spoken, modest and always professional, a true soldier's soldier. John Rodocanachi, Edward's commanding officer, did not hesitate to approve the request. It was then forwarded to the intelligence division at External Affairs, and then on to Ken Taylor in Tehran, in equally short order. "Ambassador Taylor requested that I start providing certain information to the U.S. government through the Canadian embassy," Edward confirmed.[15] As ambassador, Taylor could have declined the mission had Jim Edward expressed reservations. Neither man hesitated. "When the request was made of me to do this type of work on behalf of the Canadian government," said Edward, "I had no objection to it."[16] Clearly, despite the extraordinary risk the operation presented both to themselves and to their embassy colleagues, Taylor and Edward were confident that they could deliver on it.

The command structure for the mission was simple: Edward would report directly (and only) to Taylor. Both men would carefully document all of the information they collected. Taylor alone would then review it, collate it and have his communicators dispatch it in encrypted cables to Ottawa via U.S. warships in the nearby Mediterranean Sea. No other embassy officers would know anything about their intelligence-gathering activities. The only exceptions were communicator Master-Corporal George Edward Brian, who was posted to Tehran in early December with special cipher equipment to transmit Taylor's intel cables to Ottawa and Washington, and Mary O'Flaherty, the embassy's own communicator, who was later enlisted to help relay the information because its volume consistently exceeded Brian's transmission capacity. No one else— not Roger Lucy, John Sheardown, Claude Gauthier or any of the embassy's military staff—knew about the operation. Bruce Laingen did not know either.

As Stansfield Turner himself later acknowledged, "the Canadian Foreign Office in Ottawa served as a relay point for secret messages between Washington and Tehran."[17] Taylor's intel went directly to Louis Delvoie, and from there to the U.S. embassy in Ottawa. There, U.S. ambassador to Canada Kenneth Curtis assembled the materials for transmission, by cable or by telephone, directly to Secretary of State Cyrus Vance. "It was one of those rare times when I was in Canada that I was not free to just speak to anybody," Ambassador Curtis later recalled, "because there are usually no secrets between Canadians and Americans, so most of my correspondence and telephone conversations were with the secretary of state directly. When Ken Taylor submitted material to his government, his government submitted it to me and I submitted it directly to Washington. It went out with one of those codes, so that it would not be read by any of the underlings."[18]

(Even after he had begun active intelligence gathering, Taylor continued to send Ottawa and Washington sitrep-level information with military-intelligence value. On December 20, for example, Canada was one of many "friendly countries" asked by the U.S. State Department to provide information on strategic sectors of the Iranian economy, including foodstuffs, banking, shipping and ports, and oil production.[19] Such information-gathering was undertaken as part of President Carter's contingency planning for economic sanctions against Iran. Taylor sent off several confidential telexes in response. One of these estimated the "serviceability of USA aircraft" in Iran as "probably low," even though Iran had received "several jumbo loads of helicopter parts" just before the hostage crisis began. [20])

The distribution of Taylor's intel cables within the U.S. State Department was as restricted as it was within External Affairs. No one in the Iran Working Group knew about Taylor's intelligence work, not Peter Constable or even Hal Saunders, and neither did the Canadian ambassador to the United States, Peter Towe. The CIA's Ottawa station chief, Tim McLaren,* worked closely with Ambassador Curtis at the U.S. embassy but, significantly, received Taylor's intel cables via Admiral Rodocanachi and Canadian military intelligence. "Our CIA man in Canada had an excellent relationship with Canadian intelligence," Curtis later recalled. "They worked together. They were not looking for headlines. They just did their jobs very, very well."[21] This arrangement had the great advantage to Taylor of insulating him from direct contact with Washington, and thus from any direct meddling by Langley in his intelligence-gathering operation. (It is plausible that Taylor insisted on this command structure as a condition of accepting the assignment.) Curtis and McLaren became close friends when they worked together at the U.S. embassy in Ottawa, and remain so. Both remain friends of Taylor's to this day.

---

* "Tim McLaren" is a pseudonym.

~ ~ ~

The Canadians' intelligence mission in Tehran had three components.

The first was to monitor the activities of the U.S. embassy compound in Tehran and to carefully note all aspects of those activities, particularly as they related to the Iranians' military preparedness. "One of the first things that was requested," according to Jim Edward, "was daily surveillance of the U.S. embassy to determine the number of guards inside and outside the embassy. How they were armed? What additional ammunition or firepower that they had with them? Any gun positions that had been placed around the embassy? What time they changed shifts and virtually the daily routine of the revolutionary guard in and around the embassy compound? Virtually anything and everything that was going on, on a daily basis."[22] As well as tracking the movement of people and arms in and out of the compound, Edward monitored the movement of goods. Of particular concern was the passage of foodstuffs into the compound and of waste removal out. By calibrating the daily caloric intake of the hostages, Edward and Taylor could estimate their general health and also their capacity to withstand the rigours of the rescue mission.

Surveilling the embassy became Jim Edward's full-time job. He inspected the compound exterior several times daily, well aware that the militants were doing exactly the same thing to track the presence of foreigners. Within days, Edward had taken the measure of the entire compound. "Generally speaking," he said, "there was a loud crowd of demonstrators outside the motor pool [along the south-facing main wall]. But on the north-east and west sides of the embassy, traffic was very limited and there were very few access points to the U.S. compound itself. So it was basically a matter of either driving down those roads to the north east and west. Driving to the south was far more difficult because of the amount of traffic and because of the number of demonstrators that were continuously being filmed and demonstrating outside the motor pool."[23]

The Canadians' second objective was to locate a suitable hidesite in Tehran for the Delta Force commandos and to purchase the ground vehicles that would transport them and the hostages within Tehran. This aspect of the mission meant bringing Ambassador Taylor and his Ottawa colleagues into the secret world of Eagle Claw planning. Eagle Claw envisaged the commandos being ferried by truck from the hide-site warehouse to the embassy on the second night of the rescue mission. There they would scale the embassy walls, storm the buildings where the hostages were believed to be held, gather them up and transport them to open ground nearby, where the helicopters could lift them out of the city and fly them to Manzariyeh.

There was a broad, flat area within the embassy compound that might have served as the helicopter landing pad, but U.S. satellite photographs revealed that the occupiers had lined this field with telephone poles, a deliberate anti-helicopter tactic that reinforced the view at both the CIA and the Pentagon that they were not up against amateurs. Stansfield Turner later noted that the discovery of the poles was a setback, while obfuscating the fact that it was the Canadians who were searching for an alternative landing site. "[O]ne of our agents in Tehran," said Turner, "noted that a soccer stadium right across the street from the back of the embassy would be a satisfactory alternative."[24] That "agent" was a composite of Bob and Ken Taylor. Most histories of Eagle Claw have Bob leasing the warehouse on the outskirts of Tehran, along with six Ford trucks and two Mazdas for use by the Delta Force commandos. But this too was work in which Taylor collaborated. Many of these logistical arrangements were well under way, and possibly completed, before Bob even showed up in Tehran.

Ambassador Taylor assumed full operational control of intelligence gathering in Tehran in the weeks before Bob's arrival. Louis Delvoie's ability to insulate Taylor from interference from Langley was critical to the ambassador's ability to function in this new role, allowing him to make command-level decisions based on his understanding of what was happening on the ground in Tehran. The best example of how this arrangement worked in practice came in early December, when the CIA placed its first covert operative into Tehran. This officer spoke with a European accent and travelled on a bogus German passport. His first stop when he got to Iran was Ken Taylor's office. Unfortunately for him, Taylor was not impressed. The ambassador requested that he be replaced, a request that Michael Shenstone relayed to Kenneth Curtis, who then presumably informed Cyrus Vance and Stansfield Turner. CIA headquarters at Langley thought Taylor's veto of their man preposterous, but in the end they had little choice but to accede to his decision. As it turned out, there were no more false starts with the CIA. The next covert operative they sent was Bob, of whom Taylor approved.

As soon as Bob arrived in Tehran, he joined the Canadian intelligence-gathering operation in progress, which meant assisting Jim Edward in his daily surveillance of the embassy compound. Bob reported directly to Ken Taylor, and all of his intel was dispatched from the Canadian embassy. The volume of Taylor's transmissions to Ottawa and Washington doubled. Edward, Bob and Taylor produced reams of raw intelligence on the status of the embassy compound and its inhabitants, minutiae so detailed that Delvoie's contacts at the U.S. embassy in Ottawa thought they would go blind reading it.

The Canadians' third objective—and the one that most worried Charlie Beckwith—was to assess local logistics as they fit into the larger Eagle Claw plan. This meant, as Beckwith himself put it, "look[ing] over the hide-site because photos weren't telling the intelligence people if the nearby railroad line would interfere with the plan." It also meant "check[ing] out routes from the hide-site to the embassy gate, density of traffic flow on the possible routes and location of reaction forces, potential checkpoints and street construction in the neighborhood of the compound."[25] For the most part, it was Bob who surveilled these sites, sometimes with Taylor's help, while Edward remained focused on the embassy compound.

Jim Edward was not merely a collector of data. His opinions on Eagle Claw were, like Taylor's, actively solicited by U.S. intelligence officials. Any insights the Canadians came up with day to day were sent out in Taylor's intel cables. Edward also flew out of Tehran now and then to confer directly with CIA officials in Europe. (Whether Taylor did so is unknown.) At one such meeting, in early December 1979, Edward met with a CIA officer in Athens. That officer asked Edward's opinion of the best means of getting American troops around Tehran in light of the formidable presence of the Revolutionary Guards and their ubiquitous roadblocks. "The two easiest ways of getting in and out of Tehran," Edward told him, "were either in military vehicles or in garbage trucks. One of the suggestions that I made to the CIA was the use of garbage trucks because there were a couple hundred of them just south of the city and they were basically an armored vehicle in themselves. They weighed approximately thirty tons. They could crash virtually any barrier. And I suggested to the Americans that this might be an excellent way of reaching the walls of the embassy if in fact they did make a rescue attempt." The CIA man's response was predictable. "He was totally mortified at the thought of U.S. troops actually being contained inside a garbage truck," said Edward, "and they dismissed that idea entirely."[26]

~ ~ ~

Jim Edward had an Iranian girlfriend, named Layla,* who had no idea about his intelligence-gathering work and thus asked him repeatedly if she could accompany him on one of his many walks in the vicinity of the U.S. embassy compound. "I thought that this would actually be a good thing," Edward later reflected, "because having somebody else with you, you don't stand out as much as if you are on your own."[27] One afternoon in mid-December, he agreed to take Layla with him, even suggesting that she could assist him by translating the many revolutionary posters that were plastered all over the walls of the compound.

To the north of the embassy compound there was an apartment building that had once been occupied by the U.S. Marine Guard. It was now home to members of Iran's Revolutionary Guard. A secure but high-traffic site, the building was separated from the embassy grounds by only a small pedestrian gate. Edward knew that it served as an important base for the militants involved with the hostage-taking, but he had never been able to get close to it. Now, strolling hand in hand with his girlfriend like a curious tourist, he had the perfect cover. With Layla on his arm, he walked the circumference of the building to take the measure of its defences. "What I was really looking for was again the number of guards on the perimeter," he said, "[and] any new gun emplacements." Just as Edward and Layla were turning around to head back to the main street, the building's sentries surrounded them and took them both into custody. "They

---

* "Layla" is a pseudonym.

were heavily armed," said Edward. "They grabbed both of us, physically grabbed us and a number of others were pointing weapons at
us—automatic weapons, Uzis, G3s, etc. And they basically forced us
into the U.S. apartment building."

The Iranians began immediately to question Edward and Layla.
"During this time," said Edward, "we were being held in the living
room of the Marine Guard apartment. We were surrounded by
Revolutionary Guards, all of them fairly heavily armed with automatic weapons (and these people have a tendency to play with their
weapons). It was a very dangerous situation. Had a round been
fired in that situation they couldn't have helped but hit each other."
Edward was asked persistently who he was and what he was doing
there. "I explained to them that we were simply out for a walk," he
said, "and that my girlfriend was assisting me by translating some of
the posters that were on the wall."[28] During the questioning a series
of telephone calls took place between the Guards and what Edward
assumed was the Iranian foreign ministry. At about 10 p.m., the
Iranians called the Canadian embassy directly. One of the night staff
confirmed that Jim Edward was an employee of the embassy, but
nothing else was said.

The embassy immediately called Ambassador Taylor at home.
He alone knew what Edward had been doing at the Marine Guard
building, and what he could be made to divulge under harsh interrogation. Taylor set off immediately for the embassy, his mind undoubtedly racing with worst-case scenarios: Edward tortured and found to
be spying for the U.S. military; Bob identified; the Canadian embassy
exposed as the CIA's nefarious proxy; his own staff deported, taken
hostage or tried as spies; the houseguests exposed and hunted down.
It would be a nightmare.

Back at the Marine Guard building, Layla whispered to Jim
Edward that their captors were trying to establish who he was. At one
point, Edward whispered to her, "Let me know when I am in trouble."

About three and a half hours into the questioning she said, "You're in big trouble."[29]

Without saying anything to anyone, Edward kissed Layla, got up from his seat and walked out of the room. "This came as quite a surprise to the revolutionary guards," he said later. "I fully expected at this point in time that the guards would in fact shoot me. But due to the fact that they all had their weapons pointed at each other, it was a very difficult situation for them. As a consequence, I managed to walk out of the living room, down the steps onto the street, made a right turn and was heading for the main street, when virtually everybody that had formerly been in the room came running after me. They grabbed me physically, were prodding me with their weapons, and they physically dragged me back into the Marine Guard living room."[30] Edward knew not only that his presence at the embassy compound could be construed as spying but that his knowledge of the houseguests' situation put others at risk. "I was very, very concerned," he later recalled, "because the Iranians were known for torture and, with the information that I had, I had serious concerns as to how long I could keep the information from coming out, because of my threshold level of pain, especially when they burn and beat your feet."[31]

Once he was reunited with Layla in the Guards' living room, Edward later recalled, "things really reached a higher level of intensity." The phone calls continued. One of the Guards had a lengthy conversation in English with an MP at the Canadian embassy. "I had a cover story with the military policemen," said Edward. "In the event that they did receive any outside phone calls about who I was and what I did that they were to advise that I was in administration at the Canadian embassy and leave it at that. They obviously made that contact and were satisfied that I was who I reported myself to be."[32]

Not long after this second call to the Canadian embassy, the Iranians allowed Edward and Layla to go free. Their questioning had lasted roughly five hours. Again, Edward surprised his captors. "I told them that I was going to complete my tour around the embassy and look at the posters and have them translated," he said. "I think that they thought that I was a little bit wacky but nevertheless, they allowed me to do that. Layla and I then continued to walk inside the quartered area along the west side of the embassy and of course to the south—followed by the Revolutionary Guard who was pointing the gun at us during this whole period. After we had gotten by the motor pool entrance and the basic crowd, Layla was so upset that she said, 'I can't take this anymore.' We left the cordoned area, went back to our vehicles and returned to my residence."[33]

Jim Edward dropped Layla at his Tehran apartment and headed directly to the Canadian embassy. "As was my habit at that time," he later recalled, "I reported to the embassy immediately and submitted my reports on my observations as to gun emplacements, the number of guards that were guarding the facility and, of course, my most recent observations of the pedestrian door, or gate, that separated the north end of the compound from the U.S. marine building." As Edward was drafting his report, Ambassador Taylor showed up, more than a little relieved to see him. "At that point in time I debriefed him," said Edward of his conversation with Taylor, "and he made the decision that I was to leave the country as soon at possible. The following morning at 6 a.m. I left Iran on a Japanese Airlines flight for Paris."[34] Edward actually wanted to stay on and continue the mission, but Taylor was not taking any chances. The militants could easily change their minds and drag Edward back in for a more thorough interrogation. Taylor thanked Edward for everything he had done, and no doubt breathed a deep sigh of relief once he was out of Iran.

The Canadians had been incredibly lucky, and they knew it. Once Jim Edward was back in Ottawa, he was debriefed in full by the CIA. He gave them his blunt analysis of the intelligence failure that had caused the hostage crisis in the first place. "If they were a proper intelligence agency," said Edward, "I don't believe that the embassy would have been taken over—not once but twice—because in the intelligence community this is what it is all about. They are supposed to know what the activities are that are going on in the country. And to actually have all their agents captured in front of the facility at one time and have no knowledge whatsoever of the potential threat. I think that is *asinine!*"[35] How the CIA reacted to Edward's critique is not known.

Back in Tehran, Ken Taylor and Bob continued their intelligence-gathering work without pause, gradually shifting their emphasis from general surveillance of the embassy compound to the specific operational details of the Eagle Claw mission. Taylor's daily intel cables streamed into Ottawa and Washington until the day he left Tehran. It was extremely dangerous work—far more risky than passing information to Bruce Laingen or even harbouring the fugitive American diplomats. If at any point in the first three months of the hostage crisis the houseguests had been discovered, Taylor and his staff would likely have been pronounced *personae non gratae* by the Iranian government and expelled from the country. If, on the other hand, the ambassador had been found running an intelligence-gathering operation out of the Canadian embassy—in aid of a planned U.S. military strike against Iran—the consequences would have been incalculably worse.

Stansfield Turner later summarized the success of U.S. intelligence-gathering operations as they had taken shape over the first ten weeks of the hostage crisis. "By mid-January the CIA's intelligence was good enough for us to be reasonably sure that all the hostages were in the embassy compound," he said. "The Agency had procured eight trucks to transport Delta Force into Tehran and a warehouse to store them in until needed. Reconnaissance of the embassy's exterior was thorough and continuing. We knew where the guard posts and machine gun positions were and when they were manned. And we knew how best to navigate Delta into the city from the outskirts without arousing suspicions. Though it had taken us too long to be ready, we were finally there."[36] Never once did Turner mention the Canadians. If Ken Taylor or Jim Edward accompanied Turner and Bob to the Oval Office to allow President Carter to express his personal thanks, they have never said so.

~ ~ ~

On the balmy afternoon of July 25, 1980, a military investiture ceremony was held in Ottawa. Present to receive the Order of Military Merit— in recognition of "exceptional service displayed by the men and women of the Canadian Forces"—were George Edward Brian and Jim Edward. Both men were decorated for their extraordinary service in Tehran during the early months of the hostage crisis. After the public ceremony, a second, secret ceremony followed. There Jim Edward alone was decorated with the even more prestigious Medal of Bravery. Present at this secret investiture were only four people— Governor General Ed Schreyer and his wife, Lily; the chief of the Canadian Armed Forces Staff; and the director general of the RCMP Security Service. All were sworn to secrecy.

The cloistered ceremony concluded, the Schreyers and their guests retired to a reception at the governor general's residence. Over drinks, the newly decorated Jim Edward was approached by his brigade commander, who had been informed just minutes before that Edward had received the Medal of Bravery. He was incredulous. He had had no idea that Edward had been singled out for such an honour, and had no clue as to why. Perplexed, he asked Edward how he had come to receive his medal. Edward told him that, with all due respect, he could not say. The nonplussed commander insisted, *ordering* Edward to explain the situation. Edward kept his cool but would not divulge anything. "I was sworn under the Official Secrets Act to keep everything quiet," Edward later recalled, "and as a consequence I refused to tell him. I told him that the information was classified and that if he wanted to find out why I was awarded with the medal he could approach the Chief of Defence staff and/or the Chief of Intelligence Security."[37]

Only a handful of Canadians knew why Jim Edward had received the Medal of Bravery. None of them was present at the investiture ceremony that afternoon. If they had been, they would not have been surprised at Edward's quiet but unyielding refusal to account to his commander.

He had demonstrated the same quiet resolve in Tehran in December 1979.

PART FIVE
EXFILTRATION

Chapter 15
THE CANADIAN PLAN

As his friends and colleagues can attest, Ken Taylor is the sort of man who is always anticipating his next move. He is not one to sit on his hands, waiting for others to act.

Ambassador Taylor began thinking about the fate of the American houseguests the day he took them in, November 10, 1979. From that moment on, although he was selective about the information he imparted to them, he and the houseguests discussed possible escape scenarios practically continuously. Taylor also began conferring with Bruce Laingen about the houseguests when he was first granted access to the imprisoned chargé, on November 15. "We talked a great deal during those visits," said Laingen. "It was a matter of great concern to us that the six were in the city, secreted away. So we spent a lot of time talking with Ken about what to do about this. We had a variety of ideas. We paced the floor a great deal with him in that room, talking about this. He was as concerned as we that it was important to them, to the six and to us as a country to get them out."[1]

During the initial phase of the embassy occupation, when some kind of negotiated resolution seemed possible, there was general agreement in Tehran, Ottawa and Washington that the houseguests should simply bide their time. "The initial impulse was to wait it out," said Roger Lucy. "Nobody really believed that the crisis would go on that long. The safest thing was to sit tight, wait for things to develop and not take unnecessary risk."[2] As the standoff hardened, however, waiting it out seemed less tenable. Taylor knew that the secret of the houseguests' existence could not be kept indefinitely. And even if it could, there was no guarantee that they would be included in a deal to free the American hostages. The Iranians might single out the house- guests as CIA spies and put them on trial. Anything was possible.

Taylor's first instinct was to contrive a plan to smuggle the six Americans out of Iran overland. His thinking was influenced by the successful rescue in February 1979 of two men, Paul Chiapparoni and William Gaylord, who worked for future presidential candidate Ross Perot's Electronic Data Systems (EDS) Corporation in Tehran. On December 28, 1978, the Iranian government had thrown the two EDS employees into Qasr Prison, setting the ransom for their release at $12.75 million. Unwilling to pay, Perot took matters into his own hands. He recruited retired U.S. Army colonel Arthur "Bull" Simons to train a strike force, which included several former CIA officers, and lead it into Tehran. Perot then paid a group of Iranian revolutionaries to storm the prison, and he bribed the guards not to interfere. The mission reportedly went off without a hitch, on February 11. Eleven thousand prisoners "escaped," including Schiapparoni and Gaylord, who rendezvoused with Simons' commandos in a Tehran hotel and were then smuggled overland into Turkey. There they were met by Perot himself, who brought them and his strike force home to Dallas on his private jet. (Asked whether it had known about, or played any role in, Perot's daring escape plot, the U.S. State Department would not comment.)[3]

When the U.S. embassy in Tehran was seized, Jimmy Carter's top advisers immediately considered a rescue mission modelled on Perot's. "Ross and his people thought that if we infiltrated a military team into Tehran," said Stansfield Turner, "it could canvass the territory, purchase its weapons, and then wait for the right moment to storm the embassy and release the hostages."[4] By mid-November, however, the idea was abandoned, mainly on the grounds that the logistics of bringing out over fifty captive Americans were unworkable. Smuggling out a smaller number, however, seemed to Ken Taylor a different matter. Because the houseguests' whereabouts were unknown to the Iranians, they could be transported in secret, presumably without military assistance—driven to an Iranian port city and evacuated by a friendly ship, or perhaps flown directly out of Tehran via helicopter to neighbouring Turkey. "We had all kinds of different scenarios as to how to get them out overland," said Taylor. "We had an idea to take them to the Turkish border, because a lot of Iranians had left that way. But then you had to pay people off on the way, like Ross Perot."[5]

In contrast with Eagle Claw rescue planning, which was firmly in the hands of Zbigniew Brzezinski and his mini-SCC, Stansfield Turner initially took charge of escape planning for the houseguests on the American side. "I had a group of CIA operations experts studying how to rescue the six people hiding with the Canadians," Turner later recalled. "Since we knew that even a hint that there were six American diplomats loose somewhere in Tehran might lead to their capture, the planning group of the State Department and CIA people was kept to only a handful. There would be no SCC meetings. I was compartmentalizing this project down to a very few, just as Zbig had tried to hold the military planning group to a minimum. I did, however, keep the President, the Secretary of State, and Zbig well informed."[6]

Turner acknowledged Ambassador Taylor's critical role in planning the exfiltration. "The CIA team in Washington and Ken

Taylor in Iran," he later wrote, "exchanged ideas on how to organize the escape. Taylor went back and forth between his residence and his deputy's [Sheardown's], holding discussions with the two groups of Americans. They devised four escape options. The first was to smuggle the six hostages [*sic*] out of the country, either across a land boundary with Turkey four hundred miles to the west, where they would bribe their way past the border guards as Perot's people had done, or across the Shatt-el-Arab River to Iraq, some three hundred miles to the south. The second option was to take them in disguise right through Tehran's Mehrabad Airport and onto a commercial flight out of the country. The third was to move them only a short distance outside Tehran and have a U.S. military helicopter come and pick them up. Finally, some of the hostages [*sic*] thought the safest course would be to just wait it out, since everyone expected the Iranians would come to their senses and release the fifty-three hostages downtown before long."[7]

Only two of these four options remained on the table at the end of November 1979. From the Canadians' perspective, there could be no waiting it out. "One possibility that concerned Taylor at that time," Michael Shenstone later recalled, "was that USA–Iran relations would be broken and the hostages in the American embassy might depart immediately, posing the problem for us of what to do about the unrevealed houseguests. In the light of the overall situation, he thought we should begin thinking about ways for them to depart eventually, because some time in December there might be a need to act fast."[8] U.S. defence planners vetoed the option of a helicopter rescue mission. The houseguests would have to either be smuggled out of Tehran overland or exfiltrated through Mehrabad. Stansfield Turner discussed the two scenarios directly with President Carter. It was Turner's view that each houseguest should be free to choose his or her own exit strategy. "Each could take into account," he reasoned, "the physical stamina needed to make the long trip to one of the borders and perhaps across the mountains into Turkey, or the cunning needed to deceive the inspectors at the airport."[9]

Carter talked him out of it. "I disagree, Stan," said the president. "There is no telling about the mental and emotional state of those people. Some speak Farsi, some don't. Some can stand up under pressure better than others. My feeling is that you and the Canadians should make a decision as to which escape plan has the best chance of success and then simply tell them what they are to do. I think it would place an enormous burden on them if they had to choose their own escape route. I wouldn't know what to do."

"That makes sense to me, Mr. President," Turner replied. "And my belief is that bringing them out together through the airport is our best chance."

"Let's do it, then!" said Carter.[10]

~ ~ ~

Stansfield Turner was correct when he later observed that "only a handful of people in Washington and Ottawa knew of this operation."[11] But he overstated the extent to which the exfiltration was limited to the CIA, no doubt to preserve the appearance that Cyrus Vance's diplomatic overtures to the Iranians were free of the taint of the hated American spy agency (and also, perhaps, to downplay the extent to which the CIA was collaborating with External Affairs officials in Ottawa). In fact, Turner's "planning group," as he called it, was jointly headed from the start by Charles "Chuck" Cogan, the CIA's Near East/South Asia division chief, and Hal Saunders of the State Department's Iran Working Group. Cogan and Saunders got along extremely well, collaborating not only on rescue planning for the hostages and houseguests but on the various back-channel negotiations the Carter administration was pursuing with the Iranian government. Cogan reported directly to Turner, who requested daily progress reports from him throughout the hostage crisis. Saunders reported directly to Cyrus Vance. Neither Vance nor Saunders, both of whom later wrote extensively about the Iran hostage crisis, ever mentioned their close collaboration with Cogan, or with the CIA more generally.

What is true about Turner's characterization of exfiltration planning is that, like Ken Taylor's intelligence work for Eagle Claw, it was managed secretly at the highest levels of the U.S. government in order to prevent leaks and maintain the operational integrity of the mission. The same was true for the government of Canada, which restricted information on exfiltration planning to more or less the same handful of people privy to Taylor's intelligence-gathering. The distribution list for the ambassador's exfiltration cables included Louis Delvoie and Pat Black of the Intelligence Analysis Division at External Affairs, Admiral John Rodocanachi at DND and General Michael Dare of the RCMP. Taylor's missives also went up the External Affairs chain of command to Allan Gotlieb, and to Flora Mac-Donald and Joe Clark as needed.

The main CIA officer involved in exfiltration planning was Ottawa station chief Tim McLaren, a dedicated, cerebral individual who understood the absolute necessity of concealing from the Iranians the CIA's activities on behalf of the hostages and houseguests. A liberal Democrat with a deep personal commitment to advancing a progressive and humanitarian U.S. foreign policy, McLaren shunned the media spotlight during the hostage crisis. Working out of the U.S. embassy and bearing an official diplomatic cover, he was well connected and well liked in Ottawa. Since the main job of a CIA station chief in a NATO country like Canada was not to coordinate espionage but to liaise with local intelligence-gathering organizations, McLaren cultivated close relationships with Admiral Rodocanachi and General Dare. It was Rodocanachi who approached McLaren—on November 8, the day that Bob Anders first called John Sheardown about the houseguests—to offer the CIA whatever assistance Canada's intelli-

gence services could provide. An indebted McLaren, in turn, informed
Langley. Eric Neff, one of Chuck Cogan's regional deputies in the CIA's
NE division, went immediately to Ottawa to confer with Canadian
intelligence officials, including Louis Delvoie. The following week,
Rodocanachi flew to Langley to meet with top CIA officials, includ-
ing Cogan and possibly even Stansfield Turner.

During this first round of meetings, Cogan and Rodocanachi
established a warm working relationship, as did Neff and Delvoie.
All agreed on three key points. First, Canadian and American intelligence services would cooperate fully on exfiltration planning for
the houseguests, restricting the distribution of information to an
absolute minimum. Second, Tim McLaren alone would serve as
the conduit for intelligence moving between Ottawa and Langley.
Third, Ken Taylor would retain veto power over exfiltration planning and logistics.

While Rodocanachi was making these arrangements with Langley, Allan Gotlieb and Michael Shenstone were establishing their own
modus operandi with the State Department. "The point man in Washington," Gotlieb recalled recently, "was Phil Habib, Undersecretary of
State for Political Affairs. He was one of the most brilliant foreign-
service officers in the United States. Habib came up to Ottawa. I met
him in my office. In terms of all the exfiltration scenarios, Phil was
the top man. He was a wonderful guy. Our relationship with Habib
was almost daily—on the exfiltration scenario."[12] Alongside Habib,
Cyrus Vance appointed his chief of staff, Peter Tarnoff, as a special
envoy to Ottawa. Vance, Habib and Tarnoff were close personally as
well as professionally, which ensured that communication between
External Affairs and the secretary of state would be direct, trustworthy
and free of leaks. "I remember being called in by Vance," said Tarnoff, "and Habib was part of the conversation. They decided that they
wanted me to be involved, including to be the point person for diplomatic contacts with the Canadian government. I was inconspicuous

and somebody they could trust, obviously. I have a background in Canada as well. So I became the designated interface with Canada."[13] U.S. ambassador Curtis and CIA station chief McLaren also worked closely with External Affairs officials on the exfiltration, checking in with them every evening during the planning phase.

Everyone connected with exfiltration planning in Ottawa agrees that the Canadian–American collaboration was extensive, continuous and cordial. They recall as well that there was, over time, a natural transition from the Canadians' broad conceptualization of the exfiltration scenario to American operational control. "My recollection is one of growing confidence because the Americans seemed to be taking over the operational details," Allan Gotlieb said, "which I felt was absolutely right—subject to our input and veto—because they had the capacity."[14] Ken Curtis concurs, emphasizing that even as Washington assumed operational control, Ambassador Taylor always had the final say. "It was always a Canadian plan," Curtis recalled in 2009. "I remember one incident in particular where our State Department—our government—had an idea about how to get the six Americans out of Iran, and Ken had the guts to say to them, 'No, that plan won't work.'"[15]

Once Roger Lucy returned to Tehran from his European vacation in late November 1979, he became Ambassador Taylor's main sounding board on exfiltration logistics. By this time, none of the overland scenarios seemed practical to either him or the ambassador, Lucy having had the nerve-racking experience less than a year earlier of evacuating bona fide Canadian citizens from Iran. Taylor and Lucy agreed to keep their options open, but their strong inclination was to have the houseguests fly out of Tehran, incognito, on domestic flights. It was an obvious idea, one that occurred to many people simultaneously. Houseguest Lee Schatz later recalled getting a Christmas letter from his girlfriend in the United States. "She just didn't understand why they didn't just issue us Canadian passports and bring us all home as Canadians," Schatz said later. "I read this and everyone just absolutely cracked up that she'd hit it on the head!"[16] In Washington and Ottawa, this scenario was also the early favourite. As Michael Shenstone observed at the time, an overland escape would mean many days of arduous effort from the houseguests, but an exfiltration through Mehrabad would require only a few hours of role playing.[17]

Along with exfiltration scenarios, Taylor and Louis Delvoie exchanged ideas about cover legends for the houseguests. In contrast with James Bond mythology, standard procedure in international espionage is to create legends that are so inconspicuous as to go unnoticed. "In the intelligence business," explains one of the CIA's leading exfiltration experts, "we usually try to match cover legends closely to the actual experience of the person involved. A cover should be bland, as uninteresting as possible, so the casual observer, or the not-so-casual immigration official, doesn't probe too deeply."[18] The houseguests—five consular officers and an agricultural attaché—were ordinary office workers with no intelligence training. The Canadians thus were inclined toward banal covers, false personas that would not ask much of them as actors. One option was to have the six pose as Canadian teachers trapped in Tehran by the revolution. Flora MacDonald believed that they should pose as Canadian businessmen and women employed in oil exploration, an industry Canada and Iran have in common. Delvoie's idea, one that Taylor supported, was that the houseguests should pose as agricultural nutritionists from the University of Guelph who had gone to Iran on some kind of research project.

~ ~ ~

From the day the embassy was stormed by Iranian militants, American news media covered the hostage-taking obsessively. Never did the crisis leave the headlines. Little wonder, then, that before long the State Department's vague pronouncements about the exact number of hostages in captivity began to strike North American newshounds as suspicious. It was implausible that Secretary of State Cyrus Vance did not know how many hostages the Iranian militants had, yet his spokespersons dissembled for weeks. Before long, enterprising journalists tapped their trusted sources in the State Department and drew their own conclusions: a handful of Americans had eluded the hostage-takers and had been hiding out ever since with foreign diplomats in Iran. David Martin of CBS had the story before the end of November. So did Mike Ruane of the *Philadelphia Inquirer*.[19] Both agreed to keep it quiet in the interests of national security. The *New York Times* found out that it was Canadian embassy staff in Tehran who were sheltering the houseguests, prompting Cyrus Vance to meet personally with *Times* publisher "Punch" Sulzberger to request that the story be suppressed. It was.

At least one Canadian journalist posted to Washington, Jean Pelletier of Montreal's *La Presse*, also pieced together the houseguest story—a tale he later recounted in the book he co-authored with Claude Adams, *The Canadian Caper*. On Tuesday, December 11, Pelletier called the resident Iran expert at the Canadian embassy in Washington, Tom Boehm, and asked him point-blank whether Canadian diplomats in Tehran were harbouring American fugitives. Caught flatfooted, Boehm did not deny the story. Pelletier then knew for certain that he had the scoop, and immediately informed *La Presse* editor Claude Saint-Laurent. *La Presse* wanted to run the story immediately, but Pelletier refused. "You can imagine what the consequences would be for the Canadians in Tehran," he told Saint-Laurent, "not to mention the houseguests. I wouldn't put my by-line on this story now. No way."[20] The Canadian ambassador to the United States, Peter Towe, called Pelletier later the same day to commend him for holding off on the story, and to underscore the sensitivity of the information he now had in his possession. Pelletier's father, Gérard, an old friend of Pierre Trudeau's, was then serving as Canadian ambassador to France. His son, Towe reasoned, could be counted on to do the right thing.

Word that *La Presse* knew the houseguests' secret moved quietly but quickly through the upper echelons at External Affairs. On Wednesday, December 12, a flash telex was sent from the Canadian embassy in Washington to the Middle East Division at External Affairs and copied to Ken Taylor in Tehran. The ambassador was not surprised to hear, more than a month into the hostage crisis, that the story was leaking. Recognizing that the houseguests' security would be compromised if the leak made its way to Iran, Taylor made two decisions. The first was not to tell the houseguests that the press knew about them, in the belief that it would only add to their already considerable stress. The second was to put in motion a contingency plan for moving them if their location was discovered by the Iranians. Taylor had heard about a vacant villa in North Tehran, not far from his own residence. He asked his friend New Zealand ambassador Chris Beeby to approach the landlord and enquire about leasing the house. Beeby was happy to oblige, paying down three months' rent on the residence and later stocking it with provisions. Taylor had two of his six young Canadian Forces MP's move into the villa and maintain it in a state of readiness. He then explained to the houseguests his contingency plan for evacuating them on short notice, insisting that they run emergency-evacuation drills themselves in case their worst fears were ever realized and Iran's Revolutionary Guards came knocking on their doors. The militants never came, and in the end the houseguests were never relocated.

On December 10, two days before Ken Taylor learned that *La Presse* had the story, Flora MacDonald flew to Paris for an official three-day meeting with her French counterpart. She was scheduled to fly on to Brussels on December 13 for a meeting of NATO foreign ministers.

Before MacDonald left Ottawa for Europe, Michael Shenstone suggested that she take the opportunity afforded by the NATO meeting to urge Cyrus Vance to get the houseguests out of Iran. By this time, MacDonald was convinced that Washington, preoccupied with the hostages, had lost interest in the houseguests. "People dragged their feet," she observed, and she was not at all happy about it.[21] MacDonald no sooner arrived in Brussels for the NATO meeting, however, than she learned that Prime Minister Joe Clark had telephoned to request that she return to Ottawa. A confidence motion was scheduled for 10 p.m. that very evening in the House of Commons, and the minority Conservative government needed every vote it could muster. A good Tory soldier, MacDonald informed the prime minister that she would be back for the vote.

As her assistant David Elder scrambled to find her a flight home, MacDonald sought out Secretary of State Vance and asked him for a word in private. She told him that Jean Pelletier at *La Presse* knew about the houseguests and thus that they were at ever greater risk of discovery by the Iranians. MacDonald was forceful in her appeal. "I can remember saying that if something isn't going to happen to these people to get them out of Tehran," she said, "then I would put them on donkeys and send them across the border."[22] Vance assured her that he was in complete agreement and promised to put some of his top people on the matter. Ever the gentleman, he invited MacDonald to sit at the head table at a dinner he was hosting for the NATO ministers in Brussels that evening. She declined, politely telling him that she had to hurry home to Ottawa to vote on a budget motion that might well bring down her government.

MacDonald did hurry back, but she arrived too late to cast her vote. The Tories lost the confidence motion on a 139–133 vote, and Joe Clark's minority government fell. A federal election was called for February 18, 1980. Now that she and the prime minister were heading out on the campaign trail, MacDonald was more anxious

than ever that the secret of the houseguests might be divulged—
and that she might inadvertently be the one to do it. "We had been
catapulted into an election campaign," she said. "I was, next to
Clark, the lead request to be speaking to audiences all across the
country. Yet at the same time I had to be handling this issue, making
sure that it was kept under wraps. You'd face an audience and you'd
think, what if somebody stood up and said, now what about those
six people that you have in Iran? It was always there."[23] Though
he was not tending to the houseguests' file on a daily basis, as
MacDonald was, Prime Minister Joe Clark harboured similar concerns. "Canada had a different problem than the United States did,"
he said. "The United States defined their problem as fifty people
still in captivity. We defined our problem as having six people we
had to get out, because if we didn't get them out quickly, they would
be in danger but so would Canadians."[24]

Now in their sixth week in hiding, the houseguests were themselves apprehensive that they had been relegated to back-burner status
in Washington. "As we were there longer and longer," Mark Lijek later
recalled, "we began to feel like something needed to be done to get
us out of here."[25] At one point, Lijek and the others drafted a letter
to their superiors at the State Department expressing their frustration with the lack of progress on a plan to rescue them. Ambassador
Taylor sympathized, dutifully accepting their letter. But never did he
post it, either to Ottawa or to Washington. "I suspected at the time
that it was never sent," Mark Lijek later said. "But that really didn't
matter. I think the point was still being made whether it was sent
or not. Even if Ken didn't send it, it still communicated the feelings
that we had, and those feelings, I think, in one form or another, were
probably communicated back to Ottawa and Washington."[26]

Flora MacDonald spent Christmas 1979 in New Brunswick
with her old friend Dalton Camp and his wife. She hoped to extend
their holiday of solitary walks and fireside chats into the new year.

No such luck. On December 28, Cyrus Vance requested that MacDonald attend an emergency session of the UN Security Council to support an American resolution on sanctions against Iran. She agreed to do so, leaving the Camps' residence in such a hurry that she later had to borrow dress shoes from Vance's wife, Gay. MacDonald met Vance the morning of December 29, officially, to discuss the Americans' draft Security Council resolution on sanctions. She met again with him privately the same afternoon, pressing him once more to do something about the houseguests. "If you're not going to do anything to cooperate, to get these people out of Tehran," MacDonald told him, "then what I am going to do is put them on bicycles and have them bicycle north and west and over the border into Turkey."[27] Vance told MacDonald that, with the Soviets now in Afghanistan, the White House was more distracted than ever from the plight of the houseguests. He did, however, reiterate his earlier promise to send someone up to Ottawa to work with the Canadians on a rescue plan. "The unwavering support of Canada has been greatly appreciated," he said.[28]

Vance was true to his word. He sent his own special envoy from the State Department, Peter Tarnoff, up to Ottawa on Wednesday, January 2, 1980, accompanied by CIA officer Eric Neff. "My role as mandated by Vance and Phil Habib was to be the person who would follow the brief, follow the developments, and report to them when there were decision points or action points, so to speak," Tarnoff later recalled. He, Neff and Ottawa station chief Tim McLaren spent the day in and out of meetings with Allan Gotlieb, Michael Shenstone, Pat Black and Louis Delvoie at the Pearson Building. "It was all very collaborative," said Tarnoff of their day-long session. "The discussions were about how the escape operation could be managed—almost thinking out loud."[29] Michael Shenstone also recalls the meetings as cordial. "It was manifest during a long mutual discussion of the pros and cons, of course including the risks to Canada's own personnel, that at that stage the USA preferred for the houseguests to stay put as long as possible, but that in the event, Canadian documentation would be best, then U.S. documentation, then overland exit."[30]

By nightfall, Canadian officials had persuaded their American counterparts of the necessity of moving the houseguests out of Tehran. They had also committed their government to the provision of genuine Canadian passports for that purpose, subject to Flora MacDonald's approval. As he left the Pearson Building that cold Ottawa evening, Allan Gotlieb promised Peter Tarnoff that he would request a meeting with the minister at her earliest convenience and endeavour to have the Canadian passports approved by January 4, just two days later.

The time was right to operationalize the Canadian exfiltration plan, all agreed, subject to the approval of their governments and, of course, Ken Taylor in Iran.

Chapter 16
PASSPORTS AND VISAS

On January 2, 1980, CIA Headquarters in Langley dispatched thirty-eight-year-old Tony Mendez to the Canadian capital to help convert the exfiltration scenario into a viable covert operation. Mendez was chief of authentication in the Graphics and Authentication Division of the CIA's Office of Technical Services (OTS). He had spent fourteen years in the OTS, mostly serving abroad, where his specialty was creating cover legends for CIA assets who had to be brought in from the cold. "The 'authentication' of operations officers and their agents by providing them with personal documentation and disguise, cover legends and supporting data, 'pocket litter,' and so forth is fundamental deception tradecraft in clandestine operations," Mendez explained. "Personal documentation and disguise specialists, graphic artists, and other graphics specialists spend hundreds of hours preparing the materials, tailoring the cover legends, and coordinating the plan."[1]

Mendez brought to his work not only the intense visual acuity of an artist but the cool courage of an undercover operative. It was a powerful combination of skill sets, and it propelled him quickly up through the OTS hierarchy. By the time of the Iran hostage crisis, Mendez was in charge of logistics for all undercover CIA agents operating worldwide, estimated to number in the thousands. He not only conceptualized their disguises and false documents but regularly participated directly in exfiltrating them, inserting himself covertly into hostile foreign territories and accompanying CIA assets out. It was risky work, and Mendez loved every minute of it. "I have to admit that I was absolutely engrossed by this work," he said. "It was not just the technical challenges, but the full scope of clandestine operations that intoxicated me."[2] He reportedly exfiltrated "hundreds of friendly assets" over the course of his career.[3]

When Mendez first heard about the hostage-taking at the U.S. embassy in Tehran, he came up with a plan code-named "Operation Bodyguard." The idea was that a human corpse doctored to look like the body of the shah would be offered to the Iranian occupiers in exchange for the hostages.[4] It was rejected by the White House, but Mendez claims that Jimmy Carter later expressed regret for not approving it.[5] When Mendez learned that five American consular officials in Tehran had taken refuge in the homes of Canadian embassy staff (and that a sixth was staying with the Swedes and would soon join the others), he became haunted by their plight. "The fact that the six houseguests had evaded the militants' initial assault—a possible indication of clandestine training—might unfairly brand the Americans as members of the despised CIA and could lead to harsh treatment if they were captured," he feared.[6]

Yet Mendez did not participate in escape planning for the houseguests until being seconded to Chuck Cogan's NE division on December 11, five weeks into the hostage crisis. Only then was he told to drop everything and begin working on logistics for an exfiltration mission. Owing to standard compartmentalization procedures at the CIA, Mendez knew nothing about the assistance the Canadians in

Iran were already providing both Washington and Langley. Even after he began working closely with NE officers on the houseguests' file, he was not told that the Canadian ambassador was supplying the United States with critical intelligence for Eagle Claw. Not until he actually got to Iran, in late January 1980, did Mendez learn that ambassadors Chris Beeby and Troels Munk were assisting the Taylors and the Sheardowns in the care and protection of the houseguests and that Taylor was one of Washington's main conduits to imprisoned U.S. chargé d'affaires Bruce Laingen.

The gaps in Mendez's knowledge extended even to exfiltration planning. When Mendez set out for Ottawa, on January 2, 1980, he was accompanied by an OTS "documents specialist" (forger) code-named "Joe Missouri." The two CIA officers understood their main objective to be that of persuading the Canadians to provide the agency with passports for use by the houseguests. "We initially doubted that Canada would be prepared to overlook its own passport laws," Mendez later recalled. "We also did not think Ottawa would be willing to put Canadian citizens and facilities in Iran in the increased danger they would face if the true purpose and American use of the passports were exposed."[7] Before leaving Langley, he and Missouri had collaborated on a strategy for wooing their Canadian counterparts. "We prepared passport photos and appropriate alias bio data for the six, which we would take with us to Ottawa in the hope that we could win the Canadians over."[8]

When they got to Ottawa, however, the two CIA officers discovered that the passport decision was already well advanced. "In our discussions with Canadian officials," Mendez later recalled, "we learned that the Parliament in Ottawa had already approved the use of Canadian passports for non-citizens for humanitarian purposes."[9] This was not true. The matter had not been tabled in the House of Commons and, in the interests of secrecy, it never would be.

What was true was that Allan Gotlieb, Michael Shenstone and Louis Delvoie were working on the exfiltration file on practically a full-time basis when Mendez and Missouri arrived in Ottawa, and that most of the critical decisions on the exfiltration operation had already been made in consultation with the Americans' own senior colleagues, Peter Tarnoff and Eric Neff. "I saw immediately," said Mendez, "that our Ottawa contacts saw themselves as allies in the rescue effort."[10]

The morning of January 3, Tony Mendez and Joe Missouri met for the first time with Louis Delvoie (known to Langley by the code name "Lon Delgado"[11]).Over the course of their morning meeting, Delvoie brought Mendez and Missouri up to date on the current status of exfiltration planning, presenting them with many weeks' worth of correspondence between Ottawa and Tehran. (It is likely that Mendez was also briefed by his own superior, Eric Neff, who was still in Ottawa.) Mendez was impressed with the Canadians' progress. He immediately recognized Ken Taylor's pivotal role. "He possessed many of the operational qualities we would need on the ground in Tehran: He knew how to think ahead and keep a secret."[12] Delvoie also filled Mendez in on the previous day's sessions, including Allan Gotlieb's undertaking to get ministerial approval to issue genuine Canadian passports. When the morning meeting broke for lunch, Mendez and Missouri sequestered themselves to digest everything they had learned from Delvoie.

The three men met again the same afternoon. On their agenda was the question of the houseguests' legends, the false personas under which they would exit Iran. As one of the CIA's leading experts on disguises and cover stories, Tony Mendez knew that the best legends were the least conspicuous. Yet for reasons that he has never fully explained, he took a different tack with the houseguests' covers. "Why not devise a cover so exotic that no one would ever imagine a sensible spy using it?" he thought.[13] What if the six houseguests assumed the roles of Canadian filmmakers involved in a Hollywood movie shoot in Tehran? Mendez later wrote that the "Hollywood option," as the scenario became known, struck him suddenly while he was packing his bags to go to Ottawa. "Everybody in the world kinda knows about Hollywood," he said. "Everybody in the world would like to either be involved with Hollywood or meet somebody who is. And the thing about Hollywood is that they're so eccentric they wouldn't care what the political situation was anyway, if they were looking for the right hill or the right bazaar in which to shoot their movie."[14]

Mendez was so taken with the Hollywood idea that while he was in Ottawa he telephoned a friend, code-named "Jerome Calloway," to begin fleshing it out. Calloway was John Chambers, an Academy Award–winning Hollywood makeup artist who had worked regularly with the CIA in the past, most recently on Operation Bodyguard, where he had assisted Mendez in preparing a corpse to resemble the shah. During that first phone call, Mendez and Chambers compiled a rough list of job descriptions for a group of Hollywood location scouts. Such a team would have to include "a production manager, a cameraman, an art director, a transportation manager, a script consultant, an associate producer, a business manager, and a director," Chambers told Mendez. "The associate producer represented the financial backers. The business manager concerned himself mainly with banking arrangements; even a 10-day shoot could require millions of dollars spent on the local economy. The transportation manager rented a variety of vehicles, ranging from limousines to transport the stars to heavy equipment required for constructing a set. The production manager made it all come together."[15]

According to "Hollywood option" mythology, it was at this early stage that the Canadians had to be disabused of their amateurish ideas about covers for the houseguests. ("When the Canadian government suggested nutritionists inspecting crops," according to one such report, "Mendez dismissed the idea as preposterous: 'Have you been to Tehran in January? There's snow on the ground. And certainly no agriculture.'")[16] In truth, Mendez and Missouri discussed with Louis Delvoie all of the various cover legends that had been floated to date, including at least two of the Canadians' preferred covers: teachers and agricultural nutritionists. The latter, Delvoie's University of Guelph option, was so far advanced that Canadian intelligence officers had prepared their own alias bio data for each of the houseguests. "After the meeting," Mendez himself later wrote, "I sent Headquarters a cable outlining our progress with the Canadians and presenting the movie-team option, as well as the other two options: The six could pose as a group of Canadian nutritionists conducting a survey in the third world, or a group of unemployed teachers seeking jobs in international schools in the region. . . . Over the next ten days, I shuttled between Washington and Ottawa, struggling to flesh out the complex logistics of all three exfiltration cover options."[17]

Mendez, Missouri and Delvoie agreed that two sets of Canadian passports should be prepared for the houseguests, along with two complete sets of supporting documents—one for the Hollywood option and the other for the University of Guelph option. (Mendez later recalled asking Delvoie for Canadian passports for use by himself and a second CIA officer. He was told that the government of Canada drew the line at providing passports for CIA covert operatives.) All agreed that the cover documents would be couriered to Ken Taylor in Tehran via Canadian diplomatic bag, along with two complete sets of "redundant" American cover documents to be used on the off chance that Mendez was detained by the Iranians. Assuming that Mendez could make his way safely into Tehran, it was agreed, he would present all three cover stories to Ken Taylor and the houseguests. Then a final decision would be made on which one to adopt. "The subjects themselves would have the final vote when presented with the choice of two passports, three cover stories, and the option of moving out individually or together," said Mendez.[18]

~ ~ ~

To date, published accounts of the exfiltration operation have described how Tony Mendez, John Chambers and their friend Hollywood producer Bob Sidell created a fictitious film-production company, Studio Six, over the course of several days in mid-January 1980. This involved not only leasing office space and setting up phones and faxes, but contriving the bogus Hollywood resumés of the six "Canadians" who were stranded in Tehran. To bring even greater authenticity to the scenario, an actual film script was brought into play. Chambers had been involved in a project called *Lord of Light,* a futuristic science-fiction tale that had tanked at the conceptual stage when one of its producers was indicted on embezzlement charges. He suggested to Mendez that the moribund script could be used as the project the houseguests ostensibly were in Tehran to scout out. With its mountains and vaulted bazaars, said Chambers, Tehran would be a plausible location to shoot such a film. Mendez agreed. They renamed the film *Argo,* and announced in *Variety* magazine that shooting was to begin in March. In Hollywood, the ruse succeeded beyond anyone's expectations. Within weeks, Studio Six Productions was flooded with calls from would-be employees and investors hoping to get a piece of the project.

Among the Canadians in Ottawa and Tehran, in contrast, all of this smoke-and-mirrors activity fell flat. Trying to pass a group of U.S. diplomats off as Hollywood movie producers seemed a fanciful proposition. Flora MacDonald's recollection is that neither she nor anyone else in Ottawa ever took the Hollywood cover story seriously. "It just didn't make any sense," she says flatly. For MacDonald, the only viable scenario envisaged the houseguests working in petroleum exploration. "It was all done from the point of view of six Canadians who had a legitimate interest in oil in the Middle East," she said. "It was always the story I had. I never went along with any of the rest of it."[19] Zena Sheardown has gone even further, suggesting that the Canadians could have done the rescue without any CIA involvement whatsoever. "I thought we could have done it," she recalled in 2008. "I thought the plan that was formulated—the Hollywood cover story and all that—that was just silly."[20] Ken Taylor believes that all of the attention accorded the Hollywood option was misplaced. It was, after all, a relatively inconsequential detail in a broad collaborative effort that had been underway for eight weeks by the time Mendez came up with it. "Mendez changed the scenario," said the ambassador. "He had them as filmmakers, and we had them as nutritionists."[21]

The evening of Thursday, January 3, Allan Gotlieb, Pat Black and Michael Shenstone met with Flora MacDonald to brief her on the exfiltration operation they had spent the previous forty-eight hours fine-tuning with State Department and CIA officials. All she had to do, the mandarins informed the minister, was to sign the two sets of passports and authorize the order-in-council that would make them lawful. She immediately agreed to do so, calling Joe Clark for his consent as well. Louis Delvoie and François Mathys of the legal affairs bureau at External Affairs met at 9 a.m. the following day to prepare the English and French texts of the order-in-council and the formal memo of recommendation. Later the same morning, Allan Gotlieb presented MacDonald with a formal submission to council, which she duly signed. This document authorized her to take Order-in-Council P.C. 1980-87 to cabinet that very afternoon.

Joe Clark and Flora MacDonald collaborated on a sly strategy for winning the approval of their cabinet colleagues. "The law says that only Canadians can get Canadian passports," MacDonald later explained. "If non-Canadians were to receive Canadian passports, it would have to be done through this special order-in-council. That was going to take some maneuvering because there were only a few people—two or three others in cabinet—who knew anything about this. Mr. Clark and I worked out that somehow this would be the last item on a very heavy cabinet agenda, that we would leave until the end. Then, as I introduced it, and started to explain what it was about, Mr. Clark would interrupt me."[22] A willing collaborator in this ruse, Clark later recalled how he interjected. "I said, I don't think there's any need for discussion on this—without explaining what was at issue."[23] The session ended with Clark's and MacDonald's exhausted colleagues supporting them on what appeared to be an inconsequential initiative. "The meeting broke up," said Flora MacDonald, "and I went off with approval to issue these passports."[24]

Order-in-Council P.C. 1980-87 rendered the passports for the six American houseguests legal and placed the final authority for their actual use in Ambassador Taylor's hands. "It was left to Taylor to decide," said Michael Shenstone. "If he'd vetoed the use of Canadian passports as too dangerous for everybody, then it wouldn't have happened. He had the authority to do that. That's what the order-in-council allowed."[25] At 4:30 p.m. on January 4, less than twenty-four hours after it had first been proposed to the minister, the order-in-council was signed into law by Governor General Ed Schreyer. "It can be said that this was the fastest bureaucratic decision ever made in Canada about a major paper of state," Michael Shenstone observed recently. "Gotlieb's promise [to Peter Tarnoff and Eric Neff] had been kept, a track record of which those concerned are justly proud."[26] Within days, the Canadian passports were readied for the houseguests. "I signed the passports myself, to authorize them," said Flora MacDonald, "and then we sent them off to Washington or New York to be gussied up."[27]

Meanwhile, Tony Mendez and Joe Missouri returned to Langley to brief the CIA's document-forgers on the exfiltration operation. ("We were delighted when the Canadian government gave firm approval to go ahead," Stansfield Turner later recalled of Mendez's successful trip to Ottawa. "In view of the lackluster responses we had had from most allies on economic sanctions, this was a heartening affirmation of friendship.")[28] As well as forging all of the paraphernalia typical of Canadians travelling abroad—driver's licences, health cards, credit cards, shopping receipts and other pocket scraps—Mendez's OTS people would have to "gussy up" the Canadian passports, as Flora MacDonald put it. Ottawa issued the passports several days later and immediately had them couriered to CIA headquarters. There they were doctored to include bogus Iranian visa stamps, as well as fake stamps denoting entry and exit into other foreign countries. They were also made to look worn, as any passport would be under constant use. Flora MacDonald later recalled seeing the doctored passports and other documents in Ottawa before they were dispatched to Ken Taylor in Iran. She was impressed—the CIA's handiwork seemed perfect. "We got them properly packaged," she said, "and sent them off by diplomatic courier to Tehran."[29]

Louis Delvoie cabled Ambassador Taylor on January 4 to report that the passports had been authorized. The CIA, he wrote, was cooperating with the External Affairs Department to prepare all of the documents necessary for two, possibly even three, exfiltration scenarios. Taylor cabled back, commending his colleagues for their round-the-clock work on the operation over New Year's. The actual exfiltration, Taylor and Delvoie agreed, would take place some time in early February, a schedule that was amended just days later, with Flora MacDonald's consent, because Taylor feared that the house-guests' secret might leak in Iran. The exfiltration was moved up to the weekend of January 26, conditional upon the CIA's ability to place its operatives into Tehran by that time. The revised timetable was suggested by Taylor to coincide with the Iranian presidential election scheduled to begin on January 25. With Iranians distracted by the high drama of the first presidential election since the founding of Ayatollah Khomeini's Islamic republic, the ambassador reasoned, there would be no better time for the houseguests to pass unnoticed out of the country. As for Taylor and his Canadian colleagues, they would leave Tehran in the wake of the houseguests. The embassy would be closed "temporarily."

There remained one persistent wrinkle in the exfiltration plan, Taylor realized: how to finesse the unique embarkation/disembarkation form in use in Iranian airports. This was a two-sheet carbonless document issued to every visitor to Iran. One copy of the form, white in colour, was kept on file by Iranian immigration authorities. The other, yellow, was to be retained by the visitor for the duration of his or her stay and presented to airport officials on departure. When visitors left the country, the authorities were supposed to retrieve the white copy, compare it to the yellow and allow disembarkation only if the copies matched. It was a system designed to thwart the falsification of visas by Iranians, and to catch foreigners who had overstayed their visits. The houseguests' yellow forms could be forged, Taylor knew, but no matter how competent the forgeries, the fact remained that there would still be no white copies on file with Iranian airport security. There was no getting around it: the houseguests would be faced with a risky scenario. They would have to depart Iran on forged yellow forms and hope that the authorities would be either too lazy to fetch the white copies or indifferent if they could not locate them.

This snag in the exfiltration plan made the collection of human intelligence at Mehrabad Airport a top priority for the exfiltration planners, particularly at the Canadian embassy. Early in the crisis, Ken Taylor directed Roger Lucy, Jim Edward and other embassy staffers to carefully record their experiences moving in and out of Mehrabad, checking particularly for the authorities' scrutiny of passports, visas and disembarkation forms. One aspect of the exfiltration plan that bore directly on the Canadians' human-intelligence capability was the decision to begin reducing the number of embassy personnel.

Taylor and his Ottawa colleagues agreed that the Canadians should leave piecemeal, in small numbers, so as to avoid giving anyone in Iran the impression that the embassy was being evacuated. "We exited the various members of our staff," recalls Flora MacDonald, "one by one, two by two. And they would all report on what it had been like going through the airport."[30] These debriefings occurred throughout January 1980, providing the Canadian government and ultimately the CIA with crucial information about airport security. Fortunately, the Iranians had grown lax in their scrutiny of foreigners, seldom even bothering with the white disembarkation forms.

Not wanting to leave anything to chance, the CIA directed its deep-cover officer in Tehran, Bob, to meet with Tony Mendez in late January 1980 to brief him on the precise status of security at Mehrabad. "There are still a lot of Iranians trying to get out with forged papers," Bob informed Mendez. But since he and the houseguests would be foreigners travelling on either genuine passports or impeccable forgeries, he expected everything to go smoothly at the airport. "[Bob's] positive spirit bolstered our confidence," Mendez later recalled. "This man was a master at our craft, and he had just thrown holy water on our hazardous endeavor."[31]

~ ~ ~

On January 15, the Canadian passports arrived in Tehran via diplomatic bag, along with all of the other documents fabricated by the CIA's forgers. Embassy staff were under explicit orders from Ottawa concerning the handling of diplomatic bags, in light of the unpredictable behaviour of the Revolutionary Guards at the airport. Ken Taylor later recalled the couriers' instructions. "If the Guards gave any indication that they intended to demand access to the diplomatic bag," they were told, "you just step back onto that plane. And occasionally that happened."[32] On the day the passports arrived, Roger Lucy met the courier at Mehrabad Airport. Fortunately, the Revolutionary Guards showed no interest in hassling either of them. "The courier didn't even get off the aircraft," Lucy recalled. "I was such a regular at the airport that they all knew me. I was the one in the embassy who did all the weekly bag runs."[33]

Lucy returned immediately to the Canadian embassy. He and Ambassador Taylor began poring over the handiwork of the CIA forgers. Because he had taught himself to read Persian, it fell to Lucy to scrutinize all of the bogus documents. "Ken said, check over the documents carefully to make sure they look good," he later recalled. "So I looked at them, and I discovered that the date on the visas was incorrect. My heart sank. What were we going to do now? I thought. Are we going to have to wait for another bag to arrive with new passports?"[34] Taylor still recalls the moment when he knew all was not right with the forged documents. "I remember sitting in my office and hearing a moan of despair. I thought it was because Roger had run out of Gitanes cigarettes. But it wasn't that. It was that there'd been an error in terms of the calendar."[35]

Lucy explained the glitch he had discovered in the CIA's forged visa stamps. "The Iranian calendar begins on March 21, so it is almost three months behind our Gregorian calendar. The dates on their visas therefore showed that they had been issued sometime in the future—after they had left Iran."[36] How this simple but critical error was not caught at Langley remains a mystery to Lucy even now. Tony Mendez later wrote that "our Farsi linguist had apparently misconstrued the Shiite Persian calendar."[37] But, as Lucy insists, "no Persian speaker would make a glitch like that."[38] (Lucy adds that the Eagle Claw rescue planners appear to have made a similar error reading the Persian calendar: "If Eagle Claw had got to the point where the rescuers got to Tehran, they would have had their mission in downtown Tehran on a Sunday morning. The military planners probably thought it was a rest day, but it would have been the middle of the Monday morning rush hour, because Friday to Saturday were the rest days.")[39]

Flora MacDonald, now in her third month of nervous anxiety about the houseguests, was mortified when she heard that an error had been made in the passports carrying her signature. (Her stress was exacerbated by her sense that the secret could no longer be contained. "People would come up to me at embassy receptions," she later recalled, "and they would whisper 'How are your guests?'")[40] Tony Mendez was also informed of the dating error. He immediately surmised that it would be easy to fix once he was in Tehran. Communicating through CIA and Canadian intelligence channels, Mendez informed the minister and Ambassador Taylor that he would carry the necessary forgery equipment to Tehran to rectify the error.

Meanwhile, an emergency meeting was convened in Ottawa to prepare the second set of Canadian passports. Six CIA officers met with Louis Delvoie in his Pearson Building office, and there they doctored the new set of documents. This included placing them on the ground and stomping on them, the approved agency method of instantly aging a passport.

~ ~ ~

Believing the exfiltration of the houseguests to be imminent, Ambassador Taylor commenced a staged evacuation of Canadian embassy staff that included John and Zena Sheardown. This was not a popular directive. After ten weeks of safeguarding the houseguests, John Sheardown wanted to stay the course and leave with Bob Anders and the others. And despite the extraordinary risk that Zena was taking, lacking even the minimal protections of Canadian citizenship, she felt the same way. The Sheardowns protested Taylor's decision, but to no avail. On January 19, they bade a quiet farewell to their American friends and flew directly from Tehran to London.

John Sheardown carried with him, in a diplomatic bag, the weapons that had been artfully brought into Iran one year earlier for use by the embassy MPs. As part of his debriefing at the Canadian high commission in London, he was relieved of his secret cargo. Taylor directed Roger Lucy to move into the Sheardowns' villa to stay with the houseguests. With Sheardown now gone, the ambassador also announced the closure of the embassy's visa section. "The move has provoked some anger and frustration, a few mischievous threats and accusations that we are following the orders of the USA," Taylor cabled Ottawa about the Iranian reaction to the closure.[41] Otherwise, he was not worried.

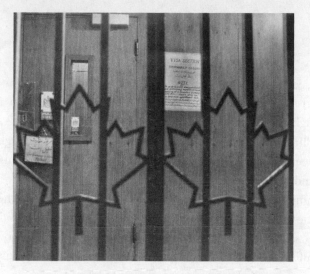

Chapter 17
THE FLIGHT OF THE HOUSEGUESTS

Tony Mendez flew to Frankfurt, West Germany, on January 21 to finalize the arrangements for the exfiltration of the Canadians' houseguests. His CIA comrade, a covert operative and expert forger code-named "Julio," flew into Geneva the same day. Both men visited Iranian consulates in person—Julio in Geneva and Mendez in Bonn—and both successfully procured one-month visas. They met up in Frankfurt the next day, and from there flew to Zurich, Switzerland, to await their final orders. Mendez had already assumed the Hollywood-option alias of film production manager Kevin Costa Harkins, but because the CIA's OTS people in Europe had provided him with various backup aliases and documents, he had the flexibility to use any number of other false personas. Julio's cover was that of a German businessman. While in Zurich, the two CIA officers received a cable from Stansfield Turner. "President has just approved the finding," it read. "You may proceed on your mission to Tehran. Good luck."[1]

With Jimmy Carter's approval in hand, Mendez and Julio boarded an overnight flight to Tehran, arriving at 5 a.m. on Friday, January 25. Julio had a close call at Iranian customs on his way through Mehrabad. Although he had a genuine Iranian visa, he was travelling on a forged German passport. On his way through security, one of the Iranian immigration officers noticed that instead of his middle name, only his initial—*H*—appeared on the document. Recognizing that this was unusual for a German passport, the officer questioned him about it. "Well, my parents named me 'Hitler' as a baby," said Julio. "Ever since the war, I've been permitted to conceal my full name."[2] The officer accepted this explanation, returned his documents and cleared him for entry into Iran.

Tony Mendez cleared Iranian security without incident. He and Julio checked into the Sheraton hotel, an ideal location because it was on the Shahanshah Expressway between Mehrabad Airport and downtown Tehran. Because they had no plans to meet Ken Taylor until the following morning, the two men had an entire day to kill. Being a Friday, Iran's holy day, the city was quiet. They decided, therefore, to do a walking tour. Their stops included the Swissair office, where they confirmed flight reservations for themselves and the six houseguests, and the U.S. embassy compound. "I felt [a] tremor erupt along my spine as reality hit me," Mendez later recalled of standing outside the embassy gate. "Fifty-three of my fellow citizens were being held in that building or at the nearby Foreign Ministry."[3]

The next morning, as planned, Mendez and Julio made their way to the Canadian embassy. Ambassador Taylor greeted them warmly. "Welcome to Tehran, gentlemen," he said, introducing them to Roger Lucy, embassy security officer Claude Gauthier and secretary Laverna Dollimore. Taylor showed the two CIA officers the documents that had arrived by diplomatic bag six days earlier, the flawed Canadian passports along with the large collection of forged paraphernalia. Their immediate task, he reminded them, was to rectify the dating error that Roger Lucy had discovered in the visa stamps. Mendez immediately produced the new set of passports that his OTS colleagues and Louis Delvoie had prepared just days before. To Roger Lucy's great relief, this set did not contain Iranian visa stamps. Mendez then produced his own visa stamp, promptly stamped all of the passports and instructed Julio to date the bogus visa stamps as directed by Lucy. "The Iranian visas were nice, simple stamps," Lucy later recalled. "So Tony just put the stamps in, and we instructed them on the proper way to date them."[4]

Mendez and Julio remained at the Canadian embassy for the rest of the day, fine-tuning the houseguests' travel covers and forging their yellow disembarkation forms. The forgeries showed the houseguests as having arrived in Tehran on an Air France flight from Hong Kong within an hour of Mendez's arrival on January 25. The information Julio wrote into the blank disembarkation forms was copied directly from Mendez's genuine one, since the immigration officer who had processed him had also processed the passengers arriving on that Air France flight. Ken Taylor and Roger Lucy, meanwhile, spent the day absorbed in the myriad tasks requisite to closing the embassy: shredding sensitive papers and anything else that might be compromising, securing less sensitive documents in the communications vault, finalizing the embassy's administrative paperwork and notifying the few remaining Canadian nationals in Tehran that consular services would be suspended temporarily.

Taylor and Lucy drove Mendez and Julio out to the Sheardown villa the following morning, Sunday, January 27. There the CIA officers met the houseguests for the first time. "We didn't know who he was," Cora Lijek later recalled, referring to Mendez. "They said that it was time for us to be taken out of Iran."[5] Joe and Kathy Stafford were driven to the villa by Chris Beeby's second secretary at the New Zealand embassy, Richard Sewell, a man Roger Lucy called "invaluable" to the exfiltration operation.[6] (It was Sewell who had procured the blank disembarkation forms from a friend at Mehrabad Airport, the station manager for British Airways.) Taylor made quick work of the visit. He made the appropriate introductions, off-loaded a large parcel of clothing and some suitcases the Canadians had put together to complement the houseguests' covers, and left to take care of administrative loose ends at the embassy. His wife, Pat, was scheduled to fly out of Tehran late that afternoon, and he was to follow twenty-four hours later. Both had much to do before leaving.

~ ~ ~

Until December 1978, roughly one-third of the scientists at Iran's Blood Transfusion Service had been foreigners. After the mass evacuation of North Americans from Iran that began that month, Pat Taylor was the only non-Iranian on staff there. She had been evacuated several times over the course of the previous year, but never for more than a week or two. Pat felt a strong attachment to her research, and also to her colleagues. "They accepted me," she later said of her Iranian co-workers. "In fact, they looked after me very, very well."[7]

In mid-January 1980, Pat Taylor broke the news to the directors of the Blood Transfusion Service and the Pasteur Institute that she would be leaving Iran along with her husband. The Canadian embassy would be closing temporarily, she explained, but she hoped to return before long to Tehran to resume her work. "That's okay," said the head of the transfusion service. "The wives of the ambassadors have to leave Iran at this time and you should go." At the Pasteur Institute, however, the director tried to persuade her to stay. "As a scientist, we need you!" he exclaimed. "We could help you find a little cottage and make sure that you have someone to help you in the house," adding that he would also look for someone to look after Douglas when he came back from school. "Don't worry, we will pay you enough to handle all of this." Pat dissembled. "I'll think about it," she said. "I'll let you know in about a month or so."[8]

Her last day on the job was Saturday, January 26, the day before she was scheduled to fly out of Tehran. Inevitably, it was a busy, chaotic day. "There were a lot of people I wanted to say goodbye to," she later recalled. "They had a lot of questions as well—scientific questions—which I wanted to try to answer before I went." At one point, in the process of hurriedly collecting some documents for her colleagues, Pat slipped on a newly polished corridor floor and twisted her ankle. "It swelled up, and everybody was worried," she said. "So they called the medical doctor on staff. He came and took my blood pressure, and he said, 'Oh, we've got to put you in hospital straight away.' I said, 'Oh no, you can't do that'—because I'm leaving tomorrow."[9] The doctor discovered what Pat had already suspected—that the stresses associated with eighteen months of revolution, the strife and tension at the Blood Transfusion Service Centre and hiding the houseguests were quietly taking their toll on her health.

Pat had not been paid for months, owing to the disruptions of the revolution. Knowing that she was leaving the next day, her boss presented her with a cheque to cover all of her accumulated earnings. Pat was grateful for the cheque but uncertain as to whether it would be possible to cash it before leaving Iran. "I couldn't change it very easily because it was the end of the day," said Pat, "the day before I was to leave."[10] As she was resting her ankle in the staff locker room and pondering the matter of the cheque, some of her Iranian colleagues entered and made a kind offer. They would be happy to pool all of their Iranian cash in exchange for the cheque. "This just shows the generous character of Iranians," she said later. "I still don't know whether whoever took the cheque was able to deposit it."[11]

Pat Taylor's colleagues' generosity turned out to be serendipitous for Ken. He and the other exfiltration planners wanted to leave nothing to chance when the houseguests left Tehran. As part of their contingency planning, therefore, it was agreed that Taylor would purchase multiple sets of tickets for various flights leaving Tehran the morning of Monday, January 28. If all went according to plan, the houseguests would escape Iran on Swissair Flight 363, departing Mehrabad Airport for Zurich at 5 a.m. But just in case of flight delays or other unexpected problems, they would also carry tickets for Air France and British Airways flights leaving the same morning. Tony Mendez had brought some cash with him to Tehran for exfiltration-related expenses, courtesy of the CIA, but it was not sufficient to purchase multiple airfares for the eight departing "Canadians." So Pat handed her cash windfall over to Ken, and he purchased the extra tickets with it.

Pat Taylor took an Air France flight from Tehran to Paris on Sunday, one day ahead of her husband and the American diplomats she had helped shelter for nearly three months. One of her research colleagues at the Pasteur Institute, a man Pat held in the highest esteem, was not so fortunate. He was later arrested and executed as a counterrevolutionary.

~ ~ ~

Back at the Sheardown villa, Roger Lucy agreed to help Tony Mendez and Julio brief the houseguests on the exfiltration mission. They poured themselves some coffee and settled into the spacious den, the room where the Lijeks had spent most of their days in hiding. There Mendez laid out the details of three possible scenarios: the Hollywood option, the University of Guelph option and Flora MacDonald's petroleum-business option. He passed around the genuine Canadian passports, the documents the CIA had forged and copies of the *Argo* script. "I've managed a lot of these operations," Mendez told the houseguests, "and I believe the *Argo* movie plan will work."[12] Although he favoured the Hollywood option, he made it clear that the final decision on cover legends would have to be theirs. "I instructed the six to go into the dining room to discuss among themselves whether they wanted to go to the airport in a group or individually and which cover story they preferred," Mendez later recalled.[13]

The most formidable challenge in preparing the houseguests for the exfiltration mission was persuading Joe Stafford to go along with the plan, and with him, his wife, Kathy. Having spent many weeks living with the Staffords, Ken Taylor had anticipated their reluctance. "Joe was not necessarily in favour of the exit plan," said Taylor. "Lee Schatz had to talk him into it. And I had to talk him into it too."[14] Mark Lijek, who knew Stafford well, later explained his reticence. "I think Joe's issue was not fear of the process of exfiltration as much as it was a sense that our departure was a betrayal of our comrades at the U.S. embassy and that we needed to stay until they were released."[15]

Unable to come to a consensus on which cover scenario to adopt, the houseguests put the matter to a vote. Bob Anders reported the result of the vote to Mendez. "We've decided to leave together as a group with the Studio Six cover."[16] With that, Mendez distributed the various Hollywood-option props he had brought along to augment the houseguests' covers. Julio followed suit with his disguise and makeup materials.

Before they had become fugitives, the houseguests had been highly visible at the U.S. consulate, seeing thousands of Iranians in the course of their work. Cora Lijek and the Staffords had worked at the non-immigrant visa unit and were especially well known, in part because enterprising Iranians sold sketches of U.S. visa officers complete with notations as to which were allegedly tougher than others. Just to be on the safe side, the houseguests all agreed to alter their hairstyles and, in the case of the men, even colour their beards and moustaches. Cora Lijek became Teresa Harris, a scriptwriter. Her husband, Mark, became Joseph Earl Harris, the transportation coordinator. Kathy Stafford became a set designer, and her husband, Joe, a producer. Lee Schatz became a cameraman. Bob Anders reportedly had the most fun with his film-mogul persona. He became director Robert Baker, donning tight pants and an open shirt and affecting an extroverted Hollywood style.

Asked later why they opted for Mendez's movie-crew option, Mark and Cora Lijek said that it struck them as the right fit for the atmosphere in Tehran. "We thought that the average person—business person, school teacher—would not be coming to Iran during the revolution," said Cora. "But film people? Yeah, they would probably go somewhere even if there was trouble because that might actually excite them or be interesting."[17] Mark agreed. "We felt, with the exception of Joe, that it was a great cover. The people who work in Hollywood have such an overweening sense of self-importance that they would actually believe that they could walk into a revolution and shoot a film and get all the cooperation they needed."[18] Reflecting on the Canadians' view that the Hollywood option seemed far-fetched, Mark Lijek suggested that it was not the practical viability of the cover that succeeded but the psychological advantage it brought him and his colleagues. "Ken Taylor was correct in one sense," he said. "As long as we were Canadians, the rest of it is kind of irrelevant, in terms of how things worked at the airport. But it wasn't irrelevant as far as how we felt about it. The confidence factor was important, especially if we had been stopped. At that stage we probably would have been in trouble anyway."[19]

Roger Lucy agrees with Lijek. "Frankly, I don't think the movie story held water for one second, but it was something that caught their imagination," said Lucy. "I think half of Tony's disguise process was psychological, a matter of convincing his subjects that their disguises would work, and thereby inducing in them a greater sense of calm so they wouldn't give themselves away by fidgeting. He was using psychology to overcome people's nervousness. We offered them the other scenarios, and nothing really sang with them. I don't think we could have sold it to them the way Tony sold it to them."[20] Mendez himself later confirmed that there was nothing accidental about his use of psychology. "Infiltrating and exfiltrating people into and out of hostile areas are the most perilous applications of this tradecraft," he wrote in the CIA journal *Studies in Intelligence*. "The mental attitude and demeanor of the subject is as important as the technical accuracy of the tradecraft items."[21]

The mission details now decided, Mendez, Julio and Lucy left the houseguests to themselves. They spent the afternoon packing, selecting their Hollywood attire and memorizing the personal information of their cover legends. (Cora Lijek later joked that she practised saying the word *Toronto* in proper Canadian fashion: "*Tronna*, like *piranha*.")[22] Lee Schatz spent much of the afternoon cajoling, and sometimes haranguing, Joe Stafford to accede to the exfiltration plan. At 4 p.m., Roger Lucy returned to the villa to walk the houseguests through various scenarios they might encounter at Mehrabad Airport. Wearing military fatigues and adopting his best Persian accent, Lucy assumed the role of an aggressive Iranian emigration officer, taking each of the houseguests through a mock interrogation. Mendez and Julio returned to the villa at 5 p.m., while the interrogations were in progress. Over cocktails, they answered the houseguests' many questions about the exfiltration plan and, as Mark Lijek later put it, "told us war stories about exfiltrations from the USSR (and one or two from Iran) that were intended to help us believe that our operation was routine."[23]

Mendez recounted how he had helped to bring the CIA's most valuable Iranian asset, code-named "Raptor," out of Tehran in April 1979. Raptor was a high-ranking military officer with close connections to the palace and to the shah personally. He was also the CIA's "top spy in the shah's government," according to historian John Prados.[24] Raptor had gone into hiding when militants loyal to Ayatollah Khomeini began rooting out and executing the shah's former officers. When Mendez got to him, he was barricaded in a drafty attic in Tehran and more than a little paranoid about being discovered, tortured and executed. The cover legend Mendez created for Raptor was that of an elderly Jordanian business person. Mendez himself had smuggled all of the requisite accoutrements for the exfiltration into Tehran and coached Raptor for hours on how to maintain his cover as he passed through Mehrabad Airport. Immobilized by fear, Raptor panicked when his flight was called and locked himself in the men's room. The quick-thinking Mendez intervened personally. He retrieved Raptor, assuming the role of a young businessman escorting a confused older colleague. A sympathetic airline agent took their boarding passes and assisted the two men onto the waiting plane. Raptor was successfully exfiltrated to Zurich hours later.[25]

His mock interrogations over, Roger Lucy returned from the den to join the houseguests and the CIA officers for a drink. Ken Taylor had arrived at the villa by this time. So had the two New Zealanders, Chris Beeby and Richard Sewell. At 7 p.m. everyone sat down to a magnificent seven-course dinner, complete with contraband champagne and liqueurs. Knowing that, with the exception of the New Zealanders, this would be their last night in Iran, all agreed that this soirée should be a "scorched earth" party, the object of which was to leave no alcohol behind. There was method in this madness, of course. Their alcohol-induced revelry would attenuate the houseguests' anxiety about their imminent flight from Tehran, scheduled for 5 a.m. that morning. Mark and Cora Lijek recall getting only two hours' sleep that night, at most. Lee Schatz and Joe Stafford got even less, staying up to continue their conversation about the feasibility of the exit plan.

~ ~ ~

Tony Mendez and Julio left the Sheardown villa at midnight, hoping to sleep for at least a couple of hours before their 3 a.m. wake-up call. The exfiltration plan called for Richard Sewell to pick them up at the Sheraton and drive them to Mehrabad Airport. Sewell got to the hotel promptly at 3 a.m. and rang Mendez from the lobby. A groggy Mendez fumbled with the phone and confessed that he had slept in. He had a quick shower and appeared in the lobby with Julio fifteen minutes later.

At the Sheardown villa, it fell to Roger Lucy to awaken everyone. "It was a matter of getting everyone up and pouring coffee down people's throats," Lucy later recalled. "Then we bundled them into the car and off they went. And then I waited to hear how it went. It was a couple of hours of biting my fingernails and hoping that nothing would go wrong."[26] The cars carrying the houseguests were limos bearing Canadian flags, a nice touch arranged by Ken Taylor. "Once we were in the car," Cora Lijek later recalled, "that's when the play-acting really started because the drivers didn't know who we were. I kept checking my pockets to see if anything had my real name on it."[27]

Mendez entered the airport first. He knew that the stakes were high. "If we had been caught," he said, "the Revolutionary Guard would have decided to make an example of us, being hung in the city square or decapitated."[28] Perceiving everything to be quiet at the terminal, Mendez checked his bags at the Swissair counter and got his boarding pass. Using a prearranged signal, he then beckoned Julio and the houseguests to enter. "I was pretty nervous going into the building," said Cora Lijek.[29] Mendez could tell that all of the houseguests—underslept and hungover—were uneasy as they queued up at the Swissair counter. Their check-in went smoothly, however, increasing their confidence. They made small talk with the flight attendants, and adopted as best they could the banter of a group of Hollywood co-workers. They then joined Mendez for what they knew would be the most nerve-racking moment of their passage through Mehrabad, the emigration checkpoint.

Lee Schatz was the first to go through. Iranian officials stamped his passport, took his yellow disembarkation form and beckoned him to proceed. It was immediately clear that, on that morning at least, no one was interested in tracking down the white copies of the disembarkation forms. All of the houseguests cleared the emigration desk without incident. Julio and Mendez brought up the rear. All were greatly relieved when they heard the announcement that their flight, Swissair 363, was ready for early departure. They tried to be as inconspicuous as possible in the departure lounge, looking through the gift shops, flipping through magazines. At one point Joe Stafford picked up a Persian-language newspaper out of habit but quickly dropped it when he realized his faux pas.

While they were killing time in the lounge, a second announcement blared across the PA. Swissair Flight 363, it said, was delayed with a mechanical problem. Knowing that Ken Taylor had equipped them with multiple reservations, the group conferred about what to do. "Tony gathered us in a corner," Mark Lijek later recalled. "We talked about it. Maybe we should switch to the British Airways flight. But there didn't seem to be any way to do that without drawing attention to ourselves."[30] Meanwhile, Richard Sewell, who had remained on hand, sought out his contact at British Airways, the friend who had earlier provided the disembarkation forms. He confirmed that the Swissair jet did have a minor technical problem but that it would not take more than an hour to fix. Hearing this, Mendez and the houseguests agreed that they should bide their time and keep to the original plan. Although they only had to wait twenty minutes, the houseguests later acknowledged that it was the longest twenty minutes of their lives. Finally, the announcement to board Flight 363 rang through the airport. The group was shepherded onto a bus that ferried them and the other passengers across the tarmac and out to the idling plane.

Climbing the stairs to the aircraft door, the houseguests noticed that the plane's name was *Argau*. Anders turned to Mendez and said, "You guys think of everything!"[31]

~ ~ ~

Having "launched" the houseguests from the Sheardown villa, Roger Lucy could do little but wait anxiously for the call from Richard Sewell to tell him that the mission had succeeded. He had by this time gone several days without sleep. At 6:30, his friend finally rang. "Word came through that the houseguests were up and away," Lucy said later, "and I must say that I heaved a great sigh of relief."[32] Lucy phoned Ken Taylor at the ambassador's residence immediately. "The party's over," he said. "The guests have gone home."[33]

Taylor and Lucy agreed to rendezvous at the embassy. Together they drafted a terse cable informing Ottawa that the houseguests had been safely exfiltrated. From the Pearson Building, where it was 2 a.m., flash cables went out to the CIA and the State Department. A series of cryptic phone calls was made. Flora MacDonald was in her hometown of Kingston, Ontario, taking a much-needed break from campaigning. "I was awakened at about two or three o'clock in the morning," she later recalled, "with the phone ringing. A voice at the other end said, 'Minister, they're out.' I just dissolved into tears from the tension."[34] The last of Ottawa's classified cables arrived in Tehran later the same morning: "BON VOYAGE TO ALL. SEE YOU LATER EXFILTRATOR."

President Jimmy Carter and CIA director Stansfield Turner, both of whom had been kept apprised of the progress of the rescue mission at every stage, were also delighted and relieved to hear that it had succeeded. "There was a surge of pride that Americans, assisted by Canadians, had finally outsmarted the Ayatollah,"[35] Turner later mused. (Carter and Turner were relieved for another reason. As former DCI Richard Helms later wrote, the Carter administration had, in fact, been "scared to death" that the houseguests' story would leak and had decided, therefore, not to inform the appropriate congressional oversight committees about CIA involvement in the exfiltration.)[36]

Once they knew for certain that the houseguests had cleared Iranian airspace, the four remaining Canadian diplomats in

Tehran—Ambassador Taylor, Roger Lucy, Claude Gauthier and Mary O'Flaherty—made quick work of shutting down the embassy. Taylor posted a note on the building's front door. "The Canadian embassy is temporarily closed," it read.[37] When the last of his flash cables had been sent to Ottawa, he directed Claude Gauthier, his burly Québécois security officer, to destroy all of the embassy's communications equipment. Gauthier was happy to oblige, wielding a massive sledgehammer to good effect, pounding the mission's rock-solid cipher machine into scrap metal. For his efforts, he earned himself the nickname "Sledge," a moniker he still uses with considerable pride.

With the embassy fully secured, Gauthier, Lucy and O'Flaherty went out for "a jolly good lunch," as Lucy himself later put it. "Then we trundled off to Mehrabad Airport."[38] Ken Taylor enjoyed his last meal in Tehran in the company of Troels Munk, Chris Beeby and John Graham, the three ambassadors to whom the houseguests and their Canadian protectors were so deeply indebted. After dining at the Danish embassy, Taylor was driven in Ambassador Munk's car directly to Mehrabad Airport, where he joined his embassy colleagues. Feeling the weight of the world lifting off their shoulders, the four exhausted Canadians boarded a British Airways flight to Copenhagen, Denmark, and bade Tehran a final adieu. When the pilot announced that they had cleared Iranian airspace, they broke out champagne and, as Taylor himself put it, "had a quiet drink in celebration."[39]

More than anyone else on that plane, of course, Ken Taylor knew that the rescue of the six American diplomats had done nothing to mitigate the broader tragedy. Fifty of the houseguests' colleagues remained imprisoned in their own embassy under conditions that could scarcely be imagined. Two others and HOM Bruce Laingen were still living under house arrest at the Iranian foreign ministry. The CIA's lone intelligence officer in Tehran, Bob, was now homeless.

In his last signed cable as Canada's Ambassador to Iran, Taylor observed with no small irony that, after three months of frenetic activity to resolve the hostage crisis, almost nothing had been accomplished. The militants were still in the driver's seat, he wrote, and their position was still unambiguous: "No shah, no hostages."[40]

PART SIX
AFTERSHOCKS

Chapter 18
THANKS, CANADA

Ambassador Ken Taylor and his three embassy colleagues flew into Copenhagen, Denmark, the evening of January 28, 1980. They immediately checked into local hotels, where they got their first decent night's sleep in days. (Roger Lucy called his parents from the airport in Copenhagen. He had been up for sixty consecutive hours and fell asleep in the middle of the call.) The following morning, Claude Gauthier and Mary O'Flaherty flew directly to Ottawa, where they were debriefed by External Affairs officers. Ken Taylor enjoyed a leisurely lunch with the Canadian ambassador in Copenhagen, Marion Macpherson, and flew off to Paris in the afternoon. Roger Lucy went to Geneva to visit a friend. Both Taylor and Lucy fully expected to return to Tehran within a week or two, and thus planned for only a limited period of rest and relaxation in Europe. Before leaving Tehran the ambassador had informed his thirty-three locally employed staff (LES) that he was closing the embassy temporarily and leaving the country. He would be back soon, he told them. The embassy would then reopen, business as usual.

Pat Taylor had flown on Sunday, January 27, directly from Tehran to Paris, where she checked into a hotel that had been booked for her by the Canadian embassy. Because Canada's ambassador to France, Gérard Pelletier, was abroad on official business, it fell to Deputy Ambassador Robert Elliott to arrange the Taylors' living accommodations. After a sleepless Sunday night, Monday brought Pat Taylor good news. She spoke to Ken by phone while he was still in Tehran, and was greatly relieved to learn that the houseguests had made their escape without incident. Later the same day she spoke with Chris Beeby at the New Zealand embassy, learning that Ken was en route to Copenhagen, along with the last of his Canadian staff. Pat was looking forward to reuniting with her husband in France, where for the first time in months they could enjoy each other's company at a slow pace, away from the myriad stresses of the hostage crisis.

Ken Taylor's Air France flight from Copenhagen arrived punctually late Tuesday afternoon at Charles de Gaulle Airport, where he was met by several officials of the Canadian embassy. As he emerged through the arrival gate, Taylor could not help but notice that the reception area was choked with television crews and journalists of every description. "I was a bit curious," he said. "I thought some celebrity must be arriving. I was thinking Charles Aznavour, or Elizabeth Taylor." One of his Paris colleagues enlightened him at once. "No, they're looking for you," he said.[1]

~ ~ ~

The story that Canadian diplomats in Tehran had hidden six Americans for three months and abetted their escape had broken earlier that day. La Presse's Washington correspondent, Jean Pelletier, had been sitting on the secret since mid-December, at the request of External Affairs. With the official announcement from Ottawa on January 28 that the Canadian embassy in Tehran was temporarily closed, Pelletier reasoned that it was only a matter of time before the houseguests' story came out. And when it did, he might lose the scoop of a lifetime. Chargé d'Affaires Gilles Mathieu at the Canadian embassy in Washington tried to talk Pelletier out of publishing what he knew. It might have repercussions for the remaining hostages, said Mathieu. But Pelletier's "instincts," as he later put it, "were now shouting that it was time to go."[2] He did not have to twist the arms of his bosses at *La Presse*. The newspaper ran the exfiltration story in the morning edition the next day. By mid-morning Montreal time, the wire services had picked it up, and it was buzzing through the world's capitals. External Affairs in Canada and the State Department in the United States confirmed that Ambassador Ken Taylor and his colleagues had indeed sheltered six American diplomats and spirited them out of Tehran. A "well-placed diplomatic source" told the *New York Times* that the CIA had provided the Canadians "technical assistance" on the passports and visas.[3]

On hearing that the Canadian embassy was temporarily closed, the Iranian foreign ministry had issued a bland statement saying that it had not been informed of Taylor's departure and that it was seeking clarification for the action from its own embassy in Ottawa. Terminating consular services would cause problems for the many Iranian students who were seeking visas for study in Canada, the statement acknowledged. But beyond that, with so many foreign diplomats already evacuating Iran, it was not surprising that the Canadians should be leaving too.[4]

When the sensational story of the Canadian rescue broke the next day, however, the Iranians had to scramble to make sense of it. "As far as I know," said Kamran Morassagghi at the Iranian embassy in Washington, "we are waiting to hear from Tehran before making further comment."[5] Foreign Minister Sadegh Ghotbzadeh, who had known about the houseguests all along, said he knew nothing of the escape. At least one Iranian newspaper, the *Daily Bamdad*, reported that the CIA had jointly planned the operation with the government of Canada. Ayatollah Khalkhali issued a statement saying that it was likely that other American "spies" had taken refuge in other foreign embassies and should be rooted out. Recriminations rolled quickly through the various factions of Iran's revolutionary government. According to a cable sent to Ottawa from the New Zealand embassy, officials in the foreign ministry, the Revolutionary Guards and Mehrabad Airport security had already begun "investigating each other's role in the affair."[6]

At the U.S. embassy compound, the hostage-takers were said to be "resentful" when they learned about the escape. A Reuters correspondent filled one of the militants in on what was known of the rescue. "That's illegal!" he replied.[7] "The foreign ministry must know the number of diplomats in Iran," added one of his comrades. "So how come more than the known number of Canadian diplomats were allowed to leave?"[8] The occupiers released their own statement later that day. It said that the rescue of the six Americans would not affect their plans for the hostages or produce reprisals against Canadians who remained in Iran. "We wouldn't take any [Canadian] hostages," said one of the militants, "because what's happened is the fault of their government."[9]

At the Iranian foreign ministry, the three imprisoned American diplomats were told that their telephone and telex communication with Washington would be terminated, and so would their visits from foreign ambassadors. "The students and others [were] suspicious," Bruce Laingen later recalled, "that the three of us had been somehow involved."[10] It mattered little to the jubilant chargé. On January 30, his eighty-eighth day in captivity, Laingen wrote his son, Bill, with the news of the escape. "We are absolutely delighted by this news," wrote Laingen Sr., "since we have worried about them ever since the beginning. We knew they were in good hands. How good has now been made apparent to everyone. I hope it reminds the American people what great and good and trusted neighbors we have to the north."[11]

The morning *La Presse* broke its story, CBC journalist Carole Jerome was in New York to interview the newly appointed Iranian ambassador to the UN, Mansour Farhang. In the middle of the interview, Jerome's phone rang. It was the CBC's Toronto desk calling to tell her that Ambassador Ken Taylor had just fled Tehran with six American diplomats he and his colleagues had been hiding since the embassy takeover. Jerome was instructed to tell Farhang of Taylor's escape while the cameras rolled. As she did so, the attitude of the nonplussed ambassador shifted instantly from one of friendly bonhomie to indignant outrage. There would be "dire consequences" for Canada, he told Jerome.[17]

Hamilton Jordan and Hal Saunders were just two weeks into their back-channel negotiation with the Iranian government the day the story broke. The two Paris lawyers who had volunteered to mediate the "scenario" deal, Christian Bourguet and Hector Villalon, were sitting in Jordan's White House office when he got word of *La Presse*'s scoop.

"Christian," said Jordan. "I have something to tell you. Six Americans who were hiding in the Canadian Embassy since the takeover have just escaped from Iran."

"The Iranians will say that once again they have been tricked by the CIA and the Americans," Bourguet replied. "We have been telling them the Americans could be trusted—and now this happens!"

Thinking quickly, Jordan came up with a tactic that might deflect the blame away from the Carter administration. "The Canadians are right in the middle of an election," he told the Frenchmen. "Tell Ghotbzadeh that it was simply a re-election ploy by Prime Minister Joe Clark. Say it was Clark's attempt to win favor with the Americans and his own people. Blame it all on the Canadians!"

"Good!" replied Bourguet. "The Iranians always look for conspiracies."

Bourguet called Sadegh Ghotbzadeh directly from Jordan's office. The call lasted ten minutes.

"He was very, very concerned about the escape," Bourguet reported to the others, after ending his call to Ghotbzadeh. "He said that he will do his best to control public opinion, but he wasn't sure what will happen at the American embassy. He will try to turn all the Iranian anger and frustration toward the Canadians."[13]

In Tehran, Ghotbzadeh convened a press conference. "We indicate that sooner or later, somewhere in the world, Canada will pay for the action they have taken," he threatened. If the escape of the six diplomats made things more difficult for the Americans being held hostage at the U.S. embassy, said Ghotbzadeh, this would not be the fault of Iranians. "Any hardness, harshness or changes which may be imposed on the hostages, it's only the Canadian government which will be responsible for it." The rescue justified the occupation of the U.S. embassy, continued Ghotbzadeh. "[The Canadians] have violated the laws they claim to defend. This gives us a particular item to justify the action of the students that these so-called international laws are only made for the suppression of small nations by the big ones." A journalist asked what he meant by making Canada pay. "Everybody is free to do whatever they want," he replied. Asked whether he knew the Canadians had been hiding the Americans, Ghotbzadeh said that was a question he would not answer. He was then asked whether the Iranian foreign ministry would have guaranteed the security of the six had they turned themselves in. "Most probably yes," he replied.[14]

Midway through his press conference, realizing perhaps that his case against Canada was thus far lacklustre, Ghotbzadeh rolled the dice. He claimed that he had received a message through an unidentified third party from Prime Minister Joe Clark. In this message Clark apologized for the rescue, saying that it had been carried out "for domestic political reasons within Canada."[15] Said Ghotbzadeh, "I was informed of the message excusing [Clark] for the unconventional action and indicating it was not against Iran but only for the internal affairs of Canada since the present government is in difficulty and needed some scheme to mobilize the people over there." Ghotbzadeh concluded his remarks with a statement clearly intended to shore up his own bona fides with the militants in his government. "It is clear now what international laws and conventions mean to the Western world," he said, "especially when everybody was talking in the past couple of months about the violation of international laws by Iran. But Canada permits itself to forge the passports, to forge the stamps and to send out some people!"[16]

The ball was now in Ottawa's court. Prime Minister Joe Clark issued an immediate denial. "I sent no message to the Iranian authorities of any kind," he said.[17] Clark's chief of staff, Bill Neville, stated bluntly that Ghotbzadeh was lying. "No apology was sent to Mr. Ghotbzadeh or anyone else in Iran for the simple reason there's nothing to apologize for."[18] Flora MacDonald was not surprised that Ghotbzadeh had threatened Canada. "I didn't expect him to come out and cheer us," she said. "I really don't believe that the threat that Ghotbzadeh issued is something that is going to suddenly take place, because I really do believe that the situation is not what it was several months ago."[19] The Canadians' denials had no effect on Sadegh Ghotbzadeh, of course. Having put this tale in motion, he had to see it through. Interviewed on CBC Radio's *As It Happens* the day the rescue story broke, he was asked if he was sticking to his story that Clark had apologized. "Absolutely," he replied.[20] For his part, Joe Clark was unflappable. Asked whether he thought Iran would retaliate for the rescue, he replied, "I don't think there will be other kinds of danger."[21]

Ghotbzadeh's allegations provided an entertaining sideline, but the real story remained the rescue and Ken Taylor's heroic role in it. Throughout the United States, the ambassador was heralded as Canada's "Scarlet Pimpernel," and Canadians everywhere found themselves "sudden blushing heroes."[22] Americans deluged local radio phone-in shows with outpourings of gratitude for their northern neighbours. Canadians all over the United States were treated to free meals by thankful restaurant owners. In Washington's National Press Club, Canadian journalists were offered free drinks. American travel agents reported new interest in Canadian tourism. "You know, we tend to take you guys for granted," a congressional aide told the press. "But when the chips are down, you always come through. What your people did in Tehran was fantastic. I can't imagine us having a better ally." "If your guy Joe Clark has any sense, this will be a good time to renegotiate the Auto Pact," joked another. "With the mood towards Canadians in this town right now, you people could ask for the moon and we'd probably give it."[23]

In Canada, editorial opinion and letters to the editor were almost uniformly effusive. The day the exfiltration story broke, the *Toronto Star* called the rescue of the six "brilliant," an affirmation that "Canada's professional diplomats are among the best in the world." The work of the Canadian diplomatic corps is normally well hidden from public view, said the *Star*. "The performance of Ambassador Ken Taylor and his staff at the embassy in Iran shows precisely those qualities all of us would most wish to find in our country's representatives abroad: skill, courage and compassion." The paper also congratulated Joe Clark and Flora MacDonald on the success of the operation. "This is an occasion that has nothing to do with the federal election, nor with the merits or weaknesses of Joe Clark's overall approach to foreign policy. It is, quite simply, an occasion for pleasure and pride."[24] The *Globe and Mail* was equally laudatory, praising the "gallantry of the band of Canadians, who might have paid dearly had their secret been uncovered at any time in the long three months since they opened their doors to mercy."[25] Across the land, the same sentiments echoed. American gratitude was matched only by Canadian pride.

~ ~ ~

Stepping into the arrivals lounge at Charles de Gaulle Airport the afternoon of Wednesday, January 30, the man at the centre of this international media storm was caught entirely by surprise. Not so his colleagues from the Canadian embassy in Paris, who had spent the last twenty hours in the eye of the international media storm that had followed on the heels of the exfiltration. They greeted Ken Taylor warmly, and then, by arrangement with the Paris police, escorted him discreetly through an emergency security exit and into a waiting car. Acting on instructions from Ottawa, they drove Taylor directly to the Canadian embassy. There he was happily reunited with Pat.

The Paris embassy, like the airport, was besieged by journalists and curious onlookers. Having had his first taste of stardom, Ken Taylor now got his first introduction to its handmaiden: security. Worried that the ambassador might be targeted by militants acting on Ghotbzadeh's threats, Prime Minister Clark directed Canada's diplomats in Paris to tighten security around him. It was prudent, said Clark, to increase security in areas where Canadian diplomats might be exposed to "actions by individuals who would be sympathetic to the Iranian cause."[26] A bomb threat received at the Canadian cultural centre in Paris reinforced the Canadians' concerns. Aware that the reach of Iranian militants might extend to Taylor's family, the French police also assigned a security detail to Douglas Taylor's lycée in the south of France. (One person who had anticipated that Taylor and his staff would be targeted for reprisals was Stansfield Turner. "The Canadians had to expect retaliation when it became known that they had abetted the escape," he said.)[27]

After a short debriefing with Deputy Ambassador Robert Elliott, Ken Taylor spoke with Flora MacDonald by phone, "mostly about the weather in Paris," he later quipped.[28] The Taylors spent Tuesday night at a hotel near the embassy but moved secretly into Elliott's private residence the next day, in the interests of security. Wednesday morning, Ken went out to a nearby brasserie for an espresso because he could not sleep. There, for the first time he felt the full weight of his instant international stardom. Glancing over the shoulders of those at the next table, he saw a picture of himself on the front page of the *International Herald Tribune*. "What do I do now?" Taylor thought to himself. "I threw some francs on the table, headed for the door, and lost myself in the crowd on the Champs-Élysées." As he was leaving, he could hear a pair of American tourists arguing.

"Yes, that was him sitting right there behind us reading our newspaper over your shoulder," said a woman.

"It was not," replied the man seated opposite her. "He's probably still in Tehran."

"Yes it was," insisted the woman. "I recognized the hair."[29]

Later the same morning, Ken Taylor held a press conference on the steps of the front courtyard of the Paris embassy. Over one hundred journalists and their camera crews showed up. Taylor knew that Ottawa wanted him to say as little as possible about his activities in Tehran, but his own sense was that it would better serve everyone's interests, including those of the American hostages left behind, if he offered a few reassuring words about his departure from Iran rather than the usual "no comment." He had by this time grown accustomed to treating his instructions from Ottawa more like guidelines than strictures. Bathed in floodlights, Taylor smiled for the cameras, his beaming, spotless grin betraying considerable bewilderment as well as immense happiness. "I in no way anticipated this acclaim, this recognition, that unfolded first in Europe," he later reflected.[30]

Taylor was described as looking fit and tanned at the press conference, and "obviously enjoying the hero's attention that his exploit has brought him."[31] Peppered by questions, Taylor gauged immediately that he would have to speak with caution—hardly a major adjustment, since he had been doing so in Tehran for months. "I really would like to answer all your questions," he told the crowd of journalists. "However, I am not able to right now."[32] Taylor was asked whether he feared for his own personal safety. "No, I feel fine," he replied. He did not think the Iranians were likely to take reprisals against Canadians or Americans in Iran, he added, nor against Canadians elsewhere in the world, notwithstanding Sadegh Ghotbzadeh's threats. The ambassador acknowledged that there had been threats against Canadians in Paris but said that he was not worried. Canada and Iran had always enjoyed good relations, he observed. "I can imagine they will remain so. Certainly that is the aim of our minister. There is a certain amount of unpredictability. But we look forward to the continuation of that relationship. I remain optimistic."[33] Some reporters wondered why he was so reluctant to say anything of substance. "There are persistent rumours," said one, "that there are more Americans hiding in Iran whose safety might be jeopardized by full disclosure of the story."[34] Others pressed him about a rumoured "seventh man," an Iranian "believed to be connected with the American embassy who later returned home with the Americans."[35] The Iranians were not alone in conjuring up conspiracy theories about the Canadians' exploits in Tehran, it turned out, but Ken Taylor was not talking. He thanked everyone for the warm welcome and disappeared with his Paris colleagues into the chancery building.

~ ~ ~

Within hours of Taylor's Paris press conference, the houseguests— Bob Anders, Lee Schatz, Mark and Cora Lijek, and Joe and Kathy Stafford—made their first public appearance since the exfiltration.

After their freedom flight into Zurich accompanied by Tony Mendez and Julio, the six Americans were met at the airport by State Department officials and driven to the U.S. ambassador's residence in Berne. (The two CIA officers were left standing in the airport parking lot, freezing, as Mendez later recalled, because they had loaned the houseguests their topcoats.) There the houseguests were informed of an aspect of the exfiltration plan that they had never heard before: their escape would remain secret for as long as the other fifty-three Americans remained in captivity. "We were told," said Mark Lijek, "that we were going to be shipped off to Florida to live under false names at an Air Force base for the duration."[36] Lijek's impression was that both the CIA and the State Department perceived this to be the appropriate strategy. "Tony Mendez was hoping to reuse parts of that exfiltration to get some of the real hostages out at some future time," he later recalled. "He didn't much care for Eagle Claw."[37]

The White House was not pleased when news of the rescue exploded onto the world's headlines. The president himself had requested of American newspapers that they hold the story, and they were continuing to do so. The day *La Presse*'s story was published, White House press secretary Jody Powell conceded that the president and his top advisers were disappointed. "Obviously," he said, "our desire was that it not come out and it was also the desire of Canada that it not come out."[38] With no reason to detain the houseguests any longer, the State Department arranged to have them flown to Dover Air Force Base on an Executive 707, the lap of luxury. There they were met by their families, who had also been flown in by the State Department. Bob Anders was reunited on the tarmac with his wife, Linda. "It felt unreal and real at the same time," he later recalled, "and I might say, very romantic. I was very, very happy to be home again."[39] Cora Lijek was reunited with her parents. "It was a very emotional reunion," she said later. "I remember my mother crying. I think she'd been holding everything inside and it all just came out."[40] Mark Lijek's mother, Wanda, said she would always be grateful to the Canadians. "The State Department called us once a week," she said, "but they didn't say [Mark and Cora] were at the Canadian embassy. I didn't care to know where he was, as long as he was all right."[41]

At Dover, a bull session was held for the houseguests to prepare them for the "rather dangerous" media attention they were likely to encounter.[42] An internal memo articulated the need for caution. "State Department briefers will impress upon them the advisability of avoiding going into detail or saying anything which might conceivably jeopardize the lives of the fifty [sic] remaining hostages," it read.[43] The next day, the houseguests were taken to Washington, DC, where, like Ken Taylor, they were treated as celebrities. Their first stop was the State Department's Dean Acheson Auditorium, where they agreed to hold a press conference on condition that no journalists be allowed to ask questions. The houseguests later recalled their reception as deeply moving. "It was even more than any of us had any reason to believe or expect," said Bob Anders. "It was a great crowd of people and employees there, and a lot of press. It was overwhelming."[44]

Anders spoke from a prepared text. Given "the sensitivity of the situation," he said, "we cannot take questions at this time or give details beyond this bare outline. We have first and foremost in our minds the continued safety and hopes for an early release of the hostages in the compound. We are certain that you understand and agree with our desire to do nothing which would jeopardize the hostages or our benefactors."[45] Anders then spoke of the time he had spent with the Canadians. "Most of our days were spent following events in the world. We avidly read newspapers and listened to overseas radio broadcasts. Also during the course of three months, we played Scrabble to the point where some of us could identify the letter on the front by the shape of the grain on the back of the tile."[46] Present at the press conference was Canadian chargé Gilles Mathieu. The embassy had been "overwhelmed" by expressions of gratitude from Americans, said Mathieu. "It reflects the depths of feeling about the fifty other people." Questioned about the Canadian rescue effort, the chargé took a page out of Ken Taylor's playbook. "We've done what would be expected, what was normal, and what any U.S. embassy would do for us," he said.[47]

The houseguests were driven from the State Department to the White House to meet President Carter. All were wearing Canadian flag lapel pins, one of which was presented as a gift to the president. Again Bob Anders read a prepared statement, this time before an audience that had brought handmade signs saying, "Thank You Canada" and "Merci Canada." "As you already know," said Anders, "the Government of Canada and its representatives in Tehran made it possible for us to avoid capture, and eventually to leave Tehran. It is difficult to fully express our appreciation for the risks the Canadians took to ensure our safety and comfort. They made us feel a part of their family, especially at such times as Christmas when our spirits needed a boost. We thank them for their brave support."[48] The president referred to the houseguests as "six brave Americans," declaring, "[W]e're grateful to have them back."[49]

~ ~ ~

At 11:30 a.m. on Thursday, January 31, President Carter called Prime Minister Joe Clark. "I wanted to call," said the president, "on behalf of the American people, Joe, to thank you and Ambassador Taylor, and the Canadian government and people for a tremendous exhibition of friendship and support, and, I think, personal and political courage." Clark replied that he hoped the remaining hostages would not be jeopardized by the rescue. Said Carter, "I don't believe that the revelation of their departure will be damaging to the well-being of our other hostages. You are nice, and very perceptive, to express that concern." The president paused. "I think it was a remarkable demonstration of mutual trust that the fact of the existence of those Americans was kept confidential so long," he continued. "The fact that it was not revealed publicly until after they had already left is very good. We are deeply grateful for this, a new demonstration of the closeness that is very beneficial to us." Carter bade Clark farewell, wishing him good luck in the upcoming election.[50]

Elsewhere in Washington, the Canadians were celebrated as heroes and as great allies. On January 30, the U.S. Senate and House of Representatives passed resolutions praising Canada for the rescue. The Senate resolution read, "The Senate, on behalf of all Americans, hereby commends the Government of Canada for its actions in protecting United States citizens."[51] House Speaker Thomas P. (Tip) O'Neill introduced the resolution in the House by noting that Congress had never before praised another nation for its actions. "History is being written," he exhorted.[52] Sought out by the media for his views on the rescue, Zbigniew Brzezinski said that Americans would "always be indebted to Canadians" for what they accomplished in Tehran, calling Taylor a "courageous Samaritan."[53] On February 12, the House of Representatives and the Senate voted to have the Congressional Gold Medal struck in Taylor's honour. Bronze copies of the medal would also be minted and sold to collectors to recoup the $20,000 cost of the original.

The following day, Americans' outpouring of gratitude for Canada made the front page of the *New York Times*. The newspaper described the atmosphere in the United States as "euphoria."[54] At the John Jay College of Criminal Justice in New York, president Gerald Lynch ordered Canadian flags flown on all campus staffs "until the American hostages in Iran are released."[55] Citibank paid $17,000 for a full-page ad in the *New York Times*. "Thank you, Canada," it read, "from the bottom of our hearts. In a world filled with hatred, anxiety and spite, you showed your unwavering compassion, reason and courage."[56] Prime Minister Joe Clark had by this time received more than two hundred telegrams from thankful Americans— business figures, politicians, diplomats, even American prisoners of war. "Your government has been the only one of our allies which has extended themselves for us and stood up for human rights," said one of them. "On behalf of the people of Milwaukee County we thank you for your noble efforts. This is a special thanks because one of the individuals, Robert G. Anders, came from Milwaukee County."[57] Everywhere along the Canada–U.S. border were signs saying "Thank you, Canada."

Editorial opinion in the United States followed suit. "Other nations have supported the United States in the hostage crisis with words," said the *Baltimore Sun*. "Canada risked its interest and may be made to suffer losses. Canada is even risking retributive violence elsewhere to Canadian lives and property by partisans of Ayatollah Khomeini."[58] The *Christian Science Monitor* said that the rescue was "a dramatic reminder that the American people still do have more than fair-weather friends in the world."[59] "A friendly nation, at no small risk to its own interests, went way out on a limb for an ally and did something truly selfless and honourable," said the *Washington Post*. "Canada has acted the way we would like this country to act, were the circumstances reversed."[60] The *New York Daily News* wrote, "A good neighbor is one who can be counted on for support and help in time of trouble. The U.S. is fortunate to have just such a neighbor on its northern border."[61]

Of the many statements of gratitude Taylor heard from Americans after his return from Iran, one of his favourites came to him via Canadian consul general Harry Horne in San Francisco. While Horne was visiting a local school to talk about the rescue of the houseguests, a child stood up in the back of the class. "Please thank Mr. Taylor very much for rescuing the six Americans," she said, "but ask him when he's going back for the other fifty."[62]

~ ~ ~

After two hectic days in Paris, Ken and Pat Taylor took an Air France flight to New York, where they were met in person by Michael Shenstone, the man who had served as Ken Taylor's main comrade in Ottawa for the entirety of his thirty-month tenure in Tehran.

Together Shenstone and the Taylors transferred to a Canadian government jet and flew directly up to Ottawa. Present to greet them at CFB Uplands on that frigid winter's night was Flora MacDonald, along with a group of roughly fifty journalists and External Affairs officials. Ken Taylor was asked how it felt to be a hero. "I'm not quite sure yet," he replied. "I'll have to sleep on it."[63] MacDonald greeted him warmly. "You've been through a number of weeks—a number of months in fact—of a job that has been difficult in the extreme. And we all know how successfully you carried it out. You've done it, and in doing so, created deep pride in Canadians."[64] As he had from the outset, Taylor insisted that the rescue had been a team effort. "What we have accomplished was entirely the work of the office as a whole. It just happens that I am here alone. But I would like to express my appreciation for my colleagues, and I'll identify them at another time."[65]

From Uplands, the Taylors were driven to the Ottawa home of Michael and Susan Shenstone, where they would themselves become secret houseguests, hidden from public view and surrounded at all times by an RCMP security detail. "We went underground," Ken later recalled. "It was such chaos. The poor Shenstones!"[66]

On February 1, Taylor gave his first Canadian press conference about the rescue, at Ottawa's National Press Club. One journalist present described him as "ruddy-faced with gray, curly hair and resembling an angelic, over-aged choir boy."[67] Taylor spoke for fifty minutes but divulged little about the operational details of the exfiltration (and, of course, nothing about his clandestine intelligence work). It was vintage Taylor, evincing his extraordinary talent for verbal misdirection. He acknowledged that the houseguests had fled Iran on Canadian passports. He would not say what identities the houseguests were given, only that they were not "real" Canadian names. He also refused to discuss their cover legends. The Canadian passports they used did not confer diplomatic status, he said, "but that's as far as I can go." When asked about how he got the bogus exit visas, he laughed, saying, "I got the passports and the rest is what you'd call a trade secret." Taylor described the houseguests as being in high sprits and "brimming with confidence" throughout their time in hiding. He was asked about how he functioned day to day in Tehran without betraying the secret. The trick, he replied, was to put the houseguests "totally out of mind" so as not to "blow the whole thing." He clarified that reports that the six had worked as embassy staffers were inaccurate. What was true, he said, was that the houseguests spent a great deal of time playing board games. "I'd nominate any one [of the six] for the world's Scrabble championship," he joked.[68]

Two weeks later, Taylor returned to his hometown of Calgary, where he was feted in separate ceremonies at city hall, the Chamber of Commerce and the Canadian Petroleum Association. Appearing with his parents, Richard and Nancy, he said, "It feels great to be home."[69] He remained tight-lipped about the details of the rescue, cracking some jokes and keeping things light instead. "I didn't bring much luggage from Iran," he quipped. "I am the only guy in town who goes to a dry cleaner to have his suit pressed and has to wait." Asked about his celebrity status, Taylor said, "It wasn't my intention to be a hero. I just did what anyone would do in the same situation."[70]

By the spring of 1980, External Affairs had not only loosened the reigns on Canada's most famous ambassador but conceded that it would be good PR for the department if he agreed to do a publicity tour while they decided what his next diplomatic appointment might be. And tour he did. For the next six months Taylor seemed to be *everywhere*, an indefatigable symbol of Canadian–American friendship. He crossed Canada six times and the United States four, in order to receive all of the honours bestowed upon him. More than once he agreed to a daily schedule of two or three appearances, only to end up doing five or six when word got out that the hero of Tehran was in town. In March, New York City mayor Ed Koch presented Ken Taylor with keys to the city. The Canadians' rescue effort, said Koch, "rivals the heroic action taken by the Dutch and Danish in World War II to save Jews from the barbarism of the Nazis."[71] Other cities to present Taylor with keys included San Francisco, Los Angeles, Dallas, Las Vegas and Kansas City. In May, Ken, Pat and all of the Canadian embassy staff from Tehran were honoured in the gallery of the Canadian House of Commons. That summer and fall, Ken opened the Canadian National Exhibition, the Pacific National Exhibition, the Calgary Stampede and the Royal Winter Fair. He gave commencement addresses to any number of graduating classes, and made cameos at countless telethons, sporting events and awards ceremonies. People remarked on how consistently gracious and charming Taylor was, often likening him to the other Canadian hero of the day, Terry Fox.

Pat Taylor later calculated that Ken made over a thousand public appearances over the course of his tour. Ever the diplomat, he never missed an opportunity to share the credit for the rescue with his Canadian embassy confrères, to celebrate Canadian–American friendship or to speak magnanimously about the future of Iran's relations with North America once the fifty-three hostages were freed. Although he was extremely careful never to say much about the exfiltration mission that had made him famous, he was always categorical about one thing. As one journalist put it after interviewing him at length, "So far as Taylor knows, there was no U.S. Central Intelligence Agency (CIA) involvement in the operation."[72]

Taylor's friends at the CIA had been right. The Canadian ambassador knew how to think ahead and keep a secret.

Chapter 19

FALLOUT

When Iranian foreign minister Sadegh Ghotbzadeh adopted his "blame Canada" strategy in response to the exfiltration story, he had more on his agenda than salvaging the hostage-release "scenario" that he had been engineering with Christian Bourguet and Hector Villalon. Though almost nobody knew it at the time, he was working secretly with Panamanian president General Omar Torrijos to have the shah extradited from Panama. If he could pull this rabbit out of a hat, Ghotbzadeh reasoned, he could overwhelm his main rival in Iran's presidential election, heir apparent Abolhassan Bani-Sadr, awe the Iranian electorate, silence his domestic critics and claim a great victory for the new Islamic republic. Hamilton Jordan later recalled how surprised he was when Bourguet and Villalon flew off to Panama on January 27, right in the middle of their talks with him and Hal Saunders.[1] The White House had no idea that while Ghotbzadeh was working toward some kind of negotiated resolution to the hostage crisis, he was also searching for a trump card that would allow Iran's elected government to consolidate power and undercut the extremists, both in the Revolutionary Council and at the U.S. embassy compound.

Ghotbzadeh's master plan unravelled the week Ken Taylor and the houseguests left Tehran. Word of his secret dealings with Torrijos leaked in Iran. Faced with the appearance that he was doing Ghotbzadeh's bidding, the Panamanian strongman denied that there had ever been an arrangement and refused to have the shah arrested. Without this *coup de grâce*, Ghotbzadeh had little to offer the Iranian electorate. He got less than one per cent of the popular vote in the presidential election, while Abolhassan Bani-Sadr walked away with 75 per cent—a landslide. President-elect Bani-Sadr agreed to allow Ghotbzadeh to remain on as Iran's foreign minister. Despite their mutual antipathy, the two men took the same view of the hostage crisis. It could be resolved, they believed, only if the duly constituted government of Iran could assert its authority over the militants, and if a back channel to the Carter White House could be maintained. Since Ghotbzadeh's was the most promising back channel, Bani-Sadr allowed him to stay.

Taking full advantage of his victory, Bani-Sadr moved decisively against the hostage-takers. For a time it looked as though the militants' influence on the Ayatollah was declining.[2] The occupiers opposed a visit from UN secretary-general Kurt Waldheim, for example, but Khomeini did nothing to prevent Ghotbzadeh from welcoming him to Tehran. Even more significantly, when the occupiers requested the transfer of imprisoned American chargé Bruce Laingen and his colleagues from the Iranian foreign ministry to the U.S. embassy compound, Khomeini said no. Bani-Sadr challenged the hostage-takers directly in his first televised interview in Iran after winning the election. Iran would not tolerate the existence of a "parallel government," he said.[3]

The following day—just as *La Presse*'s story was breaking—the *Washington Post* reported that president-elect Bani-Sadr had agreed in principle to a deal with the United States to release the hostages to a neutral third party such as the Red Cross while a UN commission investigated Iran's charges against the shah.[4] President Carter confided to his diary—in a tone of near disbelief—that despite an explicit decree from Khomeini to the contrary, "Bani-Sadr is sending word to us directly that he wants to proceed with a resolution of the hostage situation."[5] A few days later Carter got even more promising news: Bani-Sadr had been named head of Iran's Revolutionary Council. As Carter noted, he "began to make speeches in Iran designed to isolate the militants from the general public and to remove the aura of heroism from the kidnappers."[6]

Ken Taylor's friend New Zealand ambassador Chris Beeby was not nearly so sanguine. "The repercussions of the Canadian issue are likely to be severe internally," Beeby cabled his home government in Wellington on January 30. "The outcome has probably strengthened the students."[7] Despite such misgivings, the New Zealanders generously agreed to provide consular services for Canadians in Iran now that Canada's own embassy was closed. "We have not been asked to represent Canadian interests in Iran," New Zealand's acting prime minister Brian Talboys clarified in an official statement, because Canada and Iran had not severed diplomatic relations. "Bilateral relations between Canada and Iran will be conducted through the Iranian embassy in Ottawa."[8]

Ambassador Beeby's instincts proved prescient. Over the night of February 4–5, his own embassy was targeted by Iranian militants. Erecting roadblocks on either end of the street, they broke into the building and thoroughly ransacked it. Using oxyacetylene cutting equipment, they even tried to open the embassy safe—an endeavour that failed, apparently because the safecrackers ran out of gas cylinders. The militants took whatever unsecured documents they could find, none of them very important. Beeby and his colleagues arrived at work the next morning to find their embassy in shambles.

Ken Taylor was later asked whether he thought it had been ransacked because the New Zealanders were known to be close to the Canadians. "Yes," he replied. "I think in one way or another it was put together."[9] Chris Beeby decided that the time had come to follow his friend's example and get his people out of Iran. As an official memo noted, Ambassador Beeby arrived in London the same afternoon, "after hastily evacuating his embassy."[10] On hearing this news, Ken Taylor and Michael Shenstone paid a visit to the Danish ambassador in Ottawa. The Danes agreed without hesitation to represent Canada in Iran on the same basis as the New Zealanders, little knowing that they would still be doing so almost a decade later.

It fell to Iran's chargé in Ottawa, Mohammad Adeli, to register his government's official displeasure with the Canadians' rescue of the houseguests. He called the action a "flagrant violation" of international law. Canada must be "blamed and held responsible for giving in to American pressure," he said.[11] Fully expecting that Iran would level formal charges against Canada, the legal affairs bureau at External Affairs, led by Director General L. H. Legault, worked assiduously to prepare a legal defence. Canada's brief was plainly stated and endlessly repeated. "Legal, moral and humanitarian principles all support Canada's actions in protecting U.S. embassy personnel from the Iranian mob and helping them to escape from the threat of unlawful custody," Legault argued.[12] In mid-February 1980, as expected, Iran tabled its case against Canada at the UN Security Council. It centred on the undisputed fact that genuine Canadian passports stamped with forged Iranian visas had been approved by the Canadian prime minister. Such an act, according to the Iranians, was a "glaring example of duplicity" typical of the "imperialist powers" and their "back-handed approach towards the Third World."[13]

Surprisingly, though, given the international furor the rescue had precipitated, it damaged day-to-day Iranian–Canadian relations relatively little. Following Ken Taylor's example, most Canadian officials who spoke publicly about Iran—with the notable exception of Flora MacDonald—were at pains to placate rather than antagonize the Iranians. On February 8, 1980, less than two weeks after the escape of the houseguests, Governor General Ed Schreyer officially conveyed "my good wishes and those of the people of Canada" to Abolhassan Bani-Sadr for his election as president. Bani-Sadr, in turn, who was fluent in French, agreed to a lengthy interview on CBC/Radio-Canada. Although his government remained insistent that the shah be extradited to face justice in Iran, he said, he hoped that the sour relations between Iran and Canada caused by the escape of the Americans could be put behind them and that normal diplomatic relations could be restored.

Back in Ottawa, External Affairs officials noted repeatedly—and with some astonishment—that there had been no reprisals against Canadians in Iran in the aftermath of the rescue. In fact, Canada's relations with Iran were carrying on more or less as usual. The Iranian government did not close its embassy in Ottawa or recall its chargé, nor did it take any retaliatory action against Canadian property in Iran. Canadian business people remained free to come and go as they liked, and to conduct commerce in Iran. Never did Iranian militants break into the Canadian embassy in Tehran.

Despite the ongoing war of words at the UN Security Council and elsewhere, it appeared that the Iranians had already begun to make their peace with the Canadians' rescue of the six American diplomats, as Ken Taylor had expected they would. In this respect, at least, Sadegh Ghotbzadeh's "blame Canada" strategy had succeeded brilliantly.

~ ~ ~

It speaks to the depth of Joe Clark's character that he has never traded on his supporting role in Ambassador Taylor's double-edged mission in Iran—intelligence-gathering for Eagle Claw and exfil-tration planning for the houseguests. Never as prime minister did Clark seek to turn his unsung courage and decisiveness during the hostage crisis to his own political advantage, even when his adver-saries painted him as a "wimp."[14] If Ken Taylor's actions in Iran were heroic, Clark's were as well.

To the delight of his Liberal opponents, Pierre Trudeau fore-most among them, Prime Minister Clark did not even seek to cap-italize on the rescue of the houseguests during the election campaign of February 1980, when he was behind in the polls and fighting for his political life. Clark was in Kitchener, Ontario, the day *La Presse*'s story broke. In a campaign speech that evening, he said only that he wanted to express his appreciation for the "non-partisan" success of the rescue mission. "You would all want to join with me in expressing our appreciation as Canadians for the work of courage [and] dedi-cation to duty that was demonstrated under the most unthinkably difficult circumstances," he added.[15] Clark had blundered badly on foreign-policy issues during the 1979 election, most notably when he floated the idea that Canada should move its embassy in Israel from Tel Aviv to Jerusalem. Here was a perfectly timed opportunity to turn things around. Yet he did not take it.

Even when queried about Trudeau's reckless attacks in the House of Commons, the prime minister took the high road. Trudeau had never put the houseguests in jeopardy, said Clark. Nonsense, said some of his less reticent colleagues in the Tory caucus, including MP George Cooper of Halifax. "Mr. Clark told the caucus that Mr. Tru-deau's actions could have serious adverse repercussions on the lives and safety of Canadians and Americans in Iran," Cooper said flatly.[16] Flora MacDonald agreed. "My God, it was nerve-wracking, keeping quiet all that time," she later recalled. "And that rotten Pierre Trudeau attacking us when he knew what we were up against. People wonder why I dislike him so."[17] Ken Taylor, too, remained baffled as to why

Trudeau had played fast and loose with the secret of the houseguests while lives hung in the balance. "I couldn't figure out what kind of game he was playing," said Taylor. "I think it was just as well that I wasn't aware of it."[18]

Joe Clark's magnanimity also extended to NDP leader Ed Broadbent, who had suggested that closing the Canadian embassy in Tehran was a "political ploy" on Clark's part. After *La Presse*'s story broke, the prime minister was asked why he had not alerted Broadbent earlier as to what was happening in Tehran. "I wish I had," Clark replied. "That would have stopped him from making the statement he did and prevented him from being embarrassed." Clark explained that, under the British parliamentary system, only the Leader of the Opposition is given security briefings about crises affecting the government. "I decided to follow the British example," said Clark, which meant telling only Pierre Trudeau. Never did he worry that the NDP leader would have "spilled the beans," however. "He's a man of honour," said Clark of Broadbent. "He would not have breached the confidence." Clark later revealed that he considered changing the parliamentary rules so as to include Broadbent in security briefings. "I wish we had in retrospect," he said.[19]

Pierre Trudeau, of course, was not one to look a gift horse in the mouth. He took full advantage of Clark's apparent naïveté, casting the exfiltration story as a credit to Canada rather than Clark, and himself as the only leader who brought the country stature on the world stage. "This is commendable action and all Canadians and myself applaud this brave work by External Affairs officials and we commend the government for supporting it," said Trudeau. "It is in the long tradition of Canadians abroad acting to support those in danger and distress. This was true in Chile and elsewhere in the world in other crises. And if it happened in Iran we are proud of our Canadians there."[20] According to the *New York Times,* when Trudeau heard about *La Presse*'s story he cancelled a trip to Prince Edward

Island in order to give a major speech in Toronto on Canadian foreign policy. "That speech was designed to demonstrate that he, and not Mr. Clark, knew what foreign affairs were all about," said the *Times* bluntly.[21] Pollsters asked Canadians whether the rescue of the house-guests would improve Clark's chances in the election. They said no.[22] "Clark's handling of foreign policy has been so inept," quipped Liberal veteran André Ouellet, "that if he'd been ambassador in Tehran, the six Americans would have been caught within three days."[23]

Clark was not without his defenders. Columnist Joan Sutton at the *Toronto Star,* for one, was exasperated by Trudeau's opportunism. "The first shot of internal sniping came from the Leader of the Opposition, Pierre Trudeau," said Sutton, "who prefaced his comments about the rescue with the phrase, 'If it's true,' although he knew, long before the rest of us did, that the Americans had been given sanctuary. Of course, it hurts the Liberals that, in making Canada look good, Joe Clark has made himself look good. And don't kid yourself, Clark played an important role. It was the Canadians on the spot in Tehran who took the heat, who withstood the daily pressure, but the ultimate responsibility belonged to the Prime Minister."[24]

In the end, of course, Pierre Trudeau carried his Liberal Party to a decisive victory on election night, February 18, 1980. With Trudeau's "Welcome to the 1980s," Clark's short-lived minority government acquired the status of a historical footnote. As Brian Mulroney later observed of the Clark interlude, "the first Conservative government in sixteen years was defeated after thirty-eight days in the House. It passed no major legislation, left no heritage, and Pierre Elliott Trudeau was returned to office."[25] In contrast with Canada's openly pro-U.S. Tory prime ministers—Brian Mulroney and Stephen Harper—Joe Clark's relationship with the Americans is today remembered as humdrum, if it is remembered at all.[26]

Yet no other Canadian prime minister, Tory or otherwise, is known to have approved the use of Canadian passports in a covert operation to rescue imperilled Americans abroad. And no other prime minister is known to have authorized the use of a Canadian embassy as a base for clandestine intelligence gathering—at the request of an American president and in support of a U.S. military action in a foreign country. On both counts, Prime Minister Clark showed decisiveness, selflessness and courage on a scale that wholly belies his reputation as a ditherer.

As Pierre Trudeau acknowledged far more generously in retirement than he did while he was in politics, Joe Clark well deserved the acclaim that the Canadians' success in Tehran had brought him.

~ ~ ~

More hopeful for the release of the hostages than he had ever been before, Jimmy Carter dispatched Hamilton Jordan and Hal Saunders to Europe in early February for another round of secret talks with Christian Bourguet and Hector Villalon. Their mission, said the president, was to draft "a precise, written document of understanding between the Iranians and me, so that there would be no last-minute misunderstandings to abort a potentially successful effort."[27] After several marathon drafting sessions, Jordan and Saunders returned to the United States with a tightly scripted release scenario. According to this new plan, a five-person UN commission would go to Iran. The American hostages would be transferred from the embassy compound to a hospital, on the pretext that their health was to be assessed. The commission would then submit its report, including Iran's grievances, to the UN. The hostages would be released, the UN report would be made public and both presidents would issue public statements agreed upon in advance.

The dramatic climax of the scenario preparations came on February 17, when Sadegh Ghotbzadeh met Hamilton Jordan secretly in Paris. Ghotbzadeh said that he hoped that Iran and the United States could settle their differences quickly so they could start rebuilding their alliance against the Soviet Union. (He also asked a thunder-struck Ham Jordan whether his government had considered ending the hostage crisis by simply assassinating the shah.)

The UN commission envisaged by the new scenario was assembled in Geneva on February 20. The commissioners left for Iran three days later. Before they had even landed in Tehran, however, Ayatollah Khomeini announced that only the Majlis could decide the fate of the hostages—and it was not likely to reconvene for four months. Emboldened by this obvious snub to the Americans, the militants at the U.S. embassy refused to follow Bani-Sadr's and Ghotbzadeh's directives, declined to allow the UN commission access to the hostages and reiterated that they took their orders only from Khomeini. The UN commissioners remained in Iran, but it was now clear that neither Bani-Sadr nor Ghotbzadeh could deliver on the scenario. On March 6, the occupiers announced that they would consider ceding control of the hostages to the Revolutionary Council. Fatefully, Bani-Sadr and Ghotbzadeh accepted this offer, apparently in the hope that Council might, in turn, transfer the hostages into government custody. Instead, they were stonewalled—unable even to persuade the Council to meet to discuss the issue.

Together, Khomeini's rejection of the scenario and the occupiers' triumph over Bani-Sadr and Ghotbzadeh marked a fateful turning point in the hostage crisis. Jimmy Carter was heartbroken. "Khomeini, apparently deranged," he later wrote, "had overridden the government and aborted the resolution of the crisis. This failure of our best efforts was a bitter disappointment. It seemed that we had now lost our last chance to set the Americans free."[28] The UN commissioners left Tehran empty-handed on March 11, never having seen the hostages. Some observers, including Ken Taylor, believed Villalon and Bourguet had been out of their depth from the outset, but not Jimmy Carter. "These two men repeatedly risked their lives to help us," said the president, "and I and the people of our country will always be indebted to them."[29] Carter also expressed his admiration for Sadegh Ghotbzadeh, calling him "really gutsy" and applauding him for taking "a lot of personal risks in seeking a resolution to the crisis."[30]

Ghotbzadeh's courage was very much in evidence just weeks later when he publicly threatened the Soviet Union. Iran was prepared to arm the Mujahidin in Afghanistan, he said, if the Soviets did not withdraw their troops from that country. The KGB, which had always considered Ghotbzadeh one of its most formidable Iranian adversaries, retaliated with a brilliant scheme to discredit him. First, it circulated forged letters between him and Westerners that exaggerated his complicity with them in secretly negotiating an end to the hostage crisis. Then, in July 1980, it fed false information to the Iranian ambassador in Paris to the effect that Ghotbzadeh had received a bribe of $6 million for helping the Canadians smuggle the houseguests out of Iran.[31] Increasingly isolated and beleaguered, Ghotbzadeh was forced out of the Iranian government the following month. Even then, the KGB continued to circulate false documents purporting to show that he was an agent of the CIA. It is likely that this disinformation campaign contributed to his arrest and execution in September 1982.

~ ~ ~

With the scenario dead, Jimmy Carter grew more hawkish. On April 7, he broke diplomatic relations with Iran, which meant expelling all Iranian diplomats from the United States. He also imposed unilaterally the trade sanctions that the Soviets had vetoed at the UN Security Council in January. This meant a Cuba-style embargo on all U.S. exports excepting food and medicine. Carter and Cyrus Vance appealed to the leaders of Japan, France, Britain, West Germany and Canada to impose sanctions of their own. But only Pierre Trudeau

gave "a strong positive response," as Vance put it, announcing that
Canada would also embargo Iran.[32] Just before the Iranian chargé in
Washington, Ali Agah, left the United States, he met with the State
Department's director of Iranian affairs, Henry Precht. "The hostages
are really quite happy in Iran," Agah told Precht casually. "Some of
them even want to stay." The normally aloof Precht could not contain his anger. "Oh, bullshit!" he responded. Jimmy Carter later sent
Precht a handwritten note about his outburst. "One of the elements
of good diplomatic language is to be concise, accurate and clear," it
read. "You have shown yourself to be a master of all three."[33]

Just how hawkish President Carter had become came to light on
April 11. Meeting with his National Security Council, he announced
that he was now ready to authorize the Eagle Claw rescue mission.
"I told everyone that it was time for us to bring our hostages home,"
Carter later recalled with uncharacteristic bravado.[34] Cyrus Vance,
who was overseas and could not attend the NSC meeting, was pre-
dictably annoyed when he heard about it. "Stunned and angry that
such a momentous decision had been made in my absence," said the
secretary of state, "I went to see the president very early the next morning and spelled out my strong objections to the rescue mission."[35]
Vance believed that a military rescue mission would risk the lives
of the hostages unnecessarily, since they were likely to be released
safely "once they had served their political purpose in Iran."[36] Carter
obligingly convened a second meeting of the NSC six days later,
where Vance was given the opportunity to make his case. But no one,
not even Carter, could be talked out of the rescue mission. Vance told
the president that he would resign if the rescue effort went forward,
later recalling the period leading up to the Eagle Claw mission as a
time of "deep personal anguish."[37] Carter was struck by it too. "Vance
has been extremely despondent lately," he wrote in his diary.[38]

On April 19, the White House got word via Ambassador Eric
Lang at the Swiss embassy in Tehran that Bruce Laingen thought the

United States should increase the pressure on Iran. Jimmy Carter later remarked that the chargé's brave words cemented his resolve to operationalize the rescue mission. The president received an intelligence briefing on April 23, indicating that the conditions for the mission were optimal. He notified a handful of congressional leaders, insisting on total secrecy, and then gave the go-ahead for the mission. The countless hours that Ken Taylor, Jim Edward, Bob and many others had logged collecting and analyzing intelligence, and the months of secret training undertaken by Colonel Charles Beckwith and the men of Delta Force, would now be put to the test in the deserts of Iran.

"The next day was one of the worst of my life," Carter would later say of April 24, 1980, the day of the Eagle Claw rescue mission.[39] Until roughly 3 p.m. Washington time, the operation appeared to be going more or less according to plan. Two of the eight helicopters were incapacitated en route to the Desert One landing site in northern Iran, but the other six had landed and were refuelling as scheduled. Then, at 4:45, Secretary of Defense Harold Brown informed the White House that one of the six helicopters was grounded with a mechanical failure. Because the minimum number of choppers for a successful mission was always understood to be six, Brown recommended an abort. Carter and Zbigniew Brzezinski were thus faced with the agonizing choice of approving the mission with five helicopters or aborting. After conferring with Beckwith and Joint Chiefs of Staff chairman General David Jones, they agreed to call off the mission. Carter issued the abort order at roughly 5 p.m. Washington time. "Although despondent about the failure of the mission, we felt we had the situation well under control," said Carter. "I was grievously disappointed, but thanked God that there had been no casualties."[40] Brzezinski remembers Carter putting his head down on his desk after terminating the mission. "I felt extraordinarily sad for him as well as for the country," said Brzezinski.[41]

An hour after the abort order went out, President Carter got a second call from General Jones. At Desert One a helicopter had collided with a Hercules, he reported. In the explosion and ensuing fire, there were casualties. Not until five hours later did the White House receive a full debriefing on the failed mission. "All helicopter crews accounted for," read Brzezinski's real-time notes on the debacle. "Eight dead, three burned."[42] Carter was as dejected as he had ever been in his life. "I am still haunted," he would later say, "by memories of that day—our high hopes for success, the incredible series of mishaps, the bravery of our rescue team, the embarrassment of failure, and above all, the tragic deaths in the lonely desert."[43] Brzezinski called the failed mission "the most bitter disappointment of my four years at the White House."[44]

Cyrus Vance spent April 24 in Ottawa. He was there to confer with External Affairs minister Mark MacGuigan but he made a special effort to see Flora MacDonald, whom he now considered a close friend. "Cy Vance and I got along wonderfully," MacDonald later recalled of that sombre visit. "He was staying at the house near the governor general's, and he asked if he could see me. So he came and he told me—there was no one I was going to tell—that he was flying back to Washington to resign the next morning."[45] Vance did resign, and with a heart as heavy as the president's. Carter later replaced him as secretary of state with Senator Edmund Muskie.

The official Iranian reaction to the failed rescue attempt was to claim that God had delivered a great victory over the United States. Iranian newspapers published photographs of the abandoned and burned aircraft and of the bodies of the dead U.S. servicemen. Yet once the propaganda value of the failed mission had faded, as Jimmy Carter himself observed, there followed "a substantial lowering of rhetoric in Iran and in the United States."[46]

Carter resolved to maintain a high level of diplomatic and economic pressure. U.S. warships continued to patrol the Persian Gulf, the embargo remained in full force and the United States reiterated its position that Iran would suffer if it harmed or executed any of the hostages. As for the captives themselves, the failed Eagle Claw raid had the predictable effect of worsening their living conditions, in large measure because it prompted the occupiers to adopt a shell-game strategy of moving them among various sites and even cities to thwart a second rescue mission. "After we moved out of the embassy on April 24," William Daugherty explained, "I and all the others that I've talked with lived in some fairly harsh conditions as we moved around the country. Our safety was jeopardized, in that we were protected only by a few students. If outsiders had discovered hostages in their midst and decided to exact their own punishment, our guards would not have been able to stop a determined group. The Iranians purchased most of our food locally and, at least in my case, it was mostly awful, limited quantity, and at times inedible. Even the Iranians complained of the food. I weighed 180 pounds when captured and came out at 133, and much of that loss was after the rescue attempt."[47]

In the end, the occupiers' shell game mattered little. After Eagle Claw there would be no serious consideration of military action against Iran. The hostage-taking remained a diplomatic crisis and, as a dejected Jimmy Carter was forced to concede, it would have to be resolved diplomatically.

Chapter 20

YELLOW RIBBONS

When External Affairs and State Department officials expressed the hope that the exfiltration of the houseguests could be kept secret, they did not have only the welfare of the hostages in mind. Also at great potential risk were the Iranians who had been employed by Ken Taylor and his Canadian colleagues, and even those who worked for the Americans and the New Zealanders. Taylor did what he could before leaving Iran to insulate his employees from charges of collaboration, and from the moment he arrived in Paris, he stated repeatedly that his thirty-three Iranian staff had nothing to do with the exfiltration. "They didn't know we were harbouring the Americans," he insisted.[1]

Before Taylor had even left Paris, Chris Beeby cabled Michael Shenstone from Tehran. The New Zealand embassy, said Beeby, was advising Canada's local employees to stay away from the Canadian chancery, presumably because it was being surveilled by Iranian militants. "We also told Taylor's servants to retreat to an apartment they

have," wrote Beeby. "Both the local staff and the servants have been
told that these instructions stand until further notice."[2] Ambassador
Taylor and his wife Pat were justifiably anxious about their employees' uncertain status. "We kept close track of what happened," Ken
acknowledged. "We were concerned, we were preoccupied. It was a
worry to us."[3] On February 1, his first day back in Canada, Taylor
issued an official statement. "No Iranians," it read, "local staff or elsewhere, were at any time involved in sheltering or the eventual extrica-
tion of six American embassy staff members."[4]

Four months passed without incident. Then, on the night of
June 8–9, 1980, three of Taylor's Iranian staff—Ali Agha Razi, Asghar
Agha Razi and Ahad Cheragh Sepehr—were arrested on suspicion
that they had been involved in the plot to exfiltrate the houseguests.
Two of the men were embassy employees. The third was a cook at the
ambassador's residence. Ali Agha Razi's son immediately reported
the arrests to Danish embassy officials, knowing that they were
acting for Canada in Iran. "They have been told," he said of his father
and the others, "that they had assisted to give 6 U.S. diplomats passports helping them to escape."[5] The Danes notified External Affairs,
requesting explicitly that Canada "give this no publicity unless or
until the Iranians themselves make the arrests public." Canada's position on the indictments was to reiterate Taylor's earlier statement,
and to have the Danes present it to the Iranian government in no
uncertain terms. "No Iranian either on our local staff or in any other
position knew that we were sheltering members of the American
embassy staff."[6]

Two days later, Danish ambassador Joergen Adamsen cabled
External Affairs with disheartening news. "The three members of
your staff were released last night after extremely rough interrogation about their knowledge of the smuggling out of the six American diplomats."[7] The Canadians cabled back immediately. "Would
you convey to Ali Agha Razi, Asghar Agha Razi and Ahad Cheragh

Sepehr how deeply disturbed we are about the extremely unpleasant experience they are undergoing," they said. "Ambassador Taylor and other former members of the Canadian embassy staff have been made aware of the situation and are most concerned."[8]

In early July, it came to light that the informant who had delivered the three men to Iranian authorities was himself an embassy employee—an accountant. He had, in fact, been one of the last four Iranian staffers working at the Canadian embassy on January 27, the day before the exfiltration. "It is somewhat astonishing," the Canadians cabled the Danes, "that the accountant thinks he could implicate all without also implicating himself."[9] The three accused were never again detained, their "extremely rough interrogation" having yielded nothing, and in the end the charges against them were dropped. In Ottawa it was agreed, largely at John Sheardown's urging, that the Canadians' locally employed staff in Tehran should be free to emigrate to Canada. All but six of the thirty-three ultimately did leave Iran, either for Canada or the United States. The U.S. State Department later made the same offer to their own Iranian employees.

Canadian embassy staff disagree as to whether Jean Pelletier and *La Presse* acted honourably in sitting on the exfiltration story only until the houseguests were out of Iran. Ambassador Taylor believes that they were magnanimous in waiting as long as they did before going to press, and he bears them no ill will for publishing their scoop when they did. The Canadian press corps took the same view, apparently, since they honoured Pelletier with a National Newspaper Award. Not so Zena Sheardown. She remains deeply troubled about the publication of the story, particularly in light of President Carter's success in having major media outlets like *Time* and the *New York Times* quash it. One of the Taylors' household servants came to see her and John in Ottawa several years after the rescue of the houseguests. He told the Sheardowns that he and some of the other employees had been interrogated "rather brutally," as John put it.[10]

"Madame," said the man, with tears in his eyes, "they beat me, they beat me on my feet, they put something between my fingers, and. . . . I admire what you did, but why did you have to talk about it?"

"We weren't the ones to talk about it," Zena told him, sympathetically. "The news was broken by *La Presse*, and we heard about it on the BBC."

Asked recently whether she thought Jean Pelletier and *La Presse* had acted nobly, Zena did not mince words. "It's appalling that this sort of thing is allowed to happen," she said. "They should have waited until everybody was out."[11]

~ ~ ~

On July 27, 1980, the man who had been at the centre of the hostage crisis, Mohammad Reza Pahlavi—the Shahanshah Aryamehr and Light of the Aryans—died in Egypt at the age of sixty. Whether because of the shah's death or because of the mounting hardships of the U.S. embargo, the Iranians sent word to the United States via a secret German emissary that Ayatollah Khomeini was now ready to negotiate.

After several preliminary exchanges with the Iranians, using the Germans as the intermediaries, on September 10 the State Department received a proposal for resolving the hostage crisis from Sadegh Tabatabai, brother-in-law of Ahmad Khomeini. It was clearly drafted for American approval, since the most contentious of Iran's demands—an apology and an international commission to study the shah's crimes—had been dropped. Those that remained—the return of the shah's wealth, the unfreezing of Iranian government assets and a promise from the Americans not to meddle in Iranian politics—were acceptable to President Carter and always had been.

"We were ready to return those Iranian assets which were not needed to pay outstanding claims," he said, "[T]he Shah's family had long ago moved his own estate holdings to other countries; and the last thing I wanted was to become involved in Iran's internal affairs."[12] The president sent Warren Christopher to Bonn for a private meeting with Tabatabai. A new round of negotiations in Europe began.

Tabatabai was scheduled to return to Iran on September 22 to confer with Ayatollah Khomeini and other government officials about the progress of his talks with Christopher. That very day, however, Iraq attacked Iran, bombing Mehrabad Airport and sending columns of infantry over their common border. (A beleaguered President Carter could hardly believe his bad luck. "Typically," he despaired, "the Iranians accused me of planning and supporting the invasion.")[13] Tabatabai did not make his way back to Iran until a week later, and by then the invasion had thoroughly absorbed the attention of Iran's government. Once again, talks to resolve the hostage crisis stalled. When Tabatabai returned to Bonn, in early October, it was obvious to the White House that the government of Iran now understood the necessity of resolving the hostage crisis. The Iranian military needed American weapons and spare parts to fight the Iraqis. Carter acknowledged the change in Iranian attitude immediately. "We received word that all of the hostages were back in the embassy compound, in good condition," said the president, "and that there seemed to be a consensus among the top Iranian officials that it was time to free the American prisoners."[14]

On November 2, two days before the U.S. presidential election, the Iranian Majlis authorized the implementation of an agreement drafted by Christopher and Tabatabai. The question for the Americans, as always, was what Ayatollah Khomeini would do. The timing could not have been more critical for Jimmy Carter. Election day fell on the first anniversary of the seizure of the U.S. embassy, November 4, which heightened the obvious truth that his re-election hinged on whether he could bring the hostages home. "If the hostages were released," he reasoned, "I was convinced my re-election would be assured; if the expectations of the American people were dashed again, there was little chance that I could win."[15] Again things did not go Carter's way. The Iranians balked on the terms of the hostages' release, and the hoped-for news never came. Ronald Reagan defeated Carter in a landslide, the Republicans also gaining a majority in the Senate. Carter was humiliated. It did occur to him, however, that the Iranians now had no reason left to stall negotiations.

With Carter a lame-duck president, the government of Iran asked Algeria, a predominantly Muslim country, to mediate talks with the Americans. The Algerians agreed to do so, committing themselves to the process with "real determination and courage," as Carter himself put it.[16] The last major hurdle in the negotiations concerned the status of Iranian assets in the United States—and on this issue the devil was truly in the details. Legally, the White House could not unilaterally agree to matters concerning the disposition of Iranian assets, since many private-sector institutions were involved. This meant that Warren Christopher was at pains to "educate" both the Algerians and the ever-suspicious Iranians about such matters.[17] It also meant that representatives of American financial institutions had to be drawn into the talks. Just before Christmas 1980, no doubt frustrated with the Byzantine complexity of the ongoing financial negotiations, the Iranians simply demanded that the Americans pay them $25 billion to cover future claims. This was more than twice the amount of Iranian assets frozen in the United States, a request President Carter considered unacceptable.

On the bright side, the Algerian ambassador to Iran, Abdelkrim Ghraieb, was granted access to all of the hostages—even those, like Tom Ahern and his three CIA colleagues, who were kept in solitary confinement. (The hostages now numbered fifty-two in total. Richard Queen, one of the consular staff apprehended the day the houseguests fled the embassy compound, had been released and flown home to the United States in July 1980 after growing seriously ill. He was later diagnosed with multiple sclerosis.) On December 28, Ambassador Ghraieb reported to the White House that all of the American captives were in relatively good health.

As the clock ticked down on Jimmy Carter's presidency, the question on everyone's lips was whether the hostages would be freed before Ronald Reagan was sworn in on January 20. On January 18, Iran's chief negotiator, Behzad Nabavi, announced that an agreement on all outstanding financial matters had been reached, prompting an elated President Carter to make arrangements to fly to Wiesbaden, West Germany, to greet the hostages. The next day, however, the Iranians took issue with an American appendix to the financial settlement, which delayed the implementation of the agreement. Not until the morning of Jimmy Carter's final day as president, January 20, did Warren Christopher and Behzad Nabavi sign the "Algerian Accords" that finally brought an end to the Iran hostage crisis. The terms were deceptively simple. In exchange for the release of the hostages, the United States agreed to "restore the financial position of Iran, in so far as possible, to that which existed prior to November 14, 1979." The Americans also pledged that "it is and from now on will be the policy of the United States not to intervene, directly or indirectly, politically or militarily, in Iran's internal affairs." Just how tortuous the wrangling over Iranian assets had been came to light when the final text of the Accords was published. Thirteen of the document's fourteen pages set out the legal terms for the unfreezing of roughly $8 billion in Iranian assets.

~ ~ ~

For the fifty-two American hostages, rumours that they were likely to be freed meant that the last days of their captivity passed agonizingly slowly. After consultations with Algerian diplomats and doctors, each hostage was paraded before Massoumeh Ebtekar for one last filmed interview. William Daugherty later recalled Ebtekar asking him, apparently sincerely, whether he had been treated well while he was a guest of Iran. "I burst out laughing," he said, "and replied that I had been held against my will in solitary confinement for more than a year, had not been able to tell my family that I was even alive, had been interrogated, had been physically abused more than once, and had been threatened with trial and execution. And now I was being asked if I was treated well. So the answer was 'No!'"[18]

The evening of January 20, Tehran time, the blindfolded hostages were escorted by their captors onto a bus, where they were reunited with friends and colleagues they had not seen in fifteen months. They were driven to Mehrabad Airport and made to suffer the final indignity of walking to their waiting plane single file through a gauntlet of jeering Iranians. The freed hostages flew out of Tehran on an Air Algerie 727, alongside a second plane, carrying Algerian medical personnel, and a third, also a 727, that served as a decoy. Almost all of the former hostages later said that Flight 133, departing Tehran at 12:33 p.m. and bound for Algiers, was the best flight of their lives. In Algeria, they were formally transferred into the custody of the U.S. State Department by Algerian foreign minister Mohammed Seddik Ben Yahia. At 3 a.m. local time they boarded a USAF C-9 medevac plane and flew on to Rhein-Main Air Base in Frankfurt, West Germany. There the former hostages were bussed to the U.S. military hospital at Wiesbaden. Everywhere they went, they were greeted with outpourings of warmth and generosity such as they had never before experienced—surrounded at every step by seas of yellow ribbons and flowers by the truckload. At Wiesbaden they met Jimmy Carter and Cyrus Vance, the two men for whom the plight of the hostages had been such an intensely personal obsession.

The hostages' welcome when they returned to the United States a few days later was indescribable, according to most—tearful reunions with families and colleagues, a deluge of public sympathy and acclaim, all of it topped off with a joyous White House celebration hosted by President Reagan. For many of the former hostages, the most moving event of their whirlwind homecoming tour was the Blue Room reception that followed the formal ceremony at the White House. It was attended by Colonel Charlie Beckwith and the families of the eight servicemen who had died in the aborted Eagle Claw rescue mission, men to whom the former hostages feel a profound debt of gratitude to this day.

Chargé d'Affaires Bruce Laingen later recorded in his diary what was, for him, one of the highlights of that special day at the White House. "In another corner of the room is Ken Taylor and his wife, Pat, those two magnificent Canadians who had made possible the escape of my six colleagues almost a year to the day earlier," he wrote. "No truer friends for Americans exist, and yet they are Canadian to the core and deeply proud of it."[19]

It was fitting that Joe Clark should be the person to rise in the House of Commons and move that Canada "extend its congratulations to President Carter and the government of the United States for the successful conclusion of negotiations for the release of the hostages."[20] Flora MacDonald seconded the motion. The freeing of the hostages was "a triumph for international law and international humanity," said External Affairs Minister MacGuigan. The hostage-taking had been "abominable" and a "gross affront to all decent, civilized people," he added.[21] Prime Minister Trudeau sent a formal letter of congratulation to his friend Jimmy Carter. "That you have succeeded in reaching an agreement with

Iran which allows all the hostages to return home safe and sound," wrote Trudeau, "is to the great credit and the patience and wisdom which you and your advisors have shown throughout the crisis."[22]

With the hostages back in the United States, they and others were finally free to speak about the conditions of their captivity. Enforced silence, blindfolds, beatings, solitary confinement, mock executions— the stories poured forth, a harrowing litany of abuses until then unknown to most North Americans. One story in particular caught the public imagination—that of the Iranian militants forcing young American women to play Russian roulette. On January 21, 1981, Lloyd Rollins, one of the black hostages who had been released early, explained what had happened from his new post at the U.S. embassy in Ottawa. During the first few days of the embassy occupation, he said, the militants tried to get information out of the hostages. When they were unsuccessful they played Russian roulette with two of the female secretaries. "They put a bullet in the chamber," said Rollins, "spun the chamber, and then clicked the trigger off on a couple of the girls." The torture stopped only when the hostage-takers realized that they "weren't getting the information from us."[23] Elizabeth Montagne, one of the women to suffer this torment, later confirmed that the story was true. "I thought I was going to die," she said.[24]

North Americans were caught unawares by such revelations, partly because government officials who had known about the abuse had kept quiet, and also because the occupiers' own propaganda— routinely reproduced in American media—had been so effective. Ken Taylor was immediately drawn into the media furor over the abuse of the hostages. The day after the hostages' return to the United States, he told journalists that "he and the Canadian government had known for more than a year about the torture of the U.S. hostages." Speaking at a New York City press conference alongside Mayor Ed Koch, Taylor said that he had relayed information about this abuse to Ottawa. Whether the government informed the U.S. government, he could not say. Asked about Elizabeth Montagne's ordeal, Taylor said that he had heard within "a few weeks" of the embassy takeover about the hostages being subjected to Russian roulette. He decided not to reveal such incidents, he said, because he thought it "would not have added to a resolution of the situation."[25] Back in Ottawa, Taylor's remarks prompted a full-blown auditing of his cables from Tehran. "A review of departmental files," concluded the auditors, "does not reveal any reference from Tehran on Russian roulette."[26]

~ ~ ~

Revelations about the abuse of the hostages cast a long shadow over Ottawa's plans for restoring diplomatic relations with Iran. Speaking in the House of Commons the day after the hostages were freed, Joe Clark urged Prime Minister Trudeau not to appoint an ambassador to Iran "until at least these two conditions have been met: first, that there be an investigation into and report on any torture or violations of the human rights of the American hostages; and, second, that Iran has demonstrated that it will accept the normal international standards of behaviour governing diplomats abroad."[27] Trudeau replied that his government was concerned about "ill treatment of the hostages," and that it would wait until there was more information available before taking any "concrete steps."[28]

Several days later, Iran announced that it was willing to renew full diplomatic relations with Canada, but only if Canada "promises not to kidnap people, not to transfer people secretly and not to engage in espionage."[29] Communicating with the Iranian foreign ministry through the Danish government, External Affairs replied that Canada was in no hurry to restore relations with Iran. "You will be aware that there is a very real concern in the Canadian parliament, press and public at large," Ottawa wrote Copenhagen, "that Canada should not move with undue haste to normalize relations with Iran.

There is a particularly strong feeling that Canadian staff should not be sent back to Iran unless their safety is reasonably assured."[30] The Danes, and Ambassador Adamsen in particular, made this decision easy for the Canadians—by looking after Canada's consular affairs, providing a steady stream of information from Tehran and giving no indication whatsoever that it was an imposition to represent Canadian interests.

On March 6, 1981, Mark MacGuigan announced the termination of Canadian trade sanctions against Iran. Only exports of military equipment remained prohibited, he said, and only because Canada refused to sell arms to either side in the Iran–Iraq War. In Ottawa, Iranian chargé Mohammad Adeli took this as a promising sign and lobbied External Affairs officials aggressively over the following year to reopen the Canadian embassy in Tehran. Canada refused. Then, late in 1982, without any apparent provocation, Iran withdrew the olive branch. Iranian foreign minister Ali Akbar Velayati stated that Tehran would not consider restoring full diplomatic relations with Canada unless the Canadian government apologized for "smuggling" out the six American houseguests.[31]

Iran's demand for an apology remained in force for the next six years, icing any serious discussion of reopening the Canadian embassy.

~ ~ ~

On June 16, 1981, President Ronald Reagan presented Ken Taylor with the Congressional Gold Medal that the U.S. Senate and House of Representatives had approved when he had returned from Iran. It is a distinction rarely bestowed upon foreigners. (Other non-Americans to receive the honour have included Winston Churchill, Pope John Paul II, the Dalai Lama and Nelson Mandela.) Taylor was, and remains, the only Canadian recipient. The ceremony took place in the Oval Office.

Present were Pat Taylor, Bruce Laingen, Vic Tomseth, Lee Schatz and Canadian ambassador to the United States Peter Towe. President Reagan gave a lengthy introductory speech, recounting the exfiltration story and thanking the Canadians for their efforts on behalf of the United States. He was honouring an "act of courage," he said—"not only Ambassador Taylor's courage but also the contribution of all the Canadian embassy personnel in Tehran and the Canadian government in Ottawa."[32] Taylor then responded with his own remarks: "The presentation of the Congressional Gold Medal, President Reagan, not only means a great deal to myself and my family, but I think it underlines the very unique and very special relationship between Canada and the United States. The United States faces the rebuffs of history with patience, determination, and a search for justice. For this, you have gained the everlasting respect of all Canadians. Moreover, your generosity, your tolerance, cements the long-lasting and precious friendship which Canadians and United States citizens share. Thank you for this recognition. I speak on behalf of Canada, and I can say that we're very fortunate, and cherish our neighbourhood relationship with you."[33]

The gold medal, still an object of great value to the Taylors, reads, "Act of Congress, March 6, 1980. *Entre amis,* appreciation for the noble and heroic effort in the harboring of six United States diplomats and safe return to America. Thank you, Canada."

Much was said after Taylor's return from Iran of Canada's "unique and very special relationship" with the United States. Yet as much as Taylor himself promoted—and even symbolized—the idea, he also knew that American gratitude toward Canada could not by itself sustain a successful bilateral relationship in the tumultuous 1980s. By the time Taylor arrived at the Oval Office to accept his congressional medal, just eighteen months after the rescue of the houseguests, Canadian–American relations were as fractious as they had been in recent memory. Ronald Reagan's hard-nosed ambassador to Canada, Paul Robinson, freely opined on Canada's myriad flaws as he saw them—the metric system, Ottawa's flagrant overspending on social programs, its obsession with acid rain, its lackadaisical attitude toward the Soviet threat. The Reagan White House also made no secret of its opposition to nationalist policies identified closely with Prime Minister Pierre Trudeau, including mandatory reviews of foreign investment and the National Energy Program.

Allan Gotlieb, appointed Canada's ambassador to the United States in October 1981, could see which way the wind was blowing. "I attended a luncheon at the National Press Club in honour of Ken Taylor," Gotlieb wrote in his diary in July 1983. "I counted less than a hundred in the audience, at least half of whom were embassy staff, Canadian press, and other Canadians. If we had any money in the bank resulting from the great Canadian caper, the Washington branch had closed the account."[34]

Much was also made about whether Ken Taylor had handled his celebrity status well—although never by Taylor himself. Some of his colleagues in the diplomatic corps complained that fame had changed him. Others, including Gotlieb and Michael Shenstone, said that it had had no impact whatsoever. What is certain is that the culture of Canada's Department of External Affairs, built on the quiet, behind-the-scenes work of promoting Canada's interests abroad, was ill prepared when one of their own became, for a time, the world's most famous diplomat. It was said that some of the veterans of the corps, foreign-service officers who had spent their careers toiling in obscurity, were envious of Taylor's celebrity. Others were simply dismissive. "We don't have any heroes in this department," Deputy Minister de Montigny Marchand reportedly said in 1982 when asked about Taylor, "we just have good foreign service officers."[35]

Seen in retrospect, the whispering campaigns that attended to Ken Taylor's fame in the wake of the hostage crisis were rich in irony. Though he was plainly comfortable in the limelight, Taylor neither expected it nor sought it out. Never did he repeat the easy claims of the press that he was a "hero" or that he alone had acted with cunning and courage. He shared the credit at every opportunity, both with his own colleagues and with those in the United States—sometimes more generously than was warranted. In 1980, Geoffrey Pearson—career foreign-service officer and the son of Canada's *other* famous diplomat, Nobel laureate and Canadian prime minister Lester B. Pearson—was asked about Ken Taylor. He observed that the "imposed anonymity and silence of the diplomatic life" could be extremely challenging. "We're working in a public environment but we're working privately," said Pearson. "We can work patiently for months trying to get something in place and it will all be blown away because of the wrong publicity, It isn't that we're faceless men or diplomats in striped trousers. Every now and then the veil gets pulled back and someone like Ken Taylor becomes a hero. Nothing could be more difficult for Taylor. He didn't join the foreign service to become a hero, and neither did I."[36]

The worst that might be said of Ken Taylor's encounter with fame was that he did not get off the stage when his fifteen minutes were up. He did not disappear. This said, Taylor has to be credited with stage-managing his own public persona in the white-hot aftermath of the hostage crisis with extraordinary aplomb. And herein lies the greatest irony of all. For while the Canadian ambassador found himself the object of adulation for his role in the exfiltration of the houseguests, he was silent about the operational details of the mission, and also about his—and Jim Edward's—far more "heroic" intelligence-gathering work on behalf of the CIA, the State Department, the Carter White House and the Pentagon. Surveilling the militants who had imprisoned the hostages at the U.S. embassy and the Iranian foreign ministry is one of the riskiest assignments known to have been given to a Canadian diplomat in peacetime. Yet Taylor has never mentioned it publicly. He was thus accused of taking too much credit for an operation he well knew was a broad collaborative effort, and was given none at all for a second, far more dangerous mission, one that was his and Edward's alone.

In this sense, then, the *public* Ken Taylor—the smiling hero of Tehran—vanished into history as part of that unique late-seventies zeitgeist of instant celebrities, men and women whom the star-maker machinery anointed and then abandoned with equal fury. But the *private* Ken Taylor—the man known to the houseguests and the hostages, to State Department officials and CIA station chiefs, even to presidents and prime ministers—is as highly regarded today for his courage during the Iran hostage crisis as he was thirty years ago.

It is an extraordinary legacy, especially in a country like Canada, famously ambivalent about its national heroes. For every time Ambassador Taylor accepted some new honour on behalf of the government of Canada and Canadians at large, almost no one in Canada knew what he had actually accomplished in their name.

Epilogue
OUR MAN IN NEW YORK

Had Joe Clark's Tories been returned to power in February 1980, Ken Taylor would likely have gone to Washington as Canada's ambassador. But, as Allan Gotlieb later observed, "[Pierre] Trudeau had reservations, believing—wrongly, in my opinion—that Taylor personalized a broad institutional effort to save the hostages."[1] Instead, Ottawa announced in mid-July 1980 that Taylor would serve as Canada's new consul general in New York City. The diplomat he would replace, sixty-one-year-old Jim Nutt, was reportedly "very unhappy" with being shunted aside.[2] He and his wife, Grace, had been in New York less than a year, too little time even to move into their government-issued apartment because it was undergoing renovations. Nutt had hoped to finish out his career in New York but was instead reassigned to Los Angeles. If the Nutts were in fact resentful, Ken Taylor never saw it. "Jim and Grace couldn't have been more helpful and congenial towards Pat and me," he later recalled. "I knew Jim well. We had been colleagues in Ottawa, and I spent a lot of time in New York in 1980, Jim's first year there. They were always such gracious hosts, both in New York and Los Angeles."[3]

As consul general to New York, Taylor was celebrated as a new breed of Canadian diplomat, "a daring, flamboyant man who enjoyed taking chances."[4] The Taylors lived in an elegant eight-room Park Avenue apartment, complete with grand piano and original Roy Lichtenstein paintings, mingling easily with the rich and powerful who made New York their home. "There's a special kind of magic attached to the name Ken Taylor," wrote one Canadian in New York, "a magic that gives the Canadian presence here an edge that goes beyond the usual cultural, commercial and diplomatic interest."[5] New York proved fertile ground for Taylor's natural charm and affability. Despite his reputation for being Canada's "ambassador to Regine's," a reference to one of Manhattan's more famous discos of the day, Taylor served with distinction in New York, capitalizing on his celebrity as the hero of Tehran and working day and night, as he always had, to promote Canadian interests.[6]

Starting in late 1983, with a federal election looming in Canada, both the Liberals and the Tories courted Ken Taylor as a highly attractive political candidate. As the *Globe and Mail* noted at the time, "the man who hid six U.S. diplomats in Tehran in 1980 and eventually smuggled them out of Iran would be a formidable acquisition for either party."[7] Taylor was also invited by Standard Brands president Ross Johnson to join the private sector, a curious coincidence, since Johnson was an old friend of Tory leader Brian Mulroney. "Brian asked me to come up to Ottawa every two weeks for six months, trying to convince me to run for office," Taylor later recalled with a chuckle. "That's when Ross Johnson came in. Mulroney finally phoned Ross. They were close friends. He said, 'Look, here's the situation. We're all friends, the three of us, Ken and you and I, why can't you talk some sense into him, get him to join the party and run for office?' Ross said, 'I don't know if he wants that and, in fact,

I am thinking of offering him a job.'"[8] External Affairs, meanwhile, offered Taylor the position of Canadian ambassador to Rome, a posting that neither Ken nor his family relished (and one that many of his colleagues, including Allan Gotlieb, believed might expose him to reprisals from Iranian militants).

On June 1, 1984, Taylor announced his retirement from the Canadian foreign service, prompting accusations in the Canadian press and elsewhere that External Affairs had treated him poorly. Taylor was gracious about leaving the department, saying only that he was looking for a "new challenge."[9] But in truth, as he now acknowledges, he had become "more and more disengaged from Ottawa, even when I was in New York as consul general."[10] After carefully weighing his options in consultation with Pat and Douglas, Taylor decided to remain in New York, accepting a position as senior vice president, government and international affairs, of the newly merged RJR Nabisco. For six years, he worked closely with Ross Johnson, a collaboration that put Taylor at the epicentre of Johnson's attempted leveraged buyout of the company in 1988, until 2007 "the biggest deal in capitalism," as Taylor himself put it.[11] Since 1990, Taylor has worked as a strategic business consultant to foreign governments via Global Public Affairs, a firm he founded. He served two consecutive terms as chancellor of his undergraduate alma mater, Victoria University, in the University of Toronto, and continues to sit on the President's International Alumni Council, along with Michael Ignatieff and other distinguished U of T graduates.

Now seventy-five but as fit and as active as ever, Taylor sits on the boards of a broad range of companies in the energy, financial services, tourism and aviation sectors, his famous energy and enthusiasm undiminished by the passage of time.

~ ~ ~

In July 1988, Canada and Iran agreed to restore full diplomatic relations. The following October, the doors of the Canadian embassy in Tehran opened for the first time since Ken Taylor had posted his note saying that it was temporarily closed. Canada's new chargé d'affaires, Scott J. Mullin, later told Taylor that he discovered the interior of the Canadian chancery to be exactly as he and his colleagues had left it in January 1980. Four months after Mullin's arrival in Iran he was recalled by the government of Canada to protest Ayatollah Khomeini's fatwa against British author Salman Rushdie, author of *The Satanic Verses*. In 1990, Paul S. Dingledine became the first accredited Canadian ambassador to Iran since Ken Taylor.

Shortly after the Canadian embassy reopened, Flora MacDonald went to Iran with her sister at the invitation of the Iranian government. She recalls being extremely well treated. The Iranian foreign minister had put together an advisory group of about forty bureaucrats and academics, to whom MacDonald was invited to make a presentation. "I went and talked about Canada–Iran relations," she later recalled with a smile, "but all of their questions were focused on the United States." One of the people in the room asked her what changes she would like to see in Iran if she were to return in another five years. "I said, 'I would like to come back, and meet with the same group, only I would like to see half of the group made up of women.' There was dead silence. Then somebody started to laugh, and they *all* started to laugh."[12]

In recent years, ordinary Canadians and Iranians have enjoyed the fruits of a steadily deepening and broadening relationship. Almost all of the approximately 120,000 Iranians who now make Canada their home emigrated after 1980. They have proved to be one of the most successful recent immigrant groups, not merely by virtue of their high visibility in Canada's major cities (including the affectionately nicknamed "Tehranto") but also owing to their disproportionate success in business, journalism, medicine, academia and the arts.

Canada's formal relationship with the Islamic Republic of Iran has been troubled by a steady stream of bilateral *causes célèbres*, however, including the murder of Canadian-Iranian photojournalist Zahra Kazemi in 2003 while she was in Iranian custody, the police-shooting death of Iranian immigrant Keyvan Tabesh in Burnaby, BC, the same year, and the imprisonment in 2009 of Iranian-Canadian journalist Maziar Bahari. Diplomatic protests on both sides of the Iran–Canada divide have included expulsions and recalls of ambassadors and chargés. Since 2003, Canada has tabled resolutions annually at the United Nations General Assembly expressing "deep concern at serious human rights violations" in Iran. Although most Iranian officials have long since ceased holding grudges against Canada for its role in the hostage crisis, the language of Iran's recent diplomatic clashes with Canada has been eerily evocative of it. In November 2006, Iranian parliamentarian Javad Arian-Manesh threatened to shut down Canada's embassy in Tehran, calling it a "den of spies."[13] In March 2009, Prime Minister Stephen Harper told the editorial board of the *Wall Street Journal* that Mahmoud Ahmadinejad's government was "a regime with both an ideology that is obviously evil, combined with a desire to procure technology to act on that ideology."[14]

Relations between Iran and the United States remain even more strained, having never recovered from the hostage crisis. The two countries have not restored diplomatic relations since President Jimmy Carter terminated them in April 1980. The graffiti-ridden former U.S. embassy compound in Tehran has been converted into a training facility for Iran's Revolutionary Guards; the chancery building now serves as an anti-American museum. In January 2002, President George W. Bush singled Iran out as one of three countries in his imagined "Axis of Evil," along with Iraq and North Korea. After 2005 and the election to the Iranian presidency of conservative Mahmoud Ahmadinejad, the two nations' long-simmering animosities hardened into a three-year war of words that dominated the world's front pages and threatened occasionally to escalate beyond the merely verbal. Iran's nuclear program and its support for Hamas and Hezbollah together provided the pretext for the refusal of the Bush administration to countenance any sort of dialogue with Tehran. Iran thus remains one of the most challenging files in President Barack Obama's unenviable foreign-policy inheritance from Bush, albeit one on which he has demonstrated a willingness to ratchet down the rhetoric.

Some of the Americans taken hostage in 1979 have recently identified Ahmadinejad as one of the more "brutal" of the embassy occupiers.[15] Author Mark Bowden probed the matter exhaustively while writing *Guests of the Ayatollah* but could confirm only what the Iranian president himself has said about his role in the hostage crisis: that he was active in the planning phase as one of Ibrahim Asghar-zadeh's co-conspirators but he did not participate in the seizure of the embassy or the interrogation of the American captives.[16]

Notwithstanding the mass protests in Iran that followed Mahmoud Ahmadinejad's re-election in June 2009, there is a consensus in most of the world's capitals that President Obama must now engage in dialogue with him. As former U.S. chargé d'affaires Bruce Laingen remarked recently, "Thirty years is too long not to talk to each other—it makes no sense."[17]

~ ~ ~

"Do you still have those big glasses you wore 25 years ago?" Ken Taylor was asked in 2005.

"I was recently looking back at some pictures and saw those 'head-lights' I used to wear, and got nostalgic," he replied. "So I went and rummaged around in some drawers and found them and put them on. My prescription has changed so I couldn't see very well. But maybe I'll revert to them for a while to see if anybody recognizes me."[18]

ABBREVIATIONS

AIOC	Anglo-Iranian Oil Company
AWACS	Airborne Warning and Control System
CIA	Central Intelligence Agency
DCI	Director of Central Intelligence
DIA	Defense Intelligence Agency
DND	Department of National Defence
E&E net	escape and evasion network
HOM	Head of Mission
ICBM	intercontinental ballistic missile
ICCS	International Commission of Control and Supervision
NE	Near East
NIE	National Intelligence Estimate, CIA
NSA	National Security Advisor
NSC	National Security Council
OPEC	Organization of the Petroleum Exporting Countries
OTS	Office of Technical Services, CIA
PMO	Prime Minister's Office
SAVAK	Sazman-e Ettela'at Va Amniyat-e Keshvar
SIGINT	signals intelligence
SSCIA	Senate Select Committee on Intelligence Activities (Church Committee)
SSEA	Secretary of State for External Affairs

NOTES

In citations of works in the Notes, short titles have generally been used. Works frequently cited have been identified by the following abbreviations:

AP   Associated Press
BBC   British Broadcasting Corporation
BP   *Bout de Papier*
CBC   Canadian Broadcasting Corporation
CBS   Columbia Broadcasting System
CH   *Calgary Herald*
CP   Canadian Press
CPN   Canadian Press Newswire
FP   *Foreign Policy*
GM   *The Globe and Mail*
IHT   *International Herald Tribune*
IJIC   *International Journal of Intelligence and Counterintelligence*
LAC   Library and Archives Canada
LM   *Le Monde*
LP   *La Presse*
M   *Maclean's*
MR   *MERIP* (Middle East Research and Information Project) Reports

MS	Montreal Star
LHT	Les Harris Transcripts
NYT	The New York Times
NYTS	New York Times Service
PF	Pakistan Forum
PSQ	Political Science Quarterly
R	Reuters
T	Time
TS	Toronto Star
TSUN	Toronto Sun
UHR	Universal Human Rights
UP/ UPI	United Press International
WP	The Washington Post

PROLOGUE

1   Ken Taylor, interview with the author.
2   Ibid.
3   Traer Van Allen, cited in Karen Blackmore, "Family and Friends Gather to Remember Two Brave Airmen," The Labradorian (October 1, 2001), 1.
4   Ruhollah Khomeini, cited in "Seizure of USA Embassy Tehran," LAC 20-IRAN-1–4 (November 6, 1979), 1. See also "I'll Take Charge if U.S. Moves In, Khomeini Says," UPI (November 7, 1979), and Carole Jerome, The Man in the Mirror: A True Story of Love, Revolution and Treachery in Iran (Toronto: Key Porter, 1987), 135.
5   Ken Taylor, interview with the author.
6   Ibid.
7   Robert D. McFadden et al., No Hiding Place: The New York Times Inside Report on the Hostage Crisis (New York: Times Books, 1981), xi.
8   "Iran in the 1980s" (Secret report of the CIA Directorate of Intelligence, August 1977), 64.
9   Ken Taylor, "Bakhtiar's Struggle for Political Survival," LAC RG-25 20-IRAN-1–4 (February 1, 1979), 1–5.

CHAPTER 1: THE UNLIKELY AMBASSADOR

1   Ken Taylor, interview with the author.
2   Joe Clark, interview, Escape from Iran: The Hollywood Option (Saskatoon: Partners in Motion/Harmony Documentary, 2004).

3   Michael Shenstone, interview with the author.

4   Paul Malone, "Annual Report," LAC RG-25 20-IRAN-2–1 (March 28, 1967), 5.

5   Sally Jorgensen, "General Political Notes on Iran and Canada—Iran Relations," LAC RG-25 20–1–2-IRAN (November 17, 1978), 1–2.

6   Feroz Ahmed, "Iran: Subimperialism in Action," *PF* (March–April 1973), 10.

7   James George, "The Shah's Rule—Strengths and Weaknesses," LAC RG-25 20-IRAN-2–1 (October 8, 1973), 1.

8   Ibid., 6.

9   Ken Taylor, interview with the author.

10   James George, "Royal Family," LAC RG-25 20-IRAN-1–4 (January 15, 1973), 1.

11   James George, "Shah's Marriage," LAC RG-25 20-IRAN-6 (June 28, 1973), 1.

12   See Christopher Andrew and Vasili Mitrokhin, *The Mitrokhin Archive II: The KGB and the World* (London: Penguin, 2005), 171.

13   See Nikki R. Keddie, *Modern Iran: Roots and Results of Revolution,* updated edition (Princeton: Yale University Press, 2006), 158.

14   Roger Lucy, "Canada–Iran Relations," LAC RG-25 20–1–2-IRAN (November 17, 1976), 1.

15   James George, "Talk with the Shah—Economic," LAC RG-25 20–1–2-IRAN (February 23, 1977), 1.

16   James George, "Farewell Call on the Shah," LAC RG-25 20–1–2-IRAN (September 12, 1977), 1–4.

17   James George, "Iran: A Farewell Appraisal" LAC RG-25 20–1–2-IRAN (September 16, 1977), 1–5.

18   Ken Taylor, interview with the author.

19   Ibid.

20   Laverna Dollimore, interview with the author.

21   Allan Gotlieb, *The Washington Diaries, 1981–1989* (Toronto: McClelland & Stewart, 2006), 29.

22   Ken Taylor, interview with the author.

23   Joe Schlesinger, *Time Zones: A Journalist in the World* (Toronto: Random House, 1990), 231.

24   David Lancashire, "Tehran = Traffic," *GM* (October 28, 1978), 42.

25   Ken Taylor, interview with the author.

26   Ken Taylor, "Calls on PM Amuzegar," LAC RG-25 20–1–2-IRAN (November 7, 1977), 1–3.

27   Ibid.

28   Ken Taylor, "Canada-Iran Impact 1978," LAC RG-25 20–1–2-IRAN (December 18, 1977), 1–3.

29 Michael Shenstone, "Iran Program Priorities," LAC RG-25 20–1–2-IRAN (January 19, 1978), 1–4.

30 Ken Taylor, interview with the author.

31 LAC RG-25 20-IRAN-1–4 (March 23, 1978), 1–2.

32 Ken Taylor, "Iran: Political Stability," LAC RG-25 20-IRAN-1–4 (March 30, 1978), 1–2.

CHAPTER 2: A TOAST TO THE SHAH

1   Michael Shenstone, interview with the author.

2   William Daugherty, *In the Shadow of the Ayatollah: A CIA Hostage in Iran* (Annapolis, MD: Naval Institute Press, 2001), 17.

3   See ibid., 32.

4   See David Farber, *Taken Hostage: The Iran Hostage Crisis and America's First Encounter with Radical Islam* (Princeton: Princeton University Press, 2005), 59.

5   See Daugherty, *In the Shadow of the Ayatollah*, 29–30.

6   See Jerome, *The Man in the Mirror*, 47.

7   Richard Cottam, "Goodbye to America's Shah," *FP* 34 (Spring 1979), 7.

8   Tim Weiner, *Legacy of Ashes: The History of the CIA* (New York: Doubleday, 2007), 374.

9   Massoumeh Ebtekar, *Takeover in Tehran: The Inside Story of the 1979 U.S. Embassy Capture* (Vancouver: Talonbooks, 2000), 82.

10 Ruhollah Khomeini, cited in "Ayatollah's Return Climaxes 40 Years of Opposition to the Shah," NYTS (February 1, 1979).

11 Ibid.

12 Nicholas Gage, "It May Be Too Late to Save Iran," *NYT* (December 18, 1978).

13 Ruhollah Khomeini, cited in "Ayatollah's Return."

14 Ruhollah Khomeini, cited in Farber, *Taken Hostage*, 66.

15 See Ronen Bergman, *The Secret War with Iran* (New York: Free Press, 2007), 11.

16 See Carl Anthony Wege, "Iranian Intelligence Organizations," *IJIC* 10:3 (1997), 288.

17 Ken Taylor, interview with the author.

18 Eqbal Ahmed, "What's Behind the Crisis in Iran and Afghanistan?" *Social Text* 3 (Autumn 1980), 48.

19 Ervand Abrahamian, "Iran in Revolution: The Opposition Forces," *MR* 75/76 (March–April 1979), 3–8.

20 See Robert Wright, *Three Nights in Havana* (Toronto: HarperCollins, 2007), ch. 10.

21 Martin Ennals, *Amnesty International Annual Report 1974–5,* cited in Ervand Abrahamian, "The Political Challenge," *MR* 69 (July–August 1978), 3–8.

22 Amnesty International, cited in Joe Hall, "Masters of Terror Live in Fear," *TS* (February 5, 1979), A6.

23 Reza Baraheni, cited in "Nobody Influences Me!" *T* (December 10, 1979). See also Reza Baraheni, *The Crowned Cannibals: Writings on Repression in Iran* (New York: Vintage, 1977).

24 Mohammad Reza Pahlavi, cited in "Shah of Iran Admits to Police Operations in U.S.," *MR* 52 (November 1976), 23.

25 Richard Helms, *A Look over My Shoulder: A Life in the Central Intelligence Agency* (New York: Random House, 2003), 420–1.

26 Keddie, *Modern Iran*, 135.

27 "Nobody Influences Me!"

28 Ebtekar, *Takeover in Tehran*, 188.

29 Daugherty, *In the Shadow of the Ayatollah*, 41.

30 Alfred L. Atherton, cited in Hugh M. Arnold, "Henry Kissinger and Human Rights," *UHR* 2:4 (October–December 1980), 68.

31 Henry Kissinger, cited in Seymour M. Hersh, *The Price of Power: Kissinger in the Nixon White House* (New York: Summit, 1983), 137.

32 Henry Kissinger, cited in David P. Forsythe, "American Foreign Policy and Human Rights: Rhetoric and Reality," *UHR* 2:3 (July–September 1980), 50.

33 John Fraser, "Talk with Shah," LAC RG-25 20–1–2-IRAN (March 8, 1977), 1–2.

34 Jim Cockcroft, "Letter from Tehran: The Embassy Takeover," *MR* 87 (May 1980), 30–1.

35 Ken Taylor, interview with the author.

36 Ibid.

37 See Feroz Ahmed, "Iran: Subimperialism in Action," *PF* (March–April 1973).

38 Daugherty, *In the Shadow of the Ayatollah*, 46.

39 Cyrus Vance, *Hard Choices: Critical Years in America's Foreign Policy* (New York: Simon and Schuster, 1983), 314.

40 Michael Shenstone, interview with the author.

41 Stansfield Turner, *Terrorism and Democracy* (Boston: Houghton Mifflin, 1991), 31.

42 Carter Diary, cited in Jimmy Carter, *Keeping Faith: Memoirs of a President* (New York: Bantam, 1982), 450.

43 Vance, *Hard Choices*, 317.

44 Zbigniew Brzezinski, *Power and Principle: Memoirs of the National Security Adviser, 1977–1981* (New York: Farrar, Straus, Giroux, 1983), 356.

45 Alexander Moens, "President Carter's Advisers and the Fall of the Shah," *PSQ* 106:2 (Summer, 1991), 214.

46 Vance, *Hard Choices*, 317.

47   Ibid., 318.
48   Ibid., 319.
49   Ibid., 316.
50   See Richard Cottam, "Goodbye to America's Shah," *FP* 34 (Spring 1979), 11.
51   "Student Demonstrations," LAC RG-25 20–1–2-IRAN (November 28, 1977),
     1–4.
52   Carter, *Keeping Faith*, 433.
53   Ibid., 434.
54   Ibid., 436.
55   Ibid., 436–7.
56   Ibid., 437.
57   Vance, *Hard Choices*, 323.
58   "Student Demonstrations," 1–4.
59   See David Harris, *The Crisis: The President, the Prophet, and the Shah—1979 and
     the Coming of Militant Islam* (New York: Little, Brown and Company, 2004), 71.
60   Mohammad Reza Pahlavi, cited in Carter, *Keeping Faith*, 437.
61   Jimmy Carter, "Toast to the Shah of Iran" (December 31, 1978).
62   Ken Taylor, interview with the author.
63   Daugherty, *In the Shadow of the Ayatollah*, 64.
64   "Monthly Review of Current Events," LAC RG-25 20–1–2-IRAN (February 12,
     1978), 2.

CHAPTER 3: THE DOWNWARD SPIRAL

1   Vance, *Hard Choices*, 325.
2   "377 Die in Iran Theatre Fire," AP/R (August 21, 1978).
3   "Death Toll Rises to 430 in Iran Fire," R (August 22, 1978).
4   William H. Sullivan, *Mission to Iran* (New York: Norton and Company, 1981), 146.
5   Brzezinski, *Power and Principle*, 356.
6   See ibid.
7   Stansfield Turner, cited in Tim Weiner, *Legacy of Ashes: The History of the CIA*
     (New York, Doubleday, 2007), 370.
8   CIA, Directorate of Intelligence, "Iran in the 1980s" (August 1977), iii.
9   Cited in Carter, *Keeping Faith*, 438.
10   CIA, *NIE* (September 1978), 34.
11   See Daugherty, *In the Shadow of the Ayatollah*, 69.
12   See Vance, *Hard Choices*, 346.
13   See Jerold and Leona Schecter, *Sacred Secrets: How Soviet Intelligence Operations
     Changed American History* (Dulles, VA: Brassey's, 2003), 281.

14   Nicholas Wade, "Iran and America: The Failure of Understanding," *Science*
     206:4424 (December 14, 1979), 1281.

15   James Bill, cited in ibid., 1282.

16   See, for example, Senate Select Committee on Intelligence Activities,
     Alleged Assassination Plots Involving Foreign Leaders (Washington, DC: U.S.
     Government, 1975).

17   See Andrew and Mitrokhin, *The Mitrokhin Archive II*, 170.

18   Cited in ibid., 175.

19   Cited in Weiner, *Legacy of Ashes*, 369.

20   Helms, *A Look over My Shoulder*, 417.

21   Ibid., 419.

22   Ibid., 445.

23   Cited in "Declaration of Martial Law—Iran," LAC RG-25 20-IRAN-1–4
     (September 9, 1978), 1–4.

24   Brzezinski, *Power and Principle*, 361.

25   Ruhollah Khomeini, cited in "End Strike or Quit, Iran Oil Workers Told," R/AP
     (November 13, 1978).

26   Jerome, *The Man in the Mirror*, 13.

27   Ibid., 29.

28   Ibid.

29   See "Iran Arrests Former Premier," AP (November 9, 1978).

30   Carter, *Keeping Faith*, 440.

31   Vance, *Hard Choices*, 332.

32   Ibid., 333.

33   Iran was the fourth-largest supplier of oil to the world in 1978, after the USSR, Saudi
     Arabia and the United States. In the first half of that year, its production was 5.6
     million barrels per day, which constituted 10 per cent of world production and 20
     per cent of OPEC production. All but approximately 800,000 barrels per day were
     exported. Prior to the revolution, Iran supplied Canada with about 20 per cent of its
     imports, or 7 per cent of the Canadian domestic consumption of 1.8 million barrels
     per day. When strikes reduced Iranian oil output, other countries had to increase
     production. But this still left world markets short by 2 million barrels a day. See
     "Iran: Uncertain Future," LAC RG-25 20-IRAN-1–4 (January 19, 1979), 1–8.

34   Ken Taylor, "Meeting with Shah," LAC RG-25 20–1–2-IRAN (April, 10, 1978), 1–4.

35   Ken Taylor, interview with the author.

36   Roger Lucy, interview with the author.

37   "Monthly Review of Current Events," LAC RG-25 20–1–2-IRAN (August 9,
     1978), 1–2.

38   Pat Taylor, interview with the author.

39   Ken Taylor, interview with the author.

40   Pat Taylor, interview with the author.

41   Ken Taylor, interview with the author.

42   Pat Taylor, interview with the author.

43   Ken Taylor, interview with the author.

44   Douglas Taylor, interview with the author.

45   Ken Taylor, interview with the author.

46   Roger Lucy, interview with the author.

47   Ken Taylor, "Tehran Today," LAC RG-25 20–1–2-IRAN (October 23, 1978), 1–3.

CHAPTER 4: THE OVERTHROW OF THE SHAH

1   "Tehran: Effects of Rioting," LAC RG-25 20–1–2-IRAN (November 7, 1978), 1–2.

2   Roger Lucy, "Letters from the Iranian Revolution," *BP* 6:4 (Spring 1981), 31.

3   Marie Mercer, cited in "Canadians Recount Iran Horror Stories," *TS* (January 5, 1979), A12.

4   LAC RG-25 20–1–2-IRAN (November 6, 1978), 1–3.

5   Roger Lucy, interview with the author.

6   Michael Shenstone, "Iran: Contingency Planning," LAC RG-25 20–1–2-IRAN (December 1, 1978), 1–5.

7   Ken Taylor, interview with the author.

8   "Iran Situation Report," LAC RG 25 20 1 2 IRAN (December 3, 1978), 1–4.

9   "Feared Upheaval Causes Stampede to Get out of Iran," AP (December 8, 1978).

10   "Iran: Contingency Plans Update," LAC RG-25 20–1–2-IRAN (December 6, 1978), 1–2.

11   Allan Gotlieb, "Iran Contingency Planning," LAC RG-25 80–10–1-IRAN (December 13, 1978), 1–2.

12   "Iran: Ashura," LAC RG-25 20–1–2-IRAN (December 12, 1978), 1–3.

13   "Iran: Assessment after Ashura," LAC RG-25 20–1–2-IRAN (December 13, 1978), 1–3.

14   "Iranians Tortured, Report Says," AP (December 12, 1978).

15   Ruhollah Khomeini, cited in "Industry's Oil Output Rises but Industries Face Strike," AP (December 18, 1978).

16   See "Hundreds Reported Killed in Iran Clashes," R/AP (January 1, 1979).

17   "Iran: Political Situation," LAC RG-25 20-IRAN-1–4 (December 31, 1978), 1–3.

18   See "Walkout Sparks New Iran Crisis," R (January 9, 1979).

19   "Iran: Bakhtiar Government," LAC RG-25 20-IRAN-1–4 (January 8, 1979), 1–3.

20   Cited in "Canadians, Others Told to Quit Iran," CP (January 1, 1979).

21 Cited in Roger Lucy, "Letters from the Iranian Revolution," *BP* 6:4 (Spring 1981), 32.

22 Greta Murray, cited in "Canadians Recount Iran Horror Stories."

23 Kathy Storch, cited in ibid.

24 Douglas Taylor, interview with the author.

25 Roger Lucy, "Letters from the Iranian Revolution," 32.

26 Gary Goldstein, cited in David Blaikie and Marilyn Dunlop, "We're Glad to Be Out, Say Returning Evacuees" *TS* (January 5, 1979), 1.

27 Bruce Allain, cited in "Canadians Recount Iran Horror Stories."

28 See Joe Hall, "Iranian Air Force Flexes Its Muscles," *TS* (February 6, 1979).

29 Carter, *Keeping Faith*, 444.

30 Ibid., 443.

31 Vance, *Hard Choices*, 336.

32 Brzezinski, *Power and Principle*, 379.

33 Ibid., 380.

34 "Iran: Bakhtiar Government," LAC RG-25 20-IRAN-1–4 (January 8, 1979), 1–3.

35 Ruhollah Khomeini, cited in ibid.; and Ruhollah Khomeini, cited in R. W. Apple, "Iran's Civilian Cabinet Contends with Protests," NYTS (January 8, 1979).

36 "Departure of Shah: Possible Consequences," LAC RG-25 20-IRAN-1–4 (January 17, 1979), 1–7.

37 "Iran Situation," LAC RG-25 20-IRAN-2–1 (January 10, 1979), 1–2.

38 "Iran in Frenzy of Joy after Shah Leaves," NYTS/AP/R (January 17, 1979).

39 Eric Pace, "Tehran Explodes with Celebrations," NYTS (January 17, 1979).

40 "Iran in Frenzy of Joy after Shah Leaves."

41 Carter, *Keeping Faith*, 447.

42 "Departure of Shah," 1.

43 Ken Taylor, "Consequences of Shah's Departure," LAC RG-25 20-IRAN-1–4 (January 17, 1979), 1–3.

44 Ibid.

45 Pat Taylor, interview with the author.

46 "Millions on the March in Iran," UPI/AP (January 19, 1979).

47 Ibid.

CHAPTER 5: AYATOLLAH KHOMEINI IN POWER

1 Jerome, *The Man in the Mirror,* 96.

2 Ruhollah Khomeini, cited in "Cut Hand off Foreign Advisors: Triumphant Khomeini Returns," UPI/AP (February 1, 1979).

3 Ruhollah Khomeini, cited in "Iran's Premier Beset by Street Violence, Political Deadlock," AP/NYTS (January 29, 1979).

4   See "Bakhtiar Willing to Accept Khomeini's 'Shadow' Regime," AP/Reuters (February 5, 1979).

5   See Joe Hall, "Flowers Stop Guns but Rally Makes Peace Fragile," *TS* (February 17, 1979), p. A20.

6   Ken Taylor, "Bakhtiar's Struggle for Political Survival," LAC RG-25 20-IRAN-1–4 (February 1, 1979), 1–5.

7   Hamilton Jordan, *Crisis: The True Story of an Unforgettable Year in the White House* (New York: Berkeley Books, 1982), 21.

8   Joe Hall, "Iranian Air Force Flexes Its Muscles," *TS* (February 6, 1979), A17.

9   Ken Taylor, interview with the author.

10   Carter, *Keeping Faith*, 450.

11   Fred Saint-James, "These Greedy Men Must Be Punished," *TS* (February 9, 1979), A14.

12   "Fugitive Bakhtiar Sends Iran a Warning," R (March 25, 1979).

13   Vance, *Hard Choices*, 342.

14   "Iran: Recognition of Provisional Govt," LAC RG-25 20-1-2-IRAN (February 16, 1979), 1–2.

15   "Iran: Recognition of Provisional Govt," LAC RG-25 20-1-2-IRAN (February 17, 1979), 1.

16   See Joe Hall, "Masters of Terror Live in Fear," *TS* (February 5, 1979), A6.

17   Nematollah Nassiri, cited in Joe Hall, "'I Just Did Office Work' Tehran Torturer Pleaded," *TS* (February 13, 1979), 1.

18   Joe Hall, "Iranian Joy Greets Order to Execute 20 Shah Backers," *TS* (February 16, 1979), 1.

19   Ruhollah Khomeini, cited in Peter Hardy, "Iran's Khomeini Opens the Floodgates of Revenge" *TS* (February 17, 1979), 1.

20   Peter Hardy, "Iran's New Regime in Trouble," *TS* (February 21, 1979), A22.

21   Ervand Abrahamian, "The Guerrilla Movement in Iran, 1963–1977," *MR* 86 (March–April 1980), 3–15.

22   Ibid.

23   Amir Entezam, cited in "Renewed Fighting Breaks Ceasefire in Western Iran" R/AP (March 21, 1979).

24   "Iran: Short Term Prospects" LAC RG-25 20-IRAN-1–4 (February 21, 1979), 1–5.

25   Khalkhali's clerical rank was hojjat al-Islam, just below that of ayatollah, but because he was known as Ayatollah Khalkhali, I have opted for this usage.

26   See Joe Hall, "Canadian on 'Death List' Tells of Horror in Iran," *TS* (February 5, 1979), 1.

27   See Ken Taylor, "Bakhtiar/ Khomeini Confrontation," LAC RG-25 20-IRAN-1–4 (January 29, 1979), 1–2.

28   Ken Taylor, interview with the author.

29   See Joe Hall, "Iran's Not Just Bleeding—It's Broke," *TS* (February 10, 1979), C5.

30   Ken Taylor, interview with the author.

31   See Trita Parsi, *Treacherous Alliance: The Secret Dealings of Iran, Israel and the United States* (Yale University Press, 2007), 6–22.

32   See ibid., 26, 79.

33   See "Israelis Wary of New Iranian Stance," R/AP (February 20, 1979).

34   See David Landau, "Arafat's Shadow Falls on Camp David Talks," *TS* (February 24, 1979), C6.

35   Ken Taylor, interview with the author.

36   *Ibid.*

37   "Israeli representation in Iran: Possible Cdn Role" LAC RG-25 20-IRAN-1–4 (January 5, 1979), 1–2.

39   "Israeli representation in Iran: Possible Cdn Role" LAC RG-25 20–2–1-IRAN (January 7, 1979), 1–3.

40   *Ibid.*, 1–3.

41   Ken Taylor, interview with the author.

42   *Ibid.*

43   See Bergman, *The Secret War with Iran*, 27–30.

44   "Arafat's Shadow Falls on Camp David Talks," C6.

45   Ahmad Seyyed Khomeini, cited in "PLO, Iran Will Fight Israel, Arafat Says," R/AP/*NYT* (February 20, 1979).

46   See Bergman, *The Secret War with Iran*, 32–3.

47   Ken Taylor, interview with the author.

48   Ibid.

49   See Allan Gotlieb, "Israeli Interests in Iran," LAC RG-25 20-ISRAEL-1–3 (February 26, 1979), 1–3.

50   Ken Taylor, interview with the author.

51   The news that Canada was assuming Israeli interests was buried on the back pages, and did not even merit its own headline. See, for example, "Iran Oil Chief Plans to Drop Western Middlemen," AP/CP/R (March 1, 1979).

52   Ken Taylor, interview with the author.

53   Roger Lucy, interview with the author.

54   Ken Taylor, interview with the author.

55   "Iran: USA Emb [1 of 5]," LAC RG-25 20-IRAN-1–4 (February 14, 1979), 1.

56   "Iran: USA Embassy [2 of 5]," LAC RG-25 20-IRAN-1–4 (February 14, 1979), 1.

57   "We have confirmation": "Iran: USA Embassy [3 of 5]," LAC RG-25 20-IRAN-
      1–4 (February 14, 1979), 1.
58   Roger Lucy, "Letters from the Iranian Revolution," 33.
59   Ken Taylor, interview with the author.
60   William Sullivan, cited in "Americans Urged to Flee Iran Fighting" UPI/R
      (February 15, 1979).
61   Harold H. Saunders, "The Crisis Begins" in Warren Christopher et al., *American
      Hostages in Iran: The Conduct of a Crisis* (New Haven: Yale University Press,
      1985), 54.
62   Ken Taylor, interview with the author.
63   *Ibid.*
64   Turner, *Terrorism and Democracy,* 29.
65   Vance, *Hard Choices,* 370.
66   Ruhollah Khomeini, cited in "Ayatollah's Snub of Leftists Splits Iran
      Revolutionaries," R/AP (February 21, 1979).
67   "Contingency Planning," LAC RG-25 20-IRAN-1–4 (February 16, 1979), 1–3.

CHAPTER 6: FATEFUL DECISIONS

1   "Former Premier on Trial for Life," AP (March 16, 1979).
2   "9 Shot as Iranian Court Gains Sweeping Powers," R (April 7, 1979).
3   "Former PM Hoveyda," LAC RG-25 20-IRAN-1–4 (March 27, 1979), 1.
4   "Trial Hoveyda," LAC RG-25 20-IRAN-1–4 (April 4, 1979), 1.
5   "Canada values" LAC RG-25 20-1-2-IRAN (April 6, 1979), 1–2.
6   Cited in "Prime Minister Trudeau's Message Seeking Clemency for Former PM
      Hoveyda of Iran," LAC RG-25 20-1-2-IRAN (May 3, 1979), 1–3.
7   "Iran: Executions," LAC RG-25 20-1-2-IRAN (April 9, 1979), 1.
8   "Iran: Executions" LAC RG-25 20-IRAN-1–4 (April 10, 1979), 1–3.
9   Michael Pitfield, marginalia, in Jacques S. Roy, "Le Premier Ministre Hoveyda,"
      LAC RG-25 20-1-2-IRAN (April 30, 1979), 1.
10   Allan Gotlieb, Letter to Michael Pitfield, LAC RG-25 20-1-2-IRAN (May 10,
      1979), 1.
11   Ken Taylor, interview with the author.
12   Cited in Nathan Gonzalez, *Engaging Iran: The Rise of a Middle East Powerhouse
      and America's Strategic Choice* (Westport: Greenwood, 2007), 59.
13   See "Shots Fired as 20,000 Women Continue Protest," UPI (March 13, 1979).
14   See "Battle of the Veil May Decide Future of Islam in Iran Society," R/UPI
      (March 12, 1979).
15   "Iran Sitrep," LAC RG-25 20-IRAN-1–4 (March 13, 1979), 1–3.

16 Ken Taylor, "Iran: Facing the New Year," LAC RG-25 20-IRAN-1–4 (March 20, 1979), 1–2.

17 Ruholla Khomeini, cited in Ron Koven, "Iran Is Declared Islamic before the Vote Is Counted," *TS* (April 2, 1979), A07.

18 "Assembly of Experts," LAC RG-25 20-IRAN-1–4 (August 9, 1979), 1–3.

19 "Iran's Leader Demands Obedience," R (September 20, 1979).

20 Bob Graham, "Avengers Are Hunting the Shah and His Fortune," *TS* (March 3, 1979), A6.

21 See "Activities of the Shah," LAC RG-25 83–10–1-IRAN (April 3, 1979), 1–2.

22 Carter Diary, cited in Carter, *Keeping Faith*, 453.

23 Vance, *Hard Choices*, 343–4.

24 Brzezinski, *Power and Principle*, 474.

25 Jimmy Carter, cited in Harris, *The Crisis*, 188.

26 See "Executions in Iran," LAC RG-25 20-IRAN-1–4 (May 15, 1979), 1–2.

27 "Executions," LAC RG-25 20-IRAN-1–4 (May 16, 1979), 1–2.

28 Sadegh Khalkhali, cited in "Pursuit of Revolutionary Justice," LAC RG-25 20-IRAN-1–4 (May 14, 1979), 1–2.

29 See "Mecca Visit Offered for Murder of Shah," R (May 18, 1979).

30 See Nicholas van Rijn, "9 Rich Iranians Want to Bring $3 Billion to Metro," *TS* (May 21, 1979), A2.

31 Cited in ibid., A2.

32 Cited in Saunders, "The Crisis Begins," 55.

33 Ruhollah Khomeini, cited in "Delay Sending Envoy, Iran Tells U.S.," AP/R (May 21, 1979).

34 Linda McQuaig, "To the Man in the Street, Iran Is Definitely on the Right Track," *GM* (May 1, 1979), 7.

35 "Kissinger's Visits Boosted Iran's Bills," *GM* (July 18, 1979), p. 12.

36 Mehdi Bazargan, paraphrased in "Iran Adopts More Conciliatory Line toward U.S.," R/AP (May 22, 1979).

37 See "Iran Chief Wants Amnesty to Allow Work on Economy," R (May 24, 1979).

38 Ibrahim Yazdi, cited in "Iran Adopts More Conciliatory Line," R/AP (May 22, 1979).

39 L. Bruce Laingen, *Yellow Ribbon: The Secret Journal of Bruce Laingen* (New York: Brassey's, 1992), 4.

40 Daugherty, *In the Shadow of the Ayatollah*, 16.

41 Ken Taylor, interview with the author.

42 See Saunders, "The Crisis Begins," 57.

43 Ken Taylor, "Meeting with FM Ibrahim Yazdi," LAC RG-25 20–1–2-IRAN (June 19, 1979), 1–3.

44   Ibid.

45   Ibid.

46   Carter, *Keeping Faith*, 454.

47   Vance, *Hard Choices*, 370.

48   Ibid., 371.

49   Saunders, "The Crisis Begins," 55.

50   Vance, *Hard Choices*, 371.

51   Henry Precht, interview, *Escape from Iran*.

52   Bruce Laingen, LHT.

53   Carter, *Keeping Faith*, 455.

54   See Bruce Laingen to State Department, "Shah's Illness," Secret Cable 11133 (October 21, 1979), 1–3.

55   Memo from Warren Christopher, cited in Carter, *Keeping Faith*, 455.

56   See ibid.

57   Carter Diary, cited in Carter, *Keeping Faith*, 456.

58   See John Prados, *Safe for Democracy: the Secret Wars of the CIA* (Chicago: Ivan R. Dee, 2006), 22.

59   "Judge Urges Moslems to Tear Shah Apart," R (October 25, 1979).

60   Vance, *Hard Choices*, 373.

61   Ken Taylor, "The Ayatollahs Take Hold—Iran," LAC RG-25 20-IRAN-1-4 (October 29, 1979), 1–2.

62   Ibrahim Asgharzadeh, cited in Harris, *The Crisis*, 201.

CHAPTER 7: MARG BAR AMRIKA!

1   Laingen, *Yellow Ribbon*, 3.

2   Somchai Sriweawnetr, LHT.

3   Ibid.

4   James Lopez, LHT. William Daugherty's recollection was as follows: "Henry Precht, to his lasting regret I think, told us during his visit—knowing that the shah was coming to the U.S.—that Iran was 'perfectly safe.' This generated a lot of resentment towards Henry by many of us during the event. I eventually raised it with Henry years later and he said he was just trying to raise morale. I have no doubt that he was sincere in this, but it was certainly the wrong thing to say to an intelligent group of diplomats who were very well aware of the danger the admission of the shah presented" (William Daugherty, interview with the author).

5   Ebtekar, *Takeover in Tehran*, 52.

6   Ruhollah Khomeini, cited in ibid.

7   Warren Christopher, "Introduction," *American Hostages in Iran*, 14.

8   Turner, *Terrorism and Democracy*, 26.

9   See Mark Bowden, *Guests of the Ayatollah* (New York: Atlantic Monthly Press, 2006), 9.

10 Ken Taylor, "Sitrep 15 Nov Iran," LAC RG-25 20-IRAN-1–4 (November 15, 1979), 1–3.

11 See Jerome, *The Man in the Mirror*, 142.

12 Bergman, *The Secret War with Iran*, 53.

13 Charlie A. Beckwith and Donald Knox, *Delta Force* (New York: Dell, 1983), 205.

14 Ken Taylor, interview with the author.

15 Ibid.

16 Ebtekar, *Takeover in Tehran*, 95.

17 Ibid., 58.

18 Ibid., 65–6.

19 See "Ease of Takeover Surprised Students," R (November 13, 1979).

20 Jimmy Carter, cited in Bowden, *Guests of the Ayatollah*, 139.

21 See, for example, "Situation in Iran," LAC RG-25 20-IRAN-1–4 (November 8, 1979), 1–3.

22 Carter, *Keeping Faith*, 457.

23 Vance, *Hard Choices*, 374.

24 Ken Taylor, interview with the author.

25 Jordan, *Crisis*, 15.

26 Carter Diary, cited in Carter, *Keeping Faith*, 455.

27 Bruce Laingen, LHT.

28 Ibid.

29 Ibid.

30 Victor Tomseth, LHT.

31 Ibid.

32 Bruce Laingen, LHT.

33 Ibid.

34 *Ibid.*

35 Bruce Laingen, letter to Bill Laingen, November 5, 1979, cited in Laingen, *Yellow Ribbon*, 20.

36 Saunders, "The Crisis Begins," 43.

37 Brzezinski, *Power and Principle*, 475.

38 Victor Tomseth, LHT.

39 Victor Tomseth, cited in Daugherty, *In the Shadow of the Ayatollah*, 109.

40 Victor Tomseth, LHT.

41　Ann Swift, cited in Saunders, "The Crisis Begins," 41.

42　See "Ease of Takeover Surprised Students," R (November 13, 1979).

43　Victor Tomseth, LHT.

44　Ibid.

CHAPTER 8: ON THE RUN

1　Robert Anders, interview, *Escape from Iran.*

2　Mark Lijek, interview with the author.

3　James Lopez, LHT.

4　Mark Lijek, interview with the author.

5　Ibid.

6　Richard Morefield, LHT.

7　Ibid.

8　Mark Lijek, interview with the author.

9　Kim King, cited in Bernard Gwertzman, "Six U.S. Diplomats, Hidden by Canada, Leave Iran Safely," *NYT* (January 29, 1980), A1.

10　Robert Anders, LHT.

11　Cora Lijek, interview, *Escape from Iran.*

12　Mark Lijek, interview, *Escape from Iran.*

13　Richard Morefield, LHT.

14　James Lopez, LHT.

15　Cora Lijek, interview, *Escape from Iran.*

16　Robert Anders, interview, *Escape from Iran.*

17　Mark Lijek, interview with the author.

18　Kathryn Koob, LHT.

19　Ibid.

20　Ibid.

21　Ibid.

22　Mark Lijek, interview, *Escape from Iran.*

23　Kathryn Koob, LHT.

24　Ibid.

25　Ibid.

26　Ibid.

27　Laingen, *Yellow Ribbon,* 55.

28　Kathryn Koob, LHT.

29　Vic Tomseth, LHT.

30　Ibid.

31　Mark Lijek, interview with the author.

32   Robert Anders, LHT.

33   Mark Lijek, LHT.

34   Ahmad Khomeini, cited in Ken Taylor, "Seizure of USA Embassy Tehran," LAC
      RG-25 20-IRAN-1–4 (November 6, 1979), 1–2.

35   Abolhassan Bani-Sadr, cited in Fred Halliday, "Abol-Hassan Bani-Sadr: I Defeated
      the Ideology of the Regime," *MR* 104 (March–April, 1982), 6.

36   Ruhollah Khomeini, cited in ibid., 6.

37   Schlesinger, *Time Zones,* 243.

38   Carter, *Keeping Faith,* 459.

39   James Reston, "Ayatollah Acts Outside Limits of Diplomacy," NYTS (November 14,
      1979).

40   Eqbal Ahmed, "What's behind the Crisis in Iran and Afghanistan?" *Social Text* 3
      (Autumn 1980), 47.

CHAPTER 9: DIPLOMATIC MANEOUVRES

1   Bob Corbett, "Government Protest to Iran for Kidnapping of U.S. Embassy
      Personnel—Motion under S[tanding] O[rder] 43," *Hansard* (November 6,
      1979), 984.

2   Michael Shenstone, "HOFC Resolution on Occupation of U.S. Emb in Tehran,"
      LAC RG-25 20–1–2-IRAN (November 6, 1979), 1–3.

3   Editorial, *GM* (November 6, 1979), 6.

4   Shenstone, "HOFC Resolution," 1-3.

5   Ken Taylor, interview with the author.

6   Ken Taylor, "Sitrep Iran 20 November," LAC RG-25 20-IRAN-1–4 (November 20,
      1979), 1–6.

7   Christopher, "Introduction," *American Hostages in Iran,* 31.

8   Saunders, "Diplomacy and Pressure, November 1979–May 1980," *American
      Hostages in Iran,* 73.

9   Vance, *Hard Choices,* 377.

10   Brzezinski, *Power and Principle,* 478.

11   Ibid., 481.

12   Cited in "Iranian Regime Resigns," R/AP/NYT (November 7, 1979).

13   Ken Taylor, "Situation Worsening—Iran" LAC RG-25 20-IRAN-1–4 (November 7,
      1979), 1–3.

14   See "Seizure of USA Emb Iran," LAC RG-25 20-IRAN-1–4 (November 6, 1979), 1–3.

15   See "Iranian Premier Quits as Students Threaten to Execute Hostages," R/AP/
      NYT (November 7, 1979).

16   See "Stay Out or Hostages Die, Iran Mob Warns U.S.," *TS* (November 6, 1979), 1.

17 See "Iranian Premier Quits as Students Threaten to Execute Hostages," R/AP/NYT (November 7, 1979).

18 Ruhollah Khomeini, cited in "Iranian Premier Quits as Students Threaten to Execute Hostages," R/AP/NYT (November 7, 1979).

19 Ken Taylor, "Situation Worsening—Iran" LAC RG-25 20-IRAN-1–4 (November 7, 1979), 1–3.

20 Letter from President Jimmy Carter to Ayatollah Ruhollah Khomeini, cited in Saunders, "Diplomacy and Pressure, November 1979–May 1980," 76.

21 Victor Tomseth, LHT.

22 Turner, *Terrorism and Democracy*, 31.

23 Ibid., 37.

24 White House Statement, "Iranian Students in the United States Announcement on Actions to Be Taken by the Department of Justice" (November 10, 1979).

25 See Carter, *Keeping Faith*, 460.

26 Ibid., 463.

27 Ibid., 464.

28 White House Statement, "American Hostages in Iran" (November 9, 1979).

29 Cited in Jack Cahill, "U.S. Must Cure Shah—Then We Can Kill Him," TS (November 8, 1979), 1.

30 Ken Taylor, "Seizure of USA Embassy Tehran," LAC RG-25 20-IRAN-1–4 (November 6, 1979), 1–2.

31 Christie Blatchford and Helen Bullock, "Frightened Diplomats on the Run for Days before Finding Refuge," TS (February 1, 1980), A1.

32 Ken Taylor, "Situation Worsening—Iran" LAC RG-25 20-IRAN-1–4 (November 7, 1979), 1–3.

33 "Situation in Iran—Sitrep," LAC RG-25 20-IRAN-1–4 (November 7, 1979), 1–2.

34 "Iran Sitrep 19 Nov," LAC RG-25 20-IRAN-1–4 (November 19, 1979), 1–2.

35 Ken Taylor, "Sitrep Iran 20 Nov," LAC RG-25 20-IRAN-1–4 (November 20, 1979), 1–6.

36 Ken Taylor, interview with the author.

37 See Ken Taylor, "Sitrep Iran," LAC RG-25 20–1–2-IRAN (November 12, 1979), 1–2.

38 Ken Taylor, "Sitrep," LAC RG-25 20-IRAN-1–4 (November 11, 1979), 1.

39 Laingen, *Yellow Ribbon*, 16.

40 Allan Gotlieb, "U.S. Hostage in Iran" RG-25 20–1–2-IRAN (November 14, 1979), 1.

41 Ken Taylor, "Sitrep 15 Nov Iran," LAC RG-25 20-IRAN-1–4 (November 15, 1979), 1–3.

42 Ken Taylor, interview with the author.

43   Cited in Ken Taylor, "Sitrep Iran," LAC RG-25 20-IRAN-1–4 (November 13, 1979), 1–3.

44   Ken Taylor, "Sitrep 17 Nov Iran," LAC RG-25 20-IRAN-1–4 (November 17, 1979), 1–2.

45   Ken Taylor, "Sitrep Iran 26 Nov," LAC RG-25 20-IRAN-1–4 (November 26, 1979), 1–3.

46   Ken Taylor, "Sitrep Iran 28 Nov," LAC RG-25 20-IRAN-1–4 (November 28, 1979), 1–5.

CHAPTER 10: COMING IN FROM THE COLD

1   Vic Tomseth, LHT.

2   Bruce Laingen, LHT.

3   Ibid.

4   Laingen, *Yellow Ribbon*, x.

5   Ken Taylor, "Status of USA Chargé Bruce Laingen," LAC RG-25 20-IRAN-1–4 (November 8, 1979), 1.

6   See Ken Taylor, "Sitrep Iran Nov 27" LAC RG-25 20-IRAN-1–4 (November 27, 1979), 1–3.

7   Vic Tomseth, LHT.

8   Ken Taylor, interview with the author.

9   "Iran: Sitrep 15 Nov," LAC RG-25 20-IRAN-1–4 (November 15, 1979), 1–2.

10   Ken Taylor, "Sitrep 15 Nov Iran," LAC RG-25 20-IRAN-1–4 (November 15, 1979), 1–3.

11   Vic Tomseth, LHT.

12   Robert Anders, LHT.

13   Ibid.

14   Victor Tomseth, LHT.

15   Ibid.

16   Somchai Sriweawnetr, LHT.

17   Robert Anders, LHT.

18   Mark Lijek, interview with the author.

19   Somchai Sriweawnetr, LHT.

20   Cora Lijek, LHT.

21   Mark Lijek, LHT.

22   Mark Lijek, interview with the author.

23   Robert Anders, LHT.

24   Victor Tomseth, LHT.

25   Mark Lijek, interview with the author.

26   Somchai Sriweawnetr, paraphrased by Cora Lijek, LHT.

27   Mark Lijek, LHT.

28   Somchai Sriweawnetr, LHT.

29   Flora MacDonald, interview with the author.

30   Zena Sheardown, interview with the author.

31   James Edward, LHT.

32   John Sheardown, interview, *Escape from Iran*.

33   Flora MacDonald, interview with the author.

34   Ibid.

35   Allan Gotlieb, "Memorandum for the Minister," LAC RG-25 20–1–2-USA (November 9, 1979), 1.

36   Flora MacDonald, interview with the author.

37   "What Is the Situation in Iran," LAC RG-25 20–1–2-IRAN (November 9, 1979), 1–2.

38   Marc Lalonde, *Hansard* (November 9, 1979), 1136.

40   Flora MacDonald, *Hansard* (November 9, 1979), 1136.

41   John Crosbie, *Hansard* (November 9, 1979), 1137.

42   Flora MacDonald, interview with the author.

43   Joe Clark, interview, *Escape from Iran*.

44   "USA Emb Staff Iran," LAC RG-25 20–1–2-IRAN (November 9, 1979), 1.

45   Michael Shenstone, "USA Emb Staff Iran: Implications for Canadians," LAC RG-25 20–1–2-IRAN (November 9, 1979), 1.

46   Ken Taylor, interview with the author.

47   Zena Sheardown, interview with the author.

48   Robert Anders, interview, *Escape from Iran*.

49   Zena Sheardown, interview with the author.

50   Mark Lijek, interview with the author.

51   Cora Lijek, interview, *Escape from Iran*.

52   Mark Lijek, interview, *Escape from Iran*.

53   Ken Taylor, interview with the author.

54   Zena Sheardown, interview with the author.

55   Robert Anders, LHT.

56   Mark Lijek, interview with the author.

57   Bruce Laingen, LHT.

58   Ibid.

59   John Sheardown, LHT.

60   Mark Lijek, interview with the author.

61   Cora Lijek, interview, *Escape from Iran*.

62   Mark Lijek, interview with the author.

63   Somchai Sriweawnetr, LHT.

64   Ibid.

65   Executive Order 12170 "Blocking Iranian Government Property" (November 14, 1979).

66   Carter, *Keeping Faith*, 462.

67   Jimmy Carter, "Iranian Situation and United States Energy Conservation Remarks at a White House Briefing for State Governors" (November 16, 1979).

68   Ken Taylor, interview with the author.

69   Ruhollah Khomeini, cited in "Khomaini [*sic*] Rejects Pope's Mediation, Dares Carter to Use Military Force," AP/*NYT* (November 12, 1979).

70   Ruhollah Khomeini, cited in "The Answer of Imam Khomeini, Leader of the Islamic Revolution in Iran, to His Eminence Pope Jean [*sic*] Paul II," LAC RG-25 20–1–2-IRAN (November 16, 1979), 1–12.

71   Ibid.

CHAPTER 11: WALKING LAPS IN THE BALLROOM

1   "Situation in Iran," LAC RG-25 20-IRAN-1–4 (November 8, 1979), 1–3.

2   Ken Taylor, "Security of American Chargé," LAC RG-25 20-USA-1–3-MIDEAST (November 10, 1979), 1.

3   Laingen, *Yellow Ribbon*, 24.

4   Ibid., 23.

5   Ken Taylor, "Meeting with USA Chargé Laingen 15 Nov," LAC RG-25 20-IRAN-1–4 (November 17, 1979), 1–2.

6   Bruce Laingen, LHT.

7   Ibid.

8   Victor Tomseth, LHT.

9   Henry Precht, cited in Robert W. Duemling, "Memo for Michael Shenstone," LAC RG-25 20–1–2-IRAN (November 20, 1979), 1.

10   Ken Taylor, "Sitrep Iran 22 November," LAC RG-25 20-IRAN-1–4 (November 22, 1979), 1–2.

11   "Message from U.S. State Department for USA Chargé Laingen," LAC RG-25 20-IRAN-1–4 (November 22, 1979), 1–2.

12   Ken Taylor, "Iran—Message for USA Chargé," LAC RG-25 20-IRAN-1–4 (November 23, 1979), 1.

13   Ken Taylor, "Visit to Bruce Laingen Dec 1 PM," LAC RG-25 20-IRAN-1–4 (December 1, 1979), 1–2.

14   Ken Taylor, "Visit to Bruce Laingen," LAC RG-25 20-IRAN-1–4 (December 11, 1979), 1.

15   See Laingen, *Yellow Ribbon*, 41.

16   Ken Taylor, cited in Haroon Siddiqui, "U.S. Visitor Says Captives Are Anxious but Well," *TS* (November 26, 1979), A12.

17   Jimmy Carter, "Message to Prime Minister Clark from President Carter," LAC RG-25 20–1–2-USA (November 15, 1979), 1–2.

18   Michael Shenstone, "Iran Hostages" LAC RG-25 20–1–2-IRAN (November 15, 1979), 1–2.

19   Draft letter from Joe Clark to President Jimmy Carter, LAC RG-25 20–1 2 USA (November 15, 1979), 1–2.

20   Joe Clark, cited in "Clark Seeks Declaration," CP (November 22, 1979).

21   Carter, *Keeping Faith*, 466.

22   "Iran—Status Report," LAC RG-25 20-IRAN-1–4 (November 16, 1979), 1–3.

23   Zbigniew Brzezinski, cited in Peter Towe, "USA Policy on Iran: Brzezinski's Views," LAC RG-25 20–1–2-USA-1–3-MIDEAST (December 7, 1979), 1–5

24   See Bowden, *Guests of the Ayatollah*, 184.

25   Ibid., 295.

26   Ibid., 318.

27   Ibid., 146.

28   William Daugherty, interview with the author.

29   See Bowden, *Guests of the Ayatollah*, 284.

30   See Daugherty, *In the Shadow of the Ayatollah*, 108–9.

31   See Bergman, *The Secret War with Iran*, 4.

32   Ebtekar, *Takeover in Tehran*, 111.

33   Carter, *Keeping Faith*, 467.

34   See Ebtekar, *Takeover in Tehran*, 105.

35   Ruhollah Khomeini, cited in ibid., 105.

36   Ibid., 113.

37   See ibid., 114–115.

38   See "Iran Ex-Deputy PM Held as U.S. Spy," *TS* (December 20, 1979), A17.

39   Ken Taylor, "Sitrep Iran 20 Dec," LAC RG-25 20-IRAN-1–4 (December 20, 1979), 1–4.

40   Cited in Ebtekar, *Takeover in Tehran*, 92.

41   See "Iranians Threaten to Execute U.S. Hostages" R/AP (November 22, 1979).

42   *Ibid.*

43   Ruhollah Khomeini, cited in "Khomaini Backs Threats to Kill Hostages if U.S. Attacks," *NYT*/R/AP (November 22, 1979).

44   Carter, *Keeping Faith*, 466.

45   Cited in Saunders, "Diplomacy and Pressure," 90.

46   Henry Precht, interview, *Escape from Iran.*

47   Turner, *Terrorism and Democracy,* 60.

48   Jody Powell, cited in "U.S. Hostages 'Brainwashed' Ex-captives Say" UPI/AP (November 22, 1979).

49   Cited in ibid.

50   Michael Shenstone, "Iran Hostages: Canadian Views," LAC RG-25 20–1–2-IRAN (November 16, 1979), 1–3.

51   Ken Taylor, "Meeting with FM Bani-Sadr Nov 28 AM," LAC RG-25 20-IRAN-1–4 (November 28, 1979), 1–5.

52   *Ibid.*

CHAPTER 12: STALEMATE

1   Jerome, *The Man in the Mirror,* 9.

2   Ken Taylor, interview with the author.

3   See Keddie, *Modern Iran,* 247–8.

4   Saunders, "Diplomacy and Pressure," 96.

5   Ken Taylor, "Sitrep Iran 01 Dec," LAC RG-25 20-IRAN-1–4 (December 1, 1979), 1–3.

6   "Sitrep Iran 03 Dec," LAC RG-25 20-IRAN-1–4 (December 3, 1979), 1–2.

7   Ken Taylor, "Sitrep Iran—09 Dec," LAC RG-25 20-IRAN-1–4 (December 9, 1979), 1–2.

8   Carter, *Keeping Faith,* 468.

9   Saunders, "Diplomacy and Pressure," 99.

10   Jimmy Carter, press conference (November 28, 1979).

11   Turner, *Terrorism and Democracy,* 77.

12   Ibid., 81.

13   Allan Gotlieb, "Memorandum for the Minister," LAC RG-25 20–1–2-IRAN (December 4, 1979), 1–9.

14   Ken Taylor, interview with the author.

15   Ibid.

16   Pierre Trudeau, *Hansard* (November 21, 1979), 1543.

17   Joe Clark, *Hansard* (November 21, 1979), 1543.

18   Joe Clark, interview, *Escape from Iran.*

19   Pierre Trudeau, *Hansard* (November 27, 1979), 1731.

20   Flora MacDonald, *Hansard* (November 27, 1979), 1731.

21   Pierre Trudeau, *Hansard* (November 27, 1979), 1731.

22   Flora MacDonald, interview with the author.

23   Ken Taylor, interview with the author.

24   Cora Lijek, interview, *Escape from Iran.*

25 Zena Sheardown, interview, *Escape from Iran.*

26 Mark Lijek, LHT.

27 Pat Taylor, interview with the author.

28 Zena Sheardown, interview with the author.

29 Pat Taylor, interview with the author.

30 Ibid.

31 Roger Lucy, interview with the author.

32 Ken Taylor, interview with the author.

33 Roger Lucy, interview with the author.

34 Lee Schatz, LHT.

35 Ibid.

36 Ken Taylor, interview with the author.

37 John Sheardown, LHT.

38 Douglas Taylor, interview with the author.

39 Ibid.

40 Turner, *Terrorism and Democracy,* 92.

41 Cora Lijek, interview, *Escape from Iran.*

42 Carter, *Keeping Faith,* 470.

43 Ken Taylor, "Sitrep Iran 24 Dec," LAC RG-25 20-IRAN-1–4 (December 24, 1979), 1–4.

44 Ken Taylor, interview with the author.

45 "Sitrep Iran 27 Dec 79," LAC RG-25 20-USA-1–3-MIDEAST (December 27, 1979), 1–2.

46 Carter, *Keeping Faith,* 471–2.

47 Brzezinski, *Power and Principle,* 485.

48 Ken Taylor, interview.

49 Carter, *Keeping Faith,* 478.

50 "Sitrep Iran 8 Jan," LAC RG-25 20-USA-1–3-MIDEAST (January 8, 1980), 1–2.

51 Saunders, "Diplomacy and Pressure," 102.

52 "Negotiating Link," LAC RG-25 20-USA-1–3-MIDEAST (January 4, 1980), 1.

53 "Sitrep Iran 10 Jan," LAC RG-25 20-IRAN-1–4 (January 10, 1980), 1–3.

54 "Iran: Negotiating Link," LAC RG-25 20-USA-1–3-MIDEAST (January 14, 1980), 1–3.

55 See Saunders, "Diplomacy and Pressure," 115.

56 Vance, *Hard Choices,* 402.

57 See Saunders, "Diplomacy and Pressure," 122.

58 Cited in ibid., 113–14.

59 Carter Diary, cited in Carter, *Keeping Faith,* 480.

60 Ibid., 481.

61 Ken Taylor, "Sitrep Iran 15 Jan," LAC RG-25 20-IRAN-1–4 (January 15, 1980), 1–4.

62 Ken Taylor, interview with the author.

CHAPTER 13: THIS IS WAR

1 Brzezinski, *Power and Principle*, 478.

2 Ibid., 489.

3 See ibid., 482.

4 Ibid., 488.

5 Jimmy Carter, cited in ibid., 482.

6 Ibid., 488.

7 Turner, *Terrorism and Democracy*, 38.

8 Bowden, *Guests of the Ayatollah*, 136–7.

9 Turner, *Terrorism and Democracy*, 66.

10 Ibid., 67.

11 Ibid., 66.

12 Beckwith and Knox, *Delta Force*, 207.

13 Paul B. Ryan, *The Iran Rescue Mission: Why It Failed* (Annapolis, MD: Naval Institute Press, 1985), 32–3.

14 Prados, *Safe for Democracy*, 25.

15 Bowden, *Guests of the Ayatollah*, 254.

16 Carter, *Keeping Faith*, 509.

17 Turner, *Terrorism and Democracy*, 66.

18 Ibid., 66.

19 Beckwith and Knox, *Delta Force*, 205.

20 Ibid.

21 Ibid.

22 Ibid., 216.

23 Ibid., 219.

24 Ibid., 221.

25 Turner, *Terrorism and Democracy*, 71–2.

26 Beckwith and Knox, *Delta Force*, 220.

27 Prados, *Safe for Democracy*, 25.

28 Beckwith and Knox, *Delta Force*, 221.

29 Charles Cogan, "Hunters, Not Gatherers: Intelligence in the Twenty-First Century," *Intelligence and National Security* 19:2 (June 2004), 312.

30 See Prados, *Safe for Democracy*, 24.

31 See George Crile, *Charlie Wilson's War* (New York: Grove, 2003), 57.

CHAPTER 14: A NEST OF SPIES

1   See Prados, *Safe for Democracy*, 21.

2   Brzezinski, *Power and Principle*, 491.

3   Zbigniew Brzezinski, personal correspondence with the author.

4   Beckwith and Knox, *Delta Force*, 207.

5   Turner, *Terrorism and Democracy*, 71.

6   Charles Cogan's claim that the U.S. military was hobbled by poor intelligence has already been noted. Dissecting the Eagle Claw failure in 1993, Major C. E. Holzworth of the U.S. Marines was also categorical. "Human intelligence sources in Iran were virtually non-existent," he wrote. "The CIA had informed the staff that they had no agents in the objective area." See C. E. Holzworth, "Operation Eagle Claw: A Catalyst for Change in the American Military" (CSC 1997), posted at globalsecurity.org. Retired U.S. naval officer Paul B. Ryan speculated that "when the mob took over the U.S. embassy on 4 November 1979, the CIA had not one agent operating in Tehran." He also wondered whether human intelligence in Iran might have been inferior due to Stansfield Turner's stated preference for technological intelligence-gathering. Ryan was plainly unaware both of Hart's group in Tehran and of the pivotal role played by the Canadians. He wrote that Vaught's J-2 could provide only photographs of the embassy compound, satellite imagery and whatever could be "gleaned from television news programs showing the Iranian guards, the streets, and the nine-foot wall surrounding the embassy." See Ryan, *The Iran Rescue Mission*, 33–4.

7   See Ken Taylor, "Sitrep Iran 28 Nov," LAC RG-25 20-IRAN-1–4 (November 28, 1979), 1–5.

8   Ken Taylor, "Sitrep Iran 02 Dec," LAC RG-25 20-IRAN-1–4 (December 2, 1979), 1–2.

9   "Options When Diplomacy Fails," LAC RG-25 20-IRAN-1–4 (December 2, 1979), 1–4.

10 See "USA Emb Staff Safe Haven," LAC RG-25 20-IRAN-1–4 (December 3, 1979), 1.

11 Joe Clark, confidential letter to Flora MacDonald, LAC RG-25 20-USA-1–3-MIDEAST (December 3, 1979), 1–3.

12 James Edward, LHT.

13 Ibid.

14 Ibid.

15 Ibid.

16 Ibid.

17 Turner, *Terrorism and Democracy*, 90.

18   Kenneth Curtis, interview with the author.

19   "Iran—Reporting," LAC RG-25 20-IRAN-1–4 (December 20, 1979), 1–2.

20   "Situation in Iran," LAC RG-25 20-IRAN-1–4 (December 22, 1979), 1–2.

21   Kenneth Curtis, interview with the author.

22   James Edward, LHT.

23   Ibid.

24   Turner, *Terrorism and Democracy*, 71.

25   Beckwith and Knox, *Delta Force*, 221.

26   James Edward, LHT.

27   Ibid.

28   Ibid.

29   Ibid.

30   Ibid.

31   Ibid.

32   Ibid.

33   Ibid.

34   Ibid.

35   Ibid.

36   Turner, *Terrorism and Democracy*, 87.

37   James Edward, LHT.

CHAPTER 15: THE CANADIAN PLAN

1   Bruce Laingen, LHT.

2   Roger Lucy, interview with the author.

3   See "Hired Mob Staged Jailbreak in Iran, U.S. Millionaire Says," UPI (February 20, 1979).

4   Stansfield Turner, cited in David Patrick Houghton, *U.S. Foreign Policy and the Iran Hostage Crisis* (Cambridge, UK: Cambridge University Press, 2001), 114.

5   Ken Taylor, interview with the author.

6   Turner, *Terrorism and Democracy*, 48.

7   *Ibid.*, 91.

8   Michael Shenstone, interview with the author.

9   Turner, *Terrorism and Democracy*, 91.

10   Jimmy Carter and Stanfield Turner, cited in Jordan, *The Crisis*, 130.

11   Turner, *Terrorism and Democracy*, 90.

12   Allan Gotlieb, interview with the author.

13   Peter Tarnoff, interview with the author. Day-to-day operations on virtually all aspects of the hostage crisis, including exfiltration planning, were managed

jointly by Chuck Cogan at the CIA and his counterpart at the State Department, Hal Saunders of the Iran Working Group. Cogan and Saunders thought highly of one another and enjoyed a close working relationship for the full duration of the Iranian–American standoff.

14 Allan Gotlieb, interview with the author.

15 Kenneth Curtis, interview with the author.

16 Lee Schatz, LHT.

17 Michael Shenstone, interview with the author.

18 Antonio J. Mendez, *The Master of Disguise: My Secret Life in the CIA* (New York: Morrow, 1999), 276.

19 See Antonio J. Mendez, "CIA Goes Hollywood: A Classic Case of Deception," *Studies in Intelligence* (Winter, 1999–2000).

20 Jean Pelletier, cited in Jean Pelletier and Claude Adams, *The Canadian Caper* (Toronto: Paperjacks, 1981), 152.

21 Flora MacDonald, interview with the author.

22 Ibid.

23 Ibid.

24 Joe Clark, interview, *Escape from Iran.*

25 Mark Lijek, interview, *Escape from Iran.*

26 Mark Lijek, LHT.

27 Flora MacDonald, interview with the author.

28 "Iran: Security Council Debate" LAC RG-25 20-USA-1-3-MIDEAST (December 30, 1979), 1–2.

29 Peter Tarnoff, interview with the author.

30 Michael Shenstone, interview with the author.

CHAPTER 16: PASSPORTS AND VISAS

1 Mendez, "CIA Goes Hollywood."

2 Mendez, *The Master of Disguise*, 54.

3 Joshuah Bearman, "How the CIA Used a Fake Sci-Fi Flick to Rescue Americans from Tehran," *Wired* 15:5 (April 24, 2007).

4 See Bearman, "How the CIA Used a Fake Sci-Fi Flick."

5 See Mendez, "CIA Goes Hollywood."

6 Mendez, *The Master of Disguise*, 270.

7 Mendez, "CIA Goes Hollywood."

8 Ibid.

9 Ibid.

10 Mendez, *The Master of Disguise*, 275.

11   See ibid., 275, where the author uses the code name "Delgado"; and Mendez, "CIA Goes Hollywood," where he uses the code name "Degaldo."

12   Mendez, *The Master of Disguise*, 275.

13   Ibid, 276.

14   Antonio J. Mendez, interview, *Escape from Iran*.

15   Mendez, "CIA Goes Hollywood."

16   Bearman, "How the CIA Used a Fake Sci-Fi Flick."

17   Mendez, *The Master of Disguise*, 278.

18   Mendez, "CIA Goes Hollywood."

19   Flora MacDonald, interview with the author.

20   Zena Sheardown, interview with the author.

21   Ken Taylor, interview with the author.

22   Flora MacDonald, interview, *Escape from Iran*.

23   Joe Clark, interview, *Escape from Iran*.

24   Flora MacDonald, interview, *Escape from Iran*.

25   Michael Shenstone, interview with the author.

26   Ibid.

27   Flora MacDonald, interview with the author.

28   Turner, *Terrorism and Democracy*, 92.

29   Flora MacDonald, interview with the author.

30   Ibid.

31   Mendez, *The Master of Disguise*, 277–8.

32   Ken Taylor, interview with the author.

33   Roger Lucy, interview with the author.

34   Ibid.

35   Ken Taylor, LHT.

36   Roger Lucy, interview with the author.

37   Mendez, *The Master of Disguise*, 284–5.

38   Roger Lucy, interview with the author.

39   Ibid.

40   Flora MacDonald, cited in Val Sears, "A Kingston Living Room Became Escape Central," *TS* (February 1, 1980), A16.

41   Ken Taylor, "Sitrep Iran 21 Jan," LAC RG-25 20-IRAN-1–4 (January 21, 1980), 1–3.

CHAPTER 17: THE FLIGHT OF THE HOUSEGUESTS

1   Mendez, *The Master of Disguise*, 287.

2   Julio, cited in Carter, *Keeping Faith*, 484.

3 Mendez, *The Master of Disguise*, 290.

4 Roger Lucy, interview with the author.

5 Cora Lijek, interview, *Escape from Iran*.

6 Roger Lucy, interview with the author.

7 Pat Taylor, interview with the author.

8 Ibid.

9 Ibid.

10 Ibid.

11 Ibid.

12 Mendez, *The Master of Disguise*, 295.

13 Mendez, "CIA Goes Hollywood."

14 Ken Taylor, interview with the author.

15 Mark Lijek, interview with the author.

16 Robert Anders, cited in Mendez, *The Master of Disguise*, 296.

17 Cora Lijek, interview, *Escape from Iran*.

18 Mark Lijek, interview with the author.

19 Ibid.

20 Roger Lucy, interview with the author.

21 Mendez, "CIA Goes Hollywood."

22 Cora Lijek, LHT.

23 Mark Lijek, interview with the author.

24 See Prados, *Safe for Democracy*, 23.

25 See Mendez, *The Master of Disguise*, 256–67.

26 Roger Lucy, LHT.

27 Cora Lijek, interview, *Escape from Iran*.

28 Mendez, interview, *Escape from Iran*.

29 Cora Lijek, LHT.

30 Mark Lijek, ibid.

31 Bob Anders, LHT.

32 Roger Lucy, interview with the author.

33 *Ibid.*

34 Flora MacDonald, interview with the author.

35 Turner, *Terrorism and Democracy*, 94.

36 Richard Helms, cited in Loch K. Johnson, "Richard Helms: An Interview with the Former U.S. Director of Central Intelligence" *Intelligence & National Security* 18:3 (Autumn 2003), 30.

37 Ken Taylor, interview with the author.

38 Roger Lucy, LHT.

39 Ken Taylor, cited in Ron Lowman, "Ken Taylor—The First Interview" *TS* (17 March 1980), A1, A12.

40 Ken Taylor, "Sitrep Iran 21 Jan" LAC RG-25 20-IRAN-1–4 (January 21, 1980), 1–3.

CHAPTER 18: THANKS, CANADA

1   Ken Taylor, interview with the author.

2   Pelletier and Adams, *The Canadian Caper*, 225.

3   Bernard Gwertzman, "6 American Diplomats, Hidden by Canada, Leave Iran," *New York Times* (January 30, 1980), A12.

4   See "Our Embassy in Tehran Smuggled out Americans," *TS* (January 29, 1980), A1, A12.

5   Kamran Morassagghi, cited in ibid., A1, A12.

6   Tehran to Canberra, "Iran: Canadian Representation," LAC RG-25 20-IRAN-1–4 (January 31, 1980), 1–3.

7   Cited in "Americans' Escape Is Called 'Illegal,'" R (January 30, 1980).

8   Cited in "You'll Pay for This Iran Tells Canada," CP (January 30, 1980).

9   Cited in ibid.

10 Laingen, *Yellow Ribbon*, 64.

11 Bruce Laingen to Bill Laingen (January 30, 1980), cited in Laingen, *Yellow Ribbon*, 65.

12 Jerome, *The Man in the Mirror*, 157.

13 Christian Bourguet, Hamilton Jordan and Sadegh Ghotbzadeh, cited in Jordan, *The Crisis*, 130–2.

14 Sadegh Ghotbzadeh, cited in "You'll Pay for This Iran Tells Canada," CP (January 30, 1980).

15 Sadegh Ghotbzadeh, paraphrased in ibid.

16 Sadegh Ghotbzadeh, cited in ibid.

17 Joe Clark, cited in "Clark Shrugs Off Threats by Iran," *TS* (January 31, 1980), A1.

18 Bill Neville, cited in ibid.

19 Flora MacDonald, cited in "You'll Pay for This."

20 Sadegh Ghotbzadeh, cited in "Clark Shrugs Off Threats."

21 Joe Clark, cited in ibid.

22 Joe Hall, "America Hails Canada's Rescue of 6 Diplomats" *TS* (January 30, 1980), A1.

23 Cited in ibid.

24 "Iran Rescue Does Us Proud," Editorial, *TS* (January 30, 1980), A8.

25 Editorial, "Very Quiet Diplomacy," *GM* (January 30, 1980), 6.

26 Joe Clark, cited in Ron Lowman, "You Made Us Proud, Flora Tells Envoy," *TS* (February 1, 1980), A16.

27   Turner, *Terrorism and Democracy*, 92.

28   Ken Taylor, cited in Jonathan Manthorpe, "'Hero' Envoy under Guard, Changes Hotels Daily," *TS* (January 31, 1980), A1.

29   "What do I do now?" Ken Taylor, "Heroes" (Unpublished notes for a lecture at Reed College, Oregon, October 9, 1986).

30   Ken Taylor, interview with the author.

31   Manthorpe, "'Hero' Envoy."

32   Ken Taylor, cited in ibid.

33   Ken Taylor, cited in "You'll Pay for This."

34   Manthorpe, "'Hero' Envoy."

35   Christie Blatchford and Helen Bullock, "Frightened Diplomats on the Run for Days before Finding Refuge," *TS* (February 1, 1980), A1.

36   Mark Lijek, interview with the author.

37   Ibid.

38   Jody Powell, cited in "You'll Pay for This."

39   Robert Anders, LHT.

40   Cora Lijek, LHT.

41   Wanda Lijek, cited in "Diplomats in Hiding Played Endless Scrabble" UPI (February 1, 1980).

42   "Iran: USA Policy," LAC RG-25 20-USA-1-3-MIDEAST (January 31, 1980), 1–2.

43   Ibid.

44   Robert Anders, LHT.

45   Robert Anders, cited in "6 Who Fled Iran Are Greeted by President," *NYT* (February 2, 1980), 4.

46   Robert Anders, cited in ibid., 1.

47   Gilles Mathieu, cited in ibid., 4.

48   "As you already know," Robert Anders, cited in *Ibid.*, 4.

49   Jimmy Carter, cited in ibid., 1.

50   Jimmy Carter, cited in Joe Hall, "Carter Phones to Say Thank You, Canadians" *TS* (February 1, 1980), A1.

51   Cited in "Congress Praises Canadian Action," AP (January 31, 1980).

52   Thomas (Tip) O'Neill, cited in ibid.

53   Zbigniew Brzezinski, cited in Patrick Doyle, "Brzezinski Cites Soviet Threat," *TS* (December 6, 1980), A6.

54   "Canadians Are Suddenly Heroes, and Americans Extend Thanks," *NYT* (February 2, 1980), 1.

55   Gerald Lynch, cited in ibid.

56   Cited in Hall, "Carter Phones," A1.

57   Cited in "200 U.S. Telegrams Say a Big Thank-You," *TS* (February 2, 1980), A2.

58   Cited in Joe Hall, "Carter Phones," A1.

59   Cited in ibid.

60   Cited in ibid.

61   Cited in ibid.

62   Cited in Lowman, "Ken Taylor—The First Interview," A1, A12.

63   Ken Taylor, cited in Ron Lowman, "You Made Us Proud, Flora Tells Envoy," *TS* (February 1, 1980), A1.

64   Flora MacDonald, cited in ibid.

65   Ken Taylor, cited in ibid.

66   Ken Taylor, interview with the author.

67   Ron Lowman, "Mystery Call Triggered Great Escape from Iran," *TS* (February 2, 1980), A1.

68   Ken Taylor, cited in ibid.

69   Ken Taylor, cited in "Embassy Hero Feels Great Being at Home," UPI (February 12, 1980).

70   Ken Taylor, cited in ibid.

71   Ed Koch, cited in "From Coast to Coast, United States Sings O Canada," *TS* (February 1, 1980), A16.

72   Lowman, "Ken Taylor—The First Interview," A1, A12.

CHAPTER 19: FALLOUT

1   See Jordan, *Crisis*, 126.

2   See "Captors Losing Influence," *LM* (January 29, 1980).

3   Abolhassan Bani-Sadr, cited in ibid.

4   See "U.S. Approves Plan to Free Hostages," *WP* (January 30, 1980), reprinted in *TS* (January 30, 1980), A15.

5   Carter, *Keeping Faith*, 485.

6   Ibid., 486.

7   Chris Beeby, "Iran: Canadian Issue," LAC RG-25 20-IRAN-1–4 (January 30, 1980), 1.

8   Brian Talboys, cited in "Iran-Canada," LAC RG-25 20–1–2-IRAN (January 30, 1980), 1.

9   Ken Taylor, interview with the author.

10   "Iran—NZ Emb" LAC RG-25 20-NZ-1–3 (February 11, 1980), 1–2.

11   Mohammad Adeli, cited in "A 'Flagrant Violation' of the Law Endangers Hostages, Iran Says," CP (February 2, 1980).

12   "U.S. Hostages and International Law," LAC RG-25 20-USA-1–3-MIDEAST (January 31, 1980), 1–3.

13   Embassy of Iran in Canada, "Note No. 339," LAC RG-25 20–1–2-IRAN (February 15, 1980), 1–4.

14   Allan Levine, *Scrum Wars: The Prime Ministers and the Media* (Toronto: Dundurn, 1996), 303–4.

15   Joe Clark, cited in John Honderich, "Clark Sidesteps Rescue Limelight," *TS* (January 30, 1980), A15.

16   George Cooper, cited in John Honderich, "Clark Shrugs Off Threats by Iran," *TS* (January 31, 1980), A1, A17.

17   Flora MacDonald, cited in Val Sears, "Flora's Success Recipe: Homey Style with a Dash of Iran," *TS* (February 3, 1980), A15.

18   Ken Taylor, interview with the author.

19   Joe Clark, cited in Honderich, "Clark Sidesteps Rescue Limelight," A15.

20   Pierre Trudeau, cited in ibid.

21   Henry Giniger, "Escape of 6 from Iran Gives Lift to the Election Drive of Joe Clark," *NYT* (January 31, 1980).

22   See "Escape Won't Elect Clark, Most Say," *TS* (January 31, 1980), A17.

23   André Ouellet, paraphrased in "Tory Says Iran Story First Break of Campaign," CP (January 31, 1980).

24   Joan Sutton, "Why Snipe at Success?" *TS* (February 5, 1980), A4.

25   Brian Mulroney, *Memoirs* (Toronto: McClelland & Stewart, 2007), 199.

26   Robert Bothwell, *Canada and the United States: The Politics of Partnership* (Toronto: University of Toronto Press, 1992), 128.

27   Carter, *Keeping Faith*, 487.

28   Ibid., 499.

29   Ibid., 485.

30   Ibid., 504.

31   See Andrew and Mitrokhin, *The Mitrokhin Archive II*, 185.

32   Cyrus Vance, *Hard Choices*, 406.

33   Jimmy Carter, cited in Saunders, "Diplomacy and Pressure, November 1979–May 1980," 142.

34   Carter, *Keeping Faith*, 507.

35   Vance, *Hard Choices*, 409.

36   Ibid., 408.

37   Ibid., 410.

38   Carter Diary, cited in Carter, *Keeping Faith*, 510.

39   Ibid., 514.

40   Ibid., 516.

41   Brzezinski, *Power and Principle*, 498.

42　Zbigniew Brzezinski, cited in Carter, *Keeping Faith,* 516.

43　Carter, *Keeping Faith,* 518.

44　Brzezinski, *Power and Principle,* 500.

45　Flora MacDonald, interview with the author.

46　Carter, *Keeping Faith,* 525.

47　William Daugherty, interview with the author.

CHAPTER 20: YELLOW RIBBONS

1　Ken Taylor, cited in Lowman, "Ken Taylor—The First Interview," A1, A12.

2　"Confidential," LAC RG-25 20–1–2-IRAN (January 30, 1980), 1.

3　Ken Taylor, LHT.

4　See "Arrest of Canadian Embassy Local Staff in Tehran," LAC RG-25 20–1–2-IRAN (June 9, 1980), 1.

5　Cited in "Dan-Can No. 123" LAC RG-25 20–1–2-IRAN (June 9, 1980), 1.

6　"Arrest of Canadian Embassy Local Staff in Tehran," LAC RG-25 20–1–2-IRAN (June 9, 1980), 1.

7　"Dan-Can No. 124," LAC RG-25 20–1–2-IRAN (June 10, 1980), 1.

8　"Your Dan-Can 128," LAC RG-25 20–1–2-IRAN (June 18, 1980), 1.

9　"Canint Tehran NBR 121," LAC RG-25 20–1–2-IRAN (July 2, 1980), 1.

10　John Sheardown, interview with the author.

11　Zena Sheardown, interview with the author.

12　Carter, *Keeping Faith,* 558.

13　Ibid., 559.

14　Ibid., 560.

15　Ibid., 566.

16　Ibid., 580.

17　Ibid., 586.

18　Daugherty, *In the Shadow of the Ayatollah,* 206.

19　Laingen, *Yellow Ribbon,* 288. On January 27, the day of the White House reception, an angry John Sheardown told the Canadian press that he was thinking of returning his Order of Canada medal. "The wives deserve most of the credit," he said. "They had to feed and entertain the Americans and handle nerve-wracking security." Sheardown had very nearly boycotted the original investiture ceremony on July 4, 1980, he said, because neither his wife, Zena, nor Pat Taylor had been included. With the matter now in the public eye, the House of Commons recommended both Zena and Pat for the honour, effectively laying the problem at the feet of the Order's advisory council. At the end of June 1981, the council announced that the two women would indeed be named members of the Order of Canada. The investiture ceremony for Zena Sheardown and Pat Taylor took place on October 21, 1981, Governor General Ed Schreyer doing the honours.

20 Joe Clark, *Hansard* (January 19, 1981), 6305.

21 Mark MacGuigan, cited in Pamela Wallin, "Canada-Iran Ties to Resume," *TS* (January 21, 1981), A23.

22 Pierre Trudeau, cited in ibid.

23 Lloyd Rollins, cited in "Russian Roulette Played with Two Women Hostages," AP-UPI (January 21, 1981).

24 Elizabeth Montagne, cited in "Horror Tales Shock Carter," *TS* (January 22, 1981), A14.

25 Ken Taylor, cited in "Ottawa Knew of Torture—Taylor," UPI (January 22, 1981).

26 "Ken Taylor's Statement re Treatment to [*sic*] Hostages," LAC RG-25 20–1–2-IRAN (January 23, 1981), 1–2.

27 Joe Clark, *Hansard* (January 22, 1981), 6450.

28 Pierre Trudeau, *Hansard* (January 22, 1981), 6450.

29 Behzad Nabavi, cited in "Canada Must Vow Not to Spy—Iran," CP-UPC (January 28, 1981).

30 "Iran—Reopening of Cdn Emb in Tehran," LAC RG-25 20–1–2-IRAN (January 30, 1981), 1–2.

31 "Iran Wants Canada to Apologize": R (November 10, 1982).

32 Ronald Reagan, "Remarks on Presenting the Congressional Gold Medal to Kenneth Taylor, Former Canadian Ambassador to Iran" (June 16, 1981).

33 Ken Taylor, ibid.

34 Gotlieb, *The Washington Diaries*, 165.

35 de Montigny Marchand, cited in Andrew Szende, "Our Diplomats Are a Brave New Breed," *TS* (August 14, 1982), B4.

36 Geoffrey Pearson, cited in Pamela Wallin, "Don't Call Him 'Pearson's Son'" *TS* (July 27, 1980), D5.

EPILOGUE: OUR MAN IN NEW YORK

1 Gotlieb, *The Washington Diaries*, 29.

2 Andrew Szende, "Ottawa Notebook," *TS* (August 13, 1980), A14.

3 Ken Taylor, interview with the author.

4 Szende, "Our Diplomats," B4.

5 Joan Sutton, "New Yorkers Dance Social Tune to Ken Taylor's Magic," *TSUN* (March 25, 1981), A4.

6 Ibid., A4.

7   Editorial, *GM* (December 9, 1983), 6.

8   Ken Taylor, interview with the author.

9   Joan Sutton, "A Great Loss for Canadians," *TS* (May 23, 1984).

10   Ken Taylor, interview with the author.

11   Ibid.

12   Flora MacDonald, interview with the author.

13   "Iranian Legislators Want to Shut Down Canada's 'Den Of Spies' in Tehran," CP (November 30, 2006).

14   Stephen Harper, cited in "Iran's Ideology 'Evil,' Harper Tells U.S. Paper," R (March 1, 2009).

15   Bergman, *The Secret War with Iran,* 3.

16   Bowden, *Guests of the Ayatollah,* 615.

17   Bruce Laingen, cited in Michael Theodoulou, "Former Hostage Hails Obama's Iran Efforts," *The National, United Arab Emirates* (June 3, 2009).

18   Ken Taylor, cited in Jonathon Gatehouse, "Ken Taylor: 'It Was a Canadian Initiative from Start to Finish,'" *M* (January 31, 2005).

SELECT BIBLIOGRAPHY AND FILMOGRAPHY

Abrahamian, Ervand. "The Guerrilla Movement in Iran, 1963–1977." *MERIP Reports* 86 (March–April 1980).

———. "Iran in Revolution: The Opposition Forces." *MERIP Reports* 75/76 (March–April 1979).

———. "The Political Challenge." *Middle East Research and Information Project (MERIP) Reports* 69 (July–August 1978).

Afshari, Reza. "State Legitimacy: The Case of the Islamic Republic of Iran Human Rights." *Human Rights Quarterly* 18:3 (1996).

Ahmed, Eqbal. "What's Behind the Crisis in Iran & Afghanistan." *Social Text* 3 (Autumn 1980).

Ahmed, Feroz. Iran: Subimperialism in Action." *Pakistan Forum* 3:6/7 (March/April 1973).

Andrew, Christopher, and Vasili Mitrokhin. *The Mitrokhin Archive II: The KGB and the World.* London: Penguin, 2005.

Ardalan, Davar. *My Name Is Iran.* New York: Holt, 2007.

Arnold, Hugh M. "Henry Kissinger and Human Rights." *Universal Human Rights* 2:4 (October–December 1980).

Bakhash, Shaul. "Iran." *American Historical Review* 96:5 (December 1991).

Bani-Sadr, Abolhassan. *My Turn to Speak: Iran, The Revolution and Secret Deals with the U.S.* New York: Brassey's, 1989.

Bani-Sadr, Abolhassan, and Fred Halliday. "I Defeated the Ideology of the Regime." *MERIP Reports* 104 (March–April 1982).

Baraheni, Reza. *The Crowned Cannibals: Writings on Repression in Iran.* New York: Vintage, 1977.

Bearman, Joshuah. "How the CIA Used a Fake Sci-Fi Flick to Rescue Americans from Tehran." *Wired* (April 24 2007).

Beckwith, Charlie A., and Donald Knox. *Delta Force.* New York: Dell, 1983.

Beeman, William O. "Iran's Religious Regime: What Makes It Tick? Will It Ever Run Down?" *Annals of the American Academy of Political and Social Science* 483 (January 1986).

Bergman, Ronen. *The Secret War with Iran.* New York: Free Press, 2007.

Bloomfield, Lincoln P. "From Ideology to Program to Policy: Tracking the Carter Human Rights Policy." *Journal of Policy Analysis and Management* 2:1 (Autumn 1982).

Bothwell, Robert. *The Big Chill: Canada and the Cold War.* Toronto: Irwin, 1998.

Bowden, Mark. *Guests of the Ayatollah.* New York: Atlantic Monthly Press, 2006.

Brzezinski, Zbigniew. *Power and Principle: Memoirs of the National Security Advisor, 1977–1981.* New York: Farrar, Straus, Giroux, 1983.

Carter, Jimmy. *Keeping Faith: Memoirs of a President.* New York: Bantam, 1982.

Chomsky, Noam. "U.S. Aid and Torture: A Correlation." *Journal of Palestine Studies* 13:2 (Winter 1984).

Christopher, Warren, Harold Saunders, Gary Sick, and Paul H. Kreisberg. *American Hostages in Iran: The Conduct of a Crisis.* New Haven: Yale University Press, 1985.

Cockcroft, Jim. "Letter from Tehran: The Embassy Takeover." *MERIP Reports* 87 (May 1980).

Cogan, Charles. "Hunters, Not Gatherers: Intelligence in the Twenty-First Century." *Intelligence & National Security* 19:2 (June 2004).

———. *La République de Dieu.* Paris: Éditions Jacob-Duvernet, 2008.

Conover, Pamela Johnston, Karen A. Mingst, and Lee Sigelman. "Mirror Images in Americans' Perceptions of Nations and Leaders during the Iranian Hostage Crisis." *Journal of Peace Research* 17:4 (1980).

Cottam, Richard. "Goodbye to America's Shah." *Foreign Policy* 34 (Spring 1979).

Crile, George. *Charlie Wilson's War.* New York: Grove, 2003.

Daugherty, William. *In the Shadow of the Ayatollah: A CIA Hostage in Iran.* Annapolis, MD: Naval Institute Press, 2001.

Delpech, Thérèse. *Iran and the Bomb: The Abdication of International Responsibility.* New York: Columbia University Press, 2006.

Duke, Simon. *United States Military Forces and Installations in Europe.* New York: Oxford University Press, 1989.

Ebadi, Shirin. *Iran Awakening.* Toronto: Vintage Canada, 2007.

Ebtekar, Massoumeh. *Takeover in Tehran: The Inside Story of the 1979 U.S. Embassy Capture.* Vancouver: Talonbooks, 2000.

El Azhary, M. S. "The Attitudes of the Superpowers towards the Gulf War." *International Affairs* 59 (Autumn 1983).

"Everything Positive Has Come from the Masses Below." *MERIP Reports* 88 (June 1980).

Farber, David. *Taken Hostage: The Iran Hostage Crisis and America's First Encounter with Radical Islam.* Princeton, NJ: Princeton University Press, 2005.

Forsythe, David P. "American Foreign Policy and Human Rights: Rhetoric and Reality." *Universal Human Rights* 2:3 (July–September 1980).

———. "The United Nations and Human Rights, 1945–1985." *Political Science Quarterly* 100:2 (Summer 1985).

Freedman, Robert O. "Patterns of Soviet Policy toward the Middle East." *Annals of the American Academy of Political and Social Science* 482 (November 1985).

Glad, Betty. "Personality, Political and Group Process Variables in Foreign Policy Decision-Making: Jimmy Carter's Handling of the Iranian Hostage." *International Political Science Review / Revue internationale de science politique* 10:1 (January 1989).

Gonzalez, Nathan. *Engaging Iran: The Rise of a Middle East Powerhouse and America's Strategic Choice.* Westport: Greenwood, 2007.

Gotlieb, Allan. *The Washington Diaries, 1981–1989.* Toronto: McClelland & Stewart, 2006.

Granatstein, J. L., and David Stafford. *Spy Wars: Espionage and Canada from Gouzenko to Glasnost.* Toronto: Key Porter, 1991.

Green, L. C. "International Crimes and the Legal Process." *International and Comparative Law Quarterly* 29:4 (October 1980).

Griffith, William E. "The Revival of Islamic Fundamentalism: The Case of Iran." *International Security* 4:1 (Summer 1979).

Halliday, Fred. *Iran: Dictatorship and Development.* Middlesex, UK: Penguin, 1979.

———. "Iran's Revolution: The First Year." *MERIP Reports* 88 (June 1980).

———. "Testimonies of Revolution." *MERIP Reports* 87 (May 1980).

Harris, David. *The Crisis: The President, the Prophet, and the Shah.* New York: Little, Brown and Company, 2004.

Harris, Les (Director). *The Iran Hostage Crisis: 444 Days to Freedom (What Really Happened in Iran).* Toronto: Canamedia, 1997.

Hassan, Riaz. "Iran's Islamic Revolutionaries: Before and After the Revolution." *Third World Quarterly* 6:3 (July 1984).

Head, Ivan, and Pierre Trudeau. *The Canadian Way: Shaping Canada's Foreign Policy, 1968–1984.* Toronto: McClelland & Stewart, 1995.

Helms, Richard. *A Look over My Shoulder: A Life in the Central Intelligence Agency.* New York: Random House, 2003.

Hemmer, Christopher. "Historical Analogies and the Definition of Interests: The Iranian Hostage Crisis and Ronald Reagan's Policy toward the Hostages in Lebanon." *Political Psychology* 20:2 (June 1999).

Hersh, Seymour M. *The Price of Power: Kissinger in the Nixon White House.* New York: Summit, 1983.

Holzworth, C. E. *Operation Eagle Claw: A Catalyst for Change in the American Military.* 1997. http://www.globalsecurity.org/military/library/report/1997/Holzworth.htm.

Hooglund, Mary. "One Village in the Revolution." *MERIP Reports* 87 (May 1980).

Houghton, David Patrick. *U.S. Foreign Policy and the Iran Hostage Crisis.* London: Cambridge University Press, 2001.

Hunt, Michael H. "In the Wake of September 11: The Clash of What?" *Journal of American History* 89:2 (September 2002).

Hyser, Robert E. *Mission to Tehran.* New York: Harper and Row, 1986.

Ismael, J. S., and T. Y. Ismael. "Social Change in Islamic Society: The Political Thought of Ayatollah Khomeini." *Social Problems* 27:5 (June 1980).

Jeffery, Anthea. "The American Hostages in Tehran: The I.C.J. and the Legality of Rescue Missions." *International and Comparative Law Quarterly* 30:3 (July 1981).

Jeffreys-Jones, Rhodri, and Christopher Andrew. *Eternal Vigilance? 50 Years of the CIA.* Portland, OR: Frank Cass, 1997.

Jentleson, Bruce W. "Discrepant Responses to Falling Dictators: Presidential Belief Systems and the Mediating Effects of the Senior Advisory Process." *Political Psychology* 11:2 (June 1990).

Jerome, Carole. *The Man in the Mirror: A True Story of Love, Revolution and Treachery in Iran.* Toronto: Key Porter, 1987.

Johnson, Loch K. "Richard Helms: An Interview with the Former U.S. Director of Central Intelligence." *Intelligence & National Security* 18:3 (Autumn 2003).

Jordan, Hamilton. *Crisis: The True Story of an Unforgettable Year in the White House.* New York: Berkeley Books, 1982.

Kaufman, Edy, and Patricia Weiss Fagen. "Extrajudicial Executions: An Insight into the Global Dimensions of a Human Rights Violation." *Human Rights Quarterly* 3:4 (November 1981).

Keddie, Nikki R. *Modern Iran: Roots and Results of Revolution*. Princeton, NJ: Yale University Press, 2006.

Kessler, Ronald. *Inside the CIA*. New York: Pocket Books, 1992.

Khomeini, Ruhollah. *Islamic Government: Governance of the Jurist*. 1970. Trans. Hamid Algar. Ahlul Bayt Digital Islamic Library Project. http://www.al-islam. org/islamicgovernment.

Kinzer, Stephen. *All the Shah's Men: An American Coup and the Roots of Middle East Terror*. New York: Wiley and Sons, 2003.

Kissinger, Henry. *Years of Renewal*. New York: Simon and Schuster, 1999.

Laingen, L. Bruce. *Yellow Ribbon: The Secret Journal of Bruce Laingen*. New York: Brassey's, 1992.

Lake, C. M. "The Problems Encountered in Establishing an Islamic Republic in Iran 1979–1981." *Bulletin (British Society for Middle Eastern Studies)* 9:2 (1982).

Lucy, Roger. "Letters from the Iranian Revolution." *Bout de Papier* 6:4 (Spring 1981).

MacGuigan, Mark. *An Inside Look at External Affairs During the Trudeau Years: The Memoirs of Mark MacGuigan*. Calgary: University of Calgary Press, 2002.

Mahant, Edelgard. *Invisible and Inaudible in Washington*. Vancouver: UBC Press, 2000.

Makdisi, Ussama. "Anti-Americanism in the Arab World: An Interpretation of a Brief History." *Journal of American History* 89:2 (September 2002).

McFadden, Robert D., Joseph B. Treaster, and Maurice Carroll, eds. *No Hiding Place: The New York Times Inside Report on the Hostage Crisis*. New York: Times Books, 1981.

Mendez, Antonio J. "CIA Goes Hollywood: A Classic Case of Deception." *Studies in Intelligence* 43:1 (Winter 1999–2000).

———. *The Master of Disguise: My Life in the CIA*. New York: Morrow, 1999.

Mikva, Abner J., and Gerald L. Neuman. "The Hostage Crisis and the 'Hostage Act.'" *University of Chicago Law Review* 49:2 (Spring 1982).

Milani, Mohsen M. "The Evolution of the Iranian Presidency: From Bani-Sadr to Rafsanjani." *British Journal of Middle Eastern Studies* 20:1 (1993).

Mirfakhraie, Arnir Hossein. "Transmigration and Identity Construction: The Case of Iranians in Canada, 1946–1998." MA thesis, Department of Sociology and Anthropology, Simon Fraser University, 1999.

Moens, Alexander. "President Carter's Advisers and the Fall of the Shah." *Political Science Quarterly* 106:2 (Summer 1991).

Mokhtari, Ali. "Torture and Other Cruel, Inhuman or Degrading Treatment or Punishment: A Comparative Study between International Law, Islamic Jurisprudence and the Iranian Legal System." LL.M. thesis, McGill University, 2005.

Mottahedeh, Roy Parviz. "Iran's Foreign Devils." *Foreign Policy* 38 (Spring 1980).

Mulroney, Brian. *Memoirs*. Toronto: McClelland & Stewart, 2007.

Nacos, Brigitte L. *Terrorism and the Media: From the Iran Hostage Crisis to the World Trade Center Bombing*. New York: Columbia University Press, 1994.

Neff, Donald. "The U.S., Iraq, Israel, and Iran: Backdrop to War." *Journal of Palestine Studies* 20:4 (Summer 1991).

Nobari, Ali Reza. "We Started to Feel Cold Sweat on Our Brows." *MERIP Reports* 104 (March–April 1982).

Ott, Marvin. "Shaking Up the CIA." *Foreign Policy* 93 (Winter 1993–1994).

Parker, Richard B. "Anti-American Attitudes in the Arab World." *Annals of the American Academy of Political and Social Science* 497 (May 1988).

Parsi, Trita. *Treacherous Alliance: The Secret Dealings of Iran, Israel and the United States*. Princeton, NJ: Yale University Press, 2007.

Pelletier, Jean, and Claude Adams. *The Canadian Caper*. Toronto: Paperjacks, 1981.

Pesaran, M. H. "The System of Dependent Capitalism in Pre- and Post-Revolutionary Iran." *International Journal of Middle East Studies* 14:4 (November 1982).

Piscatori, James. "The Rushdie Affair and the Politics of Ambiguity." *International Affairs* 66:4 (October 1990).

Prados, John. *Safe for Democracy: The Secret Wars of the CIA*. Chicago: Ivan R. Dee, 2006.

Precht, Henry. "Ayatollah Realpolitik." *Foreign Policy* 70 (Spring 1988).

Queen, Richard. *Inside and Out: Hostage to Iran, Hostage to Myself*. New York: Putnam's, 1981.

Rafizadeh, Mansur. *Witness: From the Shah to the Secret Arms Deal*. New York: Morrow, 1987.

Ramazani, R. K. "Iran's Revolution: Patterns, Problems and Prospects." *International Affairs* 56:3 (Summer 1980).

Razi, G. Hossein. "The Nexus of Legitimacy and Performance: The Lessons of the Iranian Revolution." *Comparative Politics* 19:4 (July 1987).

Rejali, Darius M. *Torture and Modernity: Self, Society, and State in Modern Iran*. San Francisco: Westview, 1994.

Richards, Helmut. "America's Shah, Shahanshah's Iran." *MERIP Reports* 40 (September 1975).

Richelson, Jeffrey T. *A Century of Spies: Intelligence in the Twentieth Century*. New York: Oxford University Press, 1995.

———. *The Wizards of Langley: Inside the CIA's Directorate of Science and Technology*. New York: Westview, 2002.

Ritter, Scott. *Target Iran: The Truth about the White House's Plan for Regime Change*. New York: Nation Books, 2006.

Rubinstein, Alvin Z. "The Soviet Union and Iran under Khomeini." *International Affairs* 57:4 (Autumn 1981).

Ryan, Paul B. *The Iran Rescue Mission: Why It Failed.* Annapolis, MD: Naval Institute Press, 1985.

Saikal, Amin. "Soviet Policy toward Southwest Asia." *Annals of the American Academy of Political and Social Science* 481 (September 1985).

Salinger, Pierre. *America Held Hostage: The Secret Negotiations.* New York: Doubleday, 1981.

Samii, Abbas William. "The Shah's Lebanon Policy: The Role of SAVAK." *Middle Eastern Studies* 33:1 (1997).

Schecter, Jerold, and Leona Schecter. *Sacred Secrets: How Soviet Intelligence Operations Changed American History.* Dulles, VA: Brassey's, 2003.

Schenker, Hillel. "The Iranian Connection." *Journal of Palestine Studies* 16:3 (Spring 1987).

Schlesinger, Joe. *Time Zones: A Journalist in the World.* Toronto: Random House, 1990.

Scott, Catherine V. "Bound for Glory: The Hostage Crisis as Captivity Narrative in Iran." *International Studies Quarterly* 44:1 (March 2000).

Scott, Charles. *Pieces of the Game: The Human Drama of Americans Held Hostage in Iran.* Atlanta, GA: Peachtree, 1984.

"Shah of Iran Admits to Police Operations in U.S." *MERIP Reports* 52 (November 1976).

Shahidian, Hammed. "Women and Clandestine Politics in Iran, 1970–1985." *Feminist Studies* 23:1 (Spring 1997).

Shirley, Edward G. "The Iran Policy Trap." *Foreign Policy* 96 (Autumn 1994).

Sick, Gary. *October Surprise: America's Hostages in Iran and the Election of Ronald Reagan.* New York: Random House, 1991.

Skaarup, Harold Aage. *Out of Darkness Light: A History of Canadian Military Intelligence.* 2 vols. Ottawa: iUniverse, 2005.

Slavin, Barbara. *Bitter Friends, Bosom Enemies: Iran, the U.S., and the Twisted Path to Confrontation.* New York: St. Martin's, 2007.

Stiefler, Todd. "CIA's Leadership and Major Covert Operations: Rogue Elephants or Risk-Averse Bureaucrats?" *Intelligence & National Security* 19:4 (Winter 2004).

Sullivan, William H. *Mission to Iran.* New York: Norton and Company, 1981.

Takeyh, Ray. *Hidden Iran: Paradox and Power in the Islamic Republic.* New York: Holt, 2006.

Tarnoff, Peter. "America's Role in a Changing World: An Interview with Peter Tarnoff." *U.S. Foreign Policy Agenda* 1:4 (May 1996).

———. "Containing Iran." *DISAM Journal* (Winter 1995–1996).

Tarock, Adam. "The Muzzling of the Liberal Press in Iran." *Third World Quarterly* 22:4 (August 2001).

————. "U.S.-Iran Relations: Heading for Confrontation?" *Third World Quarterly* 17:1 (March 1996).

Tehrani, Shirin, and Fred Halliday. "Eyewitness from Iran: Signs of Civil War." *MERIP Reports* 98 (July–August 1981).

Thomas, Gordon. *Gideon's Spies: The Secret History of the Mossad.* New York: Thomas Dunne, 1999.

Triffo, Chris (Director). *Escape from Iran: The Hollywood Option.* Harmony Entertainment Management, 2004.

Trudeau, Pierre. *Memoirs.* Toronto: McClelland & Stewart, 1993.

"Tudeh Party Calls for a United Front." *MERIP Reports* 71 (October 1978).

Turner, Stansfield. *Terrorism and Democracy.* Boston: Houghton Mifflin, 1991.

Vance, Cyrus. *Hard Choices: Critical Years in America's Foreign Policy.* New York: Simon and Schuster, 1983.

Wade, Nicholas. "Iran and America: The Failure of Understanding." *Science* 206 (December 14 1979).

Wege, Carl Anthony. "Iranian Intelligence Organizations." *International Journal of Intelligence and Counterintelligence* 10:3 (1997).

Weiner, Tim. *Legacy of Ashes: The History of the CIA.* New York: Doubleday, 2007.

Wright, Robert. *Three Nights in Havana.* Toronto: HarperCollins, 2007.

Wright, Robin, and Shaul Bakhash. "The U. S. and Iran: An Offer They Can't Refuse?" *Foreign Policy* 108 (Autumn 1997).

Zabih, Sepehr. "Aspects of Terrorism in Iran." *Annals of the American Academy of Political and Social Science* 463 (September 1982).

Zamani, Abbasa. "Revolutionary Guard Commander: The Danger Comes from the U.S. Leftist Organizations." *MERIP Reports* 86 (March–April 1980).

Zonis, Marvin, and Craig M. Joseph. "Conspiracy Thinking in the Middle East." *Political Psychology* 15:3 (September 1994).

INDEX